MW00583716

Charles de Gaulle

Charles de Gaulle

A Thorn in the Side of Six American Presidents

William R. Keylor

ROWMAN & LITTLEFIELD
Lanham • Boulder • New York • London

Published by Rowman & Littlefield
An imprint of The Rowman & Littlefield Publishing Group, Inc.
4501 Forbes Boulevard, Suite 200, Lanham, Maryland 20706
www.rowman.com

6 Tinworth Street, London SE11 5AL, United Kingdom

British Library Cataloguing in Publication Information Available

Library of Congress Cataloging-in-Publication Data

Names: Keylor, William R., 1944– author.
Title: Charles de Gaulle : a thorn in the side of six American presidents / William R.
    Keylor.
Description: Lanham : Rowman & Littlefield, 2020. | Includes bibliographical
    references and index.
Identifiers: LCCN 2020013444 (print) | LCCN 2020013445 (ebook) | ISBN
    9781442236745 (cloth) | ISBN 9781442236769 (epub)
Subjects: LCSH: Gaulle, Charles de, 1890–1970. | France—Foreign relations—
    United States. | United States—Foreign relations—France. | France—Politics
    and government—20th century. | United States—Politics and government—20th
    century. | World War, 1939–1945—Diplomatic history.
Classification: LCC E183.8.F8 K49 2020 (print) | LCC E183.8.F8 (ebook) | DDC
    327.4407309/045—dc23
LC record available at https://lccn.loc.gov/2020013444
LC ebook record available at https://lccn.loc.gov/2020013445

To Pierre Mélandri and Maurice Vaisse

Contents

Acknowledgments

I owe such an enormous debt to a long list of individuals who for decades have contributed to my understanding of the foreign relations of the United States, the foreign relations of France, and/or the relationship between those two countries since the Second World War. On this side of the pond (as they say), these include (in alphabetical order): the late Chuck Cogan, Bob Dallek, Will Hitchcock, the late Stanley Hoffman, Steve Kalberg, Stephen Kinzer, the late Sally Marks, the late Ernie May, David Mayers, Kim Munholland, Cathal Nolan, Arnie Offner, David Schalk, Bruce Schulman, Tom Schwartz, Marc Trachtenberg, the late Nick Wahl, and Irwin Wall.

In France I have been blessed by friendships and fruitful conversations with the following outstanding historians over many years (again in alphabetical order): Denise Artaud, the late Jacques Bariéty, the late Jean-Baptise Duroselle, André Kaspi, Pierre Mélandri, Yves-Henri Nouailhat, Elizebeth de Réau, Serge Ricard, Georges-Henri Soutou, Benjamin Stora, and Maurice Vaisse. Two French scholars with whom I have become acquainted briefly at conferences, for whose scholarship I have the highest regard, and on whose work I have relied on a great deal in composing this book are André Béziat and Frédéric Bozo.

I gratefully acknowledge the financial assistance I have received from the Pardee School of Global Studies at Boston University and its founding dean, Dr. Adil Najam, which enabled me to visit numerous archives and libraries. I also was privileged to receive travel grants from the Dwight D. Eisenhower Library in Abilene, Kansas, and the Harry S. Truman Library in

Independence, Missouri. Finally, I have had such an exceedingly positive experience working with my esteemed editor at Rowman & Littlefield, Susan McEachern. She has responded promptly to my requests for advice and offered useful suggestions for revisions. As the author or editor of seven previous books, I have never before received the degree of encouragement and support that she has given me.

I am so fortunate to have a wonderful wife and best friend for the last fifty-one years, Dr. Rheta Grenoble Keylor, and two loving children, Daniel and Justine.

~

Introduction

I chose the metaphor of a "thorn in the side" as the title for this book about the relationship between Charles de Gaulle and the six American presidents with whom he interacted for one simple reason: despite the memorable transatlantic brouhahas during his service as the leader of the Free French movement during World War II and later during his time in office from 1958 to 1969, Charles de Gaulle and his policies never posed a direct threat to the vital national interests of the United States in the minds of the six American presidents and their representatives whom he confronted. But he served as a source of annoyance and irritation to five occupants of the White House: Roosevelt, Truman, Eisenhower, Kennedy, and Johnson. The sixth president found much to admire in de Gaulle. During those five presidencies, de Gaulle pursued a dogged campaign to restore France to the ranks of the great powers in the world in a manner that conflicted with the objectives of American foreign policy as seen by the presidents he encountered.

For the U.S. government during the Second World War, France was a secondary consideration, a sidelight to its main purpose, which was the defeat of the Axis powers. As head of the Free French movement, de Gaulle repeatedly clashed with Franklin Delano Roosevelt and, briefly, Harry Truman, as those two American presidents focused their attention on winning the war. But they had to cope with periodic challenges from the leader of a rag-tag army with no legitimate claim to represent the population of his occupied country, until he belatedly received in the fall of 1945 the formal recognition from Washington that he had coveted but which he had long been denied. De Gaulle's abrupt resignation in January 1946, precipitated by his adamant opposition to the restoration of a parliamentary system in postwar France that French voters had just approved, temporarily removed him from the consciousness of the American government, press, and people.

After a brief failed attempt at a comeback in the late 1940s and early 1950s, he devoted most of his attention to writing his memoirs in almost total obscurity and completely off the radar screen of the Eisenhower administration until the spring of 1958, when the threat of civil war in France caused by the Algerian War resulted in his return to power. By that time France had been toppled from its perch as one of the world's great powers in a world dominated by what had come to be called the two "superpowers" in a bipolar world. But once securely in command of what was to become the Fifth French Republic, de Gaulle pursued a series of foreign policies that would directly challenge the position of the United States as the leader of the West at the height of the Cold War.

Presidents Dwight Eisenhower, John F. Kennedy, and Lyndon Johnson found that de Gaulle's challenge to their leadership of the Western alliance, while never so threatening as to precipitate a break between these two old allies, represented a constant roadblock to their efforts to mobilize the non-Communist world to confront the Soviet Union and its allies under the undisputed leadership of the United States. His persistent campaign to detach France from the American-dominated North Atlantic alliance raised the prospect of the transformation of the postwar bipolar international system into a multipolar international order with what he hoped would be a French-dominated Western Europe asserting its independence from Washington. His stinging criticism of America's military (mis)adventure in Vietnam and his call for negotiations with the North Vietnamese government, first under Kennedy and then under Johnson, generated enormous ill will in Washington. He was the only one of Washington's allies in NATO to openly break with the United States on this issue, though some of the others privately expressed misgivings about the military intervention in Southeast Asia. Each of these three American chief executives sought to lure Gaullist France back into the corral, and each failed to do so.

When the sixth American president to confront de Gaulle, Richard Nixon, entered the White House in January 1969, he became the only U.S. chief executive to develop a respectful, even laudatory, view of the French president. But that remarkable transformation was cut short when de Gaulle resigned four months later. After de Gaulle's departure from the world scene,

Nixon and his foreign policy adviser Henry Kissinger would conduct a foreign policy that included many of the suggestions that the French president had made while in office, including détente with the Soviet Union, rapprochement with the People's Republic of China, and withdrawal of American military forces from Vietnam.

CHAPTER ONE

~

The Young Charles de Gaulle, 1890–1940

Before the Fall of France

Charles André Joseph Marie de Gaulle was born in his grandparents' house in the northeastern industrial city of Lille, France, on November 22, 1890, the third of five children to a minor aristocratic but by then thoroughly middle-class Catholic family. His father, Henri de Gaulle, taught philosophy, mathematics, and literature at a Jesuit high school (collège) in the French capital. At the age of three months, the baby was taken to Paris where his parents lived in the 7th Arrondissement. As a young child, Charles displayed the willfulness that would later inspire his followers and exasperate his opponents, as Jean Lacouture recounted in the opening pages of his superb biography, quoting de Gaulle's elder sister Marie Agnès: at the country house of an uncle, "Charles said to our mother, 'Maman, I should like to ride the pony.' 'No, you rode yesterday.' 'Then I'm going to be naughty.' And straight way he threw his toys on the ground, shouted, cried, stamped."[1]

   Although with much more finesse and dignity, he was to reenact that kind of single-minded willfulness to many of his interlocutors during the Second World War and after. Young Charles received a traditionalist upbringing and education, attending parochial schools (including the collège where his father taught) in Paris. While there he developed a passionate interest in history and military affairs and acquired the ambition to enter Saint-Cyr, the French West Point, which had been founded by Napoleon Bonaparte in 1808. An ancestor had allegedly fought against the English at the Battle of Agincourt in 1415. His father had fought against the Germans in the Franco-Prussian War in 1870–71. One might say that he had the warlike spirit in his genes. On the other hand, he also acquired an early interest in literature—poetry, drama, and short stories. Though he never fulfilled these early dreams of composing works of fiction, he produced some of the most eloquent, engaging memoirs of any political leader of the twentieth century, in the league with his future protector/nemesis Winston Churchill.[2]

His adolescent years were marked by heightened anxiety in France in the face of the blustering bravado of the impetuous emperor of Germany, Wilhelm II, who had launched an ambitious naval construction program at the turn of the twentieth century and almost precipitated a war with France in 1905 by challenging that country's claims in Morocco, one of the last remaining territories in Africa that had not been seized by the European colonial powers. In the summer of 1908, the seventeen-year-old briefly visited France's hereditary enemy to the east and took note of the burgeoning anti-French sentiment there. His country was in the midst of what the historian Eugen Weber called a "nationalist revival," a nationwide campaign to strengthen France's defenses against what was perceived to be the threat of another attack from the country that had defeated it in 1870–71 and annexed its eastern provinces of Alsace and Lorraine.[3]

Though a transplanted Parisian, young de Gaulle retained the wariness toward imperial Germany from his birthplace in the northeastern invasion path. He was strongly affected by three intellectual forces in prewar France: the mystical Catholic writer Charles Péguy, the influential philosopher Henri Bergson, and the novelist Maurice Barrès. Péguy was a man of the left who had embraced Catholicism and nationalism; Bergson was the champion of instinct over intellect, spirituality over rationalism, intuition over analysis. De Gaulle also drew some inspiration from the royalist writer Charles Maurras, who relentlessly criticized the weakness and inefficiency of the parliamentary political system of the French Third Republic and advocated a strong executive authority in the form of the restored monarchy. While rejecting Maurras's insistence that only a hereditary king could restore France to its former grandeur, de Gaulle became convinced that only a strong executive authority rather than an omnipotent parliament could achieve that result.[4] He also paid close attention to the daily column of the royalist journalist/historian Jacques Bainville, who warned about the German threat and called for a strong leader to take charge in the absence of a royal guiding hand.[5] His son Philippe confirmed that his father regarded Bainville as "the most intelligent analyst of foreign affairs that the Third Republic had produced" and had "read all his books and articles." When Bainville died prematurely on February 10, 1936, he had been denied a Catholic burial in his parish (because the royalist movement Action Française had been condemned by the papacy), a fact that caused Charles de Gaulle "much sadness."[6]

In 1910 the twenty-year-old Charles got his early wish when he entered the Saint-Cyr military academy after passing the entrance examination with the mediocre score of 199 out of 221. At six feet four inches, he towered over most of his classmates—the average height of males in France was five feet three inches at the time—and promptly acquired the sobriquet "the big asparagus."[7] Obliged to choose between the infantry and the cavalry, de Gaulle chose the former despite the romantic appeal of the latter as France consolidated its control over Algeria and Tunisia and the soon-to-be protectorate of Morocco. He graduated thirteenth in his class of 211 from Saint-Cyr in 1912, a formidable achievement in light of his poor grade on the entrance examination. The new graduate entered the armed forces amid renewed tension with Germany, whose leader had again challenged France's position in Morocco the previous year. Second Lieutenant Charles de Gaulle joined the Thirty-third Infantry Regiment that was quartered near the eastern town of Arras under the command of Colonel Henri-Philippe Pétain.

At the age of fifty-six, Pétain appeared to be near the end of his military career. Although a highly esteemed lecturer at the Ecole de Guerre, his promotions had been delayed because of his outspoken criticism of the cult of the offensive ("l'attaque à outrance"), the reigning strategic doctrine espoused by General Ferdinand Foch and General Louis de Grandmaison, which envisioned rapid infantry bayonet charges to break through enemy lines as the key to victory in the next war. He proposed instead a defensive military strategy of relying on massive artillery barrages to clear the ground before an infantry advance. It may have been this quality of a maverick, a rebel, that endeared Pétain to the young second lieutenant who would later acquire a similar reputation for challenging the new reigning consensus presided over by the older man. "My first colonel, Pétain, showed me the real value of the gift and the art of commanding," de Gaulle would later recall in his memoirs.[8] In the following year, Pétain would leave his command in Arras as de Gaulle was promoted to the rank of first lieutenant.

Two years later, the young officer was afforded the opportunity to test his fighting skills against the enemy, when German soldiers advanced through Belgium and streamed into the northeastern provinces of France in the summer of 1914. Lieutenant de Gaulle later expressed his astonishment and delight at how the entire country came together in what was proudly called the Union sacrée (Sacred Union). In the Chamber of Deputies, the leader of the royalist right strode across the floor and embraced the left-wing socialist Jules Guesde. De Gaulle's Thirty-third Infantry Regiment advanced toward the Meuse River, where Lieutenant de Gaulle was wounded by German fire. After recuperating behind the lines, he returned to the front to rejoin his regiment in the Champagne region. After being wounded two more times, he was promoted to captain in September 1915.

In February 1916, de Gaulle's regiment advanced to the besieged French fortress of Verdun in Lorraine near the border with Germany. On March 2, the young twenty-four-year-old captain was wounded and then captured by a German unit near the fortress of Douaumont amid a sea of dead French soldiers who had tried to repel the German assault. He would spend the next thirty-two months in captivity in a succession of German prisoner-of-war camps, making five daring but unsuccessful escape attempts. In a maximum security camp in Ingolstadt in central Bavaria, full of French, British, and Russian POWs, de Gaulle again tried and failed to break out. Once returned to Ingolstadt, the twenty-seven-year old passed the endless days by preparing and delivering a series of lectures to his fellow inmates in the winter and spring of 1917 on the military strategy and tactics of the French high command during the war. After another failed escape, he was put on a close watch during the winter of 1917–18.[9]

A fellow internee, the Russian officer Mikhail Tukhachevsky, executed a successful jail break and made his way to his homeland. Before his daring escape, de Gaulle and other French officers had tried to dissuade him from leaving with the ominous warning that, if successful, he would be shot by the Bolsheviks that were on the verge of seizing power in Petrograd because he hailed from a noble family. "Shot? I will be a general at twenty-five," he confidently declared. He signed up with the Red Army after the November 1917 revolution. He became a marshal at forty and was executed at forty-three in Stalin's purge of the officer corps in the late 1930s.[10]

Charles de Gaulle was absent from his country from 1916 to 1918 in Germany, just as he would later be absent from his country from 1940 to 1944 in Great Britain during the next war. After his release at the end of the war in November 1918, he sought to compensate for his years "out of action" in the German POW camps. In April 1919, he volunteered to serve as an instructor to the fledgling Polish army as it defended the newly reconstituted country's capital city of Warsaw against the threat posed by military forces of the new Bolshevik regime in Russia. The head of the four-hundred-man French military mission sent to advise the Poles was General Maxime Weygand, Supreme Allied Commander Ferdinand Foch's chief of staff at the end of the Great War, who (as we shall see) would later become head of the French army in late May 1940 and de Gaulle's nemesis as France fell. One of the Red Army commanders in the Battle of Warsaw in 1920 was the same Mikhail Tukhachevsky whom de Gaulle had befriended in the German POW camp before the former's daring escape and return to Russia. One of the Bolshevik political advisers who accompanied the Red Army advancing on the Polish capital was Josef Stalin, who would execute Tukhachevsky in 1937 and whom de Gaulle would later encounter in 1944 in Moscow under very different circumstances.[11]

By the end of the summer of 1920, the Polish military forces had driven the Bolshevik forces out of their country and began a counterattack that brought them deep into Ukraine. While on leave in October 1920, Charles de Gaulle met at a dinner party a twenty-year-old woman from a middle-class family in Calais named Yvonne Vendroux. After a whirlwind court-ship that led to an engagement on November 11—one year to the day after the armistice of the Great War—de Gaulle rejoined the French mission in Warsaw. He returned to Paris for good at the end of 1920, and before the wedding on April 6, he received an appointment that he had coveted ever since his lectures to his fellow inmates in the German POW camps: assistant professor of history at the Saint-Cyr military academy. The young captain's brilliant lectures on the history of French warfare in the nineteenth century, delivered with great panache and without notes, attracted attentive audiences that included seasoned field officers up to the rank of general. It was the extensive research he had meticulously performed in preparation for these lectures that provided the basis for his subsequent book *La France et son armée* (*France and Its Army*).[12]

In May 1922, de Gaulle entered the Ecole Supérieure de Guerre, the army war college near Les Invalides in Paris that was commanded by a disciple of Pétain (who had been promoted in 1918 a month after the armistice to the highest rank of Marshal of France in recognition for his exemplary service in the war as the "savior" of Verdun). In 1924 the young thirty-four-year-old captain published the first of four books in the interwar period that would establish his reputation as a leading military intellectual. Titled *La Discorde chez l'ennemie* (*Discord Among the Enemy*), it sought to explain why imperial Germany had lost the war. One of the major themes of the work was its criticism of the German general staff for imposing its will on the civilian government. Another was his critique of the German high command's imprisonment in established military doctrine, which de Gaulle insisted should be subordinate to the actual circumstances encountered in war. This latter theme also contradicted the received wisdom of French military thought as taught at the Ecole de Guerre, which emphasized slavish adherence to doctrine at the expense of a pragmatic, opportunistic response to changing circumstances on the ground. The impetuous junior officer's implicit criticism of the reigning orthodoxy so offended his instructors at the war college that they awarded a mediocre evaluation to him on graduation, which might have doomed his military career had his old regimental commander, Pétain, not intervened to upgrade the evaluation.[13]

The Marshal was impressed with the young captain's literary gifts as revealed in the lucid prose of his 1924 book. The next year Pétain summoned de Gaulle to Paris from his temporary assignment on the staff of France's Rhineland occupation force in the city of Mainz to join his private office in Paris. The Marshal hoped to enlist the younger man's service as a ghost writer for a book on the history of the French army in order to establish his own literary reputation and perhaps pave the way for his election to the prestigious Académie Française.[14] He also hoped to influence the French parliament, which was debating a proposal by a left-wing government to reduce the period of military service from three to two years, in order to retain the longer period to bolster French security. For his part the younger man owed a great debt to the older one for rescuing him from a tedious staff position in the army of the Rhine that made no use of his already displayed intelligence.

From 1925 to 1927, de Gaulle served on Pétain's staff, which had its headquarters at Les Invalides, the iconic former military hospital and museum (and the site of Napoleon's tomb). Although he had become one of the Marshal's protégés, de Gaulle began to develop a set of military principles that sharply diverged from the strategic theories of his patron. For Pétain, the enormous casualties of the French army during the Great War had discredited the traditional offensive doctrines of officers such as Joseph Joffre, Robert Nivelle, and Ferdinand Foch. He preached instead a defensive doctrine that emphasized the importance of shielding infantry units from gunfire and prohibited offensive operations until they could be protected by artillery barrages. This strategic vision would become the reigning orthodoxy of the war college, which trained the officers who would command the French army in the future. It was during this period that de Gaulle began to voice reservations about this hallowed doctrine of the defensive.[15]

De Gaulle had already earned a reputation as one of the finest writers in the French officer corps. He spent the second half of the 1920s drafting the study commissioned by Pétain and delivering memorable lectures on military history to officers at the Ecole de Guerre. These formal presentations had been arranged by Pétain himself, whose insistence on personally presiding over the lectures ensured that the hall would be packed. When de Gaulle's manuscript was completed, Pétain filed it away in his desk and forbade its publication, probably because some of its conclusions were at variance with the Marshal's own teachings. On his promotion to major in September 1927, de Gaulle assumed his first command of troops since his capture at Verdun in 1916 as commander of the Nineteenth Battalion of light infantry stationed in the German city of Trier in the French occupation zone of the Rhineland. The two-year occupation duty in Germany was uneventful, except for the birth of his daughter Anne on January 1, 1928. When it became evident that the little girl was afflicted with a form of Down syndrome that would prevent her from experiencing normal family life, the father developed a special connection to his daughter that would last for the rest of her life.[16]

In October 1929, he secured a post in Beirut among the French forces in Syria and Lebanon, which France had administered as mandates under the League of Nations since the collapse of the Ottoman Empire after the war. When he arrived with his family in December, this was his first and only colonial posting, indeed his first trip outside of Europe. During his two years in the Levant, he took note of the acute competition in the Middle East between France and Great Britain, which held the League mandates in Palestine, Transjordan, and Iraq. This rivalry between the two major colonial powers would later spark intense disagreements between de Gaulle and Winston Churchill during the Second World War. But unlike many ambitious French officers who craved assignments in the French empire in North Africa, sub-Sahara Africa, and Southeast Asia, however, de Gaulle regarded policing the empire as a dangerous diversion from the much more important objective of preserving France's security in Europe.[17]

De Gaulle returned to Paris at the end of 1931, to assume a staff position (on Pétain's recommendation) in the General Secretariat of the Supreme Council of National Defense (CSDN), an organization that had been created by the Marshal nine years earlier to advise the prime minister on the necessary means of preparing the country for the next war. In his mid-seventies, Pétain had finally retired as commander of the French army as de Gaulle took up his staff position. The latter would remain at this post from 1932 to 1937, during which he took part in the drawing up of plans for the defense of France while Hitler was laying the groundwork for Germany's military revival across the Rhine. At the beginning of his service in the Supreme Council, he expanded on the lectures he had delivered at the Ecole de Guerre in 1927 and published them five years later as *Le Fil de l'épée* (*The Edge of the Sword*). The book was a stirring call to arms for strong and decisive political and military leadership that reached a wide audience and helped to secure his promotion to lieutenant colonel at the end of 1933. The book was dedicated to Pétain with the additional comment, "This essay, Monsieur le Maréchal, could only be dedicated to you, for nothing shows better than your glory how clear thought can lead to correct action."[18]

From his perch in the General Secretariat at Les Invalides near Napoleon's tomb, de Gaulle had drafted a recommendation for the mobilization of the nation's economic resources in the event of war. But the acute political instability in Paris—fourteen governments from 1932 to 1937—prevented the French parliament from adopting the revised plan until the summer of 1938, five years after Nazi Germany had launched its full-scale program of national mobilization. This experience of the political disarray of the Third Republic in the face of the mounting threat from the east left a bitter taste in de Gaulle's mouth and inspired an intense skepticism about the ability of a system of parliamentary supremacy to provide for an effective defense of the country.

In the meantime, Pétain's sacrosanct doctrine of the defensive had been put into practice during the late 1920s and the first half of the 1930s in the form of a continuous fortified line that was gradually constructed all along France's border with Germany to shield the country from future aggression by its adversary to the east. Named after former minister of war André Maginot, who had promoted the concept and persuaded the parliament to finance its construction, this iron-and-concrete barrier was intended to protect stationary French infantry units from German firepower, thereby avoiding a repetition of the suicidal offensives of 1914–18. But de Gaulle had learned a different lesson from the last war. While he was languishing in German POW camps in 1916, the British had developed the tank, which restored mobility to warfare by providing armored protection against enemy firepower. Though other French military theorists after the war appreciated the value of this new weapon, they regarded it as useful only in a supportive role to accompany and protect the slowly advancing infantry.[19]

De Gaulle's first reference to the tank as the weapon of the future appears in a comment he made while serving in the French advisory mission to Poland in 1920. After the failure of the Bolshevik drive on Warsaw and the counterattack by the Polish army that summer, the observant young French officer included in a report to his superiors in Paris a prescient assessment: "Tanks should be brought into the field in a body, not separately."[20]

In May 1934, de Gaulle incorporated these ideas in a book titled *Vers l'armée de métier* (*Towards a Professional Army*), which directly challenged the strategic conception adopted by Pétain and slavishly promoted by his followers in the officer corps. He argued that since the operation of modern machines of war required highly specialized technical knowledge, France's ground forces should be dominated by an elite of professional tank commanders operating separately from the amateur citizen-soldiers of a large conscript army. At the outbreak of war, this highly mobile strike force could be thrust deep behind enemy lines to disrupt communications and sow confusion. While de Gaulle was convinced that the tank would the decisive weapon in the next war, he did not sufficiently appreciate the potential value of that other novel weapon of the last war—the airplane—as an auxiliary to the advancing armored units. The combination of daring tank offensives and supportive aerial bombardment would restore the value of individual initiative and heroism to warfare, which had degenerated into the unheroic stalemate of the disease-ridden, rat-infested trenches of the Western Front in the Great War. De Gaulle's offensive military strategy was also determined by his assessment of France's diplomatic commitment to defend its East European allies Poland and Czechoslovakia, with whom alliances had been signed in 1921 and 1924, respectively, in the event of a German attack. The defensive strategy of huddling behind the Maginot Line at the outbreak of war undermined the credibility of the French alliance system. But the book sold only 750 copies in France—half the print run of 1,500 had to be given away—and had a minimal effect on the French high command (except as a source of irritation at the heterodox principles it promoted).[21]

De Gaulle was not alone in promoting the role of mobile armored columns in warfare. The British military theorists B. H. Liddell Hart and J. F. C. "Boney" Fuller had been heralding the tank as the decisive weapon in the next war throughout the interwar period.[22] Military theorists such as General Heinz Guderian in the recently established Nazi regime in Germany were busy advocating just such a system of independent armored (or "Panzer") divisions that would strike deep into enemy territory in a "lightning war" (Blitzkrieg). They paid close attention to Liddell Hart's and Fuller's writings which supported the kind of tank and aircraft cooperation that they were developing.[23] De Gaulle's book had been translated into German and was read by Guderian, though it is difficult to establish the precise influence of the French colonel on the German general.[24]

Gradually de Gaulle's strategic and tactical recommendations began to find a following among certain people in the French political elite who took an interest in defense matters. The most important of these was Paul Reynaud, a conservative member of the Chamber of Deputies whom de Gaulle first met at the end of 1934. Reynaud eschewed the virulent anti-Communism of the French Right by supporting the Franco-Soviet Pact that was signed in 1935 on the grounds of "the enemy of my enemy is my friend." De Gaulle also distanced himself from his right-wing admirers by expressing his support for the Russian alliance. "We do not possess the means to refuse Russian help, however much we may loath their regime," he wrote to his mother. "At this moment everything must be subordinated to one single plan: to align as a group against Germany all those who are opposed to her."[25] After their first meeting in December 1934, the colonel and the politician exchanged dozens of letters for the remainder of the decade about the need to replace the defensive strategy of the Maginot Line with the kind of offensive program enunciated in de Gaulle's book.[26]

After receiving several briefings from de Gaulle about the three Panzer divisions that were being formed across the Rhine, Reynaud delivered a series of stirring speeches in the Chamber of Deputies calling for the creation of the mobile, mechanized units that de Gaulle had advocated in his controversial book. It is noteworthy that, despite his upbringing in a devout Catholic, conservative family, de Gaulle did not confine his political contacts to the politicians of the right. In October 1936, he met with the Socialist prime minister Léon Blum, whose Popular Front coalition had taken power shortly after the remilitarization of the Rhineland by Nazi Germany the previous March, to press his ideas before the unsympathetic head of government who expressed confidence in the defensive strategy in place. But Blum soon recognized the threat posed by a rearmed Nazi Germany and in September 1936 proposed a rearmament program that included plans for two armored divisions.[27]

In the fall of 1937, de Gaulle received what he had long coveted: the command of a tank regiment, the 507th based in Metz along the Maginot Line. After his promotion to colonel in December, "Colonel Motors" (as de Gaulle was disparagingly dubbed by his critics in the French high command) was free to test the concepts advanced in his book and in Reynaud's speeches in the Chamber that he had inspired. The commanding officer of the Metz region was General Henri Giraud, whom de Gaulle would later meet in very different circumstances during the Second World War. The tension between the two began at their first encounter. Giraud allegedly referred to the other officer as "mon petit de Gaulle," an inaccurate physical characterization probably intended as an insult.[28]

In this position, de Gaulle was able to study at first hand the operation of the armored units and refine his ideas. But his superiors continued to resist the concept of independently operated armored divisions. His unit operated in close coordination with the infantry instead of operating independently, as de Gaulle had forcefully advocated. While at the Metz garrison, he looked on with consternation as the government of Prime Minister Edouard Daladier signed the Munich agreement, allowing Nazi Germany to annex the German-speaking borderland of Czechoslovakia, thereby condemning one of France's eastern allies—the other being Poland—to the mercies of Hitler. As de Gaulle had earlier recognized, the defensive military strategy of the

French high command prevented France from honoring its diplomatic commitments to deter Germany from expanding to the east.

On September 27, two days before the fateful conference in Munich, de Gaulle brought out the fourth of his books, *La France et son Armée* (*France and Its Army*), which was a revised and expanded version of the manuscript he had ghostwritten in 1925–26 for Pétain, who had refused to allow its publication. While the book was in galley proofs, de Gaulle informed Pétain about its forthcoming publication. The Marshal responded with an angry letter claiming primary authorship of the work because it was the fruit of staff work under his supervision and based on revisions he had made to the manuscript. In a tense meeting at Pétain's home, de Gaulle declined the old man's request that he leave a copy of the galleys for his inspection. Even after the Marshal refused de Gaulle's request to write a preface to the work, the author agreed to acknowledge the Marshal's contributions to the work.[29]

The outbreak of the Second World War on September 3, 1939, two days after the German panzers drove into Poland, finally afforded de Gaulle the opportunity to put his ideas on military strategy and tactics into practice. The day before, Colonel de Gaulle had been named commander of the armored units of the Fifth Army behind the Maginot Line in Alsace. His unit was composed of five unconnected tank battalions rather than the single unified force he had advocated in his writings. The German Blitzkrieg in Poland had clearly demonstrated the utility of mechanized units supported by dive-bombing attack planes. But the military powers-that-be in France refused to learn the appropriate lesson from the Polish campaign. In December 1938, the French high command had grudgingly authorized the creation of four armored divisions, each with four tank battalions, but implementation of the plan had been delayed by bureaucratic snags.[30]

After the disappearance of Poland in six weeks, de Gaulle continued to issue dire warnings of the danger of such armored thrusts against the static French defenses. It was not until the beginning of 1940 and the advent of the so-called Phony War, with German forces lined up along what was called the Siegfried Line opposite the French forces deployed along the Maginot Line, that the French high command authorized the establishment of the first two armored divisions (but with deficient armament and communication capabilities). On January 30, 1940, de Gaulle expressed to Reynaud his satisfaction that the first two armored divisions had been constituted a few weeks earlier and that two others were slated to enter into service in early March and late June, respectively. He added his earnest plea that he be named commander of one of these divisions, despite the fact that he was still a colonel and it was understood that the commanders would be generals. He closed with the suggestion that he be made a "temporary brigadier general" to enable him to take a command.[31] On March 21, Reynaud replaced Edouard Daladier as prime minister. De Gaulle finally had his political patron in charge of the French government.

Five days after the German offensive against Belgium and France began on May 10, de Gaulle took command of the Fourth Armored Division, which was being hastily assembled from disparate units and headquartered in the town of Laon northeast of Paris. It soon received its infantry unit, a ragtag collection of soldiers who had never worked together that lacked artillery, antiaircraft guns, and radios. On May 17, his division waged an effective operation against the flanks of the German tank columns under General Heinz Guderian that were pouring through Belgium on their way to northeastern France. But the German panzers could not be diverted from their course. In the meantime, de Gaulle received his sought-after promotion to brigadier general "with temporary rank" at the young age of forty-nine to take effect on June 1. Then the new prime minister decided that he required the services of his protégé on the home front. On June 5, de Gaulle received a summons from Reynaud to assume his first political appointment as under-secretary of state for war.[32]

The American ambassador to France cabled to President Franklin D. Roosevelt his judgment of the new cabinet member: "Two weeks ago this general was a colonel in the tank corps," William Bullitt explained to the president. "He showed great initiative and courage in stemming the German advance on Paris. One day last week when I was talking to Reynaud he called him in to introduce him to me. He is a young man who appears to be vigorous and intelligent."[33] When he took up his post in the Ministry of War on the Rue Saint Dominique on June 6, Charles de Gaulle was finally in a position to impose his tactical and strategic doctrines on the French army.

But it was too late. The British expeditionary force of 335,000 that had been dispatched to France after the beginning of the war, together with some 120,000 French troops, had been evacuated from the continent from May 26 to June 4 at the Channel port of Dunkirk as German armored columns swarmed throughout the northeastern part of the country. On his first day in office at the Ministry of War, de Gaulle urged Reynaud to stand firm and, if need be, transfer the government to North Africa to carry on the struggle. He accepted the prime minister's assignment to fly to London to persuade the new British prime minister, Winston Churchill (who had replaced the discredited Chamberlain on May 9), to commit the Royal Air Force to the Battle of France. Before his departure, he met with the new commander-in-chief of the French armies, General Weygand, who had hastened back from

Beirut where he commanded French forces in the Levant to replace General Maurice Gamelin on May17. When de Gaulle unveiled his plan to continue the battle from France's North African Empire and support the British, Weygand exclaimed: "The Empire? But that's childishness! As for the world, once I've been beaten here, Britain won't wait a week before negotiating with the Reich."[34]

De Gaulle promptly urged the new prime minister to relieve Weygand of his duties because of his defeatist attitude. Reynaud asked for suggestions for a replacement. But when Gaulle mentioned General Charles Huntziger, Reynaud said he would need more time to reflect. On June 9, de Gaulle arrived in London for his first trip to Great Britain as Reynaud's personal emissary. He promptly met with Churchill at 10 Downing Street and then made the rounds of top British military leaders and diplomats. He describes in his memoirs how impressed he was with the resoluteness of the British leader compared to the defeatists in the French army, such as Weygand. He conveyed to Churchill Reynaud's pledge to carry on the struggle, without mentioning the option of doing so from North Africa if necessary. But de Gaulle failed in his goal of persuading the British prime minister to dispatch squadrons of the Royal Air Force to bolster the French defenses and flew back to Paris empty-handed.[35] Churchill had obviously concluded that the Battle of France was over and that his air force should be preserved for what he anticipated would be the Battle of Britain.

On June 10, the French government abandoned Paris and headed south toward the Atlantic port city of Bordeaux, where the government had temporarily relocated at the outset of World War I. De Gaulle traveled in the same automobile as the prime minister while refugees clogged the roads as the French army reeled in disarray, slowing up the ministers' retreat. Before leaving the French capital, Reynaud exclaimed to Ambassador Bullitt (in language that sounded Churchillian), "The enemy is today practically at the gates of Paris. We will fight before Paris, we will fight behind Paris, we will regroup in our provinces, and if we are expelled we will go to North Africa and, if need be, in our possessions in the Western Hemisphere."[36] The next day and the day after, the French government leaders met with Churchill, Secretary of State for War Anthony Eden, and their aides in the Château de Muguet near Briare, a small town in the Loire Valley near the city of Tours. Weygand presented a starkly pessimistic assessment of the military situation, and it became clear to the British visitors that the French political leaders were bickering over the next move. Marshal Pétain (whom Reynaud had also brought into his government to appease the right-wing defeatists) headed a faction that pressed for an immediate armistice that would spare France from further death and destruction, a position which Weygand eagerly supported. De Gaulle, who sat in on part of the high-level meeting but said nothing, spent most of his time drawing up plans for the evacuation of the government to North Africa.[37]

At dinner de Gaulle had fortuitously been seated next to Churchill, their second meeting. "Our conversation fortified my confidence in his strength and purpose," the Frenchman later recalled. "He himself, no doubt, went away with the feeling that de Gaulle [referring to himself in the third person], though without means, was no less resolute." De Gaulle then left for the city of Rennes in Brittany to chair a group of officers discussing the possibility of temporarily transferring the government to what came to be called the "Breton redoubt" in that distant western province pending the organization of resistance in France's North African Empire.[38]

In a final meeting between Churchill and Reynaud on June 13 at the prefecture of the city of Tours, a few miles from the little town where they met the previous day, the French prime minister hinted for the first time to his British counterpart that he was under enormous pressure from the "peace party" led by Weygand and Pétain to seek an armistice. With a heavy heart, he asked the British prime minister to consider releasing France from the Anglo-French agreement signed March 28 never to conclude a separate peace with the Third Reich. De Gaulle rushed back to Tours from Brittany and arrived as the meeting was approaching its end. On learning of the request to the British, he expressed his astonishment and fury to his patron Reynaud for his apparent surrender to defeatism. The next day he drafted his resignation to the prime minister and requested reassignment to a battle command.[39] As a dismayed Churchill prepared to fly to London and bade de Gaulle farewell, he revealed his high regard for the courage and determination to continue the fight displayed by the brigadier general he had briefly encountered by muttering sotto voce with his terrible French accent, "L'homme du destin [the man of destiny]."[40]

The makeshift government reassembled the following day after arriving in the Atlantic port city of Bordeaux as the invading German army occupied Paris. De Gaulle again pleaded with Reynaud to sail with his ministers to North Africa and set up a French government-in-exile in Algiers beyond the reach of the German armies. The perpetually wavering prime minister seemed to indicate his willingness to follow his protégé's advice. He agreed to send de Gaulle to London to seek the assistance of the British navy in transporting the government to North Africa. "We will meet again in Algiers," Reynaud emotionally declared.[41]

Winston Churchill's "Man of Destiny"

On the evening of June 14 in a hotel restaurant in Bordeaux, Brigadier General Charles de Gaulle strolled over to a nearby table to pay his respects to his longtime mentor, eighty-four-year-old Marshal Henri-Philippe Pétain. "He shook my hand, without a word," de Gaulle later recalled. "I was never to see him again, never." In the early morning of June 16, de Gaulle drove to see his wife and their three children who were waiting in Brittany and then sailed in a destroyer from the port city of Brest to Plymouth, whence he made his way to London for his one final mission for Reynaud.[42]

At his London hotel next to the French embassy on the morning of June 17, de Gaulle was visited by Jean Monnet, head of the joint Anglo-American Coordinating Committee that had directed the economic dimension of the Anglo-French war effort. Monnet shared with de Gaulle a hastily improvised, desperate plan drawn up a week earlier by himself, his assistant René Pleven, and Sir Robert Vansittart, permanent secretary of the Foreign Office, to avert the capitulation that Weygand and Pétain were insisting on. He proposed to Churchill, who placed it before the cabinet that afternoon and obtained its endorsement, that the British and French governments declare an "indissoluble union" of joint citizenship, a joint parliament, joint foreign and domestic policy, and a common currency. When he learned of the British parliament's acceptance of this extraordinary proposal, de Gaulle phoned Reynaud from the antechamber of 10 Downing Street with the news that he hoped would stiffen the resolve of the prime minister to resist the defeatists, putting Churchill on the line to confirm in his heavily accented French his government's solemn commitment to the project and expressing his willingness to fly to France the next day to seal the deal. "Hello Reynaud! De Gaulle is right. Our proposal may have great consequences. You must hold out."[43]

Reynaud seemed energized by the prospect, but as Churchill was preparing to fly to the Atlantic port city of Concarneau north of Bordeaux to sign the agreement, news reached London that Reynaud had resigned, that Pétain would replace him, that the Anglo-French summit meeting had been cancelled, and that the French cabinet had approved a request to the German high command for its terms for an armistice. In the meantime, de Gaulle was on the little biplane furnished by Churchill flying to Bordeaux. After learning the disheartening news on his arrival, the member of the former government who had just lost his job decided to return to London the next day with the intention of continuing the fight if Pétain opened armistice negotiations with the Germans. After arranging for the evacuation of his wife and three children from Brittany to London on the morning of

June 17, he and his loyal aide Lieutenant Geoffrey Chodron de Courcel appeared at the Bordeaux airport pretending to bid farewell to Major General Sir Edward Spears, a close friend of Churchill's and the head of the British liaison with the French government. As the small biplane containing Spears prepared for takeoff, the British liaison official pulled de Gaulle aboard and they headed off for England. It was the last time the youngest general of the French army at forty-nine would set foot on French soil for four years. Spears brought de Gaulle to 10 Downing Street as the military situation in France rapidly deteriorated.[44]

Had Charles de Gaulle decided to remain in France on that fateful mid-June day and either supported the regime of Marshal Pétain that would be soon established or refused to oppose it, as almost every one of his superiors in the French officer corps had chosen to do, the name Charles de Gaulle would be confined to the specialized studies of interwar French military strategy. No one in the United States, and very few people in France, would have ever heard of him.

On the afternoon of June 17, Pétain's address on Bordeaux radio announced to his countrymen that "it is with a broken heart that I must tell you today that it is necessary to stop fighting." This order to French fighting forces to surrender from the old hero of World War I and newly chosen prime minister of France was broadcast even before the request for an armistice had been submitted to the Germans, depriving the French government of any leverage to insist on conditions for the capitulation.

De Gaulle pleaded with Churchill for permission to speak to his countrymen on the British Broadcasting Corporation airwaves, urging support for a continuation of the war effort outside of France. After a contentious debate in the British cabinet, some of whose members opposed allowing the renegade French general to speak while there remained a slender hope of turning around the government in Bordeaux, the British prime minister finally consented. At 6 p.m. on the evening of June 18, de Gaulle recorded a four-minute address at BBC headquarters that was directed at the Frenchmen then resident in London, those who had escaped at Dunkirk, or those in France who might find ways of crossing the English Channel: "I, General de Gaulle, at present in London, invite the officers and French soldiers who are located in British territory, or who will be in the future, with their weapons or without their weapons; I invite the engineers and the special workers of the arms industries who are located in British territory or may be in the future, to contact me. The flame of French resistance must not be extinguished and will not be extinguished."[45] The speech hit the airwaves at 10:00 p.m. British standard time. That address—which had not been recorded by BBC technicians—would be rebroadcast four times the next day. But that would be the Frenchman's last broadcast for two weeks, until June 22, when the several British ministers who were reluctant to anger the new Pétainist government by allowing another speech by de Gaulle gave up their opposition. It would be the first of sixty-seven broadcasts de Gaulle would make in London from 1940 to 1944, usually about twice a month.[46]

In the following days, he took two steps that would sever whatever loose connection he may have had to the new government in France. First, he proposed that Weygand—who had acquired "in the midst of capitulation," as de Gaulle sardonically put it in his memoirs, "the astonishing title of Minister of National Defense"—place himself at the head of the resistance and offered to serve under him were he to come to London. He telegraphed a similar appeal with the same offer to a wide range of French military commanders in French territories abroad: General Charles-August Noguès, resident general in Morocco; General Marcel Peyrouton, resident general in Tunisia; and General Eugène Mittelhauser, high commissioner in the French mandates in the Levant, among others. He urged them all to violate their government's instructions and refuse to accept the conditions of the armistice.[47]

Noguès had cabled his commander-in-chief, General Weygand, that his forces were "burning" to fight in continuation of the war from North Africa and looked forward to the arrival of an intact French navy. But after a period of hesitation, he accepted Pétain's authority and scrupulously followed his orders.[48] These included the incarceration of eighty French politicians who had voted against the resolution by the National Assembly on July 9 and 10 to grant Pétain full powers and who had arrived in North Africa from southern France in the ship *Massiglia*. In short, de Gaulle's appeals to Weygand and French military commanders and colonial administrators across the globe in French North Africa, French West Africa, French Equatorial Africa, and French Indochina fell on deaf ears.[49]

In subsequent addresses, de Gaulle tirelessly emphasized that in its moment of supreme agony France held two trump cards that could be played against the German occupiers. The first was the French empire, with its vast reserves of resources and manpower that were out of the reach of the Germans and could at some point be brought to bear against the enemy. The second was the support of Great Britain and the largest colonial empire in the world that it possessed.

CHAPTER TWO

~

Fallen France, 1940–1941

Occupation, Collaboration, and Exile

Few French people heard the appeal to resistance issued by General de Gaulle on the BBC on June 18, 1940, and in later broadcasts in the summer of 1940. The Franco-German armistice was signed on June 22, at Hitler's insistence in the same railway car in the forest of Compiègne thirty-seven miles north of Paris where the armistice of the First World War had been signed twenty-two years earlier with the German army retreating on all fronts. Its military clauses required the demobilization of the French army and the French navy, whose ships were to be interned in their home ports. It split defeated France into two political units. The northern zone, which included almost two-thirds of the country and all French ports on the English Channel and the Atlantic Ocean, would be occupied directly by the German army. Hitler ordered his generals to prepare for the establishment of a naval flotilla along the French Channel coast for the invasion of the British Isles.

In the southern unoccupied zone, Pétain was permitted to set up his government at the end of June in the spa town of Vichy 225 miles south of Paris. It had been chosen because its many hotels that accommodated the summer influx of visitors seeking the supposed medicinal qualities of its famous mineral waters could serve as offices for the new government. In mid-July, Pétain had become both president and premier, assuming full legislative powers. The Chamber of Deputies and the Senate had in effect voted themselves out of existence. By formally transferring full powers to the eighty-four-year-old Marshal, the last parliament of the Third Republic had acquiesced in the establishment of an authoritarian regime to replace the French system of parliamentary democracy.

The reaction in the U.S. media was uniformly critical. The *Washington Post* on July 10 lamented that the Vichy regime was preparing to "dig the grave of the Third Republic. In that grave they also plan to bury the heritage of the French Revolution, the Rights of Man, Liberty, Equality and Fraternity, representative government and all."[1] Four days later the *New York Times* did not hesitate to publish an article titled "Fascist France."[2]

In the early summer of 1940, de Gaulle had little to show for his audacious claim to represent his occupied country in London. No high-level French military or political figure had responded favorably to his appeals. Only about seven thousand of the roughly twenty thousand French soldiers in Britain at the time of the fall of France chose to sign up with de Gaulle's fledgling movement. Two high-ranking French officials who might have been expected to rally to de Gaulle's cause gave him the cold shoulder. Jean Monnet, his former ally in the abortive Franco-British union scheme who was highly esteemed in government circles in London and especially in Washington, refused to support de Gaulle's unofficial government-in-exile on the grounds that Frenchmen would view it as a puppet of Great Britain. "My dear friend," de Gaulle admonished him, "at such a time as this it would be absurd for us to cross one another, because our fundamental aim is the same, and together perhaps we can do great things." Unconvinced, Monnet resigned from the defunct Franco-British purchasing committee he chaired and departed for the United States. Alexis Leger, who had served as secretary-general of the French Foreign Ministry from 1932 to 1940 before being dismissed by Reynaud, had fled to London on June 16, two days before the surrender. He conferred with Churchill and other high British officials but made it clear that he had never met and did not want to meet de Gaulle. He left Britain for Canada and eventually made his way to Washington, where he indulged in unrelenting criticism of de Gaulle and his fledgling movement in conversations with high American officials.[3]

But by the end of the summer, de Gaulle had been joined by a handful of lawyers and journalists who volunteered their services to the cause. The BBC had reserved airtime each day for a Free French radio service, whose head, Maurice Schumann, had escaped to London and met de Gaulle for the first time on June 30.[4] Schumann delivered broadcasts in impeccable English to a growing clientele of appreciative British and foreign listeners. Pierre Comert, former head of the French Foreign Ministry's press service, founded a Gaullist newspaper, *France*, that provided the British people with well-prepared copy on all manner of subjects. Geoffrey Chodron de Courcel was a diplomat from a noble family who had accompanied de Gaulle on the plane to London and served as his loyal aide-de-camp during the London years. René Cassin, a left-wing Jewish jurist, would become the chief legal adviser of de Gaulle's movement.[5]

The organization that was originally called the French National Committee soon acquired the sobriquet "Free France." But Free France was financially precarious from the very beginning of its operation. De Gaulle's treasury initially consisted of the paltry sum of 100,000 francs in cash that Reynaud had given him before his escape to Britain, which lost virtually all its value when converted to sterling. The French embassy and the French consulates in Britain were full of officials who supported the Vichy regime and refused to provide him with logistical support. As a result, he became totally dependent on the British government for office space, telephones, typewriters, and financing for the upkeep of his ramshackle operation. As the war dragged on, de Gaulle's organization became increasingly indebted to its British protector. The man in charge of Free French finances, René Pleven, skillfully navigated the shoals of Anglo-French monetary relations. After months of ad hoc interim arrangements, a formal agreement was eventually signed in March 1941 that provided for regular British payments to cover de Gaulle's budget.[6]

The legal status of "Free France" was equally precarious. Unlike the situation of the governments-in-exile that had been established in London on behalf of countries that had been overrun and occupied by the German army, such as Belgium, the Netherlands, Norway, Czechoslovakia, and Poland, there was a legitimate government in occupied France. Marshal Pétain had been asked to form a government by French president Albert Lebrun and had been granted emergency powers by the National Assembly—the same parliament that had been elected in 1936 and chose a "Popular Front" government headed by a Socialist with Communist support. On June 30, de Gaulle received an order from the French government to return to France and surrender himself to a prison in Toulouse to await a trial by the Conseil de Guerre. In August, he received a death sentence for desertion in absentia and was stripped of his French nationality in December.[7]

This isolated French leader in the dark days of the summer and fall of 1940 pressed on with that iron-willed determination in the face of overwhelming odds for which he would become legendary in the years to come. He gradually succeeded in patching together enough soldiers, sailors, and airmen to form a military force to fight alongside Churchill's Britain, the only country in the world still at war with Germany. Some of the Frenchmen who found themselves ensconced on British soil after retreating from the beaches of

Dunkirk elected to remain. Others who had been attached to the British expeditionary force that had failed to land in the Norwegian port of Narvik in April signed up. A light infantry division of Alpine troops and the Thirteenth Half-Brigade of the Foreign Legion decided to refuse to do what most of the French soldiers in the United Kingdom did: follow the orders of the legally constituted French government in Vichy to return to their homeland.[8]

The first high-ranking officer to join the Free French movement was Vice Admiral Emile Muselier, commander of an Atlantic squadron of the French navy stationed in Gibraltar. He had never heard of Charles de Gaulle but had had a falling out with his superior, Admiral François Darlan, a close ally of Pétain who would later become vice premier in Vichy. Just before Reynaud gave up his post of prime minister in Bordeaux, Darlan had brazenly promised to take the French fleet to Britain if an armistice were signed. But he reversed himself the next day and urged the members of parliament not to leave for North Africa, as some French politicians were planning to do.[9]

De Gaulle named Muselier commander of the small Free French naval forces that were in the process of creation. The highest-ranking military officer to sign up was General Georges Catroux, whom Pétain had dismissed from his position as governor-general of French Indochina when he rejected the Vichy regime's order to accede to the Japanese government's demand to close the French colony's border with China. On September 17, this five-star general arrived in London, where he swore his allegiance to the two-star general who headed Free France. The only other proconsul from the French empire to renounce Vichy in favor of de Gaulle was General Paul Legentilhomme, commander of the French garrison of the small colony of French Somaliland on the northeast horn of Africa (later renamed the Republic of Djibouti).[10]

The Tragedy of Mers-el-Kébir

The status of the French fleet after the fall of France and the signature of the Franco-German armistice on June 22 was a matter of utmost concern for Winston Churchill. The armistice agreements specified that the French vessels were to be assembled at the southern French port of Toulon, which was under Vichy government control, and at the naval port of Mers-el-Kébir near the Algerian city of Oran across the Mediterranean. The Vichy regime had solemnly pledged that it would never turn over its ships to Germany. But Churchill and his naval advisers were obsessed with the fear that if the French fleet—the third largest by total tonnage and the fourth largest by numbers of ships in the world—ever came under German control, the combined German and Italian naval forces could transform the Mediterranean into an Axis lake. Accordingly, on the early morning of July 3, Admiral Sir James Somerville, the British commander of a British naval task force moored at Gibraltar, dispatched an ultimatum to Admiral Marcel Gensoul, commander of the French fleet anchored at Mers-el-Kébir: the fleet must either leave its base to join up with the royal navy to continue the fight against the Axis; sail to either British or American ports; sail under British escort to the islands of the French West Indies; or scuttle the ships. The ultimatum was concluded with the threat that if none of these options were chosen by 5:30 p.m., the British task force would attack the French warships. When the French admiral indignantly rejected the ultimatum as a violation of his country's sovereignty, the British flotilla promptly opened fire on the French vessels. Within fifteen minutes, a battleship had been sunk and five other vessels had been seriously damaged, and some 1,300 sailors lost their lives in the first naval battle between the two countries since the Battle of Trafalgar in 1805.[11]

General Spears, the British liaison officer to the French, had been summoned by Churchill on July 2 and informed of the ultimatum. When Spears argued that de Gaulle should not be kept in the dark about such a momentous possibility, Churchill instructed him to delay informing the leader of Free France until the ultimatum was issued. When Spears met with de Gaulle the next day with the information, the latter replied that he hoped that Admiral Gensoul would accept one of the conditions offered him. After the attack on the fleet, Spears saw de Gaulle that evening. The British representative was impressed with de Gaulle's "magnificent dignity" and serenity in the aftermath of such a tragedy. The latter calmly said that he would have to decide by the following morning whether to remain allied to Great Britain or retire to private life in Canada.[12]

The British attack on the French fleet at Mers-el-Kébir temporarily had a devastating effect on the reputation of the Free French movement in the eyes of the French people. The government in Vichy immediately severed diplomatic relations with Great Britain while its leaders, led by the fanatically Anglophobe Admiral François Darlan, unleashed a torrent of invective against "Perfidious Albion." Some extremist members of Pétain's inner circle openly discussed forming an alliance with Germany and issuing a declaration of war on the country whose navy had just attacked its fleet. De Gaulle's recruitment efforts among soldiers and sailors remaining in Britain flagged, and members of the French community in the country were susceptible to the anti-British diatribes emanating from Vichy that were portraying the renegade brigadier general as a puppet of the murderous British. Obliged to comment on the tragic loss of French lives at Mers-el-Kébir at the hands of the British navy, de Gaulle broadcast a message via the BBC to the French people on July 8. After expressing profound sorrow at the loss of French ships and lives, he swallowed his pride and his resentment of the British action by avoiding direct criticism of the country that was hosting him.[13]

By the end of the summer 1940, the Free French "government" in London had already begun to turn its attention to developments in Metropolitan France. André Dewavrin, a twenty-nine-year-old captain in the French army who had returned from the disastrous Anglo-French landing in Norway to cut off Germany's coal supplies, found himself in London after the armistice. After a brief meeting between the two men, who had never met before, de Gaulle designated him to form a Free French intelligence service, known as the Deuxième Bureau.[14] Adopting the nom de guerre "Colonel Passy" (named after a Parisian subway stop in the fashionable 16th Arrondissement), he dispatched agents to France to report on the state of public opinion and identify potential links to groups willing to resist the German occupation and the Vichy regime.[15]

When the German Luftwaffe unleashed its air attacks on Great Britain in early August 1940, de Gaulle sent his wife and three daughters—his only son, Philippe, was serving in the small Free French navy—to the village of Ellesmere in Shropshire, four hours from London. The Free French leader stayed at the Hotel Connaught and retained his offices at Carleton Gardens, located in a cul-de-sac in central London, that was once occupied by Lords Palmerson and Kitchener.[16] In early July, de Gaulle sought to transform Churchill's recognition of the Frenchman as "the leader of the Free French" into a formal and legal relationship. René Cassin handled the negotiations on the French side. De Gaulle weighed in with a request that Britain guarantee the reestablishment of both France and the French Empire after the war. The French leader's courageous defense of the British attack on the French fleet at Mers-el-Kébir solidified the personal tie between the leader of Free France and the British prime minister, although it would be severely tested in future months and years. The exchange of letters between Churchill and de Gaulle on August 7 put teeth into the rather vague agreement of June. It stipulated that Britain would finance the Free French movement, allowed de Gaulle to set up a "civil organism [whatever that meant]" to supervise the activities of his organization, and committed Britain to support the "complete restoration and greatness of France" after the war.[17]

At the end of July, de Gaulle had been persuaded by Commandant Georges Thierry d'Argenlieu, a former Carmelite friar who had resumed his naval career and joined the small Free French navy, to attach the Cross of Lorraine to the French flag as a symbol of French resistance to the Nazi swastika—Hitler had annexed France's eastern provinces of Alsace and Lorraine after the French defeat.[18]

In the month before the formal link between the Free French and Great Britain was completed, de Gaulle had decided that the support of Great Britain would have to be supplemented by a bold attempt to rally the overseas French Empire to his cause. Already the commanders of a few isolated French imperial outposts in Asia and the South Pacific, far removed from the reach of German and Italian military power, had signed up. Those that were cheek-by-jowl with British authority were the first to accede: the two little French coastal outposts in British India, Chandernagor and Pondicherry, followed by the French half of the island of New Hebrides that was jointly administered with the British as a condominium, were the first to act in June and July, respectively. Tahiti and New Caledonia (an old French penal colony) in the Pacific soon followed.[19] But de Gaulle's hopes for rallying the French Empire to his side focused on a region closer to home. With Vichy firmly in control of Morocco, Tunisia, and Algeria across the Mediterranean, he set his sights on the French possessions in sub-Sahara Africa. After the accession of French West Africa and French Equatorial Africa, he planned to use the port of Dakar in Senegal as a base of operations from which to make war on the Axis.

The African project had received a major boost on July 17 when de Gaulle received a telegraphic message of support from Félix Eboué, the grandson of black slaves from French Guiana who had become the first black administrator of French colonies, first in Guadeloupe and then as governor general of Chad in French Equatorial Africa. On August 6, de Gaulle dispatched to that region a mission that included his top aide René Pleven and Captain Philippe de Hauteclocque. The latter was from an aristocratic family, was first in his class at Saint-Cyr, and had been severely wounded during the German invasion of France. After escaping from a German POW camp, he hobbled his way to the Spanish border and somehow arrived at Carleton Gardens on July 25, 1940, to offer his services to de Gaulle.[20] He adopted the nom de guerre "Leclerc" (and would later lead the Free French forces in France after the Allied invasion of the continent in June 1944). By the end of the month, Chad, Cameroon, and the French Congo had declared their allegiance to the Gaullist cause. Leclerc proclaimed himself governor general of French Equatorial Africa and set about recruiting a military force to do battle with the enemy in Italian-controlled Libya to the north in the name of de Gaulle.[21]

The rest of the French empire overseas remained loyal to Vichy. This included the French Caribbean islands Guadeloupe and Martinique and French

Guiana on the northeastern coast of South America. For the first time, this issue brought the government of the neutral United States into the picture. The Roosevelt administration worried that the Germans might extract from the collaborationist government in Vichy authorization to establish bases in these French territories so close to the United States. Such a dangerous situation prompted FDR to assemble representatives of the other Latin American countries in Havana, Cuba, to approve in late July the so-called no transfer resolution. This agreement prohibited any government with possessions in the Western Hemisphere from allowing a foreign power to establish military bases on its territory. After the passage of the Act of Havana, Washington promptly ensured that the French Caribbean islands would be neutralized. An agreement between the Vichyite Admiral Georges Robert, high commissioner of the French possessions in the Western Hemisphere, and American Admiral John Greenslade signed on August 6, 1940, placed the French possessions under U.S. surveillance. A French aircraft carrier was docked in Martinique with twenty-six American aircraft on its deck that had been purchased by the French government before the armistice. The Robert-Greenslade negotiations also produced an agreement to neutralize the aircraft and a French pledge to inform Washington of any operations of the French ships in the Caribbean. These negotiations with a French official loyal to Vichy greatly annoyed de Gaulle, but he was in no position to do anything about it.[22]

But the leader of Free France addressed a message to Secretary of State Cordell Hull through the American Consul General in the Free French–controlled city of Brazzaville in Africa in protest of the Havana Declaration. "The Antilles and French Guyana, as well as the islands of Saint-Pierre and Miquelon [off the coast of Newfoundland in North America], are among France's oldest possessions," he declared. "Occupation of these colonies by armed forces of a friendly power such as the United States—if decided unilaterally—would bring deep sorrow to all the French people." He asserted that Free France had the air, naval, and land forces that, in cooperation with the American navy, were capable of protecting these French territories in the Western Hemisphere.[23]

Resistance to the Vichy-controlled government of Guadeloupe had emerged by the end of summer of 1940. In late August, the leader of a so-called committee of notables on the island traveled to Martinique to meet with the U.S. consul to the French West Indies. He hoped to "make known to President Roosevelt" the decisions of the inhabitants "to be freed from [Vichy] France and placed under American protection."[24]

The sudden victories of Free France in French Equatorial Africa and the South Pacific in the summer of 1940 demonstrated that de Gaulle was no longer a lonely expatriate in London kept afloat by British money. In addition to enhancing the standing of the Free French leader, the almost effortless conquest of these Vichy-controlled colonies prompted Churchill to envision a spectacular operation against a strategically valuable French position under Vichy control: the heavily fortified French naval base at Dakar, the capital of Senegal in French West Africa on the southern end of the Cap Vert peninsula, the western-most extension of the African continent. The British worried that future German use of the port as a base for submarine warfare would gravely threaten the British naval position in the Atlantic. If Dakar could be wrested from Vichy control, it would remove that threat while affording the Free French an enormous psychological boost. Although de Gaulle was originally skeptical of the plan because the city was ruled by a fanatical Pétainist governor general and the small Free French naval forces were inferior to the Vichy French ships anchored in the harbor, he overcame his hesitations and signed on to the plan. If it succeeded, most of France's African possessions south of the Sahara would be under Free French control. Vichy would suffer a humiliating loss that could inspire opposition to the regime's French possessions in North Africa.[25]

So a Free French–British flotilla accompanied by about 2,500 army forces was assembled in Liverpool and dispatched to Freetown in the British colony of Sierra Leone south of Dakar on September 17, with de Gaulle on one of the ships. On September 23, the invasion force arrived at Dakar. De Gaulle broadcast an appeal to the inhabitants of the city from his flagship, and Free French agents landed to organize popular support. But they were unable to persuade the harbor forces to lay down their arms. Meanwhile, the onset of fog interfered with the visibility of the ships in the harbor as coastal batteries caused sufficient damage to the ships to force a change of plans. The plan for a landing south of the port also encountered fog and opposition, so both the British commander and de Gaulle agreed to call off the operation.[26] The fiasco of the Dakar expedition has been unfairly blamed on de Gaulle. As noted, he had expressed reservations about the project before he signed on to it. Nonetheless, criticism from the American media was directed at the chastened leader of Free France.[27]

But the humiliating setback for the Free French cause at Dakar was followed in the autumn of 1940 by a series of promising developments in the remainder of the French colonial empire. All the districts in French Equatorial Africa except Gabon had rallied to the Cross of Lorraine, and that last holdout would soon join the fold. Meanwhile, de Gaulle had instructed General Georges Catroux, who had resigned his command in Indochina and rallied to de Gaulle, to serve as his representative in Cairo to head Free French affairs in Africa and the Middle East. De Gaulle met Catroux for the first time at Fort Lamy, the capital of Chad, which Félix Eboué had earlier brought into the Gaullist camp. He appointed Eboué governor general of French Equatorial Africa. General Philippe Leclerc organized a Free French army that began to conduct raids across the northern border with Libya, where the Italian army was engaged in combat with the British forces operating out of Egypt.[28]

CHAPTER THREE

~

FDR and de Gaulle, 1940–1945

A Cold Shoulder from the "Stubborn Dutchman" to the "Stubborn Frenchman"

The name of Charles de Gaulle was known to very few people in the United States after the fall of France in June 1940 and the creation of the "Free French" movement under British sponsorship in London. De Gaulle's writings on military strategy, in particular his emphasis on the critical role of concentrated armored divisions that he was certain would play a key role in a future war, did not engage the interest of American military planners. In an exhaustive examination of American military journals and the military attaché reports from U.S. embassies abroad during the 1930s, Christopher Thompson uncovered only a handful of references to de Gaulle's writings before the outbreak of the Second World War. In May 1934, the military attaché in the American embassy in Paris sent a copy of *Vers l'Armée de métier* to the director of military intelligence in the War Department. He followed that up with a brief summary of the book and a translation of a favorable review of de Gaulle's book in the *Echo de Paris*. A second report in October forwarded an article in the French newspaper *Le Temps* by a retired French general praising de Gaulle's argument about armored warfare. But not a single military journal in the United States reviewed the book, despite the frequent articles in *The Cavalry Journal* about tank warfare that treated in detail the writings of Liddell Hart and Fuller, the two leading British advocates of a motorized, mechanized army. It was not until the summer of 1940 that one of de Gaulle's books, *La France et son armée*, was reviewed (briefly) by an American military history periodical. The American officer corps obviously had no knowledge of de Gaulle's writings on strategy and tactics before the fall of France, with the single exception of General George Patton, who had read *Vers l'armée de métier* in the mid-1930s.[1]

Franklin Delano Roosevelt may have considered himself a "stubborn Dutchman," but French blood flowed in his veins as well. The maiden name of his mother, Delano, was a deformation of the name of a certain Philippe de la Noye, a Franco-Luxembourgeois Huguenot who had immigrated to America in 1621. Young Franklin had accompanied his family in their annual excursions to France in the late nineteenth century. At seven years he cavorted in the Tuileries Garden and walked down the Champs-Elysées with his father.[2] He had encountered Pétain briefly on a trip to France in 1918 and was said to have an "old and deep affection" for the Marshal. When Pétain, known by many Americans as the hero of the battle of Verdun during the First World War, had visited the United States in 1931, he was wined and dined and given a ticker-tape parade in New York City.[3] By that time, of course, Franklin Roosevelt had contracted what was believed to be poliomyelitis (though that diagnosis has been challenged) while on vacation in the summer of 1921 at Campobello Island in Canada. In any case, he was paralyzed from the waist down and had to spend the rest of his life in a wheelchair.

In late October 1940, de Gaulle initiated his first contact with the U.S. government by informing the American consul in Brazzaville, the capital of the Free French territory in French Equatorial Africa, that the so-called Empire Defense Council would be formally created the next day. He offered to administer Vichy-controlled French possessions in the Western Hemisphere and to provide Free French soldiers and sailors to defend them. He even hinted that bases in areas controlled by the Free French could be made available to American military forces if they were ever needed. This bold approach to win the support of the Roosevelt administration did not receive even a cursory response from Washington.[4]

After the defeat of the last remaining pro-Vichy regime in Gabon, de Gaulle returned to London on November 18 with his prestige, which had been severely tarnished by the Dakar embarrassment, fully intact. All of France's possessions in the South Pacific and French Equatorial Africa had rallied to his cause. As we have seen, he had received the allegiance of General Georges Catroux, the former governor general of Indochina, and of General Paul Legentilhomme, former governor general of French Somaliland on the northeast tip of Africa. With the exception of French West Africa after the abortive Free French landing at Dakar, French Somaliland after the defection of Legentilhomme, and the island of Madagascar of the East African coast, all of French Africa south of the Sahara was Gaullist. More, in December 1940–January 1941, Leclerc's forces in Chad, composed of only one hundred Europeans and two hundred indigenous soldiers armed with primitive weapons, drove northward to engage Italian forces in the southern-most Italian fortress in Libya, the oasis of Koufra. After seizing the fortress on March 1, he issued a solemn pledge that he and his men would not rest until the tricolor flew again over the Cathedral of Strasbourg.[5] French forces contributed to British victories against the Italian forces in the Libyan desert at Tobruk and other villages.[6] "Free France" had become "Fighting France" for the first time. But no apparent interest in the Free French operations was forthcoming from the U.S. government.

Vichy's Active Collaboration with Nazi Germany

In the fall of 1940, the Vichy regime was continuing its downward slide toward active collaboration with the Nazi occupier. On October 24, Pétain had been maneuvered by the Germanophile vice premier Pierre Laval into meeting with Hitler in the small town of Montoire near Tours along the line of demarcation between occupied and unoccupied France to discuss relations between the two countries. The photograph of the old Marshal and the Nazi leader together sent the message to the rest of the world that France was actively collaborating with its German occupiers in order to secure a privileged place in the new European order. The Montoire meeting, together with the anti-Semitic laws passed by Vichy without German pressure, had begun to tarnish the Marshal's reputation in the United States and, by contrast, burnished that of de Gaulle after the setbacks of Mers-el-Kébir and Dakar. In December Pétain ousted the Germanophile Laval from the office of vice premier and replaced him with the Anglophobe Admiral François Darlan, who hastened to reassure his support for the former's policy of collaboration. Meanwhile, General Weygand, increasingly uneasy with the overtly pro-German policy pursued by Vichy, gave up his post as minister of defense and secured the appointment as commissioner general of France's North African possessions. With the failure of the German air campaign against Britain in the autumn, the crafty, opportunistic Weygand began to entertain the possibility that Britain might possibly thwart the Fuehrer's bid for a German-dominated Europe. His goal was to keep the Germans out of North Africa, prevent de Gaulle from winning converts to his cause, and hedge his bets in case the tide of the war turned. Darlan turned out to be no improvement over Laval from the British and Gaullist perspective, as Vichy under his tutelage continued its policy of close col-laboration with Germany.[7]

The United States, Vichy, and Free France

As it had at the beginning of the last world war, the United States immediately declared its neutrality at the beginning of the Second World War
in Europe. During the period of the "phony war" in the winter and spring
of 1940, the urgent pleas of the French government for airplanes and navel
support fell on deaf ears. Finally, in the spring of 1940, the Roosevelt administration authorized the dispatch of planes to France, but the deliveries had
just begun when France fell and they were transferred to Britain.[8]

It was only after the fall of France that Roosevelt initiated the series
of steps that broke with the isolationist past, such as the establishment of
conscription, the destroyers-for-bases deal with Great Britain, Lend-Lease,
and so forth. By the time of the Franco-German armistice of June 1940, the
United States had remained scrupulously neutral. The U.S. government had
to decide whether its ambassador in Paris should follow the French government as it began its disorganized trek toward Bordeaux. On June 9, Roosevelt
had prepared a cable to Ambassador William Bullitt instructing him to accompany the French government as it headed south in order to influence
its decision-making. But it was never sent and was superseded by a message
drafted by Secretary of State Cordell Hull that was sent the next day asking
Bullitt to use his "discretion" about which path to follow. Bullitt replied with
an emotional plea for authorization to remain in the capital city, as his predecessor Myron T. Herrick had done in the summer of 1914 while the French
government relocated (temporarily) to Bordeaux. "If I should leave Paris
now, I would no longer be myself," he exclaimed. "It will mean everything
to the French and to the Foreign Service to remember that we do not leave
though others do. J'y suis. J'y reste. (I am here, here I stay.)"[9]

Bullitt, who was fluent in French and on excellent terms with French
officials, might have stiffened the prime minister's resolve to withstand
the unrelenting demands from Pétain, Weygand, and their advocates of
capitulation. De Gaulle complained that Bullitt should have headed south
for that reason and was disappointed to meet the American ambassador in
Reynaud's office and to learn that he was intent on remaining in the French
capital.[10] The first secretary of the embassy, H. Freeman "Doc" Matthews,
and Anthony J. D. Biddle (the former U.S. ambassador to Poland who had
recently been named Bullitt's deputy) dutifully followed the French government south. But neither had the kind of influence that Bullitt might have
been able to bring to bear in this critical moment in the history of France.
Matthews later acknowledged that "if there was one man who, with his en-
joyment of French confidence and dynamic personality, might at one or two

critical moments have succeeded in giving the necessary push to swing the scales, that man was Ambassador Bullitt."[11]

As a neutral country that retained embassies in Nazi Germany and Fascist Italy, the United States was in no position to withhold diplomatic recognition of the new French government in Vichy. Pétain's regime was the legally constituted government of France. Bullitt and Robert Murphy, the embassy's political counselor since 1930, dutifully closed down the Paris embassy and headed south for Vichy. After a courtesy call on Pétain, Bullitt left on July 11 for Washington, where Roosevelt had vaguely promised him a new position. Murphy took up residence as the chargé d'affaires in a villa owned by an American heiress who used it during her visits to take the mineral waters in the famous spa city. As we have seen, the members of the National Assembly had repealed the constitution of the Third Republic on July 10 and voted the Marshal full powers to draft a new one that would create an authoritarian state to replace the democratic republic.

Murphy's instructions were to use his influence with Pétain and his entourage to prevent the remnants of the French fleet interned (according to the terms of the Franco-German armistice) at the Mediterranean port of Toulon from being seized by Germany. President Roosevelt's preoccupation with keeping the French fleet out of German hands had begun even before the fall of France in June 1940. On May 22, Secretary of State Hull had sent a top secret telegram to Ambassador Bullitt in Paris transmitting the president's warning to Prime Minister Paul Reynaud and Defense Minister Edouard Daladier that "the French fleet must not get caught bottled up in the Mediterranean," proposing that if necessary it "retire to the West Indies or to safe ports in the West African possessions."[12]

In addition to reiterating this American anxiety about the fate of the French fleet, Murphy's objective was to leave no stone unturned to pressure Vichy into preventing the Germans from gaining access to air and naval bases in the French empire (particularly in North Africa) and into resisting the temptation to collaborate closely with the Nazi regime in the hopes of becoming a favored participant in an Axis-controlled European order after the defeat of Great Britain. The American diplomatic presence in Vichy would also serve as a valuable listening post for intelligence purposes, all the more important since the British had no representation there.[13]

This became the mantra for the next two years whenever the question was raised about the U.S. recognition of the Pétain regime: the fleet, the African bases, and intelligence opportunities trumped all other considerations. Murphy's goal was to influence Pétain in any way he could to distance himself from the German occupiers and to provide as much intelligence as he could gather on German activities. Washington certainly wanted to avoid antagonizing the Vichy regime by developing any contacts whatsoever with the rebellious soldier in London who would soon be sentenced to death by a Vichy military tribunal in absentia.

Indeed, contacts between de Gaulle and the U.S. government were nonexistent in the summer and fall of 1940. The State Department dealt directly with the French Embassy in Washington. When Gaston Henry-Haye presented his credentials in early September to replace René Doynel de Saint-Quentin, who had been ambassador since 1938, he assured Secretary of State Hull that reports of his pro-German and anti-British sentiments were entirely false. The secretary asserted (inaccurately) that "the French government had signed away to Germany the entire French navy." The ambassador replied with the equally inaccurate claim that the fleet had been "sent to African harbors where Germany could not reach it." He added, prophetically, that if Germany tried to seize control of the French fleet, it would either flee or scuttle itself. Hull shot back, again inaccurately, that "the fleet could not be more securely in German hands than it is now."[14] He later insisted that Vichy officials were disposed "to keep extremely close to Hitler" while displaying "antipathy toward Great Britain," adding that the United States enjoyed normal relations with all governments "except those at Tokyo, Berlin, Rome, and Vichy."[15]

These sharp criticisms of the Pétain regime did not result in an approach by the U.S. government to the unofficial French government-in-exile in London. As noted above, despite his writings on mechanized warfare that had been duly noted among military strategists in Britain, Germany, and the Soviet Union, the new leader of the Free French had been almost totally unknown in American military circles. He was equally unknown to the American embassy in Paris, except for the brief mention from Bullitt to the State Department on June 5. Churchill also briefly mentioned de Gaulle to Roosevelt on June 12 when he praised Reynaud for opposing an armistice and noted that "he has a young General de Gaulle who believes that much can be done."[16]

Hull officially defined American policy toward de Gaulle and the Free French in a message to the American consul in Leopoldville, the Belgian Congo: "The Department desires to avoid as far as possible raising any question of principle in the matter of relations between this Government and the de Gaulle Committee."[17] The Dakar fiasco sealed the fate of the Free French movement in the eyes of the Roosevelt administration. When Roosevelt had learned from Churchill about the plan for a British–Free French operation against that port of Senegal, FDR worried that the proposed landing might provoke a German intervention that, if successful, would directly threaten the security of Brazil and the rest of South America. His advice to Churchill was simple and straightforward: "All right. But succeed."[18] Cables flowed into the State Department from American diplomats in Africa, the Middle East, and London announcing that de Gaulle had lost all popular support after his failed assault on Dakar.[19]

De Gaulle was also totally unknown to the American public as seen through the media before the fall of France. His entrance in the Reynaud government elicited brief references to the soldier "who for years has been advocating that France must have an offensive force or tanks and motorized divisions."[20] He was described in American newsmagazines as "the lanky, pale, mustached military innovator," the "'Caterpillar Prophet'" who was "Reynaud's most important appointment."[21] Although *The New York Times* quoted from the text of de Gaulle's June 18 radio broadcast from London, neither *Time* nor *Newsweek*—the two widely read newsweeklies—mentioned it in their June 24 issues. In July the American media expressed profound skepticism about the Frenchman in London. *Time* and *Newsweek* both denigrated him and his movement and questioned why Churchill had tendered him support.[22] Later *Time* mocked the French general: "The Man on Horseback who will try to make France strong again had not appeared last week. . . . Some people thought that if the British should win, General Charles de Gaulle would be such a man. More likely it would be someone as obscure as Adolf Hitler in 1918."[23]

Toward the end of the summer, the former editor of *Paris-Soir*, Pierre Lazareff, who had come to the United States, inaccurately described the head of the Free French as an "ambitious royalist."[24] The U.S. press reacted to the Dakar fiasco with sharp words. *The New York Times* bemoaned "the sad mistake" by de Gaulle for misreading the local population.[25] For *Newsweek* it was an "inglorious failure."[26] The successes won by the Free French movement in sub-Saharan Africa, together with Churchill's continuing support, eventually inspired a change of tone in the American press toward de Gaulle's movement. *Time* hailed the success of Free French forces there as a sign that the humiliation of Dakar had been erased.[27] American consuls in Africa and the South Pacific reported that the French inhabitants of the outposts were rallying to de Gaulle.[28]

Attitude toward de Gaulle among
French Nationals in the United States

Approximately 150,000 French men and women resided in the United States at the time of the fall of France, the establishment of the Vichy regime, and the formation of the Free French movement.[29] As we have seen, the last French ambassador to Washington under the Third Republic, René de Saint-Quentin, was relieved of his post by the Pétain regime and replaced by Gaston Henry-Haye, a former mayor of Versailles who dutifully obeyed instructions from the Vichy government. The new ambassador traveled to former French-speaking areas in New Hampshire, Maine, and Massachusetts, where the descendants of the Acadians who had been expelled by the British from Canada resided. In his speeches he stressed the oppression by the British two and a half centuries before, the abandonment of France by Britain at Dunkirk in 1940, and other thinly veiled denunciations of the country that sponsored de Gaulle and the Free French. The American press denounced the Vichy embassy in Washington for its acquiescence in the German occupation of France.[30]

To combat the pro-Vichy stance of the French embassy in Washington, Eugène Houdry, a French industrialist and naturalized American living in Philadelphia, founded the organization France Forever (France Quand Même) in late August to gather together Americans and French nationals in the United States who supported de Gaulle. Houdry was an industrial chemist who had amassed a considerable fortune from his invention of a process for distilling gasoline with a high octane content. The organization launched an ambitious campaign to counter Vichy propaganda in the United States.[31] For example, it organized a meeting to protest Vichy's anti-Semitic legislation.[32] At the time of Pearl Harbor, it boasted about nine thousand members, including such notables as Robert Sherwood and Herbert Bayard Swope. By the end of the war, it had established fifty-two chapters throughout the country. But France Forever was dominated by Francophile Americans and had been established as an American corporation registered in Pennsylvania. While prominent Americans enlisted in the cause of Free France, few French people in the United States joined the American-controlled organization dedicated to promote that cause. It also lacked a direct line to officials in the Roosevelt administration.[33] For the remainder of the war, the organization sponsored dinners at which the speakers would earnestly urge U.S. government support for de Gaulle's movement.[34]

Pleven Takes Charge

After hearing searing criticism of the ineffectual representation of Free France in the United States, de Gaulle sent a note to his close collaborator René Pleven beseeching him to travel to America and clean up the mess. Pleven was an ideal choice for this formidable task. He was fluent in English, had spent time in the United States as a businessman before the war (where he had served as general director for Europe of the Automatic Telephone Company of Chicago), and had worked with Monnet in the Anglo-French Coordinating Committee in 1940. He had advised the government of French Equatorial Africa after it rallied to de Gaulle and then served as director of foreign and economic affairs for the Free French movement in London. De Gaulle stipulated Pleven's mission to the United States in a May 19, 1941, memorandum: to establish liaison with the State Department, seek economic assistance from Washington, organize an information service, and seek the support of private groups in the country.[35]

Pleven left London for the United States in early June and met with Raoul Aglion, a distinguished jurist and former attaché to the French embassy in Cairo who had arrived in the United States on February 5, 1941, and settled in New York City. Pleven promptly proceeded to Washington in search of an eminent Frenchman in the United States who could represent the Free French movement in that country. He reported to de Gaulle on June 26 that Free France was not well known there. Pleven cultivated a wide circle of contacts in Washington. After traveling to the nation's capital, he got instant entrée to the top movers and shakers in the administration. His friend Under-Secretary of War John McCloy introduced him to Secretary of War Henry Stimson, who was impressed. So too was Treasury Secretary Henry Morgenthau, who arranged an appointment with FDR's top aide Harry Hopkins and wrote the president urging him to meet with the impressive Free French representative.[36]

But the seemingly irrepressible Frenchman was not granted a meeting with either Secretary of State Hull or the president. After seeing low- and mid-level State Department officials, Pleven urged de Gaulle to issue a declaration specifying the principles of the movement to combat the false impressions that de Gaulle was opposed to representative democracy. This view of de Gaulle as a fledgling dictator was reinforced by such episodes as the fact that during the first year of de Gaulle's residence in London, the radio broadcasts of the Free French movement began with the words "Honor and Fatherland," rather than the Third Republic's motto "Liberty,

Equality, Fraternity," which Vichy had replaced with "Family, Fatherland, Work (Famille, Patrie, Travail)."[37]

Pleven doggedly went the rounds of prominent French émigrés in the United States to seek their support. He approached three individuals but was rebuffed in his strenuous effort to recruit them. Alexis Leger, the former secretary-general of the Quai d'Orsay who had been dismissed by Reynaud before the fall of France, was a distinguished former French diplomat who was held in high esteem by President Roosevelt and Secretary of State Hull. But Leger turned him down on the grounds that de Gaulle had no legal right to represent the country. Pleven then approached his old friend and collaborator Jean Monnet. During his mission to procure American aircraft for France in 1938, Monnet had developed contacts with a wide array of officials in the United States who were close to the president, including Harry Hopkins, Treasury Secretary Henry Morgenthau, and Supreme Court Justice Felix Frankfurter. But Monnet refused his invitation to join the Free French and support its cause in the United States. The eminent French Catholic theologian and philosopher Jacques Maritain had left France in January 1940 to teach at the Pontifical Institute of Medieval Studies in Toronto, Canada. After the fall of France in June, he settled in New York, where he taught at the Ecole Libre des Hautes Etudes, an affiliate of the New School for Social Research and a sort of university-in-exile. Although he detested Pétain's regime, he declined to assist in promoting the Gaullist cause in the United States.[38]

In early September 1941 the patient, smooth-talking Pleven finally persuaded the State Department to accept the dispatch of an official Free French mission to Washington to explore the possibility of developing more cordial relations with Hull and Roosevelt. Failing to attract any distinguished French personalities in the United States to head the mission, Pleven temporarily settled for Raoul de Roussy de Sales, a bilingual French journalist who served as the correspondent of the Havas news agency in New York City and whose mother was American, ignoring his warning that "I am not a Gaullist and probably will never be one"[39]; the industrialist Etienne Boegner, son of the head of La Fédération Protestante de France, who lived in Washington and was well connected with American officials; Jacques de Sieyès, de Gaulle's old classmate at Saint-Cyr who headed Patou Perfumery, a French perfume company in New York; and the aforementioned Raoul Aglion, the jurist and former attaché to the French embassy in Cairo who lived in New York City and established contact with virtually all of the Free French sympathizers there. Another Frenchman in exile who aspired to the leadership of Free France in America was Maurice Garreau-Dombasle, the commercial counselor of the French Embassy in Washington who had resigned in disgust when Pétain surrendered. But the latter became a bitter rival of Sieyès and resigned his position on July 15, 1941.[40]

To head this mission Pleven shrewdly chose a Socialist union leader, Adrien Tixier, who served as the representative of the French labor movement to the International Labor Organization in Washington. Once he received assurances of de Gaulle's commitment to democratic principles, Tixier accepted the appointment. His status as a Socialist and labor leader enhanced the credibility of de Gaulle in the eyes of anyone in the United States who suspected him of reactionary tendencies. De Gaulle fully endorsed Tixier for his leftist credentials and warned Pleven to avoid all contact with Camille Chautemps, the highest-ranking former French statesman in the United States. This former French prime minister under the Third Republic had been sent to Washington on a mission by the Vichy regime, broke with Pétain, and remained in the United States. De Gaulle disparaged him as unreliable and a typical "politicien fini."[41] Pierre Cot, a former minister of air in Léon Blum's popular front government, went to London and offered his services to the Free French, but de Gaulle rejected him because of his close ties to the French Communist Party. Cot came to the United States and secured a teaching position at Yale University, while allegedly serving as a Soviet spy in the country, and spent much time in Washington.[42]

Tixier, who had lost an arm and sustained serious head injuries in World War I, lacked the diplomatic finesse of Pleven and antagonized some American officials with his bluntness. Yet the frosty relations between Free France and the United States had gradually begun to thaw. On September 11, de Gaulle ordered Pleven to offer naval bases on the Free French–controlled islands in the South Pacific—New Hebrides, New Caledonia, and Tahiti—for use by the American navy as tensions built up between Washington and Tokyo. Hull weighed in a month later with his first favorable public comment on the Free French movement, taking note of a "community of interests" between the United States and de Gaulle's operation.[43]

An American journalist named Ben Lucien Burman, who had been observing the Free French movement in sub-Sahara Africa, sent a memorandum to Anthony Drexel Biddle, the American ambassador to the European governments-in-exile in London, lavishly praising the Free French movement and recounting the favorable reception it had received. Biddle forwarded the report to Roosevelt on May 9, 1941, with a cover letter endorsing its conclusions.[44] Pleven submitted memoranda to Biddle summarizing de Gaulle's willingness to cooperate with American military forces in the French territories he controlled on the condition that the Free French administration be left in place. In his covering letter, Biddle endorsed Pleven's arguments about the strategic importance of France's African possessions and de Gaulle's willingness to act as "trustee" of all Free French territories until democratic elections could be held.[45]

President Roosevelt thoroughly rebuffed these overtures, telling Biddle he would not meet with Pleven but promised eventually to ask Undersecretary of State Sumner Welles to receive him.[46] It is hard to imagine a less sympathetic interlocutor for the Free French representative's first meeting with the U.S. State Department. Benjamin Sumner Welles was a Harvard-educated brahmin who had served as a page at the wedding of Franklin and Eleanor Roosevelt in 1905. After a diplomatic career in Latin America, he became FDR's under-secretary of state in 1937, an office he would hold for six years until being forced out amid unsavory circumstances that will be treated below. He was from the beginning a severe critic of de Gaulle and a firm advocate of the U.S. relationship with the Pétain regime.[47]

In the meantime, the French embassy in Washington and the French consulate in New York hued closely to the Vichy line. An investigation by the State Department purportedly revealed that 85 percent of French nationals in the United States did not support de Gaulle, as French refugees continued to stream into the United States during the period of American neutrality.[48] This group included former deputies Henri de Kerillis, Henry Torrès, and Edouard Jonas. A number of notable cultural figures crossed the Atlantic as well: writers Philippe Barrès, André Maurois, Jules Romains, and the famous pilot and novelist Antoine de Saint Exupéry.[49] Other arrivals included the journalists Geneviève Tabouis,[50] André Géraud (Pertinax), and Pierre Lazareff and cinema personalities such as the directors Jean Renoir (son of the artist Auguste Renoir) and René Clair and the actors Jean Gabin and Charles Boyer. They all refused to support either Pétain or de Gaulle.[51] Saint-Exupéry and his wife would often dine with Raoul Aglion and his wife in their New York City apartment. "We must credit Pétain for having saved France from destruction by the Nazis," he conceded, but he dismissed the Free French movement and its military forces as "not independent! It is paid for by the British."[52]

Hints of Pro-De Gaulle Sentiment among U.S. Officials

One of Réné Pleven's chief goals in the United States had been to secure economic assistance and access to Lend-Lease for the Free French. In late July 1941, the State Department had authorized a tripartite discussion (American-British-Free French) in Washington about the eventual extension of Lend-Lease funds to Free France. When de Gaulle learned that Pleven had been invited to attend, but only as an "expert," he poured out his resentment in a cable to his delegate on August 9: "I do not accept that you, representing France, would attend a tripartite conference only as an expert. You will attend with rights equal to the other representatives, or you will not attend."[53] But there was nothing he could do about it. Pleven was continually informed that such assistance could only be provided indirectly through Great Britain. When Pleven finally secured an appointment with Under-Secretary of State Welles in early October, the latter informed him that direct Lend-Lease aid to Free France was out of the question because the program was reserved for legitimate governments.[54] (He might have added that it would adversely affect the American influence on Vichy.)

Yet Pleven permitted himself to express a note of optimism, reporting to de Gaulle on October 13 that "influential people" supported Free France in Washington. That was a reference to former ambassador to France William Bullitt and, most importantly, Oscar Cox, legal counsel to the Lend-Lease administration. Cox had been pressing for the disbursement of Lend-Lease funds to the Free French–controlled territories in French Equatorial Africa since July 1941. In a letter to Hopkins, he opined that such funds would "strengthen de Gaulle politically," which he deemed to be "of extreme value to our own defense."[55] A Gallup Poll conducted in October 1941 found that 74 percent favored such aid and only 16 percent opposed it.[56]

When the Lend-Lease administrator (and future secretary of state) Edward Stettinius backed Cox's proposal, Hopkins replied that "it is a very touchy subject and must be explored only through the State Department. It gets into the matter of foreign policy."[57] The president adamantly refused to compromise the game with Vichy but officially authorized Lend-Lease funds to Free France through the British on November 11 with the proclamation that "the defense of the territories under the control of the volunteer French forces is vital to the defense of the United States."[58] De Gaulle's name was not mentioned in the proclamation.

From the very beginning, the Free French delegation in the United States was beset by personal rivalries and animosities. Jacques de Sieyès, de Gaulle's most loyal, some would say obsequious, member of the Free French delegation, clashed with Tixier and the others who had privately expressed misgivings about the Free French leader. Aglion recalled de Sieyès exploding at Tixier, "You are acting as though you were the enemy of General de Gaulle." When Etienne Boegner had traveled to London in late May to satisfy himself about de Gaulle's firm commitment to democracy, he was met with a violent outburst from the leader of Free France. "What is going on in New York?" he asked. He had been informed "that you are a traitor." When Boegner tried to defend himself de Gaulle stood up and yelled, "Get out, get out! Traitor."[59]

This vicious internecine struggle continued throughout 1941 and into the following year after the United States had entered the war. While Tixier was in London, he appeared at the U.S. embassy on March 26, 1942, and indiscreetly complained to the U.S. chargé d'affaires H. Freeman Matthews (who promptly reported it to Hull) that he "finds the Free French headquarters so occupied with their petty squabbles as to be unable to give that leadership 'devoid of self-seeking' which the movement requires."[60] The Free French commission in the United States gradually deteriorated and broke up in the winter of 1942–43. Roussy de Sales, who had been ill when he joined, died in early December 1942, and Sieyès (who had quarreled with Tixier) was recalled by de Gaulle. The only remaining commissioners were Aglion and Tixier.[61]

Roosevelt's early unsympathetic evaluation of de Gaulle stemmed from many sources, but it is worth noting the presence of a handful of French émigrés in the United States who refused to support the general and who had the ear of the president and his closest advisers. René de Chambrun, a well-connected aristocratic lawyer and businessman, had been sent to Washington by Prime Minister Reynaud as a special envoy on June 9, 1940, to rally support for France in its hour of despair. On June 14, the day that the Germans entered Paris, Roosevelt entertained his French guest on his yacht, *The Potomac*. Chambrun's familial connections and friendships were impressive: the great-great-grandson of the Marquis de Lafayette, his wife was the sister-in-law of Theodore Roosevelt's flamboyant daughter Alice Roosevelt Longworth. He married the daughter of Pierre Laval and become a staunch supporter of his father-in-law as well as his good friend and godfather, Marshal Pétain. He held honorary American citizenship because of the Lafayette connection. Much later, Chambrun told Jean Lacouture that FDR had said to him, "René, the show is over. I don't think that Great Britain can hold out."[62]

As we have seen, the obvious choice to head the Free French delegation in the United States was Alexis Léger, the former secretary general of the French Foreign Ministry, who enjoyed close ties with leading members of the Roosevelt administration. Like Jean Monnet, he had left London for Washington rather than throw his support to de Gaulle. He was hired by his friend Archibald Macleish, head of the Library of Congress, which gave him time to write poetry under the *nom de plume* Saint-John Perse—he was later awarded the Nobel Prize for Literature in 1960. A close friend of FDR's attorney general, Francis Biddle, Leger became strongly anti-Gaullist in part because of his dismissal from the Foreign Ministry by Prime Minister Reynaud at the same time de Gaulle was named undersecretary of defense.[63] He was also very close to Under-Secretary of State Sumner Welles, whom he had known before the war. Leger repeatedly told his American contacts that while de Gaulle was acceptable as a military leader, he had no right to form a government in exile. His denunciation of de Gaulle continued throughout the war.[64]

On September 22, de Gaulle had repeated his earlier offer to grant the United States air, land, and naval facilities in the part of Africa under Free French control. In the meantime, Pleven conveyed de Gaulle's offer to the State Department via the American minister in Cairo, Alexander Kirk, to use the airfields and ports in French Equatorial Africa for American air and naval forces. Of particular interest to the United States was the airport in Pointe-Noire in the French Congo. The War Department accepted the offer and designated Colonel Harry Cunningham, fluent in French and married to a Frenchwoman, to head a mission to evaluate the situation. Then an article by George Weller in the *Chicago Daily News* on August 27, 1941, sent from Leopoldville in the Belgian Congo detonated a bombshell. It revealed that de Gaulle had offered bases to American forces both in French Equatorial Africa and in France's possessions in the South Pacific (two areas under Gaullist control), implying that the State Department was dealing with the Free French and calling for the end of Washington's relationship with Vichy. Colonel Cunningham left New York City on October 2 for Pointe Noire. *The New York Times* reported on an interview he gave on October 16 in which he expressed the hope for closer relations with Free France.[65]

When Weygand got wind of the operation in Free French Africa, he raised a ruckus, forcing an embarrassed Hull to promise that the Cunningham mission was "in no sense" an official mission to African territory controlled by de Gaulle and pledged that there was "no change in this government's policy toward Free France."[66] Hull bluntly informed Cunningham on October 23 he had overstepped his authority. After vociferous complaints from the Vichyite French embassy in Washington, and Cunningham's memorandum to the State Department on December 12 about his contacts with Free French officials, Hull recalled him immediately to Washington.[67] De Gaulle had to issue a denial of the article's contents, which embarrassed Washington in its relations with Vichy and further damaged de Gaulle's standing in the Roosevelt administration.[68]

FDR's Vichy Gamble

After a long interval, President Roosevelt decided to upgrade the American embassy in Vichy by replacing chargé d'affaires Robert Murphy with a full-fledged ambassador. He had originally tapped General John J. Pershing, an old friend of Pétain dating from their collaboration during the First World War. But when Pershing, almost eighty years old, demurred on grounds of precarious health, the president turned to his old friend Admiral William Leahy. The latter accepted the assignment and departed from the United States on December 23, 1940, and arrived in Vichy on January 5, 1941, to assume the post of ambassador to France, presenting his credentials to Pétain three days later. A future American ambassador to France, Charles Bohlen, recounts that every time he met with the admiral at the White House toward the end of the war, after Leahy's return to Washington to become FDR's chief of staff, "he usually had some crack to make about de Gaulle, and I would go to a map on the wall and point out the crucial geographical location of France, which he knew better than I did."[69] Leahy would pepper Roosevelt with reports of talks with French people that contradicted British claims that de Gaulle had strong popular support within the country.[70] The admiral blamed support for de Gaulle and his movement in the United States on "a group of Jews and Communists in this country."[71]

Robert Murphy, a career diplomat who had served as chargé d'affaires in Vichy since the regime had been established, had lived in France for a decade. He was fluent in the language, a devout Catholic, and a political conservative, all qualities that made him the perfect choice to handle U.S. interests in Pétain's capital. He attributed the anti-Semitism of Vichy to the many Jews in the French Communist Party.[72] He had been called home in September 1940 for consultations about the best policy to adopt vis-à-vis defeated France. In Washington he and others devised plans for the dispatch of economic assistance to Vichy as part of the goal of keeping Pétain from moving toward the Germans. When Roosevelt learned that General Weygand had been appointed delegate general by Vichy in September 1940 to organize the defense of France's African possessions, he saw an opportunity. The president entertained the hope that French military forces could be recruited in French North Africa to hold the line against German pressure with Weygand's assistance.[73] Murphy was later transferred to Algiers in the hopes that he could connect with Weygand on the basis of their shared devout Catholic faith.

After intensive negotiations, the Murphy-Weygand Accords were signed in Algiers on February 26, 1941. They allowed Vichy France to purchase American products with French funds sequestered in the United States and transport them across the Atlantic on French ships that had been interned in U.S. ports. Britain was persuaded to relax its blockade to allow the arrival of these ships. To ensure that the goods were properly distributed, American vice consuls serving as inspectors would oversee the distribution—and double as intelligence agents.[74]

The Deterioration of U.S. Relations with Vichy

While Murphy in Algiers was laying the groundwork for U.S. economic aid to French North Africa, Leahy in Vichy was attempting to organize humanitarian assistance such as food, medicine, and clothing for unoccupied France. He informed Under-Secretary of State Welles of the rise of anti-German sentiment in the unoccupied zone but sensed "a feeling of disappointment in the person of M. de Gaulle."[75] Leahy never hesitated to express his visceral dislike for the Free French movement, observing that "the radical Gaullists whom I have met do not have the stability, intelligence, and popular standing in their communities" to achieve their purpose.[76]

Admiral François Darlan, the fanatical Anglophobe who had just replaced Pierre-Etienne Flandin as vice premier at Vichy and also became foreign minister, defense minister, and interior minister, traveled to Paris to confer with German ambassador Otto Abetz in early May 1941 and then flew to Hitler's mountaintop retreat above the town of Berchtesgaden for a meeting with the Fuehrer himself. In his report to the Vichy cabinet on May 14, he defended the principle of collaboration to protect French interests.[77] When Leahy had met with Darlan for the first time on February 24 after the latter's elevation to vice premier and the other key cabinet posts, Darlan informed him that Britain had lost all influence in Europe and that "France and Germany must learn to get along together." The American ambassador noted that Darlan had "an almost pathological hatred for the British navy."[78]

The Murphy-Weygand Connection

Roosevelt and his top advisers continued to cling to the hope that Weygand and Pétain would withstand German pressure in North Africa. On May 21, 1941, Hull told the British ambassador that any approach to de Gaulle and his movement was impossible because of the need to "salvage whatever we could from the situation of Weygand in Africa" and that "if Weygand should stand up, De Gaulle would have to become subordinate [to him]."[79] But to the French ambassador in Washington, the American secretary of state complained that Vichy "had gone straight into the arms of the German government" and that "pro-Hitler officials have finally taken over control" in order to "deliver France body and soul to Hitler."[80] In late July, Leahy reported to Roosevelt that the Germans had demanded the use of bases in North Africa, which Darlan resisted because of pressure from Weygand. But Murphy was worried that he could not hold out much longer. Roosevelt wrote Pétain demanding protection of the sovereignty of the French empire. The Marshal replied on September 17 that he would repel all threats from foreign powers, adding the complaint that Washington had not uttered a peep of protest against the only attack on that sovereignty at Dakar, by Britain and "French rebels" led by "the viper" de Gaulle.[81]

German pressure on Darlan to get rid of Weygand, delivered by German ambassador Otto Abetz in Paris, reached its peak in the fall of 1941. Darlan bluntly informed the Marshal on November 8 that he would have to choose between himself and Weygand. "The conduct of the current policy is impossible," he declared, as long as Weygand "is in [North] Africa." Pétain finally caved in and recalled Weygand to Vichy on November 18.[82] Leahy cabled Hull the next day after meeting with Pétain, proposing a revision of U.S. policy toward Vichy. During their meeting, the Marshal had said that he had bowed to German pressure to protect the French people and twice declared, "Je suis prisonnier" (I am a prisoner). Leahy described Vichy as a regime "presided over by an old, weak, intimidated man surrounded by ambitious conspirators." On November 20, the State Department announced the suspension of economic aid to French North Africa and a reevaluation of its French policy. But neither Leahy nor Murphy was recalled.[83]

Pearl Harbor, Saint Pierre, and the "So-Called Free French"

The Japanese attack on the naval base of the American Pacific fleet at Pearl Harbor, Hawaii, on December 7, 1941, followed by Hitler's declaration of war on the United States four days later, brought the United States into the war. The new situation forced the Roosevelt administration to redefine its relationship with the two other major nations at war with Nazi Germany— Great Britain and the Soviet Union. It also required a reconsideration of its relationship with the Vichy regime, whose acquiescence in the Japanese occupation of French Indochina in July 1941 had paved the way for the acute tension between Washington and Tokyo that had led to Pearl Harbor.

The two tiny islands of Saint Pierre and Miquelon,[84] located some twelve miles off the southern coast of Newfoundland near the entrance to the Gulf of St. Lawrence, were all that remained of the once formidable French Empire in North America. Their five thousand inhabitants, mostly fishermen and their families, had expressed strong support for the Free French cause. But they were governed by a loyal Vichy administrator, who operated under the jurisdiction of the pro-Vichy Admiral Georges Robert headquartered on the French island of Martinique in the Caribbean. After the fall of France, the Roosevelt administration had pressured Robert into immobilizing the French fleet based in Martinique in exchange for Washington's recognition of Vichy sovereignty there. After Pearl Harbor, Leahy transmitted an urgent message from Roosevelt to Pétain requesting and receiving the Marshal's assurance that the French ships would not depart from the ports of French possessions in the Western Hemisphere to avoid any conflicts with the United States. Roosevelt dispatched Admiral Frederick Horne to Martinique on December 17 to meet with Robert and sign new accords restricting French ships to their ports, immobilizing the aircraft on the aircraft carrier *Béarn,* and authorizing a U.S. observer to be stationed at the island's capital, Fort-de-France.[85]

But no similar arrangement had been made with regard to the two little French islands off of Newfoundland. They were of no strategic significance save the existence of a powerful short-wave radio station that had been established in 1938 to service Air France. Ever since the fall of France, the radio had broadcast Vichy propaganda to the French-speaking population of Canada. In September 1940, the Vichyite governor-general of the islands, Gilbert de Bournat, rejected the request from military veterans on the islands for a plebiscite to determine which France they should support, Vichy or Free France.[86] After Pétain publicly praised Germany for its invasion of the Soviet Union "in defense of a civilization" on August 12, 1941, anxiety mounted in Canada about the possible use of Saint Pierre's radio transmitter on behalf of the Axis. While some Gaullist militants in Montreal plotted to seize the islands, de Gaulle in London decided on October 13 to issue a formal request for British support for an external invasion to rally the islands. In Washington the State Department tried to avoid acquiescing in a proposal from Canadian prime minister W. L. Mackenzie King for a peaceful move by Canadian personnel to gain control of the radio transmitter, preferring economic pressure on de Bournat.[87]

As early as May 1941, de Gaulle had speculated to his man in New York, de Sieyès, about an expedition to take control of the islands for Free France.[88] When he learned that the Vichyite Admiral Robert had agreed, at the behest of Admiral Horne, to neutralize the French possessions in the Caribbean and the ships in their ports, he decided to act on the two little islands near the entrance to the Gulf of Saint Lawrence.[89]

With the U.S. intervention in the war after Pearl Harbor, de Gaulle decided that the time was ripe to topple the pro-Vichy administration on the islands and add another overseas French possession—however small and insignificant—to his expanding roster of supporters. He instructed Admiral Emile Muselier, commissioner of the Navy and Merchant Marine of the French National Committee, to prepare the takeover while Muselier was inspecting Free French naval ships docked in Halifax, Nova Scotia. When de Gaulle informed Churchill of his plans on December 10, the prime minister gave his assent to the operation before his trip to Washington to confer with his new ally in the White House. But when the Churchill informed Roosevelt of the Free French project, the president insisted on retaining the pro-Vichy administrator on the islands in accordance with the agreement reached with Admiral Robert in Martinique. On December 15, Muselier went to Ottawa on his own initiative to brief the Canadian government about his plans and asked Pierrepont Moffat, the U.S. minister to Canada, to solicit Roosevelt's views on the operation. After the president reiterated his opposition to the use of force, Hull reported that Muselier had accepted FDR's decision, which was supported by Britain and Canada. On December 17, the British foreign office informed de Gaulle of Roosevelt's objection to the project. The next day the Free French leader instructed Muselier to proceed with the plan without notifying any foreign government. On learning from the British Foreign Office that the Canadian government, in agreement with Washington, had decided to send forces to seize control of the radio, the prospect of a foreign power taking control of French territory prompted de Gaulle to accelerate his plan to seize the islands for Free France.[90] When a pro–Free French *New York Times* correspondent, Ira Wolpert, caught wind of the operation, he threatened to expose it if he was not allowed to report on it firsthand. The intrepid reporter in search of a spectacular scoop was consequently allowed to board one of the ships.[91]

De Gaulle thereupon ordered Muselier, who had reached the Canadian port city of Halifax with a small flotilla of four French ships while the Canadians and Americans were preoccupied with Christmas preparations, to land on the islands and claim them for the Gaullist cause. In his memoirs, the Free French leader recalled with some humor that he had motivated by the intention to "stir up the bottom of things, as one throws a stone into a pond."[92] On the morning of December 24, the ships arrived on Saint Pierre and occupied the island without opposition within half an hour. Muselier promptly announced that a plebiscite would be conducted and promised that if it rejected the Free French, he would withdraw. The story broke in the newspapers on Christmas Day. *The New York Times* carried an eyewitness account by Wolpert (who would later cover the D-Day landing in Normandy).[93] The plebiscite on Saint Pierre was held on Christmas Day and on Miquelon on December 28. After the result was published—783 for "Rally to Free France" and 15 votes for "collaboration with the Axis powers"—a Free French naval officer, Alain Savary, was appointed administrator of the islands.[94]

Roosevelt's secretary of state, Cordell Hull, rushed back from his Christmas vacation to deal with the crisis. The usually mild-mannered American secretary of state reacted with uncharacteristic fury to the operation, issuing a harsh condemnation of the arbitrary action by "the so-called Free French ships at St. Pierre and Miquelon." The term "so-called Free French" had been regularly used by the Vichy authorities to denigrate de Gaulle's movement.[95] Hull warned the British ambassador sternly that to do nothing in response to the "unlawful act of the Free French" would be "throwing overboard the entire problem of Vichy and French Africa, which we have been nursing for a considerable period of time and without such efforts on our part Germany would probably be in occupation of North or West Africa, or both."[96]

The angry secretary of state also implied that his government would consult with Canada about how to restore Vichy authority on the islands. When cautiously asked by British foreign secretary Anthony Eden what his response would be if British, Canadian, or American ships approached the islands to restore to status quo ante, de Gaulle contemptuously replied that he would give the order to open fire. He later claimed that he had been planning to call off the operation, but when he learned on December 17 that the U.S. government had authorized the Canadian government to take control of the radio station, he decided to assert French sovereignty by beating the Canadians to the punch.[97] Hull received the Vichy ambassador on December 26, who was full of fulsome praise for the secretary's public statement denouncing the raid on the two islands. When Hull proposed a scheme for a British-Canadian-American team to protect the wireless, Henry-Haye replied that his government insisted that Admiral Robert in Martinique designate a new governor of the islands to preserve Vichy sovereignty there.[98]

The American press lavished praise on the Free French action. Dorothy Thompson in the New York Herald Tribune jokingly referred to it as a "little diplomatic Pearl Harbor."[99] The New York Times praised the action in a sharply worded editorial.[100] The Christian Science Monitor's editorial declared that the seizure of the little islands "bespoke an initiative and flair that had often been lacking in allied strategy."[101] The New York Post weighed in against the embattled secretary of state. Hull received letters addressed to "the so-called State Department," a phrase that had been used in a blistering editorial in the New York Herald Tribune. His claim that the action had been a rogue one initiated by Muselier was contradicted by the admiral's declaration on the front page of The New York Times on Christmas day that he was working under orders from de Gaulle.[102]

Although he had approved of his secretary of state's December 25 declaration, Roosevelt did not jump to Hull's defense. At a White House meeting with Roosevelt, Hull, and Churchill on December 29, the secretary of state implored the British prime minister to pressure de Gaulle to remove the troops. When Churchill refused to do so, Roosevelt did not intervene on his secretary of state's behalf. The next day the British prime minister gave a speech to the Canadian parliament in Ottawa in which he denounced "Pétain, Darlan, and the whole Vichy gang" and praised the Free French, claiming that de Gaulle had the support of 90 percent of the French people. He declared that "I have good reasons to fear the present attitude of the State Department in Washington toward the Free French," whom he praised as "Frenchmen who would not bend their knees and who under General de Gaulle have continued the fight on the side of the Allies." These remarks elicited the fury of the secretary of state.[103]

On January 1, 1942, Roosevelt instructed Hull to let the matter die in light of much more pressing issues on the horizon. Angered at being abandoned, the secretary of state drafted a letter of resignation but did not send it. When Churchill returned from Ottawa to Washington the next day to continue his discussions with Roosevelt, Hull complained bitterly to the British prime minister that his Ottawa speech represented an insult to him personally and to the State Department in general. When Churchill refused Hull's request for a public statement approving Washington's recognition of Vichy, the secretary of state received not a word of support from his president.[104]

After the British ambassador informed the beleaguered secretary of state that public opinion in Britain and the United States "was gaining rapidly in favor of the Free French operation" and that his government "was very fearful of injuring the de Gaulle movement in Africa," Hull responded by comparing the Gaullist takeover of the two islands to acts by Nazi Germany and Imperial Japan of "invading and seizing territory that did not belong to them." He warned that "to let the de Gaulle occupation continue unchallenged" would mean that the Free French leader "would probably undertake to capture other French colonies" in the Western Hemisphere in violation of the "No Transfer" Havana Declaration that Hull had masterminded after the fall of France.[105]

On January 2, 1942, Admiral Robert in Martinique had demanded that the United States "reestablish French sovereignty over the two islands" while Vichy Ambassador Henry-Haye repeated the same request to Britain and Canada. Henry-Haye agreed on behalf of his government to accept the U.S. suggestion that a commission comprising American and Canadian naval observers assume control of the radio station, but insisted that Robert be authorized to designate a replacement for the ousted Vichy governor of the islands.[106] Darlan warned Roosevelt through Leahy that Nazi Germany might very well exploit the affair to justify a military intervention in French North Africa. Hull would not let up in his obsession with overturning the

Free French seizure of the islands. On January 8, he repeated to Roosevelt that the Free French action was an egregious violation of the Act of Havana, which prohibited the transfer of territory in the Western Hemisphere.[107] On the same day, he proposed calling for the neutralization and demilitarization of the islands, the removal of the Free French governor, and the establishment of joint control by the United States, Canada, and Britain. Roosevelt accepted the proposal and Churchill pledged to bring it before his cabinet on his return from Washington. Eden raised it with de Gaulle on January 14, but it died for lack of British support. Hull finally threw in the towel on February 2, 1942, in order to attend to much more urgent matters in the war against Germany and Japan.[108]

Free France in the South Pacific: The Back Door to Favor in Washington

To balance Japan's increasing interest in the mineral resources of the French island of New Caledonia in the South Pacific, the governor of the island, Henri Sautot, had arranged for an American representative to be sent to its capital city of Nouméa in early April 1941. But along with concerns about Japan's ambitions for the island was anxiety about American interests as well. So de Gaulle dispatched Admiral Thierry d'Argenlieu to keep his eye on both the Japanese consul and the American representative on the island. Shortly after d'Argenlieu's arrival an American military delegation turned up on the island and began an inspection tour without notifying the new governor. After Pearl Harbor, the United States requested that the island be used as an Allied base in the South Pacific.[109]

An agreement was signed on January 15, 1942, whereby U.S. military and naval forces were granted use of the island of New Caledonia, and the United States pledged to provide Lend-Lease aid to the island. The Japanese occupation of the Solomon Islands at the end of January raised the threat that Vichy would cooperate with the Japanese in the Pacific as it had in Indochina. On February 13, the State Department had informed the French National Committee that it recognized its authority in those parts of the empire that had rallied to it. Once the United States had pledged to assist in the defense of French territories in the Pacific, de Gaulle informed d'Argenlieu on February 25 that Lieutenant General Alexander Patch would arrive at the head of an American expeditionary force. On March 12, 1942, more than fifteen thousand GIs poured onto the island and Patch assumed control of its defense. Considerable friction ensued between the Americans and the French administration thereafter.[110]

High Commissioner d'Argenlieu accused Governor Sautot of excessive loyalty to the Americans. At d'Argenlieu's request de Gaulle recalled Sautot, who was arrested on May 5 and sent by ship to New Zealand. When the indigenous "Caldoches" demonstrated their support for the ousted governor, d'Argenlieu requested American protection. General Patch insisted on remaining neutral in this internal French dispute, but that did not prevent d'Argenlieu from angrily accusing the Americans of fomenting the indigenous rebellion to bolster Washington's designs on the island, despite assurances that the United States fully intended to restore French sovereignty there.[111] For the rest of the year de Gaulle never wavered in his conviction that American policies in this far-off French island were a symptom of Washington's goal to encroach on and perhaps destroy the French empire across the globe.[112]

1942: America at War and the Free French/Vichy Conundrum

The relationship between the Roosevelt administration and the Vichy regime had gradually deteriorated in the first eight months of the year 1941. But de Gaulle continued to harbor strong resentment at what he viewed as the Roosevelt administration's cold shoulder. When Churchill and Roosevelt signed the "Declaration on United Nations" on January 1, 1942, they invited twenty-six governments and the eight governments-in-exile of occupied European countries with headquarters in London to be founding signatories.[113] Eden cabled Churchill with an urgent plea for the inclusion of the Free French in the declaration, asserting that "they are in every sense an ally." When the British prime minister firmly agreed with his foreign secretary and tried to persuade FDR to add the Free French to the list, his appeal fell on deaf ears in the White House.[114] The consequences of this policy would return to haunt the United States for many years to come in its relations with Gaullist France.[115]

Both Roosevelt and Churchill were obsessed with pressuring Vichy to resolutely oppose any foreign involvement in North Africa and continued to hope that Weygand could eventually operate there in tacit alliance with the United States and Britain. Roosevelt had written to Weygand on December 27 praising his courage and expressing the hope that his work for France had not ceased. Douglas MacArthur II, nephew of the general and secretary to the U.S. embassy in Vichy, carried two messages from Roosevelt to Weygand in a Nice hotel on January 20, 1942. Weygand declined the offer to go to North Africa and take command of French forces there and said he would have to inform Vichy about the proposal despite MacArthur's insistence that it be kept confidential. Vichy had removed all military officers whose loyalty to the regime was uncertain, and Weygand refused to identify any who might be willing to work with the United States.[116]

On March 26, Leahy reported on a meeting in a forest near Vichy between Laval and Pétain, in which Laval, temporarily out of power, warned that Hitler was thinking of naming a Gauleiter for France unless Vichy adopted a policy of total collaboration. Welles cabled Leahy on March 27 affirming that Laval was totally unacceptable to Washington. But he also described a conversation he had with the president in which Roosevelt declared that it was "urgently necessary that some outstanding Frenchman of the right type come immediately to the United States to represent the Free French senti-ment" in the country. He asked Leahy to approach former French prime min-ister Edouard Herriot, whom Roosevelt had known before the fall of France, with this "personal request," to make the trip to Washington.[117]

Pétain met with Laval and Darlan on April 14 and worked out a deal for the reshuffling of the government: the Marshal as chief of state, Laval as vice premier, Darlan as commander of the army, navy, and air force, changes that went into effect four days later. On the following day, Leahy was informed that he had been recalled to Washington and that all Ameri-can residents in France were urged to leave the country in light of these troubling personnel changes.[118]

Leahy made the rounds before his departure from France. In a meeting with Herriot, who had been imprisoned by the Germans, the old French statesman lavishly praised the Free French and de Gaulle. He declared that he would be "ready at any moment to take a post in a government presided over by General de Gaulle."[119] In the ambassador's meeting with Laval, the newly designated second-in-command of Vichy predicted that France would play a major role in the new Europe after the German victory, denounced de Gaulle, and excoriated "Soviet-British bolshevism." In a press confer-ence after returning to Washington, Leahy expressed his respect for the old Marshal and his courageous resistance to German pressure. He met with the Senate Foreign Relations Committee on June 17 and submitted his resigna-tion the next day.[120]

On the same day of Leahy's resignation, American and British officials opened a week-long conference in London that produced the decision that Operation Torch, a plan for an Allied amphibious landing in French North Africa, would take place in the fall of 1942. As the Anglo-American allies agreed in London in June to launch an attack on French North Africa later in the year, de Gaulle decided to send a full-fledged member of the French resistance to demonstrate to the Americans the support he enjoyed with the anti-Vichy group within occupied France. He decided on Emmanuel d'Astier de la Vigerie of the branch of the Resistance known as Libération who was fluent in English. When d'Astier failed to secure meetings with Roosevelt's inner circle after his arrival in Washington, Tixier decided on a desperate tactic to get the president's attention. He arranged for an interview with *Life*, the popular weekly news magazine. The resulting article included a photograph of d'Astier with his back to the camera to preserve his anonymity at a meeting of Tixier and the Free French military, naval, and press attachés. In the article the mysterious resistance leader, with the pseudonym "Pierre Durand," lavished praised on de Gaulle as the hero of the resistance and submitted a black list of Frenchmen whose collaboration with the German occupation would result in their trial for treason after the liberation of the country.[121] But nothing came of this latest effort to garner support for the Free French cause in Washington.

Bir Hakeim: The Free French Become the Fighting French

In the first week of June 1942, the Free French movement got a shot in the arm when its small military force finally contributed to the Allied struggle against the Third Reich. In the early spring, Erwin Rommel's illustrious Afrika Korps had driven the British forces out of Libya and back into Egypt and drawn up plans for a massive drive to reach the Suez Canal and the oil resources beyond. De Gaulle had persuaded the British to allow the First Free French Division under General Marie-Pierre Koenig to join the British First Army's desert campaign against German and Italian forces. As de Gaulle put it with emotion in his memoirs, "In his justice, the God of Battles was about to offer the soldiers of Free France a great fight and a great glory."[122] Koenig's small force, a diverse group including foreign legionnaires and colonial troops, held out bravely against a combined German and Italian force from May 31 to June 11 at the besieged oasis of Bir Hakeim in the Libyan desert. The successful French defense of Bir Hakeim provided the much larger British army in Libya breathing space from the intense desert fighting and a chance to regroup near El Alamein. The Battle of Bir Hakeim marked the first time that French troops had fought German forces since the armistice. The French victory, after fourteen days of intense fighting that cost more than 1,500 casualties, greatly enhanced the credibility of de Gaulle's movement by demonstrating its ability to field a military force capable of holding its own against the Axis enemy.[123]

Bir Hakeim gave the French leader a degree of respectability that he had never before achieved in the eyes of the British and American public. He took the occasion to deliver a stirring speech on the radio from London on June 23 announcing that after France was liberated, "all the liberties" of the French people would be restored, pledging that "all men and *all women* would enjoy the right to vote" (italics added).[124] In recognition of the Free French military contribution to the Allied cause, the State Department designated Admiral Harold Stack and General Charles Bolte as representatives of the Navy and Army, respectively, to the French National Committee.[125] While the Battle of Bir Hakeim was raging on June 2, the French National Committee had voted to re-designate the movement as La France Combattante (Fighting France), a new title it officially adopted on July 14. Three days earlier de Gaulle had cabled to Roosevelt his "gratitude for the military assistance and support that your government has just offered" to the Free French.[126]

Operation Gymnast/Torch

At the ARCADIA conference in Washington at the end of December 1941, Roosevelt and Churchill had offhandedly discussed the possibility of an amphibious landing in French North Africa, originally code-named Operation Gymnast. Roosevelt preferred a landing in Northern France to open the second front that his ally Stalin had been insistently demanding. But the Americans reconsidered their plans for a landing in Normandy, mainly because of Churchill's preference for a drive through the Mediterranean toward the "soft underbelly of Europe." On July 16, 1942, Roosevelt sent a high-level mission to London including Hopkins, General Marshall, General Henry H. "Hap" Arnold of the Army Air Force, and Admiral Ernest King and armed with a lengthy memorandum from the president. After intensive talks from July 20 to 22, the group replaced the plan for an operation in Normandy with Operation Gymnast (renamed Torch on July 24) in French North Africa. General Dwight D. Eisenhower was catapulted above other higher-ranking officers to be given the command. Roosevelt signed off officially on the operation on July 30.[127]

After General Weygand had finally rejected the American government's approach in January 1942, Robert Murphy in Algiers struggled to find an alternative to the old French general. He met with General Charles Noguès, the resident general of Morocco, with no result. After Laval replaced Admiral Darlan as vice premier in Vichy in April, the admiral, who remained commander-in-chief of the French military forces in North Africa, resurfaced as a man the Americans might be able to work with. In the meantime, General Henri Giraud, under whom de Gaulle had served in the Metz region in 1937, had escaped from a POW prison in the fortress of Konigstein in Saxony, crossed through Switzerland, and turned up in Vichy on April 25, 1942, where he swore his loyalty to Pétain. On May 4, he signed a statement prepared by Laval in which he pledged to do "nothing which could in any way hinder your relations with the German government or upset the work which you have entrusted Admiral Darlan and President Pierre Laval to accomplish under your high authority. My past is the guarantee of my loyalty."[128]

On May 2, the American chargé at Vichy, Pinckney Tuck, who had taken charge of the embassy after Leahy's return to the United States, told Hull that Giraud had "an exceptional reputation," "hates the Germans," and could be our man. On May 6, Felix Cole, the American consul in Algiers, wrote Hull that the governor general of Algeria, Yves Chatel, had returned from Vichy after meeting with Giraud to report that the general wanted to work with the Americans. On May 19, one of the small group of non-Gaullist resisters in Algiers traveled to Lyon, where they met Giraud for the first time. They heard the general's suggestion for an American landing in the unoccupied zone of metropolitan France, after which the country would join the war on the Allied side. When apprised of the alternative project for a landing in North Africa, Giraud accepted it and offered his services as commander of the French army after a successful operation in that region. A poll conducted by the thirty-three American vice consuls in North Africa in July showed that a landing of American troops there should contain no members of Free France for fear of alienating the population of this Vichy-controlled territory. When he returned to Washington in September 1942, Murphy reported that French civilians and the French army in North Africa were both anti-British and anti-Gaullist.[129]

During the planning for the invasion of North Africa, Roosevelt feared another Dakar fiasco. He knew that General Charles Noguès, French resident general in Rabat; Admiral Jean-Pierre Estéva in Tunis; and Yves-Charles Chatel in Algiers would follow Pétain's orders as Boisson had done in Dakar in September 1940. The president also specified that "I consider it essential that de Gaulle be kept out of the picture and be permitted to have no information whatever, regardless of how irritated and irritating he may become."[130] As will be seen, the Murphy-Weygand Accords of February 1941 had little effect on French North Africa and did not dissuade the French soldiers from firing on the American landing force.

In the meantime, Roosevelt had managed to take some steps designed to allay the concerns of de Gaulle after the intervention of the United States in the war. As we have seen, the provision of Lend-Lease funds to the Free French through Great Britain as transfer agent had been authorized on November 11, 1941. That policy was modified in the summer of 1942, approved by Roosevelt on September 3, and entered into effect on October 6. It provided direct aid to Fighting France for the first time. But when de Gaulle got wind of the plans for a landing in North Africa at the end of the summer of 1942, he correctly concluded that the abandonment of the original plan for a landing in northern France signified that the Americans no longer needed the cooperation of the Fighting French, who had no standing in Vichy-controlled North Africa. On September 21, British Ambassador Halifax warned Hull that keeping de Gaulle totally in the dark about the landing plans would lead him to "bitterly resent" such cavalier treatment, but the warning fell on deaf ears.[131]

On September 22, Eisenhower informed Giraud that he would soon be designated head of the French war effort linked to the Allies. On the same day, Roosevelt told Murphy that he would be appointed director of civil affairs in North Africa after the landing. He was instructed to assure French officials that the Americans would guarantee the salaries and pensions of French military and political officials there and that the landing would be exclusively American to allay the concerns of Anglophobes. Murphy left his post as adviser to Eisenhower in Gibraltar and arrived in Algiers on October 11. He met with General Charles Emmanuel Mast, Giraud's representative in North Africa, who assured the American representative that the French army in the region would follow the orders of Giraud.[132]

Amid this frantic planning for the invasion, de Gaulle sent a twelve-page letter to Roosevelt in which he poured out his resentment at the treatment he had received from Washington. He reminded FDR that in the dark days of June 1940 none of the political and military leaders had responded to his plea for resistance. He repudiated the assertion that he sought "a regime of personal power . . . to cheat the French people of their future liberty." He noted, with a bit of exaggeration, that Blum, Herriot, and other leaders of the Third Republic had "placed themselves at our disposal" and closed with a pledge that his current authority was "provisional" until his country could be liberated.[133] In Washington Tixier followed this up a few weeks later with letters from the leaders of the principal French resistance organizations, Liberation and Combat, to the American president urging him to support de Gaulle as the only alternative to Vichy.[134]

Another of de Gaulle's spokesmen was André Philip, a Socialist and member of the French resistance who had escaped to London and signed up with the French National Committee. The leader of Free France dispatched him to Washington in October 1942 to persuade the American government of de Gaulle's popularity in the French underground. Fluent in English, he gave lectures at churches and civic associations declaring that all the resistance movements recognized General de Gaulle as the legitimate representative of their country. He brought with him a letter from de Gaulle for delivery to Under-Secretary of State Welles pleading for consideration—to no avail.[135]

On November 7, a British submarine commanded by an American transported Giraud to Eisenhower's headquarters in Gibraltar. When Pétain learned of the invasion of North Africa, he promptly broke diplomatic relations with the United States. De Gaulle, who had been completely ignored by the Americans as they launched their operation, had been awakened at 6 a.m. in London by his chief of staff, Pierre Billotte, and told of the beginning of Operation Torch. His first reaction was to shout, forgetting his role in the Dakar fiasco in September 1940, "I hope the Vichy people are going to throw them into the sea. You can't get into France by breaking and entering."[136] But when he met with Churchill and Eden at 10 Downing Street for lunch, he had calmed down. The British prime minister was also on his best behavior. He assured de Gaulle that his exclusion from the operation was solely at the insistence of the Americans. "I shall never forget those who did not desert me in June 1940, when I was all alone," he declared. "You'll see. One day we'll go down the Champs Elysées together."[137]

De Gaulle expressed satisfaction that the United States was on the verge of establishing a base of operations in North Africa. He even managed to wish Giraud well. On the evening of November 8, de Gaulle's radio speech to French citizens in North Africa papered over his resentment at what he regarded as his shabby treatment and called for all Frenchmen to rally to the Allies. It had certainly become clear that the resistance of the French North African forces to the Allied landing demonstrated the failure of Hull's Vichy policy.[138]

Amid the Allied landing in North Africa, Hollywood weighed in with a cinematic production titled *Casablanca* after the capital of Morocco. Filmed in the Warner Brothers Studios in Burbank, California, from May 25 to August 3, 1942, it was originally scheduled to appear in the early spring of the following year but was hurriedly released on November 26 in New York City and nationally on January 23 in order to profit from the world's fascination with the Allied landing in North Africa and its aftermath. Before it was released nationally on January 23, Roosevelt viewed it in the White House on December 31, during the last stages of preparations for a top-secret trip to the Moroccan capital to meet with Churchill.[139]

It had an all-star international cast: Humphrey Bogart, the only major American-born actor in the film, played Rick Blain, the owner of a café in the heart of Casablanca; the Swedish actress Ingrid Bergman played Ilse Lund, a former lover of Rick's in Paris who arrived at the café with her husband, the Czech resistance fighter Victor Laszlo (played by the Austrian émigré Paul Henreid). She had suddenly left Rick in Paris without explanation when she discovered that her husband, whom she thought had been killed, was alive after having escaped from a German concentration camp. The couple was seeking letters of transit to escape to neutral Portugal that they had learned Rick possessed, which he eventually gives to them. The German Major Heinrich Strasser (played by the German émigré actor Conrad Veidt)[140] rushes to the airport to arrest the pair after being alerted by the corrupt Vichy police prefect Louis Renault (played by the British actor Claude Rains). Rick pulls a gun on Renault and then kills Major Strasser so that Laszlo and Ilse can depart. Instead of ordering the arrest of Rick when the police arrive, Renault feigns ignorance of what he has just witnessed and orders the cops to "round up the usual suspects." At the end of the film, Renault proposes to Rick that they both travel south to join Charles de Gaulle's Free French movement in Brazzaville in the French Congo. The final scene displays a discarded bottle of Vichy water, an arresting metaphor in case any of the viewers did not grasp the blatantly political significance of the film.[141]

While this Warner Brothers production briefly introduced Charles de Gaulle to many theater-goers in the United States for the first time, by 1943 he was featured in a number of newsreels (which were shown in American movie theaters before the featured film). Frédérique Dufour has examined the newsreel footage preserved at the Library of Congress and concluded that the vast majority of these newsreels that cover the Free French leader were favorable notwithstanding the negative attitudes toward him by the Roosevelt White House.[142]

The Darlan Deal[143]

During Operation Torch Murphy discovered that Admiral François Darlan, Pétain's right-hand man and commander of all Vichy military forces, was by pure coincidence in Algiers visiting his polio-stricken son.[144] Col. William "Wild Bill" Donovan, head of the American Office of Strategic Services (the forerunner of the CIA), had written to Roosevelt as early as April 1942 proposing that the United States approach Darlan about switching sides and joining the Allies.[145] In the morning of November 8, U.S. General Mark W. Clark (whom everyone called by his middle name "Wayne") arrived from Gibraltar as Eisenhower's representative with Giraud in tow. Clark met with Darlan and threatened to imprison him if the admiral would not immediately declare a cease-fire "in the name of the Marshal." When the admiral finally caved in and gave the order, the question of French North Africa's joining the Allies was still to be resolved. In the meantime, Pétain had given in to German pressure and approved the landing of German infantry and air forces and Italian airplanes at the Tunisian port of Bizerte.[146]

Churchill became anxious about the impending political complications in North Africa. He felt obliged to warn Eisenhower that Britain had "solemn obligations to de Gaulle," who deserved "a fair deal," and urged the American commander to avoid creating "rival French Empire governments, each favored by one of us."[147] While in Algiers, Murphy was approached by one of the indigenous Algerian leaders, who asked if Roosevelt was prepared to apply the Wilsonian principles of the Atlantic Charter to the people of Algeria. Ferhat Abbas had been very pro-French earlier in the war but had evolved into a fierce defender of the rights of his people and opponent of French colonialism. When Murphy appeared sympathetic, Abbas declared that "if this war was, as has declared the President of the United States, a war of liberation for peoples and individuals, without distinction of race or religion, Algerian Muslims would join, with all their strength . . . in this liberating struggle."[148]

In response to the Allied landing, German military forces in Metropolitan France drove southward into the unoccupied zone on November 11 and extended the occupation to the entire country, thereby removing the fig leaf of respectability that had concealed Marshal Pétain's total subservience to Hitler. After Darlan issued the cease-fire order under intense Allied pressure, Eisenhower proceeded to recognize the admiral as the ranking French military authority in North Africa. Then on the night of November 26–27, German forces approached the Mediterranean port of Toulon, where the French naval ships had been interned since the armistice. The commander of the mothballed French fleet—which included three battleships, eight cruisers, and sixteen submarines—ordered the scuttling of the entire fleet. Except for five submarines whose commanders defied orders and sailed into the open sea, the once formidable French flotilla went to the bottom of Toulon harbor, in what de Gaulle later described as "the most pitiful and sterile suicide imaginable."[149] The scuttling of the French fleet removed one of the key motivations of the Roosevelt administration's support for the Vichy regime. It no longer had to worry about the French ships falling into German and Italian hands.

After informing de Gaulle of the North African landings on November 8, Churchill also laid out the entire story of Giraud and Darlan. Expressing astonishment that the British prime minister could so obsequiously defer to the Americans, the Free French leader swallowed his pride and issued a statement over the BBC that evening urging his countrymen in North Africa to support the landings: "Rise up, help our [American] allies, join them without reservations."[150] But things would soon turn for the worse from the vantage point of de Gaulle. Clark and Murphy went far beyond the cease-fire deal and pressed to a more comprehensive agreement recognizing Darlan as the supreme French authority in North Africa and Giraud as the commander of French military forces there.

De Gaulle was foaming at the mouth when news of what came to be known as the "Darlan deal" reached him. On November 12, he unleashed a broadside to Admiral Stark, the U.S. representative to the Free French, with the observation, "You can buy traitors, but not the honor of France" and later announced on radio that the Fighting French would never accept the deal. Tixier and Philip complained bitterly to Welles on November 13 and Hull on November 14.[151] "The Americans have recruited Giraud in the hope that the announcement of his name would make the walls of Jericho fall," de Gaulle bitterly complained to his supporters. "When I consider his military qualifications, I find them insufficient for the very delicate task that he intends to assume."[152] Amid this rancor between the United States and the Free French, Resident General Noguès handed General Patton a memorandum on November 18 lavishing praise on Admiral Darlan and denouncing the Gaullists for hoodwinking the Americans and the British.[153]

Roosevelt received a long cable from Eisenhower on November 14 providing an elaborate justification for the Darlan deal, which greatly impressed him. In the meantime, the American press was roundly denouncing the arrangement. Freda Kirchway, in an editorial in the Nation titled "America's First Quisling," unleashed a broadside against "reactionary diplomacy even in the interests of military gains."[154] The New York Times and the New York Herald Tribune weighed in with sharp criticism of the deal.[155] From London the CBS broadcaster Edward R. Murrow, who had a large following in the United States, severely criticized the deal: "What the hell is this all about? Are we fighting Nazis or sleeping with them?"[156]

Treasury Secretary Henry Morgenthau denounced Darlan's record as "terrible" and lamented the "awful implications" of the policy for de Gaulle and the Free French. When Secretary of War Stimson expressed tentative support for Eisenhower's choice of Darlan as a "military necessity," Morgenthau showed him a copy of Murrow's broadcast and later complained to Roosevelt on November 17 about the policy. He was assuaged when the president assured him that it was only a temporary move, citing the old Bulgarian proverb "You can walk with the Devil as far as the bridge but then you must leave him behind."[157]

FDR's public relations advisers Robert Sherwood, Elmer Davis, and Archibald Macleish, in concert with Hopkins, drafted a statement to the press in response to the public outcry. Modified and then approved by the president, it described the deal in North Africa as a "temporary arrangement" and "a temporary expedient." He and Hopkins then dispatched a cable to the Supreme Commander stating that "we do not trust Darlan" and recognizing that "it is impossible to keep a collaborator of Hitler and one whom we believe to be a fascist in civil power and longer than is absolutely necessary." But it had no mention of de Gaulle.[158] When Milton Eisenhower, Ike's brother, was visiting North Africa working for the Office of War Information, he interviewed Darlan and received this poignant message: "I know what you Americans think of me. Your president thinks that I am a lemon to be held until all the juice has been squeezed out. That is all right with me. I am cooperating with you not for the benefit of the United States or Great Britain, but for the good of France."[159]

On November 17, *The New York Times* issued a blistering editorial denouncing the decision to work with Darlan while casting aside "our friends the Fighting French."[160] The next day de Gaulle sent a note to the Allied governments expressing his "stupor" and "disgust" at the deal and its devastating effect of the morale of the French resistance.[161] Roosevelt responded favorably to de Gaulle's request that the president receive the general's representatives in Washington to clear the air. When Roosevelt finally met with Philip and Tixier, he cheerfully informed them that he would be happy to meet with de Gaulle. Phillip, who had been active in the French resistance and had been sent to Washington as proof of its strong support for de Gaulle, recalled to Jean Lacouture many years later the tenor of the conversation: "I am not an idealist like Wilson," he recalled Roosevelt declaring. "I am concerned above all with efficiency; I have problems to solve. Those who help me solve those problems are welcome. Today, Darlan gives me Algiers, and I cry *Vive Darlan*. If Quisling gives me Oslo I will cry *Vive Quisling*! Let Laval give me Paris tomorrow and I will cry *Vive Laval*!"[162] One can only imagine de Gaulle's thoughts as he contemplated the extraordinary situation: two loyal former servants of the collaborationist Vichy regime installed as the rulers of French North Africa by the Americans, while the leader of Free France was left on the sidelines.

While the White House and the State Department continued to champion the cause of General Giraud, the War Department began to warm to de Gaulle. Assistant Secretary of War John McCloy noted that "the Fighting French have been fighting for us and with us for some time now, in fact we hold some valuable bases made available to us by them." General Marshall balanced his opposition to closer links to the Free French because of the fear of leaks with the observation that closer relations should be contemplated.[163]

The Postponed Plans for a Landing in Normandy

On November 19, Roosevelt ordered Eisenhower to free all political prisoners in French North Africa and French Equatorial Africa. In Dakar the former Vichyite Boisson refused to release his political prisoners—most of whom were Gaullist and British—until the Vichyite prisoners in Gaullist-controlled French Equatorial Africa were freed. On December 3, Roosevelt cabled Churchill that Boisson should be informed that both sets of prisoners must be released, a solution that Eisenhower endorsed on December 7.[164] In the meantime Boisson, with his finger to the wind, had arrived in Algiers from Dakar on November 30 and began working with Murphy and Darlan to resolve the issue.[165] Boisson pledged to make all facilities in French West Africa available to the Allies.[166]

Vichy had voted to apply a set of anti-Jewish laws in North Africa on October 7, 1940, prohibiting Jews from employment in administration, teaching, the press, the army, radio, and the film industry. It repealed the Cremieux Decree of October 24, 1870, which had granted French citizenship to Jews in Algeria. On December 5, 1942, Hopkins sent a memorandum to General Marshall proposing the abolition of those laws.[167] In the meantime, Churchill became concerned about the Darlan situation. On December 11, he announced that Harold Macmillan would be sent to represent Great Britain in North Africa. Three days later the French admiral announced his program: French North Africa would fight alongside the Allies; the French people would be allowed to choose their government after the final victory against the Axis; an amnesty for those who helped the Allied landing and Allied prisoners would be freed; Jews would recover their rights; North African territory would be available to the Allies as they pursued the Germans and Italians in Tunisia; and Giraud would command French troops dispatched to fight alongside the Allies in Tunisia.[168]

But all the plans and recriminations related to the "Darlan Deal" were rendered moot on New Year's Eve. The admiral was assassinated with a pistol in his office by a twenty-four-year-old named Fernand Bonnier de la Chapelle, son of a French journalist father and an Italian mother. When he had reached North Africa from France after the German victory in June 1940, Bonnier had joined a group of monarchists intent on restoring to royal power the Orléanist pretender, the exiled Count of Paris. Conspiracy theories abounded, particularly after the gunman was convicted by a secret court-martial and executed two days after the murder. Charles Noguès, the Vichyite resident general in Morocco who had ordered French troops to engage the American forces landing in the country, informed his old adversary

General George Patton on December 31 that the conspirators who organized the assassination intended to stage a coup the next day after Giraud, Noguès, and Robert Murphy had been murdered as well. The plot, the French general stated, was "backed by a group of men principally De Gaullists."[169] Whatever the conspiracy theories, General Clark was moved to remark that Darlan's death was "like the lancing of a troublesome boil."[170]

Two days later Hull learned that Giraud had been named Darlan's successor owing to pressure from Eisenhower, who did not want the Vichyite Noguès, and publicly expressed his acceptance. Earlier in the month Roosevelt had agreed to a meeting with de Gaulle in Washington to sort out their differences. The murder of Darlan led to the postponement of the visit, which had been set for December 27, greatly annoying the Free French leader who had packed his bags and was about to leave for the airport.[171]

Toward the Rendezvous at Casablanca

After the removal of Darlan from the North African scene, de Gaulle cabled Giraud on December 25, asking to meet him on French territory, preferably in Algeria, but got no response. After he renewed the request on January 1, 1943, Giraud responded five days later agreeing only to a meeting of each French general's military representatives. On January 17, the leader of the Free French sent his officers to consult with Giraud's military representatives. This was the first contact, however indirect, between the two rivals. In early January, de Gaulle had asserted in a radio address that he could work with Giraud only if all Vichy personnel were removed from his entourage. De Gaulle claims in his memoirs that the American president and his representative Robert Murphy were behind Giraud's dilatory response to his urgent requests to meet. The Free French leader was convinced that Roosevelt was intent on playing off French leaders against each other, first de Gaulle against Pétain, then de Gaulle against Darlan, and finally de Gaulle against Giraud, "until the moment when he himself would impose on both parties the solution of his choice."[172] Leahy insisted in his memoirs that "it was certain that de Gaulle's followers were at this time interfering with our war effort," while Britain was taking no action to halt this interference.[173]

On January 5, 1943, Eisenhower expressed his view that unified French political leadership behind the lines during the American military campaign against the Germans and Italians in Tunisia was essential if that effort was to succeed. Roosevelt thereupon decided to take the matter into his own hands at the forthcoming conference in Morocco, in which he and Churchill would meet to plan strategy without Stalin, who declined the invitation to attend because of the ongoing Battle of Stalingrad. On the same day, British Ambassador Halifax asked if the United States would allow de Gaulle to sit on a proposed "European Committee on the Administration of Territories" that would be set up in London and include the various refugee governments. Hull replied coldly that "we would not want to become a party either directly or indirectly to De Gaulle being placed in a position where he could maneuver to make himself or one of his choice the political head of the French Empire."[174]

Two days after Churchill, the American president arrived in Casablanca on the evening of January 14. He promptly retired to the resort suburb of Anfa, where he resided at the lush Villa Dar-es-Saada with Harry Hopkins and his son Elliot. At the opening of the conference on January 15, Roosevelt received more troubling reports from Eisenhower and Murphy about Giraud's political naiveté and lack of administrative ability.[175] When he met with Churchill the following day, the president spontaneously decided that both French generals should be invited to the meeting to endorse the proposal for French political unity that his representative on the spot, Harold Macmillan, had prepared. "I'll tell you what," FDR proposed. "We'll call Giraud the bridegroom and I'll produce him from Algiers, and you get the bride, de Gaulle, down from London and we'll have a shotgun wedding."[176]

When de Gaulle received Churchill's respectfully worded invitation from Anthony Eden, who had remained in the British capital during the meeting in Morocco, he hit the roof. Two foreign powers, even if they were allies in the war against Germany, had no right to invite the leader of Free France with no advance warning to attend a conference on French territory. In his reply de Gaulle brusquely declined Churchill's invitation, informing the British prime minister that he was renewing his request to Giraud for a one-on-one meeting between Frenchmen. Roosevelt chortled over the embarrassing position Churchill found himself in with his French protégé. "I have got the bridegroom, where is the bride?" he cabled Eden in London. "The temperamental lady de Gaulle . . . is showing no intention of getting into bed with Giraud."[177]

After strong pressure from Churchill, de Gaulle uncharacteristically referred the matter to his hand-picked French National Committee, which decided to recommend that he should go. So much for de Gaulle as an imperious dictator! On January 17, the American president finally met with Giraud, who had come from Algiers with General Mark Clark. But in his talks with the French general Roosevelt was aghast at Giraud's ignorance of the political realities on the ground and did not hesitate to chastise Murphy for recommending such a man for such an important post.[178]

Charles de Gaulle and Franklin D. Roosevelt finally met face-to-face for the first time on the evening of January 22 after a dinner honoring the Sultan of Morocco. The president (who spoke passing French but with an almost incomprehensible American accent) insisted on talking to the French leader alone without interpreters. De Gaulle could not help but notice the presence of Secret Service agents armed with machine guns behind the window curtains and on a balcony overlooking the room.[179] With an aide surreptitiously taking notes behind a door slightly ajar, the American president patronizingly described France as "a little child unable to look out and fend for itself." He complained about the instability of the French parliamentary system before the war, with such frequent changes of government. He vaguely suggested political reforms to introduce more stability and informed de Gaulle that there had been too many political parties in prewar France.[180]

The next day de Gaulle met with Giraud for a long one-on-one conference. He unleashed a blistering attack on Giraud's past expressions of loyalty to Pétain and current support of the former Vichyites Noguès and Boisson. He proposed that he, de Gaulle, establish in Algiers a Provisional Government in North Africa with Giraud as its military commander and demanded the removal of the remaining Vichy officials from their positions, both of which Giraud rejected out of hand. The leader of the Free French had thus prevented the conference from achieving Roosevelt's stated objective of establishing French unity. In de Gaulle's farewell meeting with an incensed Churchill, the British prime minister figuratively took out his meat axe and brought it down on de Gaulle's head. "He declared that on his return to London," de Gaulle reported in his memoirs, "he would publicly accuse me of having obstructed the agreement, would rouse public opinion in his country against me personally, and would appeal to the people of France."[181]

When de Gaulle made his farewell call on Roosevelt on January 24, the president implored him to give some public expression to the cause of French unity by signing a joint declaration with Giraud. "In human affairs the public must be offered a drama," the American chief executive lectured the Frenchman. "The news of your meeting with Giraud in the midst of the conference in which Churchill and I were taking part, if this news were to be accompanied by a joint declaration of the French leaders . . . would produce the dramatic effect we need."[182] De Gaulle replied that he would produce his own communiqué that would differ from the Anglo-American draft. Churchill and then Giraud joined the meeting. Roosevelt used all of the charm for which he was renowned to persuade de Gaulle at least to pose for a photograph in the company of Giraud and the two Allied leaders and shake his rival's hand. When the Free French leader magnanimously replied, in English,

"I shall do that for you," Roosevelt got his photo-op. After four chairs were placed on the lawn, with photographers at the ready, the two French generals awkwardly shook hands before a smiling Roosevelt and a scowling Churchill. As the photo was distributed to the world's media, de Gaulle drew up a vague statement indicating that the two groups would exchange liaison missions and pledging to work together against the common foe.[183]

But FDR could not resist a final dig. He wrote to Churchill on May 8: "I am sorry, but the conduct of the BRIDE continues to be more and more aggravating," he complained. "The war in North Africa has terminated successfully without any material aid from de Gaulle, and the civil situation with all its dangers seems to be working out well. . . . However, de Gaulle is without question taking his vicious propaganda staff to Algiers to stir up strife between the various elements." He suggested naming Giraud to the top post and dismissing de Gaulle.[184] A few months earlier he had shocked Eden by proposing that after the war France be partitioned, creating a new state called Wallonia (which could comprise French-speaking Belgium and Luxembourg) and possibly include the Ruhr, northern France, and Alsace-Lorraine.[185]

A New Source of Tension: French Ships in New York Harbor

In the meantime, a minor dispute between the two French generals placed the Roosevelt administration in an embarrassing situation. Soon after the success of Operation Torch, Giraud's representatives in the United States had opened a military bureau in New York City on Fifth Avenue near its Free French counterpart. The two organizations promptly began competing to recruit French sailors residing on ships docked in New York harbor for service in their respective naval forces. The Free French organization succeeded in inducing hundreds of French sailors to abandon their commitments to the Giraud group and sign up with the Gaullists. On February 15, 1943, the battleship *Richelieu*, which had fired on Free French ships during the assault on Dakar in September 1940, steamed into New York harbor for repairs. In the following weeks, 350 of its crew "jumped ship" to the Free French movement, enraging Giraud and his agents in the United States. Since Roosevelt was still very much committed to Giraud, the latter's sharp protests prompted Secretary of the Navy Frank Knox to declare the French sailors deserters on March 3. Twelve of the sailors were arrested and detained on Ellis Island in New York Harbor to dissuade others from joining the Gaullists.

The pro-Gaullist American press rushed to the defense of the Free French and the sailors who sought to join them. Several sailors sent messages to Roosevelt denouncing their officers as Vichyites and demanded that they be released. An agreement between Giraudists and Gaullists was finally concluded on April 22 to form a joint commission to review the appeals of each sailor. The sailors were eventually set free after a trial before the New York Supreme Court and most set sail for Great Britain, where they joined the Free French navy.[186]

The Two Generals Resume Their Bid for Roosevelt's Favor

During the Casablanca conference, Roosevelt had decided to ask the well-connected Jean Monnet to come to Algiers to advise Giraud on how to navigate the swirling political waters in which he was floundering. When Monnet had arrived in late February at Roosevelt's behest, he dutifully pursued his mission to strengthen Giraud's position. He retained his earlier suspicions of de Gaulle that dated from his refusal to join the Free French movement in 1940. "De Gaulle stands for arbitrary action with all the risks of Fascism," he declared. "Giraud stands for the preservation of the right of the people and democratic process."[187] But as he gradually perceived that Giraud was hopeless and that de Gaulle had strong support and formidable political abilities, he decided to switch sides. Instead of weighing in on the dispute between the two French generals, he remained disengaged as de Gaulle gradually outmaneuvered Giraud, to Murphy's profound displeasure.[188]

The major point of dispute remained the question of leadership of the refurbished French National Committee, and it would eventually be resolved on de Gaulle's terms. Amid this jockeying for position, de Gaulle received in London on March 23 Cardinal Francis Spellman, the archbishop of New York. There is no indication that the prelate was undertaking a mission for the White House. The cardinal pressed de Gaulle to abandon his policy of isolating Giraud and to establish a cooperative relationship on the political level. De Gaulle replied that while he esteemed the rival general as "a good and great soldier," he brushed aside the suggestion for a political entente.[189]

Under the influence of Monnet (who worked closely with Macmillan), Giraud finally succumbed in mid-May and invited de Gaulle to come to Algiers from London. The two soldiers would serve as co-presidents of a planning committee to establish a new unified national committee. De Gaulle arrived in Algiers on May 30 and immediately plunged into conferences attended by representatives of the two rival generals. De Gaulle forcefully reiterated his familiar two demands: the subjection of the military command to the political leadership and the removal of the Vichyites Noguès, Boisson, and Peyrouton to demonstrate that French North Africa had definitively broken with the collaborationist regime on the continent. When Giraud rejected both conditions out of hand, de Gaulle stalked out. But when passions had cooled and under Monnet's patient mediation, the two generals met and agreed on June 3 to formally establish the seven-person French Committee of National Liberation (CFLN), with Giraud and de Gaulle serving as co-presidents. It was soon enlarged to fourteen members, giving de Gaulle a clear majority.[190] This dramatic turn of events represented the first stage in what would soon become total victory for de Gaulle over the rival French general.

Throughout the summer of 1943, de Gaulle gradually elbowed Giraud and his supporters aside as he consolidated his power over the committee. After Peyrouton resigned as resident general of Algeria, the committee voted, over Giraud's objections, to remove Noguès from Morocco and Boisson from French West Africa. On June 5, the Committee of Seven had met to appoint a cabinet. Most of the key posts went to prominent supporters of de Gaulle: René Massigli to Foreign Affairs, André Philip to Interior, Réné Pleven to Colonies, Adrien Tixier to Labor. Three days later the committee definitively subordinated the military command to the political direction, thereby revoking Giraud's membership on the Committee. Roosevelt responded to the news of the displacement of his favorite French general with fury. "I am fed up with de Gaulle and the secret personal and political machinations of the French committee," he fulminated. "I am absolutely convinced that he has been and is now injuring our war effort, and that he is a very dangerous threat to us. It is time that we must break with him." He proposed that Washington and London set up a new French committee free of his influence.[191]

But other U.S. officials were beginning to stray from the path that the chief executive laid out. Robert Sherwood, the playwright, presidential speechwriter, and director of the U.S. propaganda agency, the Office of War Information, urged Roosevelt on June 6 to announce the admission of "United France" to the United Nations roster to enhance American propaganda in Europe. The president peremptorily brushed aside the proposal as "premature."[192]

After receiving an invitation from Roosevelt to visit Washington, Giraud left Algiers on July 2 for a two-week visit to the United States that was billed as a strictly military affair. Soon after his arrival on June 5, he was greeted warmly by Roosevelt and then by his counterparts in the American officer corps. "At 5 pm intimate tea with the president," he recalled in his memoirs. "We spoke only in French. At 8 pm, a grand dinner on the [presidential yacht] Mayflower hosted by General Marshall. I met the senior military authorities in Washington. Sumptuous feast. French wines."[193] But July 9 the French general, who spoke not a word of English, gave an awkward press conference in Washington under the auspices of the War Department.

Journalists were instructed to ask only questions related to military affairs. In a press conference on the same day, even Roosevelt declared that the French general's visit was "only that of a soldier."[194] On the previous day, Hull had sent a memorandum to Roosevelt reminding him, as if he needed such a reminder, that the CFLN was not a full-fledged government until free elections were held in France.[195]

Giraud made the rounds of Washington officialdom. On July 6, he met with General Marshall and Admiral Leahy to inform them of his goals for France. He lunched with the president along with Marshall and Leahy, which he strangely claims in his memoirs was conducted "almost exclusively in French"—a language that neither Marshall nor Leahy spoke.[196] Nothing of substance came from his sojourn. Churchill had advised Murphy against inviting Giraud to Washington for fear that de Gaulle would stage a putsch in his absence.[197] When he returned to Algiers on July 27, he naively assumed that the trip to Washington had strengthened his hand in his rivalry with de Gaulle. In reality he had lost all semblance of political power while retaining his military position. Four months later Giraud and an ally were eliminated from the FCNL, thereby ending the co-presidency. Churchill recognized such a development as logical in light of Giraud's failure as a political leader. But the prime minister continued to distrust de Gaulle and cabled Roosevelt suggesting that the two leaders "maintain an attitude of complete reserve until we can discuss the position together."[198]

Roosevelt and the Future of the French Empire

The American president periodically returned to his obsession with securing control of key military bases in the French Empire after the war with a succession of harebrained schemes that would have enraged de Gaulle had he known about them: the port of Dakar in French West Africa could be converted into a naval and air base under the joint auspices of the United States and Brazil, while Australia and New Zealand could administer the French bases in New Caledonia.[199] As plans for the invasion of northern France began to take shape in late January 1944, Roosevelt repeated to his secretary of state what he had often said about the future of the French empire after the war, particularly French Indochina: "France has milked it [Indochina] for 100 years. The people of Indochina are entitled to something better than that." He reiterated his vague and ambiguous belief that after the war "it should be administered by an international trusteeship."[200]

During FDR's brief stopover in Cairo after returning from the Teheran Conference of the Big Three on November 23–December 1, 1943, Macmillan recalls him reiterating his belief that Indochina should not be returned to France but held under "tutelage" by China and the Tunisian Mediterranean port of Bizerte should be placed under British protection.[201] But Churchill's government strenuously opposed Roosevelt's plans for the French Empire, presumably because it worried about their implications for the British Empire after the war. In February 1944, the British cabinet approved a message from the Foreign Office recommending that Indochina be returned to France after the Japanese defeat. In April Great Britain authorized Admiral Louis Mount-batten, the Supreme Allied Commander for Southeast Asia, to equip the French forces in India under General Roger Blaizot, who had been named by de Gaulle commander of the Far East French Expeditionary Forces, for future missions in Indochina.[202]

Preparations for D-Day

Just before he left Algiers for Washington and then London to take charge of his new assignment for what came to be designated as Operation Over-lord, the cross-Channel invasion of northern France, Eisenhower had paid a courtesy visit to de Gaulle in his villa on December 30. He assured the French leader that "he could not imagine entering Paris" without French troops and believed that they should be involved in the landing, even if only as "a token force." When Eisenhower confidentially apologized for the treatment that de Gaulle had received in North Africa, de Gaulle replied with some emotion, "You are a man." The supreme commander assured de Gaulle that the liberating army would need to depend on de Gaulle's admin-istrative support after the landing and his rallying of French public opinion in support of the operation. He also affirmed that he intended to recognize no political authority in France after the invasion other than de Gaulle's. This and similar conversations convinced de Gaulle that Eisenhower's views toward the Free French movement were very different than those of the American commander in chief.[203] In early January 1944, Eisenhower and then his aide-de-camp General Walter Bedell ("Beetle") Smith pleaded with the War Department in Washington for full authorization to deal with the French Committee of National Liberation. Smith asserted that "the French National Committee, whatever its faults may be, represents the beginning of civil government in France, and has received the allegiance of practically all of the French resistance groups."[204]

But de Gaulle's hopes that Ike's and Bedell Smith's assurances reflected the president's thinking were not borne out. Indeed, the Roosevelt adminis-tration remained very wary of de Gaulle as the preparations for the opening of a second front in France intensified. In January 1944, the State Department drafted a report titled "Reasons underlying this government's lack of confidence in de Gaulle." The report trotted out the familiar complaints: the narrow, chauvinistic nationalism, the "threat of dictatorship," and (curiously) his "subservience to the Russians." An earlier report on the French resistance asserted that the Free French leader "seeks a military socialistic dictatorship in alliance with the Communist party."[205]

It is fair to conclude that a sharp distinction was developing within the Roosevelt administration on the issue of relations with Charles de Gaulle. General Eisenhower, Secretary of War Henry Stimson, and presidential aide Harry Hopkins were pragmatic and realistic when it came to the Free French movement. Secretary of State Cordell Hull and Franklin Roosevelt let their emotions intervene in their judgment.[206] When Eisenhower was in Washington in early 1944, he met with Stimson and Under-Secretary of War John McCloy at the War Department. The general stressed the importance of maintaining good relations with Free France in order to promote the success of the projected landing in Normandy. When Stimson and McCloy met with Hull on January 14, they pressed the secretary of state to agree that the time had arrived to completely revise American policy toward de Gaulle. Stimson wanted to establish contact with the resistance groups in France with de Gaulle as intermediary to prepare them to support the planned landing. He also noted that the invading army would need the support of the Gaullist movement to establish the first administrative organisms in Normandy behind the lines of the fighting. Hull refused to agree to this fundamental change in policy and urged Stimson and McCloy to see the president. On January 19, Eisenhower told Chief of Staff George Marshall that it was essential that plans for civil affairs in liberated France be drafted in the near future in conjunction with the Gaullists. He added that de Gaulle should be asked to designate an official in London to establish liaison with the War Department so that administrative authority could be seamlessly turned over to the Free French representatives in France as soon as possible after the landing.[207]

But Roosevelt continued to stand firm. In mid-January he chided Churchill for pressing him to publicly support the Free French, declaring that "I have no intention of withdrawing support from Giraud. He is a fine old fellow and represents certain decencies which I still like."[208] At a press conference on February 11, he denied reports that the U.S. government was in the process of revising its policy toward Free France in the direction of formal recognition.[209] In the same month a startled British ambassador to Washington learned that Leahy, FDR's chief of staff, had told the president that Pétain was best suited to rally the French people after the liberation began.[210]

In March the president approved a message to Eisenhower, which Stimson had modified to remove the limits on the commanding general's authority to deal with the Free French. It granted Eisenhower wide latitude to arrange for the civil administration of liberated French territory in consultation with the CFLN but, as always, stipulated that this new policy did not constitute recognition.[211] What was notable about this directive is what it did *not* include. There was no reference to the implementation of the plan for an American military occupation of liberated France that had been discussed and very tentatively approved after the Allied landing in North Africa.[212]

The Specter of AMGOT

Early in the war the question arose about how liberated countries would be administered to protect the rear of the liberating army. In early 1942, Secretary of War Henry Stimson, who favored a military occupation of liberated territory, set up a Military Administration School in facilities provided by the University of Virginia in the city of Charlottesville. Its official title was the American Military Government for Occupied Territories (AMGOT). In the spring of 1943, Roosevelt wrote Churchill suggesting that he and the British prime minister agree to a military occupation of France after its liberation "run by British and American generals," joking that "I do not know what to do about de Gaulle. Possibly you would like to make him Governor of Madagascar."[213] In September 1943, Roosevelt had signed a project prepared by Hull for the administration of France after its liberation. The following month he had informed his secretary of state that "the thought that the occupation when it occurs should be wholly military is one to which I am increasingly inclined."[214]

In the liberated zone, the Supreme Commander would have total authority and would favor no French political group. Monnet had arrived in Washington in mid-November of the previous year as a representative of the CFLN to discuss the provisioning of France after liberation. When he learned that the United States planned to print banknotes identical to those that would be circulated in liberated Italy, francs replacing lire, he forcefully urged that the French currency be used.[215] In the meantime, the War Department in Washington was buffeted by an internal debate about AMGOT for France. Assistant Secretary of War John McCloy took the lead in opposing the measure. "It would be 'dynamite' to intervene in the internal affairs of France as we use to do in small Central American states," he declared, noting that it "would be obnoxious to the French people, regardless of their political views." This position was supported by Eisenhower's chief of staff, General Walter Bedell Smith.[216]

Hull's Change of Heart

In the spring of 1944, Cordell Hull began to soften his earlier harsh criticism of Charles de Gaulle and the Free French.[217] He announced in a radio speech on April 9 that the United States had "no purpose or wish to govern France or to administer any affairs save those which are necessary for military operations against the enemy" and affirmed that the U.S. government was "disposed to see the French Committee of National Liberation exercise leadership to establish law and order" in future liberated regions of France "under the supervision of the Allied Commander-in-Chief."[218] He added frosting on the cake by affirming that the CFLN has been "a symbol of the spirit of France and of French resistance."[219] It is unclear whether the president authorized this statement by his secretary of state.

In the meantime, the position of Giraud had become entirely untenable and led to his disappearance from the world scene. When the CFLN officially designated de Gaulle head of the French army and president of the Committee on April 4, Giraud resigned from the Committee and declined the honorific post of inspector general of the French Armies. Hull learned the opinion of Robert Murphy on April 7 that Giraud was hopeless and widely regarded in Algiers as "nothing more than an 'American agent' or an 'American valet,'" to the detriment of American prestige. Murphy urged that the U.S. government "should not only interpose no objection to Giraud's departure but facilitate it." Hull promptly responded with full approval of this final blow to the French general on whom FDR had pinned his hopes to circumvent de Gaulle.[220]

But on April 15, with the Normandy landings only six weeks away, Hull learned that Roosevelt was adamant in opposing any hint of recognition of the CFLN, despite pleas from Churchill and McCloy that he deal directly with the Gaullist organization.[221] British foreign secretary Anthony Eden chimed in on the matter during a question period in Parliament. In response to a question about whether the British government would deal exclusively with the CFLN in liberated France, Eden replied, "Yes sir! I do not know of any other [French authority] except Vichy."[222]

But in the light of FDR's continuing opposition, an irritated de Gaulle delivered a speech in Tunis on May 7, which consisted of a strategy that he would later repeat seven months later when he flew to Moscow for direct negotiations with Stalin: he played the "Russian card." Hinting at a possible reorientation of French policy toward Stalin's Soviet Union (probably intended for Churchill's ears), he called for direct and practical cooperation with "dear and powerful Russia, a permanent ally." At a press conference two weeks earlier, he had declared that "we are linked with the USSR, although there exists no formal treaty between us."[223] However, a month after the liberation of France began, the American ambassador to the Soviet Union, Averill Harriman, reported that when the French representative in Moscow had requested Soviet recognition of the French committee as the provisional government of France, he was told by Soviet foreign minister Vjacheslav Molotov that his government would take "no action vis-à-vis the French at variance with the Anglo-American position," a policy repeated by Molotov on several occasions to Harriman.[224]

On May 11, Eisenhower warned the War Department of the dire consequences of keeping the Gaullists out of the loop of information about the plans for the landing, which would constitute a grave insult to General Marie-Pierre Koenig, the Free French delegate to Eisenhower's headquarters. He urged that de Gaulle be summoned to London to apprise him of the Allied plans. Eisenhower's headquarters had dispatched a directive to American and British army groups that would land in Normandy, and it constituted a preemptive strike against AMGOT. "Military government will *not* be established in liberated France," the directive clearly stipulated. "The French themselves will conduct all aspects of civil administration in their country, even in areas of military operations."[225]

Roosevelt finally authorized an invitation to the leader of the Free French to proceed to London but repeated the familiar refrain that it would constitute no recognition of de Gaulle's movement until free elections could be held in France after its liberation.[226] This declaration would have been music to de Gaulle's ears and a source of immense relief. He did not yet know whether the United States would permit French authorities to administer his country after the liberation. He recalled to his son, Philippe, that just before the embarkation on June 6 he had encountered an American colonel who, with a cigar between his teeth, informed the French leader that "you are headed for France. So am I. I have been designated head of the Gare de l'Est [a Parisian railroad station]."[227]

On May 16, the French National Committee decided to rename itself "the Provisional Government of the French Republic." A few days later Eisenhower complained to his diary that both Roosevelt and Churchill "have been absolutely unwilling to give the French any information whatsoever" about the impending plans for the landing.[228] At the end of the month, Roosevelt let it be known through an emissary that de Gaulle was free to visit the United States after what he hoped would be a successful landing but could not be invited as a head of state.[229] But after FDR implored Churchill to persuade de Gaulle "to actually assist in the liberation of France without being imposed on the French people as their government," the British prime minister (with Roosevelt's reluctant permission) invited de Gaulle to come to London from Algiers in total secrecy in a British plane to bring him into the loop about the impending invasion of his country.[230]

The French leader left Algiers for London on June 3, the same day of the official announcement that the CFLN had assumed the title of Provisional Government. De Gaulle was greeted at the airport by a military band playing the "Marseillaise" and was invited by the prime minister to join him in his train compartment near Eisenhower's headquarters at Widewing, where Eden and several other British officials were present.[231] Churchill informed him that, although Franklin Roosevelt was not in a position to issue a formal invitation, the American president would welcome the opportunity to discuss political matters with de Gaulle in the United States. The French leader testily replied, "Why do you seem to think that I need to submit my candidacy for the authority of France to Roosevelt? The French government exists. I have nothing to ask in this respect from the United States of America nor of Great Britain." It was at this point that an enraged Churchill scowled at de Gaulle and blurted out, according to de Gaulle's memoirs, a statement that would color the French leader's attitude to his British allies for many years to come: "There is something you ought to know: Each time we have to choose between Europe and the open sea, we shall always choose the open sea. Each time I have to choose between you and Roosevelt, I shall always choose Roosevelt." Although Eden and Ernest Bevin, the Labour Party opposition leader, both promptly disassociated themselves from the prime minister's outburst, de Gaulle derived from this statement the certainty that France could never depend on Britain to be anything else but a subservient servant of the other English-speaking power across the Atlantic.[232]

On June 4, after lunching with Churchill in his railroad car, de Gaulle drove to Eisenhower's command post nearby. The Supreme Allied Commander filled him in on the details of the planned landing and told him that he expected to deal with the French Committee in the territory that was liberated. Eisenhower proceeded to show de Gaulle the proclamation he planned to issue to the French people during the landing and expressed the hope that the French leader "could prepare a statement to be broadcast as well."[233] Eisenhower informed him that it had already been printed and could not be modified before the projected landing. The planning for the address did not please the leader of the Free French. The Supreme Commander's speech had been translated into Dutch, Flemish, Norwegian, and Danish as well as into French.[234] The leaders of all the governments-in-exile in London would address their fellow countrymen. Eisenhower would then speak on behalf of the Allies, and then de Gaulle would issue his own proclamation. De Gaulle initially refused to speak after the Allied commander to avoid giving the impression of endorsing all his statements. Recriminations soon followed from Eisenhower, Churchill, and General Marshall.[235]

In a last-minute dispute, de Gaulle refused to allow the two hundred French liaison officers stationed in Britain to accompany the Allied soldiers on the landing beaches, though he eventually relented and permitted about eighty to make the voyage.[236] So the question of who would administer the liberated territory was left unresolved. In the end de Gaulle decided to backtrack, and he dutifully delivered his speech to the French people on June 6, as the landing unfolded.[237] The British Foreign Office was prepared to cut short the speech, the draft of which neither the Americans nor the British had been permitted to vet, if it sounded disagreeable. There proved to be no need for such measures. After urging all French people to do their duty to engage the enemy "by all means in their power," he expressed his heartfelt thanks to his allies for their support of France, causing tears to well up in Churchill's eyes.[238] A small contingent of some 177 soldiers, a small detachment of French paratroopers, and air and naval forces participated in the amphibious operation.

The day after D-Day de Gaulle dined with Eden in an effort to settle the issue of the administration of liberated France on the basis of a September 1943 memorandum drafted by the French Committee in Algiers. Roosevelt had continually refused to appoint a representative to such talks on the grounds it was a purely military affair of concern only to Eisenhower. But intense criticism in the American press prompted the president to issue on the same day a formal invitation to de Gaulle to visit Washington as soon as possible to settle the matter, suggesting June 22 to June 30 or July 6 to 14 as convenient dates.[239] De Gaulle replied much later with a tentative acceptance but asked whether any restrictions would be placed on his visit, in other words, that he would be received as only a military leader.[240] On June 13, a *New York Times* editorial stated the obvious: there was no other French group deserving of recognition.[241]

After an abortive effort by Churchill to postpone indefinitely de Gaulle's plan for a brief visit to Normandy, the Free French leader boarded the French destroyer *La Combattante* on the morning of June 14 for the four-hour voyage from Britain to the France's Channel coast in Lower Normandy. On the fourth anniversary of the entrance of German troops in Paris, he set foot on metropolitan French territory for the first time since his hasty flight from Bordeaux to Britain four years earlier. He was accompanied by several loyal aides. The small group that accompanied the Free French leader included François Coulet, whom de Gaulle planned to leave behind to assume administrative control of liberated French territory according to top-secret plans that had been drawn up in Algiers without the knowledge of British or American officials.[242]

De Gaulle landed at the village of Courseulles in the beachhead established by Canadian and British forces. He dispatched aides to Bayeux, the largest town liberated by then, to prepare the way for his planned visit there. With its medieval cathedral and its famous tapestry depicting the cross-Channel invasion in the opposite direction by William the Conqueror in 1066, it was replete with historical symbolism. The advance party dispatched earlier to Bayeux included Rear Admiral Georges Thierry D'Argenlieu, General Marie-Pierre Koenig, the civil administrator François Coulet, and Maurice Schumann (who had served as the Free French press spokesman in London). Schumann circled around the town with a bullhorn announcing that de Gaulle would soon arrive in the town square. Coulet had brought with him a trunk containing twenty-five million francs that were printed under the auspices of the French provisional government. The Americans had already begun to distribute their "fausse monnaie" as de Gaulle contemptuously called it, in the liberated Norman towns within the expanding Anglo-American beachhead. But Coulet was under orders from de Gaulle to remove them from circulation and replace them with the provisional French government francs.[243]

On his way to the town square in a jeep, he came upon a priest, who announced that he was the local curé and said that he had heard de Gaulle's broadcast on June 18, 1940: "I have sheltered parachutists, I had been in touch with the Maquis, and you have passed through my village without even shaking my hand." The leader of Free France leaped from the jeep and put his arms around the priest. "Monsieur le Curé, I do not shake your hand," he declared. "I embrace you."[244] He stopped off at the office of the prefecture and shook hands with an assembly of local notables, including the Vichy-appointed sous-préfet who had served the French state for almost the entire period of the occupation. In his first speech on French soil in four years, de Gaulle invoked a theme that had become, and would remain, a central element of the Gaullist legend: "What the country expects of you, here behind the front, is to continue the fight today as you have never ceased from fighting since the beginning of the war, and since June 1940."[245] De Gaulle's speech in Bayeux, and many others that he would deliver for the rest of his career, repeated the assertion that the French people had been betrayed by a small band of traitors—with his old mentor Pétain at their head—and had never acquiesced in the defeat and degradation of their motherland. Four hours after his return to France, the leader of the Free French boarded the French destroyer and headed back to England.

While de Gaulle was in Bayeux, Secretary of War Henry Stimson received a call from Roosevelt. In a conversation that lasted almost an hour, the president adamantly refused to grant de Gaulle some degree of recognition until national elections could be held in France. Stimson recorded the conversation in his diary: "I pointed out the impossibility of actually supervising elections and he fully agreed. But he believes that de Gaulle will crumble. . . . This is contrary to everything that I hear. I think de Gaulle is daily gaining strength as the invasion goes on, and that is to be expected. He is becoming the symbol of deliverance of the French people."[246]

While the Anglo-American forces were struggling to break out of their beachheads in Normandy, a group of high-level American officials were spending a long evening on the yacht of Secretary of the Navy James Forrestal on the Potomac on June 22. In addition to Forrestal, the party included Under Secretary of State Edward Stettinius, FDR's Chief of Staff (and former ambassador to Vichy) Admiral William Leahy, Assistant Secretary of War John McCloy, and Jean Monnet. Forrestal (who had long been a strident critic of the Free French movement) and Leahy unleashed a ferocious attack on de Gaulle. Leahy reviewed the long history of what he considered to be the Free French leader's disgraceful behavior against the former Vichyite Boisson and Giraud (erroneously claiming that the latter had been thrown into prison by de Gaulle). Monnet offered a feeble defense of the leader of Free France but was outnumbered by the angry American officials.[247] In the meantime, Hull had totally reversed himself on the topic of recognizing the Free French "government." He told State Department official Adolph A. Berle that "this is entirely a presidential matter" and would wash his hands of the issue.[248]

AMGOT: The Controversy That Would Not Die

The issue of the currency was the hardest nut to crack. As we have seen, it had been broached in the fall of 1943 and then revisited in the spring of 1944, but not been officially resolved when the landing began. In his talk with Churchill at Portsmouth on June 4, two days before the invasion, de Gaulle had complained bitterly that he had just learned that the troops to be landed had "a so-called French currency printed abroad" without his approval. "Go ahead," he yelled, "wage war with your fake currency." On June 9, with Allied troops still ensconced on their Normandy beachheads, an alarmed Churchill implored Roosevelt to look into the situation and Eisenhower urged the Allied general staff to demand that the currency issue be clarified. The next day John McCloy informed Roosevelt that the currency issue was for de Gaulle "the touchstone of the political problem of recognition."[249]

But FDR would have none of it. He complained to Churchill that the bank note issue "is being exploited to stampede us into according full recognition" to de Gaulle's committee (studiously avoiding using the term "Provisional Government of the French Republic"). He insisted that the supplementary currency be utilized "in exactly the same manner we have planned," concluding his message with a familiar blast at de Gaulle: "It seems clear that prima donnas do not change their spots."[250]

De Gaulle in the United States

In the meantime, de Gaulle's position was bolstered between June 8 and June 20 by a succession of declarations by six governments-in-exile in London (Czechoslovakia, Poland, Belgium, Luxemburg, Yugoslavia, and Norway) recognizing the Provisional Government of the French Republic. On June 15, de Gaulle thanked the American president for the list he had sent of convenient dates for his visit to Washington, and promised to settle on a date in the near future. On the same day, Eden visited de Gaulle at Carlton Gardens and predicted that Roosevelt was waiting for de Gaulle's visit to announce a change in U.S. policy toward Free France.[251] Yet Elmer Davis, director of the Office of War Information, reported that his agency considered the "De Gaulle situation" to be "the most currently dangerous point in American foreign policy—dangerous because of the reactions at home as well as abroad."[252] In the meantime, de Gaulle's agents on the ground won widespread support from the inhabitants of the liberated towns and cities, leaving no doubt about his popularity in the country.[253]

De Gaulle finally accepted Roosevelt's invitation on June 25 to visit the United States. Before departing for Washington, he issued two statements designed to calm the waters. The first was a cable to Roosevelt on the eve of American Independence Day conveying "warm best wishes that the provisional government and myself retain for the greatness and the prosperity of the United States" and expressed his country's "profound gratitude" for the role of American troops in the liberation of France. The second was a public declaration the day of his departure taking note of "the blood spilled by the brave young Americans on the soil of Europe."[254]

Charles de Gaulle left Algiers on July 5 on a plane sent by Roosevelt for the almost thirty-six-hour flight to Washington. He arrived the following day—exactly a month after the beginning of Operation Overlord in Normandy. It was the first meeting of the two men since their brief encounter in Casablanca in January 1943, but this time without Giraud (who had lapsed into total irrelevance). On the president's orders, his French visitor received a seventeen-gun salute as a military officer rather than the twenty-one-gun salute for a head of state. He was greeted by General Marshall, Admiral King, and General Arnold but no member of the U.S. cabinet, to underscore the military rather than political nature of the visit. He was brought directly to the White House where he met with the president, Hull, and other dignitaries as well as Roosevelt's daughter, Anna, in the first of three encounters with the American chief executive. After greeting the French leader in French—"si content de vous voir" ("so happy to see you")—he offered tea to those present. Turning to Leahy, he allegedly joked, "For you Admiral, Vichy [mineral] water would be more appropriate," a quip that did not amuse his French guest.[255]

De Gaulle was intent on preventing the kind of dustups he had had so often with Churchill in London. On his arrival he gave a brief speech in English: "I am happy to be on American soil to meet President Roosevelt," he declared. "Our ardent desire is that the United States and France continue working together in every way, as today our fighting men are marching together to the common victory."[256] Both protagonists were on their best behavior, avoiding all issues that might cause controversy. De Gaulle's low-key performance in meetings with the American president in the course of four days impressed even such former antagonists as Admiral Leahy and Cordell Hull, the latter of whom rejoiced that the "agreeable" French leader had assured his interlocutors "that he had no intention of forcing himself or his committee on France as her future government."[257]

But the president did not mince words when the conversations addressed the issue of the postwar world and France's role in it. Gently turning aside de Gaulle's pointed inquiry about possible French participation in the military occupation of postwar Germany, Roosevelt mapped out in very general terms his vision of the future after Germany's defeat. It was a vision that was guaranteed to displease the French leader and to confirm his conviction that he must resume his efforts to reassert the position of France in the face of American opposition. "In his opinion, a four-power directorate—America, Soviet Russia, China, and Great Britain—should settle the world's problems" without France, de Gaulle complained in his memoirs. "As for the horde of small or medium sized states, he would be in a position to impose upon them by virtue of the help he could provide."[258]

The American president raised the possibility of deploying military forces under the auspices of the projected new international organization in bases across the globe, including French overseas possessions. When de Gaulle expressed his concern that this project would seriously undermine the postwar position of his country, the president replied caustically what he had said so many times earlier: that he had lost respect for France after its military defeat in 1940 and its collaboration with Nazi Germany for the next four years. He recalled the chronic instability of the governments of the Third Republic in the interwar period, confessing that he sometimes forgot the name of the current French prime minister.[259]

Swallowing his patriotic pride, de Gaulle cautioned the president that to allow his Soviet allies, which were driving the Germans out of their war-torn country, to exercise hegemony over Eastern Europe would upset the equilibrium of Europe and stressed how the restoration of France's position was essential for such a balance on the continent. When the question of France's overseas empire came up, he agreed with Roosevelt that a reevaluation of European colonialism was in order. But he warned that a rapid dismantling of the empires would risk "unleashing a xenophobia and an anarchy that would be dangerous to the entire world." Before leaving Washington de Gaulle paid a courtesy visit to eighty-four-year-old General John J. Pershing at Walter Reed Hospital on July 6. When Pershing told his visitor that if his army had gone all the way to Berlin at the end of the last war, perhaps there would not have been a second war, De Gaulle responded with vigor, "At least this time we'll go through."[260] The ailing, confused former commander of the American Expeditionary Force in France during World War I (who, as we have seen, had been Roosevelt's first choice to become U.S. ambassador to Vichy) asked his French visitor, "Ah, how is my old friend Marshal Pétain?" After an embarrassed silence, de Gaulle gently replied that "la dernière fois que je l'ai vu, il se portait bien" ("the last time I saw him he was doing well").[261]

After his talks with the president, de Gaulle made a quick trip to New York City, where he received a warm introduction at City Hall Plaza by an admiring Mayor Fiorello La Guardia. On learning about the mayor's invitation before leaving Algiers, he had specified to his representative in Washington that he did not want to meet any of the French personalities in the city that had refused to support him, mentioning, among others, Alexis Leger, the journalist Geneviève Tabouis, the former Deputy Henri de Kerillis, and the journalist André Géraud.[262] The New York mayor had been a staunch supporter of Free France and had declared an official "Free French Week" in the city in July 1942. The day before Bastille Day he had delivered a fiery speech at the City Hall in which he denounced "those [French people] who are in friendly negotiations with the Nazis" and lauded the organization "that is fighting the Nazis."[263]

After the diminutive mayor's welcome, de Gaulle delivered a short speech in heavily accented English. The "Marseillaise" was belted out by a French soprano from the Paris Opera, followed by the "Star Spangled Banner" sung by a singer from the Metropolitan Opera, in the presence of uniformed military from both countries. The emotion-laden event formed a spectacular counterpoint to the chilly relations between de Gaulle and the president. But the two leaders exchanged exceedingly cordial messages after de Gaulle's departure. The latter thanked the president for his "warm hospitality" and the "sentiments of friendship and confidence" he had received in Washington. Roosevelt replied with an expression of "real pleasure" at their conversations and thanked de Gaulle for his gift of a small model submarine.[264]

After a trip to Québec City and Montréal, whose mayor urged his constituents to "show General de Gaulle that Montréal is the second French city of the world," he returned to Algiers on July 13 in time to celebrate Bastille Day. Six days later he received the text of Roosevelt's declaration announcement in a press conference that the United States "recognizes that the French Committee of National Liberation is qualified to exercise the administration of France." Though the announcement omitted the term "provisional government," the departing leader of Free France had obtained what he yearned for most of all: the final nail in the coffin of the idea for the American military occupation of liberated France. After negotiations between de Gaulle's representatives in Washington, Henri Hoppenot and Hervé Alphand, and a team from the War Department's John McCloy, he also obtained U.S. recognition of the right of the CFLN to administer the zone behind the combat lines.[265]

In Algiers de Gaulle began to make plans for a triumphant return to France as the Allied armies recorded victory after victory against the retreating German forces. On August 15, the day of the landing of the French First and American Sixth and Seventh Armies on the coast of southern France, he informed Roosevelt of his ardent desire to return for good to his homeland. Eisenhower expressed no objection, adding that if the agreements on civil administration had not yet been signed, he would receive de Gaulle as the head of the French army; if they had been signed, he would receive him as the "head of the provisional government of France." The next day the War Department replied it had no objection to his returning to France, but only as head of the French army.[266]

On the same day, the War Department submitted to the Inter-Allied General Staff in Washington a memorandum dividing the administration of liberated France into two zones. A representative of the CFLN would be consulted on administrative questions in the combat zone. In the liberated zones in the interior, French authorities would be in charge. This project would form the basis of an agreement on August 23 in Washington among CFLN delegates, the U.S. government, and the British government. It was forwarded to Eisenhower the same day with an accompanying letter drafted by the Inter-Allied General Staff for transmission to General Koenig: the CFLN would henceforth be treated as the "de facto authority" to administer all liberated regions of France.[267]

Pierre Laval's Last Gambit

In the meantime, de Gaulle had become exercised by a murky development as the Allied armies moved eastward in pursuit of the retreating Germans. On August 12, Pierre Laval, the pro-German Vichy prime minister, visited Edouard Herriot, a three-time prime minister and the last president of the National Assembly of the Third Republic who had been incarcerated by Vichy in the city of Nancy. After securing Herriot's release and while driving with him back to Paris, Laval unveiled a harebrained scheme whereby Herriot would reconvene the old National Assembly that Pétain had dissolved in July 1940 and install it in the capital city to form a "French government" before the Allies arrived as an alternative to de Gaulle.[268]

Once in Paris on August 16 Herriot saw the handwriting on the wall and adamantly refused to enter a government that had jailed him for four years. The Germans promptly arrested Herriot and Laval and sent both to Germany. They took Pétain into custody three days later, shipping the Marshal and his dwindling entourage off to the eastern city of Belfort and eventually to an old Hohenzollern castle in Sigmaringen in southern Germany where they set up a sham Vichy "government in exile."[269]

When de Gaulle got wind of the absurd plan as he prepared for his triumphal return to France, he promptly suspected an Anglo-American role in delaying and perhaps preventing his return to Paris in cooperation with the expiring Vichy regime. In fact, Douglas MacArthur II, a nephew of the general and an American diplomat in France, had been briefed on the "Laval-Herriot Affair" and passed the information on to Chief of Staff Leahy. No evidence has surfaced of any U.S. participation in or even knowledge of it.[270] But this development, coupled with Roosevelt's occasional declarations that "de Gaulle is on the wane" and expressions of hope that "new parties will emerge" in liberated France, further damaged relations between the two leaders. Already defensive about the escalating domestic political criticism of his lack of support for de Gaulle, Roosevelt would have been insane to lend his support to a Laval-initiated plot to block the Free French leader as he prepared to campaign for his fourth presidential term.

In the meantime, despite a number of minor skirmishes between de Gaulle and Anglo-American officials about the logistics of his return to France for good, he finally flew from Gibraltar to an isolated airfield near the city of Cherbourg on the morning of August 20, 1944. He received word from Eisenhower about his military plans: Patton's Third Army would bypass Paris on its way to Lorraine, with Montgomery's British forces at his left. In his memoirs de Gaulle indicated his preoccupation with the liberation of Paris and his determination to persuade Eisenhower to permit Leclerc's Second Armored Division to enter the French capital. In *his* memoirs Eisenhower recalled that the fear of a bloodbath and wholesale destruction in the French capital prompted him to advocate by-passing the city. But when the Parisian resistance rose up on August 19, Eisenhower decided it was critical to lend it Allied military support.[271]

The Liberation of Paris

In early August the Free French Second Armored Division under General Philippe Leclerc had arrived in Normandy from Britain. On August 7, as the breakout from Normandy began, it was attached to General George S. Patton's Third Army and then transferred to General Courtney Hodges's First Army. The famous *deuxieme division blindée* intended to spearhead the Allied liberation of the French capital. General Dietrich von Choltitz, whom Hitler had recently named German commander of the city of Paris, was under orders to put the capital city to the torch if German defeat there seemed imminent. His subordinates had placed huge quantities of dynamite in the cellars of Les Invalides, behind the pillars of the Chamber of Deputies, under the Ministry of Marine near the Place de la Concorde, on the southeast leg of the Eiffel Tower, and under more than a dozen bridges on the Seine. But the German commander disobeyed orders and ordered the demolition specialists of the combat engineers to evacuate the city.[272]

After returning to France on August 20, de Gaulle had moved across Normandy to the town of Le Mans on August 22, when General Leclerc received Eisenhower's order to advance on the French capital. That night de Gaulle and Leclerc met in the château at Rambouillet southwest of Paris to map out the plan for the liberation of the city as the resistance took control of the streets and the Germans retreated to their barracks in the city. De Gaulle said to Leclerc, "Go quickly. We cannot afford another Commune."[273] The

Free French leader complained about the "reserved, even bitter, tone of the Voice of America" broadcasts about the impending liberation of the French capital compared to the "warm satisfaction" expressed over the BBC.[274]

Leclerc began the assault on the early morning of August 24, using armor to break German pockets of resistance. The U.S. First Army was approaching from the northeast of the city near the famous airport city of Le Bourget, where Charles Lindbergh had landed after his historic solo transatlantic flight in 1927. On the early morning of August 25, Leclerc's four hundred armored vehicles and infantry began their advance into the city. Their objective was the Hôtel Meurice on the rue de Rivoli facing the Tuileries gardens, the headquarters of the German high command. General von Choltitz was taken prisoner in mid-afternoon and taken to the Prefecture to meet with Leclerc to sign the surrender documents. The leader of the Communist resistance group demanded that the document be amended to include a reference to the Parisian resistance and insisted on the right to co-sign the surrender document with Leclerc. De Gaulle's commanding general agreed in order to avoid an embarrassing internal row in the presence of the German commander. De Gaulle made his way past cheering throngs to Leclerc's temporary headquarters at the Gare Montparnasse, where the Gaullist commander and the Communist leader, Henri Rol-Tanguy, waited with written proof of the German surrender. De Gaulle berated Leclerc for agreeing to the changed wording and the inclusion of the Communist leader's signature as an insult to his status as head of the provisional government.[275]

He then headed off for the Ministry of War on the rue Saint Dominique rather than proceeding directly to the Hôtel de Ville (city hall), where tens of thousands of *resistants* and their leaders had gathered in celebratory anticipation. When he entered the War Ministry, he found it unchanged with the furniture exactly where it had been when he and Reynaud had left the building on the evening of June 10, 1940.[276]

De Gaulle initially resisted the entreaties of his allies in the Gaullist wing of the resistance to make a dramatic appearance at the City Hall, pointing out that he represented a state rather than a movement and therefore would visit the Ministry of War and then the Prefecture, to prove that he was in control of state power. The leader of the Gaullist wing of the resistance was Georges Bidault, a devout Catholic who was in the process of founding the Mouvement Républicain Populaire, a center-left political party that would play an important role in the French political system in the years after the war. During the German occupation, he had become one of the founders of the Conseil National de la Résistance with Jean Moulin. He replaced Moulin as chairman of the Conseil after the latter, as we shall see, was captured, tortured, and sent to Germany by the Gestapo in 1943.[277]

Finally at 8 p.m. de Gaulle strode across the Seine and ascended the stairs of the Hôtel de Ville. The resentment at him for his cavalier treatment of the Parisian resistance leaders dissipated as the assembled crowd finally got a look at the man who had kept alive the flame of French patriotism for four years while the German occupation oppressed them. When Bidault asked de Gaulle to go out on the balcony and "proclaim the Republic," the general replied, "No. The Republic has never ceased to exist. Vichy was and still remains null and void. I am the president of the government of the Republic. Why should I proclaim it now?"[278] Here again was the argument that de Gaulle had consistently insisted on: Vichy was a total aberration in French history. After raising both arms in a brief appearance before the thousands of people assembled in the square below, he issued the following brief announcement, which totally ignored the role played by American, British, and Canadian military forces: "Paris liberated by itself, liberated by its people with the support of the armies of France, with the support and backing of all of France, of the France that fights, of France alone, of the true France, of eternal France."[279]

He promptly stepped back, ignored the resistance leaders who were preparing a champagne toast to the liberation of the city, and abruptly left the building to return to the War Ministry. He refrained from acknowledging, let alone congratulating, the many Parisians who had risked their lives in the recent uprising against the occupiers. His sole objective was to establish his position as the head of state, beholden to no one. Again, he also uttered not a word of gratitude to the American soldiers or their officers who were approaching the capital city.[280] On de Gaulle's orders Leclerc organized a parade down the Champs Elysées for the next day, August 26, without inviting officials of the Council of National Resistance to participate. When General Leonard Gerow, commander of the U.S. Fourth Infantry Division, heard of the planned procession he curtly informed Leclerc that the French division, which operated under Gerow's command, was needed to help drive the Germans out of the northeastern sector of the city. Reminding Leclerc that he was his subordinate, Gerow forbade him to participate in the procession and ordered him to "accept no orders from any other source." When informed of what he regarded as this latest American challenge to his authority, de Gaulle ordered Leclerc to proceed with the planned promenade.[281]

When de Gaulle later appeared at the Arc de Triomphe to lay a huge wreath adorned with the Cross of Lorraine at the tomb of the unknown soldier, Bidault and the Communist leaders were waiting uninvited alongside

Leclerc and other Gaullist officials. When the march down the broad avenue toward the Place de la Concord began, they were instructed to walk several steps behind the general so that none of the one million spectators lining the route would have any doubt about who was in charge. As the march transpired, de Gaulle had succeeded in the twin tasks of holding off the Americans and elbowing aside the Communists and other non-Gaullist members of the resistance. His position as absolute leader of a France that was being liberated was untrammeled. At the Place de la Concorde, he boarded a military staff car for the trip to Notre Dame Cathedral. The city was honeycombed with German snipers. There were ninety German bombers on the airfield of Le Bourget waiting for the order to attack as the American forces approached. As he got out of the car, two shots were fired by snipers, forcing people into the cathedral or onto the pavement. After de Gaulle entered the building, more shots rang out. After a brief service he left.[282] On Sunday, August 27, Generals Eisenhower and Omar Bradley drove to Paris from Bradley's headquarters in the city of Chartres south of the capital and visited de Gaulle. Eisenhower later described this gesture as "a kind of de facto recognition of him as the provisional President of France. . . . This was of course what he wanted and what Roosevelt had never given him."[283]

On the day before he had summoned the Council of National Resistance to his headquarters at the Ministry of War and after belatedly congratulating them on their role in opposing the enemy occupation, de Gaulle announced that all resistance groups would be disbanded and the fighters would be integrated into the French army with the uniforms Eisenhower had promised. In the south of France Gaullist and Communist resistance groups were struggling for predominance, the latter ignoring the announcement from Paris that the resistance had come to an end. On September 9, de Gaulle established a new provisional government with Bidault as foreign minister (a position he would later hold at key points under the Fourth Republic) and the young Pierre Mendes-France as minister of finance (who would later become prime minister). He awarded two ministries to Communist leaders— Charles Tillon as minister of air and François Billoux as minister of health, a reluctant recognition of the party's important role in the resistance.[284]

The record of the Free French army in the war justified its designation "Fighting French." The North African Army under Giraud had fought the Germans in Tunisia. The Free French army in Italy under General Alphonse Juin, which had been active in the Italian campaign since December 1943, entered Rome with other allies on June 4 and took control of the Napoleonic isle of Elba on June 17. (Juin was revered for his Basque beret and his left-handed salute—his right hand had been injured in World War I.) The

Second Armored Division under General Leclerc, which had landed in Normandy on August 1, would march into liberated Paris on August 25. In the meantime the First French Army under General Jean de Lattre de Tassigny was withdrawn from Italy to join the Allied landing in Southern France on August 15 in Operation Dragoon. De Lattre, known to his men as le Roi Jean (King John), was a flamboyant officer who had fought as a cavalry lieutenant in World War I with a saber his grandfather had used in the Napoleonic wars. He defected from the Vichy army in 1943 and rallied to de Gaulle.

CHAPTER FOUR

~

France's Role in the Postwar International Order

On August 21, less than a week before the liberation of Paris, thirty-nine delegates from across the globe assembled at Dumbarton Oaks, a magnificent estate in the Georgetown neighborhood of Washington, D.C., to lay the groundwork for the new international organization that Roosevelt had been pushing for since the Teheran Conference of 1943 to replace the defunct League of Nations.[1] It became clear from the outset that four countries would represent the real powers behind the new world organization: the United States, Great Britain, the Soviet Union, and China. The first time the American president had used the metaphor of the "four policemen" to dominate the new organization was during Soviet foreign minister Vjacheslav Molotov's visit to Washington in May 1942.

Since the Soviet Union had not yet declared war on Japan, it was agreed that the Dumbarton Oaks conference would meet in two separate stages—the U.S., Great Britain, and the USSR joining the first and China replacing the Soviet Union in the second. Edward Stettinius led the American delegation, Sir Alexander Cadogan headed the British delegation, the young Soviet ambassador to the U.S. Andrei Gromyko led Stalin's delegation, and the Columbia University–educated V. K. Wellington Koo represented China. The French had not been invited to send a delegation to the early part of the conference in July–August.[2] When Stettinius reported the tentative findings of the conference to the president on August 28, Roosevelt strenuously objected to the position pressed hard by Cadogan, reflecting Churchill's wishes, that France should be given a permanent seat on the projected Security

Council of the new organization. On August 31, the head of the U.S. delegation presented a memorandum to the president, which Roosevelt promptly
signed, recommending that the French seat be held in abeyance until the
country had a legitimate government but insisting that any one of the Big
Four have the power to veto any such agreement.[3] The conference continued
its deliberations until October 7. The French provisional government had
neither been consulted nor invited to attend, but was promised a permanent
seat on the proposed Security Council "in due course." On October 14, de
Gaulle protested vehemently this "kind of relegation" imposed on France by
its allies, perhaps doubting that they would convert this theoretical recognition of her equal status into reality at some future date.[4]

In the meantime, De Gaulle's representative in the United States, Henri
Hoppenot, had officially requested authorization to occupy the French embassy in Washington, which had been closed since the departure of the Vichy ambassador in November 1942. On August 31, Hull sent a memorandum
to Roosevelt declaring that he had no objection to the move. FDR replied
two days later in a last-ditch effort, urging a delay of a few weeks. But when
the latest request from Hoppenot arrived on September 13, Harry Hopkins
pointedly reminded Roosevelt that the British had allowed de Gaulle's representative Réné Massigli to occupy the French embassy in London and urged
his boss to do the same, adding that if we refuse it will "stir up some feeling against us in France." The president finally backed down and approved
Hoppenot's request to take up residence in the embassy, whose business had
been handled by the Swiss since the fall of 1942. The next day Hull officially
authorized this agreement, but with the customary caveat that it constituted
nothing more than the recognition of "the provisional government."[5]

The career diplomat Jefferson Caffrey, who had served in the American
embassy in Paris during the last two years of World War I, was designated as
the American representative to the "de facto French authority"—in effect as
an ambassador. A convert to Catholicism, Caffrey was the first career foreign
service officer appointed ambassador to Paris. Compared to the flamboyant Bullitt and the outspoken Leahy, the new U.S. envoy was self-effacing,
humble, and pragmatic.[6] Four days before the announcement of the appointment on September 21,[7] Hull had sent a long memorandum to Roosevelt
arguing that "the time has come to recognize the de facto French authority
as the provisional government of France." He noted that de Gaulle had been
accepted by the French people as the leader of the resistance, so there was
no longer the danger that the United States could be accused of imposing
him. (Fat chance of that!) He had demonstrated his commitment to preserve
the democratic form of government and had pledged free elections when the

country was completely liberated. He warned that further delay in recognition could jeopardize the current popularity of the United States in France, invoking Eisenhower's authority for that judgment, and noted that British and Canadian plans to grant recognition soon would leave the United States as a recalcitrant outlier. Roosevelt was the lone holdout after Stimson, Hull, and Hopkins had overcome their earlier suspicions of de Gaulle and favored recognition. Churchill had continued to press de Gaulle's case to the American president during the second Quebec Conference, September 11 to 16. Roosevelt erroneously claimed in reports to Hull that he and Churchill were "very much opposed to it at this time. The provisional government has no direct authority from the [French] people. It is best to let things go along as they are for the moment."[8] In the meantime, Hull had come to favor recognition on the condition that the term "provisional" be included in the label until a free election was held in France and so informed the president.[9]

Churchill renewed the pressure on October 14, claiming that relations between Eisenhower's troops and the French government were excellent and reiterated that the provisional government enjoyed the support of the vast majority of the French people. Roosevelt replied four days later that no recognition would be possible until France had "a true interior zone" under the authority of the French provisional government. He repeated to the British prime minister that he would not be satisfied with de Gaulle's merely saying that he was going to enlarge his consultative assembly to include non-Gaullist members.[10]

It became obvious that after Eisenhower had declared an "interior zone" in France, there would be no reason to continue to withhold recognition of de Gaulle's government. On October 20, the Supreme Commander replied to a question from the Inter-Allied General Staff about recognition four days earlier by declaring that from the military point of view a strong central authority in France was "essential" to the success of his ongoing operations. With all his military concerns he did not want the responsibility of dealing with the economic situation in France, especially the obligation to provide food to the civilian population during the approaching winter. After the interior zone was finally officially delineated on October 23, the new acting secretary of state, Edward Stettinius, publicly announced the de jure recognition of the French provisional government under Charles de Gaulle and announced that Caffrey would take up his post as ambassador in Paris.[11]

Stettinius was fully aware that Roosevelt "despised de Gaulle personally" and doubted that the Gaullist group was truly representative of France.[12] Sir Alexander Cadogan, head of the British Foreign Office, exclaimed to his diary, "At last! What a fuss about nothing! Due to that spiteful old great-aunt

Leahy. Hope he's feeling pretty sick."[13] When Caffrey rushed to the Quai d'Orsay to officially present the good news, he was encountered by the British, Canadian, and Soviet ambassadors. All four of them went into Bidault's office as a group. Caffrey reported from the capital city that the French newspapers celebrated the event but complained about the long delay.[14]

Monnet had been working assiduously to arrange for the provision of economic aid to France as it embarked on its recovery. On November 11, he finally unveiled his program for the purchase of consumer goods and equipment for $2.5 billion for eighteen months. The Treasury Department had earlier insisted that France pay for the proposed economic aid with their dollar holdings and gold reserves rather than relying on Lend-Lease. In the meantime, de Gaulle had been urgently requesting equipment for eight new French divisions. On January 2, 1945, Monnet dispatched a plaintive plea for immediate American industrial and consumer goods and the requisite shipping to stave off what he described as an approaching economic catastrophe, which Stettinius approved on January 13 with Caffrey's strong endorsement.[15]

The issue of the postwar political situation of Germany became the subject of intense discussion between the French government and the new American ambassador in Paris. De Gaulle had told Caffrey that France opposed the "setting up of any sort of central government in Germany" because he was certain that any such government "would inevitably come under Soviet control," a warning repeated a month later by Bidault.[16] On November 13 and 14, Caffrey had sent two cables enumerating France's three principal demands on postwar Germany: the first was the separation of the Ruhr and the Saar from Germany and both regions be placed under international control; the second was that France be granted an occupation zone in Germany; the third was the arming of eight supplementary divisions to endow France with more authority after the war. In response to a plea from Churchill on November 18 repeating those requests, Roosevelt had informally approved the proposal for a French occupation zone but rejected the request for more military aid to France on the grounds of the shortage of arms and shipping. He also opposed inviting de Gaulle to future allied conferences on the grounds that it would complicate the negotiations.[17]

The Strasbourg Imbroglio

Harsh conflicts continued to simmer between the United States and France over an issue of military strategy. On September 6, de Gaulle had placed the French Second Armored Division at Eisenhower's disposition with the suggestion, approved by the Supreme Commander on September 23, that it be deployed in the direction of Strasbourg in Alsace so that this iconic symbol of the "lost provinces" that had been annexed by Imperial Germany in 1871, regained in 1919, and then lost again to Nazi Germany in 1940, could be liberated by the French army. De Gaulle received word from General Leclerc on November 23 that the Second French Armored Division had liberated the city. But the next month the German counteroffensive in the Ardennes forest of Belgium precipitated what came to be known in America as the Battle of the Bulge. American General George Patton promptly called on the Second French Armored Division to counterattack against the Germans near the Belgian town of Bastogne.[18]

Since the Second Division in Strasbourg occupied a deep salient far in front of the Allied line, it was exposed to a flank attack by nearby German forces while the Americans were concentrating on blunting the German counteroffensive in the Ardennes. So on December 30, Eisenhower issued orders for the French to evacuate Strasbourg. De Gaulle promptly informed Eisenhower, Roosevelt, and Churchill that a withdrawal from recently liberated Strasbourg would be a severe psychological blow to the inhabitants of the city and would expose them to horrific punishment if the Germans were able to return. After the Second Armored Division was replaced in Alsace by the First Free French Division, Eisenhower ordered the Sixth American Army under General Jacob Devers to bolster Patton's forces, which meant the temporary withdrawal from the capital of Alsace. As early as September 31, 1944, de Gaulle had stressed to Eisenhower "the great importance I attach to seeing French troops participate in the liberation of Strasbourg."[19] Two weeks before the conflict exploded, Devers engaged in a sharp exchange of messages with Leclerc and the French minister of war about Strasbourg.[20]

Refusing to abandon the Alsatian city, de Gaulle ordered General de Lattre de Tassigny on January 1, 1945, to defend it with the First French Army if the Allied forces departed. As we have seen, the leader of the Free French often sought (and occasionally received) support from the Supreme Allied Commander to soften or circumvent the policies of the American president toward de Gaulle. But the day after his order to de Lattre to defend Strasbourg, de Gaulle reversed field and implored Roosevelt to countermand Eisenhower's order to Devers's army to abandon the Alsatian city.[21]

On January 3, de Gaulle and Juin visited the Inter-Allied Headquarters at Versailles, where both Eisenhower and Churchill were present. De Gaulle emotionally recounted the symbolic importance of Alsace to the French people. "Alsace is sacred ground," he declared, eliciting from Churchill the supportive remark: "All my life I have remarked what significance Alsace has for the French."[22] After Churchill supported de Gaulle's position,

Eisenhower reversed course and phoned Devers with instructions to remain in the Alsatian capital and prevent the return of German forces.[23] This was a rare case of Churchill and de Gaulle working together to induce Eisenhower to change a military policy without the participation of Roosevelt.

Just prior to the Franco-American dispute over Strasbourg in late December 1944 through early January 1945, de Gaulle's representative in Washington, Henri Hoppenot, prepared to leave his post. He submitted a long farewell letter to Bidault summarizing his analysis of the Roosevelt administration's attitudes and policies toward France during his long tenure in Washington. Full of recriminations about almost every aspect of the U.S. government's relationship with France, he recounted all the examples of what he denounced as the insulting treatment the Free French had received at the hands of Roosevelt and his representatives that collectively constituted a litany of "confusion, incoherence, and ignorance" coupled with "bad faith" toward de Gaulle and his organization: the cordial relationship with Vichy, the Darlan deal in North Africa, the energetic support of Giraud, the refusal to recognize the Free French entity for so long, and the plans to dismantle the French overseas empire after the war. He attributed all this hostility to the "aging, unstable, superficial man" who had recently been elected to his fourth term.[24]

On January 2, Hull's successor as secretary of state, Edward Stettinius, forwarded to Roosevelt a report from Ambassador Jefferson Caffrey detailing de Gaulle's demand that France participate in the surrender ceremonies and then the occupation of Germany. For months the French leader had been pressing Eisenhower for an iron-clad commitment, declaring that in light of the efforts of the French army in France "the entire nation could not imagine that its army would not go unto enemy soil."[25]

Stettinius endorsed these French demands two days later in a memorandum to Roosevelt. He conceded that de Gaulle's demands were completely out of proportion to France's actual power and that the addition of a fourth power in Germany could complicate the occupation. But he emphasized the importance of restoring France to its previous position of influence in the world, a development that had already begun: the Dumbarton Oaks Conference had awarded France one of the five permanent seats on the proposed United Nations Security Council. "This government may well wish, after the early period of occupation, to withdraw a considerable proportion of its troops from Germany," Stettinius remarked. Since it "would be logical to assume that they would be replaced by French forces," France should be "fully associated with plans for the occupation from the outset."[26]

This memorandum from his secretary of state, backed by his aide Harry Hopkins's championing the French cause, prompted the president to moderate a bit his previous animosity toward France in general and de Gaulle in particular. In his January 6 State of the Union Address, which was twice as long as usual, Roosevelt (at Hopkins's suggestion), went out of his way to celebrate the historic friendship between France and the United States. He praised the "heroic efforts of the [French] resistance groups" and praised "all of those Frenchmen throughout the world [without mentioning names] who refused to surrender after the disaster of 1940."[27]

De Gaulle and the French Resistance

What of the relationship between de Gaulle's movement in London and then Algiers with the resistance within France? The beginning of that relationship may be traced to fall of 1941, when an escapee from Vichy France arrived in Great Britain. A left-wing activist who had become prefect of the cathedral city of Chartres south of Paris, Jean Moulin had been dismissed by the Vichy regime. In the 1920s, he had met the left-wing Radical Pierre Cot, a leading advocate of a Franco-Soviet alliance in the 1930s. When Cot was named air minister in the Popular Front government of Léon Blum in 1936, Moulin was designated as his chief of staff.[28] Throughout the year 1941 Moulin had moved freely around the unoccupied zone under the pseudonym Joseph Jean Mercier, developing contacts with the fledgling resistance groups that had begun to sprout up. In the fall of that year he traveled to Lisbon, where he met a representative of the British Special Operations Executive (SOE), who arranged for a flight to Britain. After several meetings with de Gaulle, the Free French leader appointed him as his representative to the resistance in the unoccupied zone of France. In the early morning of January 2, 1942, a Royal Air Force twin-engine bomber parachuted Moulin and two colleagues into Provence. He worked meticulously to unite several key resistance groups, secretly moving from one group to the next. After a brief return visit to London in February 1943, he returned to France when he was betrayed to the Gestapo chief in Lyon, Klaus Barbie, on June 21, 1943. After a brutal interrogation, during which he refused to disclose any of the resistance leaders with whom he had met, he died on a train on July 8 at Metz en route to Germany.[29] Two other Resistance heroes met a similar fate: Comte d'Estienne d'Orves was executed as a spy; Pierre Brossolette jumped to his death from the window of Gestapo headquarters in Paris on the Avenue Foch.[30]

Meanwhile André Philip had been appointed commissioner of the interior in the Free French government in July 1942. He supervised the growing links between de Gaulle's staff in London and the disparate resistance groups that had emerged. De Gaulle had little experience dealing with the various political factions that jockeyed for position in the French underground. The Free French leader resented the activities of British intelligence in France, the Special Operations Executive (SOE), which had successfully recruited many French militants and operated with no coordination whatsoever with de Gaulle. Conflicts developed between the British-backed resistance groups and the major Free French resistance group, the Confrérie Notre-Dame network that had been founded by Gilbert Renault (nom de guerre "Rémy").[31] In order to coordinate a Gaullist resistance intelligence network, de Gaulle had also designated André Dewavrin (nom de guerre "Passy") for this task.[32]

An obscure development in neutral Switzerland brought the American secret services into the picture as well. On June 13, 1942, President Roosevelt had established an agency authorized to conduct covert and paramilitary operations abroad. In November Allen Dulles, the younger brother of the future secretary of state John Foster Dulles, had arrived in the city of Bern in neutral Switzerland to set up a station of the Office of Strategic Services (OSS), the forerunner of the CIA (which he later directed). The upper echelons of the OSS comprised a group of young men who would become influential in America after the war, including Richard Helms, William Colby, Arthur Schlesinger Jr., C. Douglas Dillon, William Casey, and Ralph Bunche.[33] From his perch in Switzerland, Dulles arranged for U.S. financing to be distributed to resistance groups in France that were completely separate from and hostile to those supporting de Gaulle that had been unified under Jean Moulin.[34]

Anti-Gaullist American officials opened up a barrage of attacks on de Gaulle's intelligence agent Passy as a former member of the extreme right-wing organization the Cagoule in the 1930s. From his position as counselor to the American embassy in London, H. Freeman "Doc" Matthews, who had served as first secretary of the American embassy in Vichy, inundated the State Department with reports of harsh criticism of the Gaullists, especially Passy, by French citizens. Matthews was so passionately anti-Gaullist that he did not hesitate to denounce Pleven as "one of those who fanatically believes that Charles d'Arc is really France's twentieth-century messiah." He compared Giraud, who "desires only to liberate France," to de Gaulle, who "is aiming to be the ruler of France for a long, long period of time." He urged that the United States do everything possible to prevent "this French Hitler" from gaining total control of the country and complained that the British had "built up this French Adolf for the past three years."[35] FBI director J. Edgar Hoover later weighed in with a broadside against Passy, whom he designated as "De Gaulle's Himmler" who ran a "Gestapo-like organization" that was purging anti-Gaullists in the French resistance.[36]

Ever since the fall of France, the French Communist Party—which had slavishly followed Moscow's line after the signing of the Nazi-Soviet Pact in August 1939—did not lift a finger against the German occupation and even sought to obtain German authorization for the publication of the party's newspaper, *L'Humanité*. But Communist militant Charles Tillon took it upon himself, without coordinating his activities with the party leader, Jacques Duclos—the original party leader, Maurice Thorez, had deserted from the French army and escaped to Moscow—to found the Francs-tireurs et partisans français, a Communist resistance group, before the German invasion of the Soviet Union in June 1941.[37]

As planning for the liberation of France continued, an anomalous situation developed concerning William Bullitt, the U.S. ambassador to France during the collapse in June 1940. Bullitt had returned to the United States after the formation of the Vichy regime and fell out of favor with the Roosevelt administration. He had greatly antagonized the president by his role in exposing an incident in which Undersecretary of State Sumner Welles, a close associate of the president and a closeted gay person, had solicited sex with two Pullman car porters on a train to Alabama to attend the funeral of Speaker of the House William B. Bankhead. Roosevelt had known about the incident, as did many in Washington. But after Bullitt met with the president in May 1941 to expose the situation, Roosevelt had to accept Welles's resignation the following September. He never forgave his former ambassador for this act against a longtime Roosevelt friend.[38]

As the D-Day invasion was about to begin, Bullitt failed to secure a commission in the U.S. army (for obvious reasons). He thereupon offered his services to the Free French army just before the invasion of Normandy. Writing from Algiers on May 25, de Gaulle responded to the former American ambassador with uncharacteristic warmth: "Come now! Good and dear American friend. Our ranks are open to you. You will return with us into wounded Paris. Together we will see your star-spangled banners mingled with our tricolors." Bullitt eventually joined the Free French army as an officer with the rank of commandant (roughly equivalent to an American major). He served under the command of General Jean de Lattre de Tassigny and participated in the drive to expel the Germans from his beloved country. When he returned to Paris, he unlocked the gates of his former embassy that had been shut for more than four years and received the cheers of the Parisians from the balcony resplendent in his French uniform.[39]

The Purge

Immediately after his return to Paris, de Gaulle ordered the new administrative apparatus he had installed to conduct a prompt set of trials of accused
collaborators in order to forestall vigilante justice. But the rage of the population short-circuited this attempt at institutionalized justice. Some forty
thousand accused collaborators were summarily executed without a trial
during and after the liberation. In some cases the purge was carried out for
purely personal reasons to settle scores with business competitors or political
or personal rivals. French women who had slept with German officers or officials were accused of "horizontal collaboration" and were publicly humiliated by having their hair shaved to their scalp.[40] Some, like the entrepreneur
Gabrielle "Coco" Chanel and the actress Léonie Marie Julie Bathiat (known
professionally as "Arletty"), were spared the humiliation and remained un-
repentant. Arletty famously announced that "my heart is French but my ass
is international."[41] Eventually the regular wheels of justice replaced these ad
hoc extrajudicial "trials."[42]

Marshal Pétain had been sequestered by the Germans in the town of Sigmaringen in Bavaria until he requested the right to return to France and was
transported to Switzerland. De Gaulle had preferred that he be left there to
live out his few remaining years.[43] But the eighty-nine-year-old soldier insisted
on returning to his country to explain his actions in the last four years to his
people. He was driven across the French border from Switzerland on April 26,
1945, and was promptly taken to Paris and imprisoned in Fort Montrouge. His
trial opened at the Palais de Justice on July 23 in a special court established
by de Gaulle. The presiding judge and the prosecutor had previously sworn
allegiance to the man they were now trying. The old Marshal was charged
with the crimes against people that had been carried out under his authority.
The judge recommended that the jury consider the minimal punishment of
banishment for five years and loss of civil rights. At the end of the trial on
August 15, the jury decided by a one-vote margin to impose the death penalty, followed by a recommendation that the sentence not be carried out. De
Gaulle, who had himself been condemned to death by Vichy, promptly com-
muted the death penalty to life imprisonment.[44] The old man spent the rest
of his life in a prison on a small island off the Atlantic coast, where he died at
ninety-five in 1951. The Marshal and his former protégé had never laid eyes
on one other since that fateful day in the Bordeaux restaurant in June 1940.

Pierre Laval had fled in a German airplane to Spain in April 1945. During
the Pétain trial, the Spanish leader, Generalissimo Francisco Franco, under
pressure from the Allies, deported him to Germany, where he was taken

prisoner by American soldiers and turned over to French authorities. He appeared as a rather unconvincing witness in the Pétain trial. At the end of his own trial that began on October 4, he received a death sentence, which de Gaulle declined to commute. After a failed suicide attempt in prison with a cyanide pill, he was executed by firing squad on October 15.[45] A total of 2,071 death sentences were decreed in the purge trials, and more than 40,000 collaborators were sentenced to prison. De Gaulle personally considered each death sentence and approved 768 executions.

De Gaulle and the United States after the Liberation

While de Gaulle toured the country in the early fall of 1944 to confirm and consolidate the authority of his government, Eisenhower stole time from his primary obligation of commanding the Allied military forces driving the Germans out of France to make the case yet again to his commander-in-chief for official U.S. recognition of de Gaulle's political status. As we have seen, Jefferson Caffrey arrived in Paris in early October with instructions to set up shop when the American embassy was reopened. Hence the anomalous situation: an American ambassador to a "government" that had not been recognized as such de jure.

Knowing that they had the full backing of the British government, Secretary of State Hull, Secretary of War Henry Stimson, and Eisenhower met with Caffrey and sent a message through him to Roosevelt warning that if de Gaulle failed to reestablish law and order in liberated France or was superseded by some other French leader the result would be a chaotic situation that would adversely affect the Allied armies that were pushing the Germans out of the country. But Roosevelt again demurred, and Eisenhower was obliged to send a strongly worded cable on October 20 confirming that the French provisional government was establishing effective control of the liberated portion of the country and that the Allied Supreme Commander would welcome the complete assumption of civil responsibilities by the French government. The president finally succumbed to persistent pressure from the American press, his military commander in Europe, cabinet members such as Hull and Stimson, and the British government. Without warning either Churchill or de Gaulle, he peremptorily announced that the United States would officially recognize the government of France on October 23. De Gaulle's reaction, after waiting a couple of days, was a frosty "The French government is satisfied to be called by its name."[46]

Caffrey eventually held a long meeting with the French leader on November 3. De Gaulle announced that it was in America's interest to have a strong and independent France "at the head of Europe," noting that "neither Russia nor England are European powers." He ended his monologue with a plea for Roosevelt to visit the country, where "we will give him a warm welcome." The next day Henri Hoppenot, the French delegate to the United States in Washington, issued the official invitation in Bidault's name.[47]

Playing the Russian Card and De Gaulle's Mission to Moscow

De Gaulle always referred to the Soviet Union as "La Russie," making it clear that he regarded France's eastern ally at the beginning of the Great War as a traditional great power for which its Communist ideology was ephemeral. His relations with Moscow had been good ever since he had got in touch with the Soviet ambassador to Britain, Ivan Maisky, a few days after the German assault in the Soviet Union in June 1941 and proposed the opening of relations between Free France and the Kremlin. After months of negotiations, the Soviet government designated as its representative to the French National Committee Alexander Bogomolov, who had served as ambassador to Pétain during the period of the Nazi-Soviet Pact. On January 20, 1942, de Gaulle had issued a radio broadcast affirming the de facto alliance between the Free French and the Kremlin. The next month he dispatched the diplomat Roger Garreau to Moscow as delegate of the National Committee. Garreau worked tirelessly for the rest of the war to strengthen the bilateral relationship.[48]

In the autumn of 1944, de Gaulle decided to test the waters about beefing up this bilateral connection to counteract the tense relations he had been having with Washington and London by accepting Ambassador Bogomolov's invitation to visit the Soviet capital. He left Paris for Moscow on November 24, accompanied by Bidault, Juin, and Palewski. After a long sojourn through Egypt, Iran, Azerbaijan, and Stalingrad, he was met by Foreign Minister Molotov at the train station in the Soviet capital on December 2.[49]

The talks in the Kremlin lasted eight days. The first meeting between de Gaulle and Stalin was held between 9 and 11 p.m. on the very day the French delegation arrived, with Molotov, French ambassador Roger Garreau, and Soviet ambassador to France Alexander Bogomolov in attendance. Stalin accepted without objection de Gaulle's adamant insistence that the western border of Germany be established at the Rhine River. But the Soviet leader insisted that the Soviet Union and France could not settle by themselves the question of the Rhine frontier and asked if de Gaulle had "already addressed the issue with London and Washington." De Gaulle had to back down and agree that the four powers would have to address the issue. When de Gaulle asked about the Soviet leader's wishes concerning Germany's eastern frontier, Stalin confirmed that the western border of Poland should be extended to the confluence of the Oder and Neisse Rivers, which the French leader accepted, adding that the same geographical considerations applied to France's demand for the Rhine frontier.[50]

On December 5, Bidault expressed his appreciation for Moscow's support for France's claim to a permanent seat on the Security Council of the planned United Nations Organization at the Dumbarton Oaks Conference as well as for its backing for French representation on the European Consultative Commission (which would deal primarily with the future of Germany). But the two foreign ministers sparred over Molotov's abortive attempt to get France to recognize the Soviet-installed Polish government in Lublin, which was challenging the right of the Western-backed Polish government-in-exile in London to govern the country.[51]

The final bilateral decision about the future government of Poland was left for de Gaulle and Stalin to address. The French leader began by affirming his acceptance of the proposed Soviet annexation on Poland's eastern border on the condition that Poland be compensated with German territory. But he declined to recognize the Lublin Communist government in Poland. No one seemed to notice the irony of de Gaulle's refusing to recognize the Lublin Poles because they had not achieved power through a national election—the exact treatment that he had received from Roosevelt. Finally, they reached agreement on a proposed Franco-Soviet Pact. When Stalin raised the possibility of a tripartite Anglo-French-Soviet security pact, de Gaulle reviewed the history of Great Britain's hesitation to defend France, in 1914 and again in 1939, implying that the Soviet Union would be a more valuable ally. (No mention of the Nazi-Soviet Pact of August 1939!). In the end the two leaders agreed that such a bilateral agreement was the right move for both countries.[52]

At around 4 a.m. on December 10—the Soviet leader was fond of late night and early morning negotiations—de Gaulle and Stalin signed a Franco-Soviet Pact. Both leaders pledged not to sign a separate peace and to oppose a new German threat. When de Gaulle asked Marshal Stalin if he would be willing to come to Paris, the Soviet leader responded, "How can I? I am an old man. I'm going to die soon." De Gaulle had summoned American ambassador Averill Harriman and British chargé John Balfour two days before the signing ceremony to fill them in on the state of negotiations. Harriman confirmed that France had stood firm on the issue of recognizing the Lublin government but accepted the Oder-Neisse Line as the revised border between Poland and Germany.[53]

For his part, Stalin declined definitely to endorse the French position on the Ruhr, the Rhineland, and the Saar before consulting with Washington and London. The Soviet leader was careful to keep Churchill and Roosevelt fully apprised of the state of the talks with the visiting French delegation. When the British prime minister learned from Stalin about the outcome of the negotiations, he suggested substituting the proposed Franco-Soviet Pact with a tripartite Anglo-Franco-Soviet treaty, an updated version of the old Triple Entente before the Great War. Though Stalin took the proposal under consideration, de Gaulle rejected it out of hand, as did Roosevelt, the latter because such a regional security organization might undermine the proposed United Nations Organization and its objective of collective security. But the mere discussion of including France in such a postwar security system marked a major change of attitude toward that country on the part of the Big Three.[54]

The Empty Chair at Yalta

After Roosevelt's re-election to his fourth term in November 1944, he, Stalin, and Churchill prepared their plans for a summit conference, which would eventually be scheduled to be held in the old Czarist playground of Yalta on the Crimean Peninsula of the Soviet Union. By the middle of January 1945, reports reached France that the Big Three were planning to meet in a few weeks and that de Gaulle would not be invited to join them.[55] Vigorous attempts by Eden to promote an invitation to de Gaulle in order to secure French participation in the formulation of policies toward the occupation of Germany fell on deaf ears with Churchill. De Gaulle later observed simply that "I was offended that we were not invited, but I was not surprised." He suspected that his refusal to back Stalin on the Polish issue during his trip to Moscow in the fall of 1944 played its part, but he naturally placed primary blame on Roosevelt for the snub.[56]

During their exchanges in preparation for the summit conference on the Crimean Peninsula, the British prime minister and the American president addressed two major issues concerning France. First, Roosevelt's warning that "after Germany's collapse I must bring American troops home as rapidly as transportation problems will permit" greatly alarmed Churchill. "If the French are to have no equipped postwar army," he lamented, "how will it be possible to hold down western Germany beyond the present Russian occupied line?" He urged that France be given as large a zone in occupied Germany as possible in anticipation of the withdrawal of American forces, after which "all would therefore rapidly disintegrate as it did last time."[57] The second issue was whether de Gaulle should be invited to Yalta.

On January 4, 1945, Secretary of State Stettinius wrote to FDR in support of London's sweeping proposals concerning the end of the war in Europe that would bring France into the fold: France should participate in the signing of the surrender document. France should receive an occupation zone in Germany and a sector in Berlin. The control machinery in occupied Germany would be transferred from a tripartite to a quadripartite arrangement. Stettinius argued that such an arrangement would be compatible with the Dumbarton Oaks proposal that France would become "in due course" a permanent member of the proposed United Nations Security Council. He insisted that such an upgrading of France's role in postwar Germany was necessary because of the likely withdrawal of U.S. soldiers from the occupation: "It would be logical to assume that they would be replaced by French forces and this replacement is likely to be facilitated if the French are fully associated with plans for the occupation from the outset."[58]

On the second issue, whether de Gaulle should be invited to the conference, Roosevelt adamantly opposed such an invitation because it "would merely introduce a complicating and undesirable factor" to the proceedings.[59] On January 16, 1945, the matter came to a head when Bidault formally requested that his president participate alongside Roosevelt, Churchill, and Stalin. Ambassador Caffrey forwarded the request to Washington with his strong endorsement, noting that military operations were taking place on French territory; that France was making a growing contribution to the war effort (not only with French armed forces, but also providing the Allies with port and transportation facilities); and that France could not be expected to support any decision made at the conference without her participation.[60]

But Roosevelt refused to budge on the issue, for the usual reasons. His trusted aide Harry Hopkins traveled to London on January 21 and then went to Paris to confer with Bidault in the presence of Caffrey to seek ways to repair the conflictual relations between the two governments before a meeting he had scheduled with de Gaulle. In his meeting with the French president on January 27, Hopkins again expressed his grave concern about the poor relations between Paris and Washington. He repeated Roosevelt's explanation for his attitude toward France, which he had expressed during de Gaulle's visit to Washington the previous July: the collapse of the French army in May–June 1940 and the behavior of certain French military officers and political leaders after the armistice. He ended with the blunt assertion that the United States would find it difficult to have confidence in France's ability to recover its role in the world in light of its activities during the war.[61] This assertion seemed to contradict the president's warm praise of "all of those Frenchmen throughout the world who refused to surrender after the disaster of 1940" in his State of the Union message cited above.

After admitting that the liberation of his country would not have been possible without the sacrifices of American soldiers, de Gaulle responded to this dressing down from one of his supporters in the Roosevelt administration with his own familiar list of complaints about U.S. foreign policy before and after the fall of France: its rejection of the Franco-American security pledge after the Versailles Conference of 1919; its refusal to grant France the reparations from defeated Germany that she was due in the 1920s; neutrality in the face of the Nazi menace until Pearl Harbor; and its refusal to respond to his old patron Reynaud's desperate plea for assistance as the German army swarmed into the country in the spring of 1940. (He shrewdly refrained from mentioning Washington's recognition of Pétain's collaborationist regime.) De Gaulle then asked bluntly why France had not been invited to the forthcoming conference in the Crimea. Hoping to keep the dialogue open, Hopkins announced at a lunch with Bidault and other cabinet ministers that Roosevelt would like to meet de Gaulle in a French city along the Mediterranean before his return to Washington from Yalta to fill him in on the decisions taken there. He also suggested that de Gaulle could participate in the last meetings at the conference, which would address purely European issues. Bidault said he would forward the invitation to his boss.[62]

So certain that the invitation to attend a small part of the conference would be turned down by de Gaulle, the French foreign minister refrained from passing it along. But he did forward an invitation from Roosevelt to meet with de Gaulle after the conference to discuss the decisions reached. As the American delegation arrived in Yalta on February 2, Bidault informed a surprised Hopkins that de Gaulle had accepted the American president's desire to meet with the French leader "on French soil." But de Gaulle hastened to deliver a radio address informing the world that his country was washing its hands of the postwar planning that was about to take place at the Allied conference from which it had been excluded: "France will of course be committed to absolutely nothing she has not been in a position to discuss and approve in the same way as the others."[63]

The minutes of the one-on-one meeting between Roosevelt and Stalin before the opening of the conference—at which only the two chiefs of state and interpreters were present—reveal that the Soviet leader and the American president shared similar views about de Gaulle and France. Despite having signed a bilateral alliance with de Gaulle two months earlier, Stalin evinced no interest in promoting the French cause. In response to Roosevelt's question about how he had got along with de Gaulle during their meetings,

Stalin responded that he found the French leader "unrealistic in the sense that France had not done very much fighting in this war." He complained that the Frenchman had "demanded full rights with the Americans, British, and Russians who had done the burden of the fighting," whereas "in actual fact the French contribution at the present time to military operations on the Western Front was very small and that in 1940 they had not fought at all."[64]

At the conference itself, Churchill and Eden labored tenaciously to defend France's rights to an occupation zone and membership on the Allied Control Council, a circumstance that an ungrateful de Gaulle never acknowledged. "France must take her place. We need her defense against Germany," the British prime minister exclaimed. "I do not know how long the United States will remain with us in occupation. Therefore the French should grow in strength and help us share the burden." He urged that France be allotted a zone that would be carved out of the American and British zones and that she be included in the Allied Control Council.[65]

When the question of France's future role came up at the first plenary session of the Crimean Conference on February 4, both Roosevelt and Stalin expressed contempt for de Gaulle. The American president repeated the old saw about a megalomaniac who fancied himself Joan of Arc, while Stalin described him as "unrealistic." The Soviet leader repeated his complaint about France's negligible contribution to the war against Germany, from its defeat in 1940 to the French military forces after the liberation of France. He questioned the wisdom of France's effort to place military forces in the Rhineland "in permanency." Stalin had earlier given lukewarm support to a French zone in Germany, though he adamantly opposed French participation in the Yalta conference from the beginning.[66]

At the second plenary session on February 5, Churchill pushed hard for including France in the occupation after learning from Roosevelt that "he did not believe that American troops would stay in Europe much more than two years." The British prime minister feared (though he could not say it with Stalin in the room) that the result would be to leave Britain facing the Russians alone. The Soviet leader repeated his condemnation of the French military collapse in 1940, eliciting from Churchill a veiled reference to the Molotov-Ribbentrop Pact of August 1939 with the remark that all the Allied nations "had their difficulties at the beginning of the war and had made mistakes."[67] Hopkins, who had been pressing France's case with Roosevelt, reported that "Winston and Anthony [Eden] fought like lions" for the French zone, fearing the prospect of facing the Russians alone in occupied Germany after the American troops departed. Roosevelt, who had accepted a French zone in principle since November 18, 1944, offered no objection.[68]

Roosevelt and Stalin finally accepted Churchill's compromise proposal that France should be offered a zone in Germany but that her "status" (i.e., membership on the Allied Control Commission [ACC], which would supervise the occupation) should be the topic of "separate discussions." Hopkins, Charles Bohlen (Roosevelt's interpreter at Yalta), and senior U.S. diplomat H. Freeman "Doc" Matthews—who, as we have seen, detested de Gaulle—successfully worked behind the scenes to persuade Roosevelt to agree to a French seat on the Commission.[69] Matthews recalled in a later interview that FDR "had been influenced by his dislike of de Gaulle and his activities in the earlier stages of the war" and that "Stalin also showed no interest in bringing France in at Yalta." But Roosevelt "was finally persuaded that it was the thing to do—but we had to work on him, and luckily we had Harry Hopkins' very strong support."[70] The president finally changed his mind and grudgingly aligned his position with Churchill's, remarking that it would be easier to deal with the French if they were in the Commission than if they were outside it. In his memoir Bohlen describes how Stalin fell into line, "raised his arms above his head and said 'Sdaiyous,' which in Russian means 'I surrender.'"[71]

When the discussions heated up over the question of which government of Poland ought to be recognized—the Communist government that had recently been transferred from the city of Lublin to the Polish capital or the anti-Communist Polish government in exile in London—Stalin exploited what he knew to be Roosevelt's antipathy for the French president, shrewdly observing that "the Warsaw government has as great a democratic basis in Poland as de Gaulle has in France."[72]

In the midst of the conference, Hopkins received a message from Bidault, transmitted by Caffrey, rejecting the presidential aide's earlier suggestion that de Gaulle be invited to the final portion of the conference. But when Caffrey asked if Roosevelt could come to France after Yalta, the French foreign minister added that de Gaulle would be happy to meet with him after his departure from the conference, at a time and place of his choosing.[73] On February 11, Roosevelt responded with instructions to Caffrey to inform de Gaulle that he looked forward to a meeting on French territory and suggested Algiers around February 17.[74] Two days later the president informed Caffrey that he would arrive in Algiers on February 18 and hoped that the two leaders could meet on an American ship for an afternoon discussion. De Gaulle replied on the same day that he regretted not being able to travel to Algiers, reminding Roosevelt that he had invited the American president in November to come to Paris and would be pleased to welcome the American president in the French capital if he wished to come at any convenient date.[75]

In his memoirs de Gaulle asked rhetorically, "Why should the American President invite the French President to visit him in France?" wondering if Roosevelt was aware that Algeria was French territory. He explained that a meeting with Roosevelt after Yalta would imply acceptance of the decisions made at a conference from which France had been excluded and complained about Roosevelt's refusal in November to accept his invitation to come to Paris. So a third meeting between the two leaders would never take place. Hopkins received word of the non-meeting while aboard the USS *Quincy* moored adjacent to the Suez Canal in Egypt's Great Bitter Lake after his boss had conferred with Egyptian King Farouk, King Ibn Saud of Saudi Arabia, and the diminutive Emperor Haile Selassie of Ethiopia. Caffrey said that when he reminded Bidault that de Gaulle had indicated his willingness to meet with the president, a message that had been communicated to Roosevelt via Hopkins, the French foreign minister indicated that he had done everything possible to persuade de Gaulle to see the president, but the general had changed his mind in light of what he considered his exclusion from Yalta.[76]

Roosevelt was so enraged at de Gaulle for this snub that he dictated to his secretary the outlines of an insulting response. When a horrified Hopkins persuaded Bohlen, FDR's interpreter at Yalta, to speak to the president about the danger of antagonizing the French people with such a broadside, Bohlen got FDR to moderate the wording of the response, but only after eliciting a smile from the president with the remark that "we can all admit that de Gaulle is being one of the biggest sons of bitches who ever straddled a pot."[77]

The supreme irony of the Yalta Conference, from the perspective of France, was that de Gaulle received more tangible benefits from the Big Three summit conference than he or any other observer could have been led to expect. France was awarded one of the four seats on the Allied Control Council that would administer the occupation of postwar Germany. She obtained a French occupation zone in western Germany. She was invited to be one of the sponsoring powers of the San Francisco Conference in the spring that would establish the new United Nations Organization. She was awarded one of the five permanent seats in the new organization's Security Council, which included the right to veto any resolution brought before it.[78]

Nevertheless, when the French leader received word of the extraordinary gains his country had obtained without any participation in the conference, he took a swipe at the Big Three by declining the invitation to serve as one of the sponsoring powers of the forthcoming United Nations inaugural conference on the grounds that his government had not participated in the drafting of the UN Charter at the Dumbarton Oaks Conference by representatives of the four other nations that would eventually become the permanent five members of the U.N. Security Council.[79]

After a journey of 13,842 miles, an exhausted president returned to the White House on February 28. Franklin Roosevelt delivered what would be his last public speech, to a joint session of Congress on March 1, summarizing the results of the Crimea Conference. He took a swipe at de Gaulle, referring to certain "prima donnas" who had made life difficult for him. In what turned out to be his final communication with de Gaulle, Roosevelt informed him on March 24, as he was preparing to travel to Warm Springs, Georgia, that the Allied Joint Chiefs of Staff had rejected the French leader's urgent request at the beginning of the year for additional military aid to France to equip eight more divisions. [80] The reason given for this decision was that the request exceeded the production capability of the American economy and the availability of shipping to transport the equipment.[81]

The day after Roosevelt's death on April 12 in Warm Springs, Georgia, from a cerebral hemorrhage de Gaulle dispatched a message to his vice president and successor, Harry S. Truman: "Roosevelt . . . was from the first to the last, France's friend. France loved and admired him."[82] The references were to "France" and not to its leader.

~

CHAPTER FIVE

Truman and de Gaulle, 1945–1946

A Brief Encounter with Pinpricks

Harry S. Truman had spent a year in France as a captain in General John J. Pershing's American Expeditionary Force during World War I. His letters to his fiancée, Bess Wallace (whom he married on June 28, 1919, coincidently the same day that the Treaty of Versailles was signed), reveal a simmering Francophobia that would color his views of the country he was defending. On his first visit to Paris in April 1918, he remarked that the French capital was "some town. Wine and beer are sold here," noting that his fellow doughboys on leave "are trying to drink all they can here. They can't as the supply seems inexhaustible." He later complained, echoing a sentiment shared by many U.S. soldiers on leave from the front lines, that the French shopkeepers he had encountered "love francs better than thier [sic] country and they are all extracting just as many of them as they possibly can."[1] After participating in the Meuse-Argonne offensive, this midwestern farmer returned to the French capital after the armistice in December 1918 and saw the sites. He visited the Folies Bergères and was shocked by the "disgusting performance" he witnessed. As he visited the small villages between the front and Paris, he was put off by "the narrow streets" and "malodourous atmosphere" he encountered.[2]

There is no indication of the evolution of Harry Truman's attitudes toward France during his subsequent career as a country judge as part of the Kansas City Democratic machine of Tom Pendergast, then as a U.S. senator from Missouri after his election in 1934. When President Roosevelt decided to run for a fourth term in the summer of 1944, he bowed to pressure from Democrats who regarded Vice President Henry Wallace as too far to the left and replaced him with Truman, who had won nationwide publicity for his senatorial investigation of waste and fraud in government projects related to the preparation for war. After the Democratic ticket won in November 1944, FDR totally ignored his vice president, meeting with him one-on-one only twice and failing to inform him of any important foreign policy issues, such as the results of the Yalta Conference and the project in New Mexico to develop an atomic bomb. When Truman was summoned to the White House on April 12, 1945, by First Lady Eleanor Roosevelt to inform him of her husband's death, he promptly asked if there was anything he could do for her. Her famous reply hinted at the new occupant of the White House's total lack of preparation for the office: "Is there anything we can do for *you?* For you are the one in trouble now."[3]

In addition to all the momentous foreign-policy challenges he faced in the last stages of the Second World War, Harry Truman would soon find himself at odds with the current leader of France on a number of issues, notably pin-pricks over the German city of Stuttgart, the Middle East, and northwestern Italy. Although the Yalta Conference had awarded France an occupation zone in postwar Germany, de Gaulle was intent on using French military forces that had participated in the liberation of France after their landing in the south of the country on August 15, 1944, to drive as far east as possible to strengthen the country's position when the war came to an end. General Eisenhower had decided that American and British units would advance in the north in the Ruhr Valley and then drive through the German city of Frankfurt and along the Main River. The First French army, which was positioned in the southern end of the Allied front, was to be held in reserve until it could bolster the Anglo-American position after the northern Rhine crossings had succeeded. General George Patton's Third Army crossed the Rhine at the city of Mainz on March 22 and Montgomery's British forces fol-lowed suit the next day. On March 29, de Gaulle ordered the commander of the First French Army, General Jean de Lattre de Tassigny, to cross the river "even if the Americans do not help you and you are obliged to use boats."[4]

De Lattre crossed the river on March 31, and his roughly 125,000 men continued moving east, capturing the German city of Karlsruhe. U.S. General Jacob Devers, under whose orders de Lattre operated, ordered the French general to avoid any "premature advance" and to engage the German Nineteenth Army in the Black Forest. De Gaulle instead ordered de Lattre to move farther east to capture the city of Stuttgart, which had been slated to be taken by U.S. General Alexander Patch's American Seventh Army. After de Lattre arrived in Stuttgart on April 23, Patch showed up the next day to order him to evacuate the city. De Gaulle in turn ordered de Lattre to refuse Devers's order and to set up a French military government there for one overriding reason: Stuttgart was a key point leading to an advance eastward to Bavaria and Austria, which the French leader claimed "would support our intentions as to the French zone of occupation," which had not yet been formally delineated.[5]

A plaintive plea from Eisenhower to de Gaulle got nowhere. As often had been the case during Roosevelt's presidency, Eisenhower was willing to back down. When the U.S. VI Corps arrived in the Danube city of Ulm on April 24, Devers discovered that de Lattre's forces had arrived eight hours earlier, forty-five miles outside the designated French sector.[6] The new American president was livid. Truman wrote to de Gaulle, in a letter drafted by Secretary of War Stimson, that he was "shocked by the attitude of your government in this matter and its evident implications." He warned of a "storm of resentment" in the United States if the French persisted and implied that "an entire rearrangement of command" might be necessary. He threatened to cut off all supplies to the French army unless it withdrew.[7] Privately, Truman reacted to the Stuttgart incident with his customary bluntness in a summary evaluation of de Gaulle: "I don't like the son of a bitch."[8] Having made his point, de Gaulle reduced the French contingent in the city to a nominal presence as the Americans took control.[9] Later de Lattre's forces and Leclerc's Second Armored Division drove east, crossed the Danube, and eventually occupied Hitler's Alpine retreat above Berchtesgaden.

Another quarrel between the Allied leadership and the French broke out concerning northeastern Italy in the first week of May as the German surrender approached. On May 4, de Gaulle ordered French General Paul-André Doyen to occupy the small French-speaking Alpine enclave of the Aosta Valley.[10] Without any coordination with Allied leaders, French troops near Nice burst across the Italian border and occupied the area. British Field Marshal Sir Harold Alexander, the Supreme Allied Commander in Italy, with the full support of American military authorities, ordered the French to withdraw so that he could set up the Allied military government that had been planned by Washington and London. De Gaulle had assured Ambassador Caffrey that he hoped to discuss the matter of "very minor" border "adjustments" directly with the Italian government.[11]

Under orders from de Gaulle, General Doyen refused to evacuate the region and intimated to Alexander that he would resist the Allies with force if necessary. An enraged Churchill cabled Truman that he considered the French leader "one of the greatest dangers to European peace. . . . De Gaulle's present program of defiance and scorn to Britain and the U.S. leads only to unimaginable misery and misfortune."[12] Amid this controversy, de Gaulle did not hesitate to implore Truman to allow French military forces to participate in the final months of the war against Japan in Asia, which of course the American president would not agree to.[13]

Churchill and Truman exchanged messages expressing their exasperation with the French leader throughout the crisis.[14] In a sharply worded message to de Gaulle, Truman vigorously denounced the implied threat of military action against Allied troops and demanded that the French forces leave the area forthwith. "While this threat is outstanding against American soldiers," he added, "no further issues of military equipment or munitions can be made to French troops." The situation dragged on into the summer. On June 10, Ambassador Jefferson Caffrey called in Bidault and Pleven for a dressing down on the northwestern Italy issue. The French foreign minister, who claimed that he knew nothing about the affair until the U.S. government complained to him, telephoned the American ambassador several hours later informing him that de Gaulle had given orders to evacuate the area, which the French forces did forthwith.[15] French General Alphonse Juin had privately admitted to the Americans that de Gaulle's position was "unreasonable and impetuous" and that the French cabinet did not support him on the dispute.[16]

A third source of conflict between de Gaulle and his Anglo-American allies/antagonists broke out in the Levant. Under pressure from the British during the war, de Gaulle, as we have seen, had announced France's intention to withdraw from and grant independence to France's League of Nations mandates of Syria and Lebanon, which had been formally established in 1922. In the summer of 1943, indigenous nationalists in both countries had won their citizens' support by large majorities in referenda and promptly demanded independence, a development that resulted in the French arresting the Syrian leader and his cabinet. After strenuous protests from other Arab states, the French released the nationalist leaders. But Churchill had ironically complained to Roosevelt that the French action was a violation of the Atlantic Charter—which he had specifically indicated did not apply to the British Empire—as a way of eliminating de Gaulle from his position. He denounced the "lamentable outrages committed by the French in Syria," describing them as "a foretaste of what de Gaulle's leadership means." If the French leader did not promptly rectify the situation in the Levant, Churchill proposed "bringing the issue with de Gaulle to a head," by suspending recognition of de Gaulle and ending the provision of arms to French troops in North Africa since "there is nothing this man will not do if he has armed forces at his disposal."[17]

With the end of the war in Europe, nationalist demonstrations in favor of immediate independence broke out in Beirut, Damascus, and other cities. As French troops moved in to quell the demonstrations, Britain urged the French to negotiate treaties with the independence movements. De Gaulle paid no attention to the genuine anti-French sentiment in the Levant, preferring to see the demonstrations as part of a British plot to replace France in the region. He ordered French military forces to disperse the demonstrators, despite repeated British pleas to negotiate with the Lebanese and Syrian leaders who were anxious to take control of their countries and for the French to depart. The French troops even briefly shelled the city of Damascus. De Gaulle apparently hoped to pressure Lebanese and Syrian independence leaders to sign agreements allowing the former mandatory power to retain certain economic privileges and military bases.[18]

On June 1, an enraged Churchill told the House of Commons that British troops stationed in Syria were being deployed to halt the violence between French forces and indigenous demonstrators. When de Gaulle got word of the Churchill speech, he called in the British ambassador to France, Alfred Duff Cooper, and unleashed a tirade that ended with a stern warning: "I admit that we are not in a position to wage war against you at the present time. But you have insulted France and betrayed the West. This cannot be forgotten."[19] The French leader called in Caffrey to express his outrage at the British, while Bidault was indiscreetly sharing with the American ambassador his strong opposition to de Gaulle's Syrian policy and indicated that he might resign over the issue.[20] Eventually de Gaulle was forced to back down, and in the summer, British and French troops left the two countries. In recalling the Syria-Lebanon affair, Truman expressed himself in his usual salty language: "Those French ought to be taken out and castrated."[21]

As these conflicts began to simmer in the spring of 1945, plans were well developed to convene an international conference in San Francisco to establish a new world organization to replace the League of Nations. De Gaulle had to decide definitively what France's role would be in the proposed new organization. When French ambassador Henri Bonnet had visited the State Department on March 16, Stettinius bluntly complained about France's refusal to accept sponsorship of the forthcoming conference and wondered if France would be a spoiler or a cooperative delegation in San Francisco. Bonnet assured him that the latter would be the case.[22] Toward the end of the month, de Gaulle designated a high-level French delegation to the San Francisco meeting that would be headed by Foreign Minister Georges Bidault. It included Minister of Finance René Pleven, Minister of Public Health François Billoux (of the Communist Party), Joseph Paul-Boncour (former premier, foreign minister, and delegate to the League of Nations), and Ambassador Bonnet. Before he left Paris for San

Francisco, Bidault publicly aired a number of grievances about the forth-coming conference and the organization that it was expected to create. The first was that French had not been designated as one of its official languages in the preliminary planning.[23]

The instructions to Bidault had clearly specified that the French language be established as one of the two official languages of the new world organi-zation, as it had been in the League of Nations. The foreign minister was forbidden to sign any document that did not include a French text at the San Francisco Conference.[24] His more substantive concern was that Washington was reportedly considering a proposal to convert France's overseas possessions into trusteeships to be administered by the new international organization, an idea, as we have seen, that Roosevelt had toyed with during the war.[25] De Gaulle was so wary of the "trusteeship" idea that his government reiterated its refusal of the invitation to become one of the five "inviting powers" of the conference.[26] After a month of haggling, it was agreed in late April to designate French as one of the official languages of the new organization, to the French foreign minister's relief and delight.[27]

Bidault stopped in Washington on May 18 and 19 during his return trip from the San Francisco conference to meet the new president for the first time. Truman assured the French foreign minister that he hoped to see his country recover from the ravages of the European war because a "strong France represents a gain for the world." He noted that American economic aid to France had continued to flow unabated despite the recent Franco-American dustups. Bidault pressed hard for the redrawing of Germany's western frontier and got a sympathetic response from the ill-informed presi-dent, until Acting Secretary of State Joseph Grew discreetly reminded Tru-man that Washington had not gone beyond its promise agreed to at Yalta of a French occupation zone carved out of the British and American zones (which Truman promptly confirmed to Bidault). In his public statement, the new American president emphasized that "there was a full appreciation by the United States government of the part France could and should play" in the postwar world. He also affirmed that he would welcome a de Gaulle visit to Washington.[28] In the summer, American press comments underscored the importance of repairing the relationship between Washington and Paris and assisting France in its economic recovery.[29]

Defending the Vichy Gamble

In the fall of 1944, as Cordell Hull was preparing to resign his position as secretary of state, he had asked the distinguished Harvard historian William

L. Langer, who was on leave as head of the Research and Analysis Branch of the Office of Strategic Services, to write a book explaining the reasons for Washington's decision to recognize the government of Marshal Pétain. Langer was given unrestricted access to State Department records that would be closed to other researchers for thirty years. A few weeks before Roosevelt's death, Admiral Wilson Brown, his naval adviser, informed the president's secretary that FDR had agreed to Langer's request for access to the White House files as well. The president had asked a young lieutenant in the U.S. Naval Reserves named George Elsey to compile a report of the files that Langer had not yet seen. Elsey forwarded a summary of the material he had found to the president, who reviewed and approved the summary in a note to Elsey from Warm Springs on April 6, a week before his death.[30]

On June 7, Admiral Brown asked Elsey to prepare for the new president a summary of the relations between Roosevelt and de Gaulle, followed by another lengthy recitation of FDR's correspondence with Churchill on various subjects. As we have seen, FDR almost totally ignored his vice president, so the Elsey report was valued by the White House for clarifying in particular U.S. relations with Pétain's regime. The resulting report, submitted on June 21, brought the new president up to speed not only on the Vichy policy but also on the disputatious relationship between Roosevelt and de Gaulle on so many matters, of which Truman had been totally unaware.[31] Two years later, Langer brought out his ringing defense of Roosevelt's policy toward Vichy France and the Free French movement.[32]

The Empty Chair at Potsdam

To de Gaulle's bitter disappointment, France had not been invited to the Big Three conference that was held from July 17 to August 2, 1945, at Cecilienhof, the residence of former Crown Prince Wilhelm in the Berlin suburb of Potsdam. Truman, Churchill, and Stalin and their advisers were in attendance until Churchill was replaced by Clement Attlee, the leader of the Labour Party, after the Conservatives were defeated in the parliamentary election in the middle of the conference. Of the two main items on the agenda, one was of no importance to France—the ultimatum to Japan to surrender unconditionally or face "prompt and utter destruction," a reference to the atomic bomb that had been tested in New Mexico at the beginning of the conference. The European portion of the agenda focused on implementing the decisions about the occupation of Germany and the question of German reparations—two issues that were obviously of great interest to France.[33] Despite his absence from Potsdam, de Gaulle secured for his country membership in the Council of Foreign Ministers, which would work for a formal peace treaty formally terminating the European War (a treaty that would in fact never be concluded). In short, though France had suffered some humiliations in the months after the war, it was now a member of the "Big Four" (and would remain so during the Cold War).

De Gaulle's Last Visit to Washington:
U.S. Aid, Germany, and Indochina

Truman's thoughts about inviting de Gaulle to visit Washington had swung from one extreme to the other. At his first press conference on April 17, he indicated a willingness to receive the French leader: "If he wants to see me I will be glad to see him." But the subsequent imbroglios over Stuttgart, northeast Italy, and the Middle East had soured him on the idea. When asked by radio news correspondents on June 16 if de Gaulle would be visiting, he replied, "Not by my invitation. I have no ambition to see him."[34] But he finally relented and issued a formal invitation for a visit in late August. Before his trip, Ambassador Caffrey reported that the French Foreign Ministry indicated that de Gaulle "hopes that his visit will serve to clear up all the old misunderstandings so that the United States and France can work together in close harmony."[35] He arrived in the American capital on August 22 for his first meeting with Roosevelt's successor. When he stepped off the plane, he delivered a short greeting in near-perfect English that delighted the large crowd in the audience. "Without you, the American people, led by your great presidents, Roosevelt and Truman," he declared, "there would be no future for Europe and Asia, but only intolerable servitude."[36]

The three-day visit was accompanied by all the pomp and circumstance reserved for important visitors. The front page of *The New York Times* included a photo of the two leaders standing at attention on the White House lawn as the two national anthems were played. De Gaulle was honored with a twenty-one-gun salute (finally), state dinner, wreath laying at Arlington Cemetery, and a visit to the U.S. Naval Academy at Annapolis. The substantive conversations in the afternoon and evening of August 22, which were attended by their respective foreign ministers, enabled de Gaulle to repeat the well-known French refrain about the political future of Germany: the defeated enemy had lost territory in the east but not in the west; the Rhine River represented France's security frontier, so the separation of the Rhineland was a "psychological necessity" for the French people. He also mentioned his oft-repeated proposal that the Ruhr Valley be placed under international control. Truman countered with the observation that "the

German danger should not be exaggerated," that the country had been permanently weakened by the Potsdam agreement, and that the country was unlikely ever to present another threat to its western neighbor. In what must have sounded like a repetition of Woodrow Wilson's faith in collective security that had so dismayed Georges Clemenceau at the Paris Peace Conference of 1919, he declared that the future of global peace and security must and would be guaranteed by the new United Nations organization.[37]

But the president provided his French guest with some good news. He approved the beginning of loan negotiations for a resumption of American economic assistance that had been interrupted by the termination of Lend-Lease aid at the end of the war. That presidential commitment eventually led to a $550 million loan agreement negotiated by Monnet in December. This in turn led to the presentation by France of the country's financial requirements for the next four years, which would become the basis for what would become first the Blum-Byrnes accords later in 1946 and the more expansive Marshall Plan the following year. After leaving Washington, de Gaulle visited West Point and then Hyde Park to lay a wreath at FDR's grave and express his condolences to Eleanor Roosevelt.[38]

France, the United States, Japan, and Indochina

General Yuichi Tsuchihashi, the commander of Japanese occupation forces in Indochina, had seized the French garrisons in the country on March 9, 1945; arrested the French governor general, Admiral Jean Decoux; and announced that Tokyo was liberating the country from its European colonists. Approximately 2,500 French military forces were killed or missing, and Japanese soldiers imprisoned another 12,000. The next day the Japanese government declared that "the colonial status of French Indochina has ended." Emperor Bảo Đại (the last in a long line of emperors of Annam, 1802–1945) declared the independence of his country, which was renamed Vietnam (March 11), followed by declarations of independence by King Norodom Sihanouk of Cambodia (March 13) and King Sisafong Vong of Laos (April 8).[39]

After the Japanese announcement, Roosevelt had been informed by American Office of Strategic Services (OSS) Chief William Donovan that the French forces in the protectorate had requested American assistance against the Japanese troops that were massacring French soldiers and civilians. On March 12, French Ambassador Bonnet in Washington formally asked the United States to intervene in the Inter-Allied General Staff (IAGS) to provide assistance to the French troops still fighting. The next day the head of the French military mission in Washington pleaded with the

IAGS for Allied air support and other assistance to aid the French resistance to the Japanese crackdown in Indochina. He asked that General Roger Blaizot, head of the French mission to the Southeast Asia Command, be accredited with the commander of the Allied operations in China (including Indochina) to coordinate such aid. Roosevelt approved the Blaizot request the same day. On March 15, he instructed Charles Taussig, the State Department specialist in colonial affairs, to secure from France a pledge to treat Indochina as a trust territory with independence the ultimate goal.[40]

Perhaps the president was influenced by de Gaulle's pointed question to American ambassador Jefferson Caffrey about America's objectives in Indochina. The French leader who had flown to Moscow to sign a bilateral alliance with Stalin demanded: did Washington wish to push France into becoming "one of the federated states under the Russian aegis"? And he continued: "When Germany collapses, they [the Russians] will fall on us. . . . We do not want to become communists; we do not want to fall into the Russian orbit and we hope you will not push us into it." On April 3, the State Department issued an official statement, approved by the ailing president, confirming that the Big Three at Yalta, in consultation with France and China, had approved a plan on the establishment of trust territories for colonial possessions to submit to the San Francisco conference that would establish the new United Nations Organization. De Gaulle had already proposed on March 24 a statute for Indochina specifying that "the inhabitants of the Indochinese Federation will be citizens of Indochina and citizens of the [planned] French Union, which would be governed by a governor general with ministers selected by both Indochinese and French nationals living in Indochina."[41]

After Roosevelt's death later that month, the question of the future of French Indochina would become a major topic of discussion between de Gaulle and the new man in the White House. As we have seen, Franklin Roosevelt had made no secret of his conviction that European imperialism should come to an end after the end of the war. He had bitter disputes with Churchill about the future of the British Empire and had often expressed his belief that many of the French overseas possessions should be transformed into trust territories administered by the new international organization he envisioned as a successor to the League of Nations.

In March 1945, shortly before his death, Roosevelt had consented to support a temporary return of French military forces to the protectorate after the end of the Japanese occupation on the condition that a trusteeship be set up with the intention of laying the groundwork for independence. When informed by Ambassador Caffrey of de Gaulle's solemn warning that if France were not allowed to regain control of Indochina, the region would soon fall under Soviet control, Roosevelt had ordered the American army air force to support the French in Indochina if it would not detract from the military operations against Japan.[42]

There has been a vigorous historiographical debate about Roosevelt's inchoate plans for the establishment of a trusteeship in French Indochina after the end of the Pacific War.[43] The standard version after the war was that FDR's trusteeship policy died with him.[44] The authors of the Pentagon Papers contended that Roosevelt had merely paid "lip service to trusteeship and anti-colonialism" and did not attempt to translate that inclination into policy.[45] Edward R. Drachman concluded that FDR wished that "Indochina would be placed under trusteeship only with the permission of France, which was highly improbable."[46] Walter LaFeber argued that once Roosevelt recognized that one of his proposed "Four Policemen," China, was too weak to fulfill its assigned role as the replacement of France in Asia, he "agreed to turn his head while the French moved back into Indochina."[47] In any case, just before his death in April 1945, FDR had reluctantly recognized that Washington would have to accept the return of France to its Southeast Asian colony.[48]

At their meetings on August 22–24 during de Gaulle's visit to Washington, less than a week after the Japanese emperor had announced his country's surrender, de Gaulle formally asked Truman to support the return of French troops there, and the American president offered no objection.[49] Truman knew and cared very little about the unfolding events in Southeast Asia. With regard to Indochina, he informed Foreign Minister Bidault that he would not oppose French rule in the protectorate.[50]

Anticipating the evacuation of Japanese troops from Indochina, de Gaulle dispatched a French expeditionary force under his old comrade-in-arms General Philippe Leclerc to reestablish French military control of the territory, whose colonial administration had collaborated with the Japanese occupation. He designated his loyal follower Admiral Thierry d'Argenlieu as high commissioner.[51] Contradicting de Gaulle's well-known suspicion that Great Britain was intent on encroaching on France's overseas empire after the war, the British military forces that had arrived in the south of Vietnam to receive the Japanese surrender facilitated the return of the French forces even as the new Labour government in London was beginning to lay the groundwork for its own withdrawal from the old colonial outposts of India, Burma, and Malaya. Mark Lawrence's depiction of Britain's active support for the restoration of French colonial rule in Indochina as the Second World War drew to a close leaves no doubt about the Labour government's concern about the consequences of a Communist takeover under the control of the Vietnamese revolutionary Ho Chi Minh.[52]

In May of 1941, Ho had assembled a gathering of the Indochinese Communist Party's central committee in a remote area in northeast Vietnam. The group established a patriotic coalition designed to work for the liberation of the country from foreign domination. The name of the new group was the Vietnamese Independence League (Viet Nam Doc Lap Dong Minh Hoi), soon shortened to Viet Minh.[53] Toward the end of the war in Asia, the OSS had parachuted the so-called Deer team into the northern part of the country to establish contact with the Viet Minh to work together against the remnants of the Japanese occupation forces in the French protectorate. The members of the small intelligence band were greatly impressed with the activities of the Viet Minh they witnessed. The two leaders of the group, Archimedes Patti and Alison K. Thomas, met several times with Ho Chi Minh in July and August 1945, implying that Washington supported the Viet Minh's strategy and tactics.[54]

Ho persuaded Emperor Bảo Đại (who had ascended the throne of Annam in 1932 and had been used as a puppet ruler by the Japanese after their takeover) to abdicate on August 25, 1945. The Viet Minh leader proceeded to declare his country's independence in Hanoi's Ba Dinh Square on September 2, 1945, the very day that the Japanese surrendered to General Douglas MacArthur on the battleship *Missouri* in Tokyo Bay. In his speech, he famously recited portions of the American Declaration of Independence, which Ho asked the OSS leader Patti to look over to see if they were quoted properly.[55]

At the end of the First World War, a young Ho Chi Minh had addressed an appeal to President Woodrow Wilson during the Paris Peace Conference of 1919 for the recognition of his country's right to "self-determination," a key component of the American president's ideology. There is no evidence that Wilson ever saw the appeal, but even if he had, he certainly would not have been interested in antagonizing French Premier Georges Clemenceau during the two leaders' struggles over so many issues at the conference. In any case, Ho turned his back on Wilsonianism and became a charter member of the French Communist Party in 1920, when the left wing of the French Socialist Party broke away to form the French Communist Party at the Congress of Tours.[56] In his brief speech at the conference where this parting of ways occurred, he devoted the balance of his address to a full-fledged denunciation of the French imperial policies in the country. They had "shamelessly exploited our people, driven them into the worst misery, and mercilessly plundered our country."[57] Those words were very similar to the harsh language used by Franklin Roosevelt when he addressed the role of France in its Southeast Asian possession. In any case, Ho traveled to Moscow in 1923 and became an outspoken member of the Communist International (Comintern).

After his declaration of Vietnam's independence in September 1945, the Viet Minh leader appointed the deposed emperor "supreme adviser" of the fledgling Communist government. As French colonial administrators, troops, merchants, and bankers streamed back into Indochina in the fall of 1945, Ho's hope of receiving American and French recognition were dashed. De Gaulle fully planned to incorporate the country into his new project for a "French Union" (loosely modeled on the original plan for a British Commonwealth of Nations). On March 24, 1945, de Gaulle had issued a governmental declaration that called for the creation of an Indochinese Federation with substantial autonomy for its five parts. As noted above, the appointment of Leclerc and later d'Argenlieu was designed to thwart the objectives of the Viet Minh.[58]

The British commander, General Douglas D. Gracey, who received the Japanese surrender in the southern part of Vietnam, was a dyed-in-the-wool colonialist (nicknamed the "Bruiser") who actively supported the restoration of French colonial control. He had declared martial law on September 21 to prevent anti-French demonstrations. In October and November, British troops, mainly Indians, expelled Viet Minh soldiers from Saigon and its environs. The first full division of French troops arrived in late October under Leclerc's command, after which they received supplies of British equipment from General Gracey.[59] By the beginning of 1946, French forces no longer required the backing of the British, and at the end of January, Gracey and most of his Indian troops had begun to evacuate the country. Although he had been delayed, D'Argenlieu arrived to take up his position as high commissioner several months later.[60] This British support for French imperial designs in Indochina was in sharp contrast to the situation in Syria and Lebanon, where, as we have seen, de Gaulle suspected the United Kingdom of supporting the indigenous rebellion against French colonial rule.

The Viet Minh leader was stymied at every turn. He eventually decided to make one last effort to persuade the French to loosen their control of his country. In September 1946, Ho and a delegation of his colleagues made the long trip to France to attend a conference with French government representatives in Fontainebleau outside of Paris. Although he had secured an ambiguous and ultimately meaningless "modus vivendi" agreement, he was under no illusions that it would be honored.[61] Before returning to Hanoi, he stopped by the American embassy in Paris to request assistance from Ambassador Caffrey, to no effect. Similar appeals from the Viet Minh leader to

Truman and Secretary of State James Byrnes on October 17, 18, 20, and 22 and November 1 went unanswered as well.[62] De Gaulle, as we shall see, had resigned from his post at the beginning of 1946, leaving the issue of French Indochina to his successors. But the stage was set for a thirty-year war in that country before the constituent parts of Indochina achieved their independence, first from the French, then from the Americans.

Creating the New Republic in France

In October 1945, elections were conducted in France to choose a Constituent Assembly that would both serve as a parliament and draft a new constitution for what was to be called the Fourth Republic. De Gaulle's Provisional Government included Communists, Socialists, Radical Socialists, and the new Christian Democratic Party named the Popular Republic Movement (MRP). The parties on the left, animated by spirit of the resistance, called for radical social and economic reforms to break not only with Vichy but with the discredited Third Republic as well. De Gaulle's dismissive policy toward the Resistance leaders during the Liberation left a legacy of bitterness toward him in the French left, particularly on the part of the powerful French Communist Party. In any event, he was totally unprepared to engage in the kind of political compromises endemic to a parliamentary system.

But de Gaulle fulfilled the promises he had made in a speech at the Palais de Chaillot on September 12, 1944, to introduce radical economic reforms when the war was over. In that address, he pledged to abolish "the coalitions of interests which have so weighed on the life of ordinary people" and to ensure that French society in the future would be "managed not for the profit of a few individuals but for the benefit of all."[63] While the British Labour Party was laying the groundwork for the British welfare state after coming to power in the summer of 1945, de Gaulle's government nationalized the electricity industry, the gas industry, the coal industry, Air France, the Bank of France, and the four largest private banks—Crédit Lyonnais, the Banque National de Paris, Société Générale, and Crédit Commercial. Preparations were made for the nationalization of the Renault automobile company (whose president, Louis Renault, had been accused of collaborating with the German occupiers). In a set of sweeping social reforms, the French state vastly expanded the old age and retirement system, family allowances to encourage more births, unemployment insurance, and a national health care system. Though France was one of the first European countries to grant the vote to all men in the Constitution of 1875, it was among the last of the Western countries to extend suffrage to women. At the end of World

War I, women had obtained the vote in Great Britain, Germany, and the United States but not in France. French women were given the right to vote by the Provisional Government in Algiers on April 21, 1944. They voted in municipal elections for the first time on April 29, 1945, and in national elections on October 21.

A majority of French people agreed that the 1875 Constitution of the Third Republic had to be redrawn. During the debates about the new constitution in the summer of 1945, the major parties expressed a preference for a unicameral parliament—the National Assembly—that would choose the prime minister and the cabinet. De Gaulle favored a strong executive who could operate without the constraints of a powerful legislative chamber. In the elections of October 21, 1945, the Communist Party won the most legislative seats with 26 percent, followed by the Socialists and the centrist MRP with 24 percent and other parties. At its first meeting in early November, the National Assembly voted to designate de Gaulle interim president of the republic to form a government until the new constitution was ratified by the voters. De Gaulle rebuffed the Communist Party's demand for top cabinet positions such as foreign minister, defense minister, or interior minister (which controlled the police). The government that he finally formed after a month of haggling on November 21 had to face a parliament dominated by Communists and Socialists. He realized that his dream of a powerful presidency had no chance of being enacted amid these political conditions. Again, he was unaccustomed to the give-and-take of parliamentary maneuvering, a process totally foreign to a military officer who had exercised iron control over the Free French movement during the war.[64]

Meanwhile, the constitutional drafting committee of the Constituent Assembly had proposed a new constitution that preserved the system of parliamentary supremacy that had proved so unworkable under the Third Republic. The president of the republic should be elected by the National Assembly and could not preside over cabinet meetings, and discussions were being held on whether he should be authorized to name the prime minister.[65] When apprised of these developments, a gravely disappointed, furious de Gaulle denounced the Assembly for having taken "no account of the absolute necessities of authority, of dignity, of the responsibility of government" and predicted that if the new constitution were adopted, "you will bitterly regret you have taken the path you now follow."[66] To add insult to injury, he was still smarting from the news he received through the newspapers in early December that a meeting of American, British, and Soviet foreign ministers would take place in Moscow in two weeks to discuss peace treaties with Nazi Germany's allies Bulgaria, Romania, Hungary, and Finland.[67]

Modernizing the Postwar French Economy
and the American Reaction

At home de Gaulle recognized that radical reforms were necessary to jump-start the French economy that had suffered from four years of German requisitions and the destruction of infrastructure by both the occupier and the liberators in the summer of 1944. While in Washington in August 1945, the French leader had conferred with Jean Monnet, whom he had first met in London on the eve of the fall of France and who had been handling negotiations on Lend-Lease government credits to France among other matters. Since the fall of 1943, Monnet had been working assiduously for an infusion of U.S. financial assistance to France after its liberation. De Gaulle presented a memorandum to Truman that had been drafted by Monnet pledging to present an economic modernization program to Washington in the hope that it would unlock funding that would begin when Lend-Lease would terminate at the end of the Pacific War.[68]

The Lend-Lease agreement with France that had been signed on February 8, 1945, granted the country access to some $2.5 billion worth of products through July 1946. But after receiving only $400 million of these credits, the abrupt termination of the Lend-Lease program after the Japanese surrender left France in the lurch as it faced a postwar economic crisis.[69] Never one to despair, Monnet continued to seek postwar financial assistance from Washington to promote the modernization of the French economy. He pressed for a one-time credit of roughly $4.5 billion in credits for three years to prime the pump for investment and productivity. The State Department was planning to issue $1–2 billion of credits for the same purpose. So the prospects for postwar reconstruction in France seemed bright.[70]

Monnet appealed to de Gaulle's obsession with recovering French grandeur with a lecture about what the country would need to recover its position in the world: the French, he implored, "must modernize themselves—because at the moment they are not modern. They need more production and greater productivity. Materially the country needs to be transformed."[71] In early November 1945, Monnet returned to Paris to preside over the economic recovery of his country, with de Gaulle's full support. Working behind the scenes, he formed a series of commissions charged with proposing schemes to modernize the antiquated sectors of the nation's economy. The commissions for each sector would include relevant civil service experts, business leaders, union representatives, and economists. They would draw up comprehensive plans for the modernization of each sector: steel, transportation, agriculture, energy, financial services, and so on. Once the recommendations were made, the government would have full authority to implement them without having to obtain parliamentary approval.

When Monnet submitted his scheme of government planning to de Gaulle in December 1945, the latter (who had minimal interest in or understanding of economic matters) endorsed it wholeheartedly. On January 3, 1946, de Gaulle issued a decree creating a "Commissariat General for the French Modernization and Investment Plan."[72] Monnet became the first planning commissioner, a post he would occupy for seven years until he left to create the High Authority of the European Coal and Steel Community (the distant forerunner of the European Union). Monnet's Commissariat du Plan represented the kind of technocratic approach that greatly appealed to de Gaulle and helped to lay the groundwork for the full recovery of the French economy.[73]

Concerns by U.S. government officials that de Gaulle would attempt to implement radical economic reforms had been aired in the early fall of 1944. Simon Milner of the Foreign Economic Administration in New York City predicted that the French leader would institute widespread nationalization of French industry. He cited a de Gaulle speech in Lille on October 1, 1944, calling for the creation of a vast public sector. This reiterated a declaration made by de Gaulle in a speech to the Provisional Consultative Assembly in Algiers in March that "the French democracy must be a social democracy" based on government control of many industries.[74] These American anxieties about the statist direction that de Gaulle reportedly planned for France after the war continued to increase in intensity.

Tapping the Economic Resources of Postwar Germany and the U.S. Reaction

The hope that the United States would provide financial assistance to help France recover from the devastation of the war seemed a good prospect at the fall of 1945. This situation represented a sharp contrast to the developments after World War I, when Woodrow Wilson's government suspended all wartime financial aid to France and soon demanded reimbursement for the Treasury Department funds that had been lent to France during the American participation in the war. But de Gaulle and his inner circle also demanded that defeated Germany contribute to France's economic rehabilitation, as Georges Clemenceau had done at the Paris Peace Conference of 1919. The French government specified this requirement in a memorandum to the Conference of Foreign Ministers in London on September 11, 1945, which formally called for the detachment of the Ruhr and the Rhineland from Germany for economic as well as security reasons.[75]

Since France had not been a participant in the Potsdam Conference, de Gaulle felt under no obligation to honor the Potsdam agreement that Germany would be treated as a single political and economic unit. At a press conference on November 12, he repeated his Rhineland-Ruhr demands. When asked about the issue of central political and economic agencies in defeated Germany, he responded: "Consider this: that we are neighbors of Germany, that we have been invaded three times by Germany in a single lifetime, and you will conclude that we want no more of the Reich."[76] His memorandum to the Foreign Ministers Conference indicated that France would block any effort to create any agreement on central administration, which it proceeded to do.[77] Whereas the Truman administration vigorously opposed such actions and pressed for an agreement linking the four occupation zones, the British were briefly tempted by the French proposal. But after representatives of the two countries discussed the French plan from October 12 to 26, French officials failed to persuade their British counterparts to endorse the program. London feared that the separation of the Ruhr, which was located within the British occupation zone, would force Britain to bear the cost of feeding its malnourished population.[78]

Although the security of its eastern border was the main reason for de Gaulle's call of the separation of the Ruhr and the Rhineland from Germany, economic considerations played a role as well. The Monnet Plan for France's industrial recovery would require massive deliveries of coal and coking coal from western Germany.[79] Pressed by American High Commissioner Lucius Clay to address the issue, a meeting of economic specialists in the State Department took place from November 15 to 20, 1945. The French representative reiterated the demand that the Ruhr and the Rhineland be detached from Germany and that heavy reparation payments be required. The American delegates strongly opposed the French proposal because it would stifle the exports that Germany needed to pay for the reparations stipulated in the Potsdam Agreement.[80]

In Washington, Secretary of State James Byrnes bluntly informed France that the U.S. planned to ask London and Moscow to implement a common administrative machinery for the U.S., British, and Soviet zones with or without French participation.[81] By the end of 1945, the fate of de Gaulle's aggressive bid to separate the Rhineland and the Ruhr from Germany had been stifled by Washington. But London and Moscow had not decided to follow suit until after de Gaulle's departure in January 1946, and the plan to create central administrative agencies for occupied Germany still had not been implemented. Monnet had succeeded in persuading de Gaulle that the only hope for France's postwar economic recovery lay in large credits from the only country in the world that could provide them: the United States. He recognized that France would have to abandon its strident demands for territorial amputations in Western Germany—and the security and economic advantages to France they would entail—in exchange for the influx of American credits that the battered French economy so desperately needed.[82]

As noted above, the French Communist Party had won 26 percent of the popular vote as a result of the October 1945 elections. The Communists obtained a number of cabinet posts, though not important ones. Along with the radical economic reforms approved by de Gaulle, this development did not sit well in Washington in the early stages of what would later become the Cold War. On November 20, 1945, de Gaulle's head of intelligence, André Dewavrin (Passy), dropped in on Ambassador Caffrey to say that de Gaulle wanted to remove the sources of Franco-American conflict by affirming that the combination of the rise of the French Communist Party and the Soviet threat to Western Europe trumped the potential danger of a recovered Germany. He assured the American ambassador that de Gaulle would continue to freeze the Communist deputies out of sensitive ministries, as he had up to then. René Pleven, de Gaulle's finance minister, came to the embassy with assurances that the nationalizations of French industry would not adversely affect American interests.[83] In the meantime, as we have seen, de Gaulle had appointed Monnet to launch the negotiations that resulted in the Blum-Byrnes accord that would be reached under de Gaulle's successor.[84]

As the year 1945 drew to a close, Charles de Gaulle was coming to the conclusion that he could not work with the left-wing political forces that had come to power in the October elections amid the turn toward a regime of parliamentary supremacy that seemed to him a return to the unwieldy government institutions of the Third Republic. In a speech to the Assembly on January 1, 1946, he hinted that it would be his last address from that podium and unleashed a broadside against the legislators: "If you proceed without taking account of the lessons of our political history over the last fifty years and especially what occurred in 1940, if you do not take account of the need for the authority, dignity, and responsibility of the government," you will lead the country into "a situation where, one day or other, I predict, you will bitterly regret having taken the road you have taken."[85]

Amid this political in-fighting, de Gaulle and his extended family momentarily escaped the winter chill of Paris on January 6 for the warmth of the Côte d'Azur in a villa in Antibes—the first vacation he had taken in seven years. After intensive discussions with his brother Pierre and his brother-in-law Jacques Vendroux about what his next move should be, he returned to Paris on January 14. After a few days of reflection, he convened an emergency meeting of the cabinet on Sunday, January 20, at the Ministry of War and immediately informed the astonished members: "The exclusive regime of the parties has come back. I disapprove of it. But short of establishing by force a dictatorship, which I don't want and would probably turn out badly, I lack the means to prevent this experiment. I must therefore withdraw."[86] His resignation stunned everyone.

De Gaulle's major failing during the years of the German occupation and the liberation was his lack of interest in developing a political apparatus that could run the country after it was freed of enemy control. As the leader of the Free French movement, he brooked no opposition and was able to operate without interference from political parties and political figures with interests and concerns of their own that did not always coincide with those of the general. His high-handed treatment of the left-wing leaders of the Resistance left a legacy of resentment, despite his alliance with Stalin, his acceptance of Communist members in his government, and his approval of radical social and economic reforms during the brief period between the liberation and his resignation.

He may have been tempted to follow the Napoleonic precedent and seize power from the squabbling politicians. He told Jean-Raymond Tournoux in 1952: "I had the material means to establish a dictatorship. Of course, I could have called in Leclerc and expelled the Assembly. I must confess, without requesting absolution, that events forced me to exercise a dictatorship for nearly six years. But France was gagged at the time and was in mortal peril. Should I have maintained that dictatorship? My answer to my own question was No. Dictatorship always ends badly in France if it is maintained when circumstances have returned to normal."[87] He probably assumed that the rebirth of parliamentary democracy in France would soon result in such political instability that the French people would willingly recall him to power as a man above parties who had only the nation's well-being as his cause. But the time he was required to wait for such a circumstance was much longer than he had anticipated—more than twelve years.

~

CHAPTER SIX

De Gaulle in the Political Wilderness, 1946–1958

Failed Attempt at a Comeback before Success

The only house Charles de Gaulle ever owned was a country home amid a three-acre wooded estate 120 miles northeast of Paris in the little village of Colombey-les-Deux-Eglises that he and his wife, Yvonne, purchased in 1934.[1] Designated as "La Brasserie" after a brewer who had once occupied it, it was intended to afford the couple and their disabled daughter, Anne, a rural respite from the hectic life of the capital while he pondered his next move. After the damage had been inflicted on the house by the Germans was repaired, he and his family left the dilapidated old hunting lodge near Versailles that the government had provided to him and returned to the stone country house in May 1946. His financial situation was hardly comfortable for someone who had served the country so well. He lived on a brigadier general's pension, supplemented by modest payments by the state. His daughter Elizabeth had married an army officer, Captain Alain de Boissieu, who had served as an aide to the general. His son Philippe, a naval officer who had participated in the liberation, married Henriette de Montalembert and provided him with a grandson, named Charles de Gaulle. His mentally disabled daughter, Anne, to whom he was utterly devoted, died of pneumonia at age twenty in 1948 and was buried in the little churchyard in the village, where her father and mother would later join her. The de Gaulles lived a simple life at Colombey, focusing on family matters and receiving a dwindling number of old friends and colleagues with simple meals.

Meanwhile, the new Fourth Republic began its life with the type of political instability that had plagued its predecessor and would eventually contribute to its demise twelve years and twenty-four governments later. In April, the Assembly's drafting committee unveiled a new constitution that would have caused de Gaulle nightmares had he remained in power: it provided for a unicameral parliament empowered to designate and remove the prime minister and a president with only ceremonial powers like those of the British monarch. When the draft constitution was submitted to the people in a national referendum on May 5, it was soundly defeated by the electorate, in part because of the widespread fear that it would enable the French Communist Party, the largest in parliament at the time, to come to power legally. Elections for a new Constituent Assembly were held the following month. After refusing to become involved in the first referendum, de Gaulle decided to make known his views in a speech in Bayeux on June 16, the second anniversary of his appearance in that same Norman town after D-Day. In this widely followed address, he warned the French people of the fate of parliamentary democracies without a strong executive authority—he mentioned the previous three French republics, the Weimar Republic in Germany, and the Spanish Republic, all of which had succumbed to the rule of the strongman.[2]

But he rejected the appeal of a dictator—military or civilian—in favor of a strong president who would appoint the prime minister and the cabinet, conduct foreign relations, and command the armed forces while the parliament would concentrate on passing legislation. The speech did not persuade the voters to oppose the new constitution drafted by the Constituent Assembly, which was similar to the earlier one that was rejected except that it comprised a bicameral parliament. But the power of the executive was nil and the parliament supreme. De Gaulle campaigned strenuously against the new constitution. But with the strong support of the Communist Party, the referendum in October resulted in passage of the constitution—one-third of the voters voted no, one-third abstained, and slightly more than a third voted yes. In November, the first elections under the new constitution of what would henceforth be known as the Fourth Republic returned a parliament with the Communists boasting the most seats, followed by the Christian Democratic Mouvement Républicain Populaire (MRP).

The Failed Attempt at a Comeback

When de Gaulle's resignation was announced in January 1946, *The New York Times* hailed him as "a towering figure, physically and morally. That France is whole today is due to his single-minded, inflexible faith." The article noted it was likely that he would soon be recalled to power.[3] Within a few months, the *Times* was predicting that he would seek a comeback with a program of establishing in France "a new constitution drawn on the American model" (that is, with a strong executive authority).[4] After a year in self-imposed internal exile, de Gaulle traveled to Paris in February 1947 to reconnect with some of his old wartime associates—Jacques Soustelle, his former spokesman and director of intelligence; Michel Debré, the former Vichyite turned Gaullist (and later first prime minister of the Fifth Republic); the famous novelist and resistance fighter André Malraux (and later cultural minister in the Fifth Republic); Gilbert Renault (Colonel Rémy of the Resistance);[5] and many others.

He enlisted their support in a bid to launch a political movement to rescue the Republic from what he deemed its serious weaknesses. Soustelle and Renault took charge of organizing resistance veterans loyal to de Gaulle while Malraux orchestrated mass rallies to drum up support for the general. In public speeches, he castigated the politicians in power for betraying the ideals of the Resistance and weakening the country amid delirious cries of "De Gaulle au pouvoir (De Gaulle to Power)." Socialist Premier Paul Ramadier secretly visited Colombey to inform him that if he insisted on entering the political arena, he would lose the privileges bestowed upon him by a government grateful for his wartime services, such as a police bodyguard when he left his house and guaranteed airtime for his public speeches. As the premier prepared to leave, de Gaulle declared, "You may assure the worriers—I am not going to be a Boulanger." When the Socialist President Vincent Auriol heard this remark, he replied, "Let him take note that I'm not going to be a Hindenburg."[6]

In April 1947 came the announcement of the formation, not of a new political party, but rather of a Rally of the French People (Rassemblement du Peuple Français [RPF]), under the leadership of Jacques Soustelle. One of the cardinal features of the new movement was anti-Communism. The man who had flown to Moscow to sign a pact with Stalin and included Communists in his provisional government was now horrified that Communists occupied posts in the government of Socialist Paul Ramadier.

In late April 1947, the workers at the recently nationalized Renault automobile plant struck for higher pay after the imposition of a wage freeze decreed by the Socialist government. The Communist members of the Ramadier cabinet announced their support for the striking workers, prompting the Socialist prime minister to evict them from his government. As the Cold War set in, the French Communists endured a long exile from power until awarded cabinet positions thirty-four years later by another Socialist government under François Mitterrand in 1981. Relieved of their governmental responsibilities, the French Communists launched a wave of violent strikes for the rest of the year, partly on the orders of the Kremlin in reaction against the Marshall Plan. American Ambassador Jefferson Caffrey worried that the Ramadier government was so weak that it was incapable of addressing the country's serious social-economic-political crisis. He concluded that de Gaulle was the only alternative to a lunge for power by the French Communist Party, and he alone could overcome the "incoherent, impotent" paralysis of the anti-Communist forces in France. On October 2, the American ambassador, not yet prepared to approach de Gaulle himself, discreetly met with the general's close adviser Gaston Palewski about the possibility of a de Gaulle administration supported by the United States. He later met with the Gaullist Jacques Soustelle to discuss the same topic.[7]

It helped matters that de Gaulle had taken public positions that fit in perfectly with the foreign policies of the Truman administration that had been adumbrated in the Truman Doctrine. First was his vociferous campaign against the French Communists in the summer of 1947, denouncing them in a campaign speech in Rennes on July 15 as a "fifth column" intent on turning France over to the Soviet Union. The second was his endorsement of the Marshall Plan as critical to the national security of the country.[8]

Amid this mounting class conflict in France, de Gaulle's fledgling movement exploited the fears of the middle classes with a massive campaign to attract supporters. Hundreds of thousands of people wrote the RPF headquarters offering to join the movement. The boisterous mass rallies stage-managed by Malraux were replete with loud music, floodlights, and squads of tough-looking young men. The political fortunes of the RPF began with a blaze of glory. In the municipal elections of October 1947, Gaullist candidates won an astonishing 38 percent of the total votes cast. Gaullist mayors took office in 52 of the 92 principal cities and towns of the country, including Paris, where de Gaulle's brother Pierre—who resembled Charles so much that he was sometimes saluted by military officers on the street—was installed as president of the capital city's municipal council. De Gaulle promptly called for the dissolution of the National Assembly and national elections to reflect the new state of affairs in the country: "An immense power has risen in France and the regime of division and confusion has been condemned."[9]

But de Gaulle's brazen attempt to short-circuit constitutional procedures amid his victory in the municipal elections emboldened the three main political parties in the country—the Communists, the Socialists, and the Christian Democratic MRP—to overlook their differences and band together to block his bid for power. Throughout 1948, the general crisscrossed the country delivering provocative speeches against the regime, demanding the dissolution of parliament and the holding of nationwide elections. These Gaullist rallies took on a sinister quality as Malraux's stage-managed extravaganzas generated conflicts between Gaullist and anti-Gaullist militants. In September, a rally in Grenoble addressed by de Gaulle degenerated into a melee in which one Communist demonstrator was shot dead and fourteen people seriously injured. The police report noted that the Gaullist strong-arm squads commanded by Renault comprised some six thousand men in Paris and ten thousand in the provinces that followed the general on his speaking tours. Some were beginning to see in these shock formations a private army reminiscent of the Nazi movement before Hitler took power.[10]

But amid these Gaullist political shenanigans, the American embassy in Paris labored to keep open channels of communication with the general. In mid-March 1948, Ambassador Caffrey, who had earlier relied on intermediaries, requested a one-on-one meeting with de Gaulle. The general cordially replied that such a meeting would be possible but not immediately. When French foreign minister Robert Schuman complained about such an approach, the American embassy halted all efforts to develop direct contact with de Gaulle, though contact through intermediaries continued.[11] In any case, Caffrey had by the end of 1948 became convinced that the Socialist-MRP coalition had rendered de Gaulle irrelevant by its crackdown on the Communist agitation in the streets while American funds had begun to flow into France under the Marshall Plan.[12]

Early Attitudes toward the Atlantic Alliance

De Gaulle expressed support for the signing of the North Atlantic Treaty in April 1949 and continued to honor that endorsement until his return to power in 1958.[13] He had long complained that Article Five of the Washington Treaty lacked a guarantee of automaticity, leaving unanswered the question of whether the United States would immediately intervene on Western Europe's behalf in response to a Soviet attack. His attitude toward the Alliance evolved substantially after the transformation of NATO from a conventional security agreement into something very different in early 1951 during the Korean War. The headquarters of the alliance was established in the city of Rocquencourt near Versailles, and the various national military forces of the Alliance were integrated under the command of an American general, his old comrade-in-arms from World War II, Dwight D. Eisenhower. He found intolerable a situation in which a foreign state enjoyed effective command of France's military forces, a theme that would recur throughout his entire career. He opposed the Schuman Plan for the pooling of France's

coal and steel resources with West Germany, Italy, Belgium, the Netherlands, and Luxemburg as an intolerable loss of control over the country's
heavy industry.

He also condemned the Pleven Plan—proposed by his old wartime
collaborator—for a Western European army as an intolerable loss of national
sovereignty.[14] The American embassy was pleased by "the fact that de Gaulle
was emerging virtually as the self-contained French spokesman for certain
important American concepts."[15] Roosevelt would have been astonished at
this turn of events.

In June 1951, France held its first nationwide parliamentary elections
since the formation of the RPF. The results of the election heralded the
beginning of the movement's demise. The Gaullist vote declined by four
points to 21.5 percent, behind the Communists with 25.6 percent. The RPF
retained the most seats in the National Assembly, with 121 deputies. But 27
of them broke ranks to support the investiture of the non-Gaullist conservative Antoine Pinay as prime minister. When RPF leader Jacques Soustelle
tried to enforce party discipline, a quarter of the deputies bailed out to form a
new parliamentary group. In the municipal elections of April 1953, the party
was crushed, losing two-thirds of the city council seats. De Gaulle thereupon
abandoned his campaign to regain power. The RPF deputies voted as they
liked while he brooded in silence.[16]

Disillusioned with the French voters for their failure to see the light, the
sixty-two-year-old retiree reduced his contacts with his Parisian supporters
and concentrated on composing his war memoirs. Written in a difficult long-
hand that was deftly deciphered by his loyal daughter Elizabeth, who typed
them, the first volume appeared in 1954 and sold 100,000 copies in five
weeks. His literary productivity of the interwar period had been interrupted
by the burdensome obligations of running a government-in-exile, then a
government, and finally an abortive political movement. He was now free to
put down his thoughts about his experiences. His wartime memoirs, as noted
above, rank with Churchill's as literary masterpieces. Sales of the complete
work would reach two million.[17]

After he returned to his isolation at Colombey, the Fourth Republic faced
its greatest challenge because of its colonial policies. The French fortress of
Dien Bien Phu in French Indochina near the border with Laos was captured
by the Viet Minh rebel forces on May 7, 1954. This French military disaster,
the worst since the capitulation in June 1940, brought an end to the country's desperate attempt to cling to its Southeast Asian empire. The French
politician who was called to power amid this foreign-policy calamity was
Pierre Mendès-France, de Gaulle's old collaborator who had resigned from

his government in 1945. He took office on the iconic date of June 18 with the pledge to negotiate a military withdrawal within one hundred days or resign. He rushed to the Geneva conference (which had opened on April 26 and would last until July 20) with the thankless task of finding an honorable means of extricating his country from its old protectorate. De Gaulle remained uninvolved in the controversy, rejecting the idea that he might join the new government as a demonstration of national unity in this terrible time.[18] The agreement that was reached constituted the swan song of France's long and bitter struggle to maintain control of its last remaining possession in the region. The absence of a clear public statement on the matter suggested that he too recognized that the cause was lost.

Within a month of the conference, Mendès-France's government caused an acute crisis in France's relationship with the United States by refusing to ratify the agreement for the creation of the European Defense Community (EDC), a project for a supranational West European military force. Drafted in 1950 by the omnipresent Jean Monnet and proposed by French foreign minister René Pleven—both former collaborators of de Gaulle during the war—it was designed to fend off pressure from American secretary of state Dean Acheson after the outbreak of the Korean War to allow the rearmament of West Germany by incorporating West German troops into NATO's supranational military force. The foreign ministers of France, West Germany, Italy, and the Benelux counties signed the treaty on May 27, 1952. When the Eisenhower administration took office in January 1953, Secretary of State John Foster Dulles adopted the French proposal as his own. When the French government dragged its heels on submitting the treaty to parliament for ratification, Dulles issued a stinging rebuke to Paris by threatening an "agonizing reappraisal" of the United States' commitment to the defense of Western Europe if the EDC treaty were not ratified in Paris.[19]

Horrified at the loss of French sovereignty represented by the EDC, de Gaulle had vigorously opposed the plan from the moment it surfaced. In the previous year, he had publicly declared that if the United States considered placing national troops under foreign control, "why does she not merge [her own military forces] with Mexico and Canada and South American countries?"[20] When the EDC treaty went down to defeat in the French parliament on August 20, 1954, he must have breathed a sigh of relief. But the failure of the EDC deprived de Gaulle's RPF a portion of its remaining justification. In December 1954, de Gaulle announced that the party had ceased to exist, confirming its demise in a press conference on June 30, 1955, announcing his abandonment of politics.[21]

The Gathering Storm in Algeria

Within a few months of the Geneva Conference in the summer of 1954 that ended France's role in Indochina, a rebellion by the Muslim majority in Algeria plunged the country into its latest travail. De Gaulle had made few comments about the Algerian war in its early stages while he concentrated on writing his war memoirs, which he completed in 1957.

France had begun its conquest of Algeria, a territory more than three times larger than France itself, in 1830 and had achieved effective control of the country by the mid-nineteenth century. Unlike the other French overseas possessions, Algeria was legally a part of France, an overseas département (state), just as Hawaii would become in 1959 a part of the United States. Algeria was administered by the Ministry of Interior in Paris rather than by the Ministry of Foreign Affairs, which supervised the "protectorates" of Tunisia and Morocco. Unlike Indochina, French West Africa, French Equatorial Africa, and other French overseas possessions, Algeria had a large and vocal settler population from France and other European countries. More than 80 percent of them had been born there. In the 1950s, the entire country consisted of about ten million inhabitants, of whom some one million (10 percent) were of French or other European (mainly Spanish and Italian) origin. The 90 percent majority were Muslim, divided between Arabs and Berbers. The French and European minority controlled about 90 percent of the territory's wealth, owned most of the arable land in the countryside and most of the businesses in the cities, and enjoyed full political and civil rights, which were denied to the Muslim Arab and Berber inhabitants.[22]

The rebellion against French rule in Algeria that broke out in November 1954 had been launched by the National Liberation Front (FLN in its French acronym), a group of Arab and Berber Muslims seeking to achieve independence. The government in Paris had occasionally considered the possibility of "integration," that is, the granting of citizenship rights to the Muslim majority, but each time the Pied Noir[23] (French Algerian) lobby killed it. In the next four years, the Algerian War raged across the Mediterranean from France. Roughly 475,000 million French soldiers, airmen, and sailors—most of the army contingents were conscripts, unlike the professional soldiers who had fought in Indochina—were dispatched to the country in a vast counterinsurgency effort that resulted in horrific cases of brutality and torture on both sides.[24]

The French army stationed in Algeria came to be seen by the European settlers as the only force that protected them from an Algeria independent of France and controlled by the Muslim majority. As for the officer corps of the army, its leading members gradually became suspicious of the government in Paris that was vacillating between a policy of repression and the opening of negotiations with the rebels to seek a diplomatic settlement. In February 1956, the government of Socialist Prime Minister Guy Mollet— the nineteenth premier of the Fourth Republic since its formation a decade earlier—decided to dismiss the governor general, Jacques Soustelle, a dedicated Gaullist who had been named to the post by Pierre Mendès-France in 1954 as a moderate but had become a fanatical convert to the cause of Algérie Française. Mollet named General Georges Catroux to the newly elevated position of Minister Resident in the hopes of reaching a compromise settlement. As we have seen, Catroux had been a strong supporter and close collaborator of de Gaulle during the Second World War and had developed a reputation as a moderate progressive on colonial issues. The European settlers took to the streets of the Algerian capital in protest against his appointment, while the army stood aside. Catroux withdrew from the post before he had occupied it and was replaced by a hard-liner committed to supporting the military in its counterinsurgency campaign. The *pieds noirs* were energized by this successful campaign to impose their will on the government. As early as the spring of 1957, the Eisenhower administration in Washington had begun to establish contact with the Gaullists to discuss methods of dealing with the crisis. Within a year, the American embassy in Paris was concluding that only de Gaulle had the "ability and prestige" to settle the Algerian mess.[25]

In Colombey de Gaulle did not reveal his thoughts about the brewing conflict across the Mediterranean. Did he favor "Algérie Française"? Did he support full independence for the territory? As we have seen, de Gaulle had never been an enthusiastic supporter of French colonialism. Many of his classmates at Saint-Cyr, imbued with the romantic image of suppressing native rebellions in the sands of the Sahara or the jungles of Indochina, had sought postings in French possessions abroad. De Gaulle preferred to remain at home. His principal preoccupation from his earliest years was strengthening France's position in Europe and the necessity of protecting it against the military threat from the east—Germany in the 1930s and then Soviet Russia after 1945. While Britain had already begun to relinquish control of its vast overseas empire, de Gaulle increasingly saw colonialism as a diversion of money and manpower from where they were needed in Europe to provide French security. On the other hand, he was revered by most of the officers in the French army in Algeria, some of whom had fought in his Free French forces during the Second World War, such as Jacques Massu, who was in command of the French paratroopers in Algeria. They fully expected that he would lend his support to the campaign to suppress the Muslim rebellion and keep Algeria French.[26]

At Colombey de Gaulle continued to maintain a discreet, enigmatic silence, refusing to tip his hand. But by the early spring of 1958, amid the escalating conflict across the Mediterranean, several of de Gaulle's closest confidants began a subtle campaign in France to promote his return to power as the only viable solution to the war. Jacques Soustelle, Michel Debré, and other figures who would later play important roles in French politics actively worked for his return. In March de Gaulle received a distinguished visitor, the acclaimed writer Albert Camus, a progressive of *pied noir* origins who worried that the simmering situation might explode into a massive loss of life. Camus had joined the French Resistance during the German occupation, writing for and eventually editing the underground journal *Combat*. In 1947 he had been awarded the Nobel Prize for Literature, at forty-four the second-youngest recipient of that honor (after Rudyard Kipling at forty-two).[27] On hearing Camus's expression of anxiety about the possibility of mass violence in his home, de Gaulle discounted this possibility with the casual utterance, "I have never known Frenchmen to kill other Frenchmen."[28]

When the government of Premier Félix Gaillard lost its majority in parliament over (among other things) the Algerian issue on April 15, 1958, President René Coty took an entire month to designate a successor. That long interregnum allowed Gaullist agents to fan out to cultivate contacts in the parliament and the business world, while they reactivated the old RPF network. They sent agents to Algiers to drum up support for de Gaulle in the French army. In the meantime, the officer corps in Algiers, commanded by General Raoul Salan, in consort with leaders of the *pieds noirs*, had decided to cut loose from the bewildered and impotent government in Paris—there was not even a government in place at the time—and to form their own "Government of Public Safety" to defend the French Algerians and defeat the FLN. When both President Coty and de Gaulle got wind of the planned military coup, the former anxiously established contact with the latter amid the severe political crisis that could lead to civil war. When Coty, who as a deputy had voted full powers to Pétain in 1940, inquired on May 5 about the conditions de Gaulle would insist upon to form a government, de Gaulle replied that he would consider the invitation if it were offered to him but refused to reveal his intentions.[29]

A highly respected Alsatian named Pierre Pflimlin of the MRP won parliamentary approval on May 14 to head what would become the last government of the Fourth Republic as the best alternative to de Gaulle. He was regarded as a progressive on Algeria and was well liked by the American embassy.[30] In the meantime, rioting by the *pied noir* population had broken out in Algiers. As the army looked on, a mob invaded the headquarters of the governor general, ransacking its files and throwing the contents out of the window. The following day de Gaulle's agents in Algiers arranged for General Salan to address the crowd from the balcony of the governmênt building. After announcing the imposition of martial law, he cried, "Vive l'Algérie Française, Vive la France," and then, at the suggestion of the chief Gaullist agent in the city who was standing behind him, "Vive de Gaulle!" to roars of approval from the crowd. From Colombey a statement promptly announced that "once before, from the depths of the abyss, the country gave me its confidence to lead it back to salvation. Today, with new trials crowd-ing in upon it, it is right that it should know that I am ready to assume the powers of the Republic."[31]

The instigators of the coup in Algiers planned to name de Gaulle's old foreign minister Bidault, who had become an avid supporter of French Al-geria, head of the "Government of Public Safety" and sent agents to Paris to prepare the groundwork. On May 19, the sixty-seven-year-old de Gaulle journeyed to Paris and gave a news conference severely criticizing the vacil-lating policies of the government for contributing to the FLN violence and the military insubordination. The next day he responded to a fawning letter from Bidault with a sardonic expression of contempt for the current govern-ment's paralysis in the face of the challenge, "Voluntary prisoners like those captive birds who refuse to fly out when their cage is open."[32]

In the meantime, Jacques Soustelle, the longtime Gaullist fixer and for-mer governor general of Algeria, arrived to lusty cheers from both Algérie Française militants and Gaullists in Algiers. Eager to buy time for de Gaulle to take power in Paris, Soustelle persuaded General Salan to postpone plans for a military coup in metropolitan France in favor of one on the island of Corsica. A group of paratroopers landed on Napoleon's island on May 25 and linked up with sympathetic local troops to install a Committee of Public Safety with no resistance, a development that de Gaulle declined to publicly condemn.[33] In the meantime, an envoy from de Gaulle had assured American ambassador Amory Houghton, who had presented his credentials in April 1957 and was completely in the dark about these developments, that if de Gaulle gained power, he would keep France in the Atlantic alliance and pursue European cooperation.[34]

The day after the Corsican landing, de Gaulle proposed to Prime Minister Pflimlin that the two hold a top-secret meeting late that night at the Châ-teau de Saint Cloud outside Paris. Beginning at midnight, the conference lasted for two hours but ended in a stalemate. On May 27, news reached both de Gaulle and the government that the army was planning a coup in Paris. Early that afternoon de Gaulle mounted a preemptive strike against the military's plans to install a Committee of Public Safety in the French capital. He issued a public statement calling for constitutional means of reestablishing order and stability in the country, specifically warning the military forces in Algeria "to maintain exemplary behavior."[35]

De Gaulle's stern warning to the coup plotters had its intended effect. To stage a military putsch against the wishes of the most revered public figure in France was seen as too risky by Salan and his close collaborators. On May 28, Prime Minister Pflimlin, who had already concluded that de Gaulle alone could rescue the Republic from a rebellious army, handed his resignation to President Coty. In response to the invitation of the president, de Gaulle met with the heads of the two houses of parliament to discuss procedures for forming a new government. The next morning de Gaulle received a phone call from President Coty offering him the post of premier and reading him the message he would send to the National Assembly that afternoon. Citing the extreme danger of civil war, the text of the letter, which the legislators received in total silence, announced that the chief of state had "called on the most illustrious of Frenchmen, who during the darkest years of our history was our leader for the conquest of liberty and who, having achieved national unanimity around his person, spurned dictatorship, to reestablish the Republic."[36]

When de Gaulle arrived in Paris from Colombey in the early evening of May 29, he went straight to the Elysée Palace[37] to state his terms to an emotional Coty, who officially asked him to form a government. The general demanded and received full emergency powers for a six-month period enabling him to govern by decree while the parliament would be in recess until its next session scheduled for October 7. He announced his intention to draw up a constitution for a new republic that would separate the executive from the legislature and would be submitted to public approval by a referendum. The National Assembly of the Fourth Republic would never meet again. Air Force pilots displayed their delight at de Gaulle's return to power by repeatedly flying over his country home and dipping their wings in salute.[38]

~

CHAPTER SEVEN

Eisenhower and de Gaulle, 1958–1961

Two Wartime Buddies in Power

Charles de Gaulle mounted the rostrum of the National Assembly at the Palais Bourbon on the edge of the Place de la Concorde in Paris on June 1, 1958, to ask the parliamentarians to vote him in office and grant him full powers for six months. It was the first time he had sat in the august legislative body since leaving power twelve years earlier. He issued a brief statement of his goals and refused to engage in discussion before leaving the rostrum. After a desultory debate, the parliament voted for the investiture of his government 329 to 224, with 32 abstentions. The no vote was cast by all 47 of the Communists; 46 Socialists, including the future President François Mitterrand; and 18 of the Radicals, including former prime minister Pierre Mendès-France. The new government included three longtime supporters of de Gaulle: the suave Maurice Couve de Murville, a former director of external finances under Vichy who had defected to the Free French movement in 1943 and became a member of de Gaulle's Provisional Government in Algiers before serving as ambassador to several countries under the Fourth Republic, became foreign minister (a position he would occupy for a decade);[1] the future prime minister Michel Debré became minister of justice and chaired the committee charged with drafting the new constitution of what would become the Fifth Republic; André Malraux, the renowned adventurer and novelist who had served as de Gaulle's minister of information in the latter stages of World War II and then propaganda czar under the RPF, became minister of culture with ambitious plans to restore his country's reputation as the center of civilization.

For his ambassador to Washington, de Gaulle chose to retain Hervé Alphand in that post. Alphand had been an economics attaché to the French embassy in the United States at the outbreak of the Second World War. Refusing to serve the Vichy regime, he eventually resigned his post in a strongly worded letter to Vichy ambassador Henry-Haye on June 14, 1941, and soon joined the Free French movement.[2] He would remain a loyal exponent of de Gaulle's foreign policies to three U.S. administrations until his departure from Washington on December 19, 1965, to become secretary general of the French Foreign Ministry in Paris. He would be replaced by the veteran diplomat Charles Lucet, who would present his credentials to American president Lyndon Johnson on December 15, 1965.

The first item on the new premier's agenda was the volatile situation in Algeria. He promptly arrived in Algiers on June 4, which reminded some of the Algérie Française diehards of his arrival in liberated Paris on August 25, 1944. Just as he had imposed his will on the Resistance leaders fourteen years earlier, he snubbed the fiery members of the Committee of Public Safety by insisting on meeting with foreign representatives, Muslim and Catholic leaders, and other notables first. When he finally met with the leaders, he said nothing of consequence, saving his words for a direct address to the citizens of the city. Later in the afternoon, about two hundred thousand European settlers assembled in the square facing the Government General building to hail de Gaulle, who appeared on a balcony with arms outstretched and fists clenched. In response to their enthusiastic expressions of support, he uttered a brief sentence that elicited even more rapturous cheers but whose meaning has been debated by historians ever since: "Je vous ai compris" (I have understood you).[3]

In his short speech, he called for reconciliation and pledged that after the referendum for the new constitution to be held in a few months, he would tackle the crucial question of Algeria's future status. To the dismay of many in the crowd, he studiously avoided using the term "Algérie Française." But he satisfied the diehards in the city of Mostaganem a few days later with the single utterance "Vive l'Algérie Française," the first and only time he used those words in public.[4] In his visits to other Algerian cities, he cautioned the *pieds noirs* to be patient and to maintain discipline. But on returning to Paris, he promoted General Salan to the new position of "Delegate General" in Algiers and named General Jacques Massu prefect of Algiers.[5]

The new French chief executive immediately set out to resolve the contentious problem of Algeria. Though he had been a defender of France's colonial mission overseas and counted many former comrades-in-arms among the mutinous military officers in Algeria, de Gaulle would eventually come to recognize that the cause of Algérie Francaise was doomed. As we shall see, he would initiate secret negotiations with the rebel leadership in the National Liberation Front (FLN) and exploited his unassailable reputation as a French patriot to prepare French public opinion for the eventual granting of independence to Algeria in 1962. In the meantime, he would liquidate the remainder of the French African empire with such consummate skill that most of the newly independent states of the former French West Africa and French Equatorial Africa would retain close cultural, political, economic, and military ties to France.[6] He had concluded that France's status as a great power in the world would require that it focus its energies on Europe rather than Africa.

While Debré's committee of jurists labored on a draft constitution, de Gaulle visited several French possessions south of the Sahara that had been carved out of French West Africa and French Equatorial Africa. He offered the inhabitants of sub-Saharan Francophone Africa a stark choice in the forthcoming referendum: a "yes" vote would bring membership in a newly created "French Community," successor to the moribund "French Union" that had been formed in 1946 and a sort of Gallic counterpart to the British Commonwealth. A "no" vote would lead to total independence and the severing of all ties to the former colonial power. All of the thirteen French African countries voted for membership in the French Community except Guinea, whose fiery leader Sekou Touré led his country to independence with a "no" vote. De Gaulle responded to Guinea's defiant stance with what has been called "shock tactics," by ordering the immediate return to France of all civil servants, military personnel, teachers, and physicians together with all of their portable equipment.[7]

These vindictive measures, including the destruction of infrastructure such as the ripping out of French telephones from the government buildings, set a terrible precedent for decolonization that would be copied by the Belgians when they abruptly withdrew from their only colony in Africa, the Belgian Congo. Those Francophone African countries that voted to be part of the French Community would achieve full independence in 1960. In that year no less than ten Black African states were granted independence.[8] They would be rewarded with a lavish array of economic assistance, preferential trade arrangements, advantageous currency links, and other instances of what critics would label a form of "neo-imperialism," which, despite their achievement of political independence, would tie them closely to the former colonial power for many decades to come.[9]

The draft constitution produced by the Debré committee embodied the political principles de Gaulle had adumbrated in his speech in Bayeux on

June 16, 1946, after his abrupt resignation. The president would have the power to appoint and dismiss the prime minister, would preside over cabinet meetings, and would exercise total control of foreign and defense policy. If the government lost its parliamentary majority, it could not be overturned by a vote of no confidence, as had been the case in the revolving-door cabinets of the Fourth Republic. The president, who would be chosen by a grand council of electors comprising members of parliament, mayors, and city councilors, would serve for a seven-year term. He was empowered to circumvent the parliament by submitting major issues of public policy directly to the electorate through referenda. On September 28, 1958, the new constitution was overwhelmingly approved by almost 80 percent of the electorate on the mainland and an average of 95 percent in the overseas possessions. The constitution of the Fifth Republic would officially enter into force on October 5, 1958.[10]

In the following month's elections for the new National Assembly, the Gaullist Union pour la Nouvelle République (UNR) obtained slightly more than 200 of the 465 Assembly seats. In alliance with a few minor parties, it easily enjoyed the majority it required to run the country. On December 21, 1958, when the roughly eighty thousand ballots cast for the presidential election by the grand council of electors were tallied, the result was a decisive victory for de Gaulle with 78 percent of the vote.

The Reaction from the White House

After the ballots were counted, the new French chief executive promptly received a warm letter of congratulations from President Eisenhower for becoming the president of "the great country which we are proud to call our oldest ally."[11] When de Gaulle entered the Elysée Palace for the first time as the president of the Fifth Republic on January 8, 1959, the American chief executive pulled out all the stops in his congratulatory message. "France has a special place in the hearts of the American people," he gushed. "You yourself have come to symbolize for us not only French valor and resolution in the face of adversity but also a dynamic and youthful [!] France determined to go forward with renewed vigor and strength."[12] The new French president responded to Ike's kind words by dispatching a nostalgic recollection of their "very cordial relations" during the Second World War to his "très cher et grand ami" and voiced the expectation that "our shared idea of liberty will allow us to renew and strengthen our alliance."[13] In fact, de Gaulle had been attempting to secure American favor as he contemplated a return to power. He had told American ambassador Douglas Dillon that in his opinion, "it was a great blessing to the world that the U.S. existed today as it does" and offered his eternal "friendship."[14]

But amid the euphoria about a new constitution, a new republic, and a new president with extraordinary powers, the crisis in Algeria continued to fester. It would take him another three years to bring closure to this issue, which would become one of the most contentious periods in the country's history. But it was one of his most notable achievements. De Gaulle's first challenge in the Algerian situation was to confirm his total authority over the rebellious French officer corps in the army. Six months after he had designated General Salan as commander of the army in Algeria in order to quell mutinous sentiments in the ranks, the president recalled the commander to Paris to assume the ceremonial and powerless post of military governor of Paris. Officers in Algeria suspected of disloyalty to de Gaulle were transferred to posts on the mainland or in the French army in West Germany. But at the same time, he supported a vigorous prosecution of the war against the FLN waged by Salan's successor, Maurice Challe, an air force general who had supported de Gaulle's return to power probably on the assumption that he would be a staunch defender of French interests in Algeria.[15]

Having eliminated the disloyal officers and demonstrated his support for the army's tough counterinsurgency campaign across the Mediterranean, de Gaulle took up the second challenge in Algeria. That was the necessity to explore the possibility of a diplomatic settlement over an issue that he had already decided could not be solved by brute military force alone. Such a policy would inevitably mean opening up some kind of dialogue with the FLN. On June 14, 1960, he issued a televised appeal to that organization's leaders to dispatch representatives to Paris to discuss a cease-fire. On June 25, three FLN delegates showed up in the town of Melun near Paris. The three days of desultory talks led to a stalemate.[16]

But the die had been cast. The extreme devotees of Algérie Française lost all hope that the French president would rely exclusively on military operations to crush the Muslim rebellion. Automobile horns blared out the five-syllable signal "Al-gé-rie fran-çaise" in France's major cities, while militant supporters of the French settlers clashed with riot police. More ominously, de Gaulle's willingness to negotiate with officials of what the extremists deemed a terrorist organization dedicated to the expulsion of Europeans from Algeria resulted in a veritable explosion of violence in France orchestrated by the die-hard opponents of negotiation. Plastic bombs went off in cars and cafés on a regular basis. The president himself would become the target of nine assassination attempts organized by the fanatics of Algérie Française and the terrorist group they had formed, the Secret Army Organization (OAS in its

French acronym), which was dramatized in the popular book and film *Day of the Jackal*. In one incident, an explosive placed on a road leading from Paris to Colombey went off only seconds after his car passed. In another ambush in a Paris suburb, machine gun bullets barely missed de Gaulle and his wife in the back seat of their automobile.[17]

This unrest did not deflect de Gaulle from his overriding objective to find a peaceful solution to the Algerian problem so that he could focus his attention on a host of other matters that he deemed crucial to the security and prosperity of his country. In the summer of 1960, he took the first step in disengagement from the troubled land by announcing the withdrawal of the first French military contingent of the half million conscripts stationed in Algeria. The following November, he declared that a referendum would be held in both metropolitan France and Algeria to determine whether the Algerian people should be accorded "self-determination." The result was a landslide: 76 percent in France itself and 70 percent in Algeria (despite frantic efforts by the French settlers) for "yes." So by the end of 1960, as the Kennedy administration prepared to take office in Washington, de Gaulle had secured the strong popular backing he required to open serious negotiations with the FLN leading to independence. He had come to recognize the enormous costs, economically, politically, and morally, of the conflict across the Mediterranean. "The Algerian war is a thorn in the foot of France which infects the entire body," he complained to a confidant. "This ridiculous conflict prevents France from taking its place in the world, and first in Europe. We must focus France on the true problems, and not waste substance, energy, and money abroad."[18]

In the waning months of the Fourth Republic, officials in the American embassy in Paris, despairing of the country's political instability and beginning to look forward to the return of de Gaulle to restore order, had established links to de Gaulle's entourage. Officials in the U.S. Defense Department even discussed the necessity of relocating American military bases and installations from France in light of the acute instability in the country and transferring them to West Germany, which is "more stable politically" and "more suitable than France as a military anchor" of the alliance.[19] As for Eisenhower, he had developed an ambivalent attitude toward his French counterpart. On the one hand, he recalled with great fondness his close cooperation with de Gaulle during World War II. He had made a point of stopping off at de Gaulle's headquarters in Paris in September 1944 to informally accord him the type of "de facto recognition" that Roosevelt was not yet prepared to grant. On the other hand, as Supreme Allied Commander Europe (SACEUR), he had complained to President Truman in March 1952 that, were de Gaulle to return to power, "he has so blatantly attacked NATO and American policy and positions" that "I don't know what would be the results of such a development."[20] During the debate in France about the European Defense Community in the spring of 1954, Ike had expressed grave concern about the instability of the Fourth Republic to General Alfred Gruenther, his successor as SACEUR, and wondered if "the only hope is to produce a new and inspirational leader—and I do not mean one that is 6 feet 5 [sic] and considers himself to be . . . the offspring of Clemenceau and Jeanne d'Arc."[21]

But as it became clear that de Gaulle was about to return to power, the American president had overcome his ambivalence about his wartime colleague. One of the last times that de Gaulle (as a private citizen) and Eisenhower had met was April 1952, when Ike was the Supreme Allied Commander for NATO and was preparing to run for president. The two had been invited to a dinner of members of the Order of Liberation, which de Gaulle had established to honor those who had made major contributions to the liberation of France. After dinner the two men retired to a porch overlooking the garden, with General Vernon "Dick" Walters serving as interpreter. According to Walters, de Gaulle told Eisenhower that "we both will be called upon to lead our nations. You will be called before me, but I will be inevitably called upon to lead France, as there is no alternative to me." He trotted out his concerns about NATO as too unwieldy with too many members and foreshadowed a proposal he would make much later that a tripartite group of the United States, Great Britain, and France should manage the alliance. When Eisenhower drove off with Walters, he began to reminisce: "Roosevelt didn't like him, a lot of people didn't like him," he recalled. "But I can't help but feel that he is truly and sincerely devoted to his country and to restoring its self respect, . . . and you can't really fault him for that."[22]

At a meeting of the National Security Council on May 23, 1958, CIA director Allen Dulles had predicted de Gaulle's imminent accession to power and insisted that "we have nothing to worry about with respect to de Gaulle's attitude toward the United States, toward NATO, or on the subject of U.S. bases in France." His brother, Secretary of State John Foster Dulles, indicated that Ambassador Hervé Alphand, who had just returned from France, confirmed that de Gaulle was not anti-American and that he would "certainly not quit NATO."[23]

But immediately after de Gaulle assumed power at the beginning of June 1958, Allen Dulles reported to the National Security Council that his agents in Algeria were convinced that "the French Army authorities in Algiers were ready to send paratroops to Paris" if de Gaulle's investiture had been blocked.[24] In reply to Eisenhower's warm message of congratulations, de Gaulle replied in an emotional letter recalling "the memory of the great hours when France and the United States joined their efforts in the coalition of liberty and when you gloriously assumed the command of the Allied armies."[25] Former president Truman weighed in on June 2 with the declaration that "De Gaulle is the man to save France."[26]

The most widely read American newsweekly, *Life Magazine*, issued a cover story followed by a seven-page lead article, replete with photographs about de Gaulle's accession. It included quotations from the new French leader that calmed the nerves of Americans as well as French people, such as "Is it credible that at the age of 67 I am going to begin a career as a dictator?"[27] In fact, for about a year after his accession, de Gaulle enjoyed widespread support in the United States for what appeared to be his skillful handling of the Algerian situation.[28]

While attempting to divest France of what he had come to regard as the albatross of Algeria, de Gaulle set to work on what was to be his top priority for the rest of his term in office, namely, to emancipate France from the domination of its two "Anglo-Saxon" allies, particularly the one more than three thousand miles across the Atlantic. In fact, he made his first move in this direction shortly after coming to power. By the time he became prime minister and then the first president of the Fifth Republic, France had been a close ally of the United States and Great Britain in the North Atlantic Treaty Organization. These were also the three non-Communist powers with residual occupation rights in Germany and in Berlin. They were also the only three Western powers that enjoyed privileged status in the United Nations as veto-wielding permanent members of its Security Council.

But in fact France was the "odd man out" in this Western Alliance. The United States and Great Britain were the only members of NATO to possess nuclear weapons and the means of delivering them. Although the headquarters of the North Atlantic Alliance were located near the French capital, the Supreme Commander of the integrated command (SACEUR) was, and always would be, an American general. A British general served as his second-in-command in the Supreme Headquarters, Allied Powers Europe (SHAPE) that had been set up in 1951 with Eisenhower, who had resigned as president of Columbia University to become the first SACEUR. Lower down the chain of command, a French officer was relegated to the command of the European Central Front, including all Allied forces stationed in West Germany. All decisions about the use of nuclear weapons rested firmly in the hands of the occupant of the White House.

When de Gaulle came to power, his two counterparts in Washington and London were familiar faces. As we have seen, all three men had been in

Algiers together for seven months in 1943, Harold Macmillan as Resident British Minister, Eisenhower as Supreme Commander in the Mediterranean (SACMED), and de Gaulle, who was campaigning to win Washington's support for his Free French movement. Both Eisenhower and Macmillan had used their influence with their two imperious superiors to advocate for de Gaulle's position, and he knew and appreciated it. Both had warmly welcomed his return to power in 1958 in the hopes that he would clean up the mess in France caused by the political instability of the Fourth Republic. The Algerian War was draining French manpower from the Central Front of the Cold War in Europe. The bewildering succession of French governments was complicating NATO strategy. De Gaulle seemed to offer the kind of decisiveness that would restore order to a disorderly political situation.[29] In short, the relations between France and its two main allies should have gone smoothly, with these three former wartime associates at the head of their respective countries.

But such would not be the case. Shortly after assuming power in the late spring of 1958, de Gaulle launched the first in a long series of initiatives designed to achieve his most cherished goal: French independence from the United States and Great Britain in the realm of foreign and security policy. His perspective on international developments between his resignation in 1946 and his return in 1958 is succinctly summarized in the postwar memoirs that he managed to complete before his death: "Once the declaration of principle known as the Atlantic Alliance had been adopted in Washington, the North Atlantic Treaty Organization had been set up, under terms of which our defense and hence our foreign policy disappeared in a system directed from abroad, while an American generalissimo with headquarters [in the town of Rocquencourt] near Versailles exercised over the old world the military authority of the new."[30]

De Gaulle's first moves in opposition to Washington's control of the policies of the West Europeans came in the months after his accession as the last prime minister of the Fourth Republic. A few days after he took power, the American ambassador to France, Amory Houghton, who had taken up his post on April 17, 1957, warned Dulles that when he met with the new French leader, nuclear weapons would dominate the discussion and de Gaulle would insist on "France being a member of the club."[31] At a meeting among Macmillan, Eisenhower, and their foreign ministers on June 9, they explored strategies for dealing with the new French leader. Dulles speculated, with uncanny accuracy, that he would press for some type of tripartite relationship among the U.S., Britain, and France and proposed that "we will have to find some way of keeping him out of things that we don't want him in, such as Middle Eastern problems." Both Macmillan and Dulles predicted strong opposition from Italy and West Germany to "any sort of political standing group in NATO on a tripartite basis." The secretary of state also warned his boss that strong congressional opposition would probably prevent the extension of nuclear assistance to France in the same manner as the British.[32]

Eisenhower suggested that Dulles confer with de Gaulle about all the issues that separate Washington and Paris, and the French prime minister agreed to receive him. In preparation for this important trip, the State Department prepared a series of "Points for Conversation with General de Gaulle." Among the points emphasized were the following: (1) the total rejection of the "Communist-inspired rumor" in France that the U.S. "is seeking to displace France from North Africa in order to exploit its natural resources, notably oil"; (2) that while Washington has "no objection in principle" to France's acquiring nuclear weapons, in light of the "enormous cost" of such weapons, if each Allied nation seeks independently to develop them "there would be no real strength anywhere and bankruptcy everywhere." The only practical solution would be to "avoid duplicating this cost."[33]

John Foster Dulles had a long familiarity with France in his career before his service as secretary of state. He had studied at the University of Paris before World War I, where he attended lectures at the nearby Collège de France in 1908–1909 by the illustrious philosopher Henri Bergson (who was also to inspire the young Charles de Gaulle).[34] At the age of thirty, he had been chosen by President Woodrow Wilson to accompany his uncle, Secretary of State Robert Lansing, in the U.S. delegation at the Paris Peace Conference in 1919. Dulles served as legal adviser to the Reparations Commission at the conference that determined defeated Germany's obligation to pay France and other Allied countries for the substantial damage done by its soldiers on the Western Front during the war. Dulles and his colleague Norman Davis were responsible for the inclusion in the peace treaty of Article 231, which became the notorious "war guilt clause" of the treaty. The term "guilt" appeared nowhere in the treaty but was exploited by Hitler in the 1930s to demonize the entire peace settlement. Dulles later lamented the misreading of the clause that had contributed to the outbreak of the Second World War.[35]

On arriving at Orly airport in Paris on the morning of July 4, the American secretary of state issued the obligatory expression of gratitude for France for its support during the U.S. war for independence that his own country was celebrating on that very day. In his first meeting with the general the next day, which turned out to be a two-and-a-half-hour conversation, Foster Dulles executed a charm offensive. His task had been facilitated by a very warm letter from Eisenhower to de Gaulle, which Dulles had solicited, expressing the earnest hope that "the man who symbolizes the liberation of France and who guides its present difficulties" would pay a visit to the United States in the near future.[36]

The American secretary of state conceded to his host that in recent years France had "not enjoyed the consideration it is due in American opinion" and hoped that "under your direction it will recover its position" as "the most beloved country of all our allies." Focusing on the issue of nuclear weapons (as the American ambassador had predicted he would), de Gaulle informed Dulles that France definitely intended to join the nuclear club and would gratefully accept any assistance the United States could provide in that effort. But he added that, with or without help from Washington, France would never allow the American president or the American Supreme Allied Commander to decide whether France's nuclear weapons would be used. The French leader also emphasized "the importance of France feeling that she was a world power. Unless the French people felt that, France would quickly degenerate."[37] Dulles listened without comment. But when news reports suggested that the American secretary of state had tried to dissuade de Gaulle from pursuing an independent nuclear program for France, he quickly consulted with Eisenhower and promptly issued a firm denial, remarking that the question of nuclear armaments "is for each country to decide for itself."[38]

In his conversations with de Gaulle, Dulles also took the occasion to inquire about the new French premier's future plans for Algeria and the rest of the French empire in Africa. As for the French holdings in sub-Sahara Africa, Dulles suggested that they be treated on the model of the U.S. commonwealth of Puerto Rico, which would give the inhabitants of French West Africa and French Equatorial Africa self-government without independence. With regard to the challenging case of Algeria, Dulles suggested a gradual process of independence for ten years. He noted that the United States "had spent 50 years preparing the Philippines for independence."[39] Irwin Wall has written a lucid summary of the Eisenhower administration's difficulty in devising a rational policy toward the Algerian War. During the Fourth Republic, Dulles continually tried to walk a tightrope between standing behind America's Gallic ally, the lynchpin of NATO defense in Europe, and honoring his country's anti-colonial heritage as well as its desire to court public opinion in what was increasingly referred to as the "Third World."[40]

The Tripartite Proposal

During the months of July and August 1958, two crises far from Europe would have an important influence on de Gaulle's thinking about France's security relationship with the United States and the United Kingdom. The first was the response of Washington and London to a coup that overthrew the pro-Western monarchy in Iraq on July 14. The dispatch of U.S. marines to protect the pro-Western president of Lebanon and the arrival of British military forces to bolster the pro-Western Hashemite monarchy in Jordan were both undertaken to prevent the spread of the Pan Arab ideology of Egyptian strongman Gamal Abdel Nasser to those two pro-Western countries. The French president did not hide his distaste for this "Anglo-Saxon" coordination of a military intervention. De Gaulle was particularly angry that the intervention in Lebanon, a former French mandate under the League of Nations with historic ties to France, was executed without consultation with his country.[41] In his meeting with Dulles less than two weeks before the intervention, de Gaulle had insisted that France be consulted before the taking of military action in Lebanon under the cover of the Eisenhower Doctrine.[42] The secretary of state refused to make such a pledge, noting that France would represent a liability in the Arab world because of its involvement in Algeria and its close ties to Israel.[43]

The second overseas crisis to catch de Gaulle's notice was Washington's response to Communist China's shelling of the small offshore islands of Quemoy (Kinmen) and Matsu in the Taiwan Straits that had been garrisoned by Nationalist Chinese soldiers after the end of the Chinese Civil War in 1949 and the Nationalist government's escape to the island of Taiwan. De Gaulle was concerned that by sending the Seventh Fleet to bolster the Chinese Nationalists without consulting with its NATO allies, the United States ran the risk of dragging France and other European states into a possible conflict with mainland China over issues of no vital interest to them.[44] Ambassador Hervé Alphand remarked that his foreign minister Couve de Murville "thought that all the agitation around these islands is absurd. He would freely abandon Quemoy and Matsu and would recognize the government in Peking." Alphand was certain that Couve's opinion "exactly reflected the opinion of General de Gaulle."[45]

The direct outcome of the crises in Lebanon and the Taiwan Straits in the late summer of 1958 was the controversial memorandum that was drafted by de Gaulle on September 17 and presented to Dulles by Ambassador Alphand on September 25, while a copy was dispatched to Macmillan in London.[46] Recalling the "recent events in the Middle East and the Formosa [Taiwan] Straits," it asserted that since the threats to the countries of NATO were no longer confined to the Atlantic region, the alliance should be broadened to include the entire world. The three Western countries with global responsibilities—the United States, Great Britain, and France—should form what would in effect function as a tripartite inner directorate that would have sole decision-making power in the alliance, including the use of nuclear weapons anywhere in the world.[47] The idea of such a three-power director-ate had first surfaced before de Gaulle came to power but was never taken very seriously by Washington or London.[48] Three days after de Gaulle let the Belgian NATO Secretary General Paul-Henri Spaak see his memorandum on September 24, Spaak told Dulles that the plan might well result in "the end of NATO."[49]

What a presumptuous claim for French global power this was! The French Empire had dwindled to include only Algeria in the midst of a full-scale re-bellion, the countries of French West Africa and French Equatorial Africa that would soon to be granted independence in 1960, and a handful of small possessions in the Caribbean, the South Pacific, and the Indian Ocean. It was not yet a nuclear power. It may be that de Gaulle never expected the au-dacious proposal to be accepted and that it was merely a ploy to develop the justification for loosening France's ties to the mutual defense organization.

Dulles's immediate reaction (in private) was to denounce the tripartite proposal as "wholly unacceptable to the United States."[50] While publicly assuring de Gaulle that the proposal would be carefully considered in Wash-ington, he privately called for delaying tactics.[51] Accordingly, the secretary of state suggested that the president respond favorably to de Gaulle's request that tripartite discussions be undertaken. In mid-October Eisenhower au-thorized the opening of such talks, but only at below the level of foreign ministers and only after instructing his secretary of state to assure the West Germans and Italians (who were certain to be upset about the proposal) that they would only be preliminary discussions.[52] Macmillan informed the French that while he was opposed to shutting out the other twelve members of the alliance, Britain was willing to join exploratory talks about de Gaulle's proposal. When they learned about it, the West Germans and the Italians vigorously protested against the very concept of an exclusive inner director-ate of NATO in which they were not permitted to participate.[53]

In the midst of the brouhaha over the tripartite proposal, the longtime editor of Le Monde, Hubert Beuve-Méry, established contact with de Gaulle in the hopes of securing an interview. He had joined the Resistance during the German occupation of France, after a brief flirtation with the Vichy regime. As the war drew to an end, he founded Le Monde as a successor to the old newspaper Le Temps, with de Gaulle's blessing. Having lost contact with de Gaulle after the war, he secured an interview with the French leader on September 18. In this wide-ranging discussion, the two men covered the gamut of burning issues that confronted the country. On one matter the editor extracted a concession: he noted that de Gaulle had maintained friendly contact with the monarchist pretender, the Comte de Paris. The French leader replied: "Naturally you believe that I am a monarchist. I have great respect for the monarchy. It constructed France." But he promptly added: "But it did not know how to adapt when it was necessary to do so. Today, all that it is ended."[54]

Eisenhower's official reply on October 20 to de Gaulle's tripartite memorandum raised the concern about antagonizing all of the other members of the alliance by reserving the decision-making process for these three powers. It in effect represented a clear-cut refusal despite the stated willingness to engage in discussions. He also frankly informed de Gaulle of his opposition to "any effort to amend the North Atlantic Treaty so as to extend its coverage beyond the areas presently covered." U.S. officials made the point that the North Atlantic alliance was established as a *regional* security system under article 51 of the United Nations Charter.[55] French diplomats, taking their cue from de Gaulle himself,[56] regularly implied that Eisenhower had never responded to de Gaulle's tripartite memorandum. Much later ambassador to France Charles Bohlen urged that Eisenhower's response be published to discredit that myth.[57]

The first tripartite meetings were held in Washington on December 4 and December 10 in which the French and British ambassadors and Under-Secretary of State Robert Murphy—de Gaulle's old nemesis from the wartime days in North Africa—achieved nothing.[58] After several meetings at the ambassadorial and foreign minister level and follow-up letters among the three leaders, the matter was put on hold. Eisenhower complained to an interviewer after he left office about de Gaulle's "obsession about the Anglo-Saxons. He had this fixed misconception and he would not forget it." And yet the tripartite directorate scheme included the two Anglo-Saxon powers! Eisenhower exclaimed that "you can't have just two or three pals acting as a self-contained unit in the diplomatic and strategic world, and that's all there is to it."[59]

On December 15, the American president met with de Gaulle in Paris the day before attending a two-day NATO Ministerial Meeting in the French capital. They agreed to oppose Soviet pressure on West Berlin. But de Gaulle took the occasion to complain about a U.S. abstention in the United Nations General Assembly on a resolution asserting Algeria's right to independence. Ambassador Alphand claimed that he had been assured by Eisenhower, the secretary of state, and the U.S. representative to the UN that such an abstention would not take place.[60] In fact, the FLN had sent a delegation to New York, which was received by the State Department and was able to plead its cause in the corridors of the United Nations.[61] After the NATO meeting on December 16 and 17, Dulles reported that British foreign secretary Selwyn Lloyd got the impression during a meeting with de Gaulle that he felt that "NATO might as well be scrapped and a fresh start be made under triumvirate auspices."[62] After several tripartite talks, Murphy assured the Joint Chiefs of Staff that the United States had refused to engage in military discussions "on any other than an ad hoc basis."[63]

Meanwhile, the broader issue of the Atlantic Alliance's organizational structure continued to hover over the relations among the United States, Great Britain, and France. After a one-on-one meeting with the French president in the early spring of 1959, Macmillan reported to Eisenhower that he had spoken "very firmly" about the need to preserve the existing structure of NATO, to no avail. "I fear that he does not really understand the modern concepts of integration and interdependence," the British prime minister complained. "He is fundamentally an Eighteenth Century figure, and therefore the problem of dealing with him is largely a psychological one, as you and I know well."[64] Eisenhower immediately replied with the quip "The only disagreement that I would have with your description [of de Gaulle] as Eighteenth Century is that I place the period of in the Early Nineteenth Century" (an obvious allusion to Napoleon I).[65]

In a press conference on March 25, 1959, de Gaulle mentioned publicly for the first time his total opposition to the integration of NATO's military forces. In reporting this development, *The New York Times'* Paris correspondent reminded his readers that de Gaulle in the early fifties had opposed French membership in two "supranational" entities, the European Defense Community and the European Coal and Steel Community, for precisely the same reason: the threat to French national sovereignty.[66] During a meeting at the presidential retreat of Camp David with Eisenhower, Under Secretary of State Christian Herter (who had replaced the ailing Dulles), and others, Macmillan warned that "de Gaulle is quite capable of asking [Supreme Allied Commander Lauris] Norstad to vacate SHAPE [the headquarters of NATO outside of Paris]."[67]

Eisenhower agreed with Macmillan about de Gaulle's "harmful" actions. It reminded him of the conflict he had with de Gaulle during World War II over the Free French occupation of Strasbourg. When de Gaulle had threatened to remove the French troops from Eisenhower's command, Ike had brought the French general into line by suspending all ammunition deliveries to him. "Unless we are prepared to deal with him in this way," Eisenhower remarked, "there is no point in trying to be tough with him."[68] Here the matter stood for the next six months, with Eisenhower, Macmillan, and de

Gaulle remaining wary of each other but not taking drastic steps to address the issue at hand.

During his trip to Europe in the early fall of 1959, the American president met with de Gaulle in the Elysée Palace on September 2 for a lengthy discussion of the alliance. De Gaulle repeated his assertion that the integration of NATO forces was entirely obsolete because of technological innovations in nuclear strategy. The United States should no longer bear full responsibility for the defense of Europe. France needed to be able to participate in the decision-making process of the Alliance to preclude its total destruction "without even having had the opportunity of expressing its views and without having any role." In short, *integration* must be replaced by *coordination* of forces and consultation among the Big Three powers that had global responsibilities. Eisenhower heatedly responded that a war in Europe could not be won if it were fought with "a series of national forces" operating on their own. "Under this concept," he asked, in what may have been seen as a veiled threat, "where would United States forces fit into the picture? Would they not have to go home?"[69] The French president periodically revived the stalled proposal for the tripartite management of NATO and its expansion beyond the North Atlantic area during the rest of Eisenhower's second term. Macmillan indicated that he was "anxious to persuade Eisenhower" to more actively engage the topic.[70]

After receiving another letter from de Gaulle trying to revive the tripartite scheme, so that the three countries could and should abandon their focus on Europe in favor of a global strategy on August 9, 1960, the American president dictated a memorandum for the file in which he complained that neither he nor his secretary of state "understands exactly what de Gaulle is getting at." Every time the French president raised the topic of this "tripartite world strategy," he has always been "so hazy in propounding his theories. . . . He speaks of 'our West,' but he names only our three countries." In short, he seems to be proposing that we "set up our three nations as the controlling groupment [sic] of NATO."[71]

In an unsigned, undated memorandum for the files (probably in early 1960), Eisenhower conceded that "France is right when she speaks of the necessity of a global strategy." Noting that NATO was "subject to a flank attack through the Middle East and Africa," he asserted that the Alliance should not "get bogged down in the concept of the 'Maginot Line.'" He proceeded to speculate about "a redistribution of commands on a worldwide basis" and considered the possibility of setting up a series of special restricted committees within NATO for Africa, the Middle East, the Far East, and South Asia, which would then report to the other members of the alliance.[72]

The Berlin Crisis (1958–1961):
A Different Type of Tripartism

Since the end of World War II, the United States, the Soviet Union, Great Britain, and France enjoyed quadripartite occupation and access rights in the city of Berlin, which lay 110 miles within the Soviet zone and then the Communist German Democratic Republic (East Germany). After Stalin had tried and failed to oust the three Western powers of the city in 1948–49 with the Berlin blockade, the status of the divided city remained a simmering sore point for East-West relations.

Under intense pressure from East German Communist boss Walter Ulbricht, Soviet leader Nikita Khrushchev dispatched on November 27, 1958, a note to the three Western powers with residual rights in the divided city proposing that control of a newly established "free city" and access to it be transferred to the East German government, in effect abolishing the right of the United States, Great Britain, and France to maintain access to their military forces in the divided city. At a high-level conference in the French prime minister's office, the Hôtel Matignon, in mid-December 1958, de Gaulle pressed hard for an uncompromising position on Berlin, while Dulles proved more reticent. The French president announced to the press that "if Russia issues a threat of war, we must face the threat, even if that means war."[73]

The ensuing Berlin crisis would give a shot in the arm to de Gaulle's languishing plan for Anglo-French-American coordination and cooperation. The French president's position on the unfolding Berlin crisis was somewhat paradoxical. Even as he took potshots at NATO on a variety of issues, he acquired the reputation as the most hard-line, uncompromising defender of Allied rights in the divided German city. In effect, the Berlin crisis enabled him to pose as the Federal Republic's most ardent defender on this issue that meant so much to the West German people, while both Eisenhower and especially Macmillan seemed willing to explore a diplomatic settlement of the issue with Khrushchev. In the spring of 1959, de Gaulle sent several pointed warnings to Eisenhower about the absolute necessity for the three Western powers to stand shoulder to shoulder in opposition to any changes in the future status of Berlin: "We must be firm and determined to maintain our rights" in the German city and ensure "a total unity of views in the interest of the defense of the free world."[74]

As the Berlin crisis heated up throughout 1959, de Gaulle continued to stake out the hardest line. Macmillan's trip to Moscow in late February of that year had signaled that London might be backing down from a unified Western response. Macmillan deeply resented de Gaulle's implication that

London would not take a firm stand. Before meeting with de Gaulle on March 10, he complained to his diary that "the French really agree with us entirely over the German problem. But they are trying to pretend that we are weak and defeatist, and that they are for 'being tough.'" At their meeting the British prime minister got the French president to admit that "one cd not have a nuclear war in Europe on the question of who signed the pass to go along the autobahn or the railway to W. Berlin—a USSR sergeant or a DDR sergeant."[75]

During his last trip to Europe before the cancer that afflicted him took its toll, Dulles and his French counterpart Couve de Murville had worked out a contingency plan—approved by de Gaulle—in case access to Berlin was closed down: the establishment of a joint American, British, and French general staff dubbed "Live Oak" to coordinate joint military operations in Berlin if necessary.[76] Such a tripartite general staff might have reminded observers of the stillborn memorandum of September 1958, except that it lasted until the end of the Cold War.

The Berlin crisis continued to fester for the remainder of 1959, with Paris and Washington in general agreement to hold firm. But this Franco-American cooperation on the status of Berlin would be severely threatened (in de Gaulle's eyes) by Eisenhower's invitation to Khrushchev to become the first Russian leader in history to visit the United States.[77] After arriving in Washington on September 15, he traveled to New York City before embarking on a cross-country tour that brought him to Los Angeles and Hollywood, where he chatted with several film stars. On returning to Washington, he spent two days meeting with the American president at the presidential retreat in the Catoctin Mountains of Maryland, which had been named Shangri-La by Franklin Roosevelt but which Eisenhower renamed Camp David in honor of his father and grandson, both named David. Eisenhower promptly briefed de Gaulle about the content of the two meetings with Mr. K.[78] In late October, the French president let Eisenhower know about his apprehension about such a meeting on the grounds that it would signal "a retreat on the part of the West." But in the end he backed down and obtained the American president's support for a meeting with the Soviet leader "at the end of May or June" 1960 in Paris, which would give the three Western powers time to prepare a common strategy.[79]

Although gratified that the planned summit would be held in Paris, signifying the French capital's apparent restoration as the hub of European international diplomacy, de Gaulle worried that Eisenhower and Macmillan would cave in to Khrushchev's intimidation and so alienate West German chancellor Konrad Adenauer that the Federal Republic might be tempted to lapse into neutrality in the hope of gaining reunification with Moscow's support. But by the time de Gaulle accepted Eisenhower's standing invitation to visit the United States in order to coordinate their strategy for the Paris summit meeting tentatively scheduled for mid-May, the French president was fully on board with Western plans to reach a settlement of the Berlin issue.

When Charles de Gaulle arrived at Washington's National Airport on April 22, 1960, it was the first time he had set foot on American soil since his trip to meet with President Truman fifteen years earlier. He was accorded a lavish welcome everywhere he went. He laid wreaths at the tomb of the unknown soldier at Arlington National Cemetery and at the statue of Lafayette in Lafayette Square near the White House and spoke at the National Press Club. He took a brief trip to Eisenhower's farm in Gettysburg, Pennsylvania, which he later described to his son, Philippe. While there Ike gave his guest a brief historical lesson about the iconic battle that was fought there and about the American Civil War in general. The American president then took the French president aside and complained about Franklin Roosevelt's "permanent unwillingness to understand" de Gaulle's point of view during the Second World War.[80]

De Gaulle returned to Washington to speak at a joint session of Congress, with an English translation distributed to the representatives and senators before the address. On April 26, he traveled to New York for a parade and a reception for the city's French community. The next day he flew to San Francisco where he toured San Francisco Bay and held another reception with the French community in that area. Two days later he visited the Hewlett-Packard Electronic Company near Stanford University in what would later become known as Silicon Valley. He concluded his visit with a trip to New Orleans, where he gave another reception with the French community there before leaving for a brief visit to French Guiana, his country's only remaining possession in South America.[81]

During his talks with the president, no progress had been made on the nuclear issue when Eisenhower suspended the conversations as he knew he would only be in office for another six months. De Gaulle took the occasion to reiterate his refusal to tolerate nuclear missiles and warheads on French territory that were under American control. The resulting redeployment of U.S. Air Force F-100 bombers from their French bases to Great Britain and West Germany did not adversely affect the military plans for the planes' mission. But Secretary of State Christian Herter, who had replaced the dying Dulles on April 22, 1959, lamented its corrosive political effects on the alliance.[82] In their first meeting, the two presidents had explored possible strategies for the encounter with Khrushchev.[83] At a conference in the

White House with their respective foreign ministers and other high-level officials, the two presidents agreed that disarmament and Berlin should be the two critical topics in Paris.[84]

The Summit That Never Was

The elaborate plans for the Big Four summit conference in mid-May 1960 in Paris were disrupted by the shooting down over Soviet territory on May 1 of a CIA reconnaissance plan, (the U-2), which had been conducting such flights since 1956 with impunity out of range of Soviet anti-aircraft missiles. Assuming that the fragile plane would have been destroyed as it hit the ground and that the pilot would commit suicide with the cyanide pen he was carrying, Eisenhower ordered the National Aeronautics and Space Administration (NASA) to put out a fake cover story that one of its planes conducting meteorological research in Turkey had unintentionally veered off course. Thereupon Chairman Khrushchev publicly revealed that the pilot, Francis Gary Powers, had been captured and confessed to conducting espionage deep in Soviet air space. Despite Eisenhower's embarrassment at having to acknowledge the cover-up, he adamantly refused to apologize to the Soviet leader and punish those responsible for the violation of Soviet air space, as the Soviet leader had demanded. Khrushchev hinted to Macmillan on May 10 that the summit was in serious jeopardy because of the U-2 flight. A nervous Macmillan beseeched the Kremlin leader to accept de Gaulle's proposal that the meetings taking place without reference to the controversy.[85]

As the four heads of government converged on Paris in mid-May to prepare for the high-level meeting, Khrushchev warned de Gaulle that he was seriously considering abandoning the conference without a formal apology from the American president for the U-2 flight. In the course of their brief meeting on May 15, the French president reminded Khrushchev that all countries conduct espionage and declared that if this incident led to war, "France as an ally would stand with the United States."[86]

At a meeting between Eisenhower and de Gaulle (later joined by Macmillan) on May 16, the French president was handed a press release about an impromptu press conference Khrushchev had held in front of the Soviet embassy announcing his intention to depart from Paris in protest. De Gaulle promptly made every effort to coax Mr. K. to attend the next meeting of the conference, tentatively scheduled for that afternoon, with such finesse that both Eisenhower and Macmillan lavishly praised the "skill and dignity" with which the French president "had handled an extremely awkward situation."[87]

Macmillan recorded in his memoirs that the day of May 16, 1960, was "one of the most agonizing as well as exhausting I have ever been through, except, perhaps in battle."[88] (Both he and de Gaulle has been wounded in the First World War.)

When the Soviet leader arrived at the Elysée Palace on the afternoon of that day, he brusquely interrupted the proceedings as Eisenhower was about to make a brief statement, demanding to have the floor. De Gaulle glanced at Eisenhower, who signaled his willingness to stand aside. The Soviet leader, reading from a prepared text, promptly unleashed a scorching attack on the United States with a red-faced Eisenhower sitting directly opposite him at the conference table. He repeated his earlier demands for an apology contained in letters to de Gaulle and Macmillan and took the occasion to revoke his invitation issued during the Camp David meeting the previous September for a return visit by Eisenhower to the Soviet Union. De Gaulle responded with a blast of his own in defense of his American colleague: "At this very moment a Soviet satellite is passing over France eighteen times every twenty-four hours. How can we be sure that all the machines of every sort now flitting across the skies may not suddenly rain down terrible projectiles on any country in the world? The only possible guarantee would be a peaceful détente backed up by adequate measures of disarmament. That is the object of our conference. I therefore propose that the debate be opened."[89]

Khrushchev would have none of it. He brusquely made good on his threat to walk out of the conference, announcing his intention to sign a separate peace treaty with East Germany and challenging the three Western allies' occupation status in Berlin. De Gaulle responded with haughty contempt. After the Soviet leader's abrupt departure, the French president took Eisenhower and his interpreter, Vernon (Dick) Walters, aside. "I do not know what Khrushchev is going to do," de Gaulle declared, "but whatever he does, or whatever happens, I want you to know that I am with you to the end." As Eisenhower and Walters entered the car, Ike remarked with some emotion, "That de Gaulle is really quite a guy."[90] Eisenhower was pleasantly surprised by and entirely appreciative of the strong support he received from the French president.[91]

At a somber meeting of the three Western leaders at the Elysée Palace two days later, Eisenhower urged the establishment of "closer consultation" among the three governments but without "large ponderous machinery," a veiled reference to de Gaulle's old tripartite scheme.[92] The French president was delighted to hear these words and periodically raised the issue of "organizing our [American, British, and French] cooperation more effectively in the future," a sentiment which Eisenhower heartily approved.[93]

The subject of Berlin occupied the attention of the three Western leaders as the plans for the summit unraveled. De Gaulle urgently pressed the British to state unequivocally their pledge to hold firm on the subject. On May 15, he had turned to Macmillan and asked him point blank, "How far will you go on Berlin, and how far will you not go?" but received no reply.[94] A hint of the British position was forthcoming a day later in a conference at the Quai d'Orsay when British foreign secretary Selwyn Lloyd took Herter aside to declare that it was "unthinkable that the British government should ask the British people to go to war over the formalities of access to West Berlin . . . for the sake of a stamp on travel documents."[95]

Adenauer was summoned to a hastily arranged conference of the three Western leaders on the afternoon of May 16. With regard to Khrushchev's suggestion that the issue of Berlin be put on ice for two years, de Gaulle insisted that "we should stand by our rights." He shared the West German chancellor's belief that "any backing down on Berlin would be a grave blow to the prestige of the West."[96] In a remark to Macmillan, he had earlier warned that the West must stand firm: "If that means war, well then there will be a war."[97]

Initial French Attempts to Woo West Germany

One of the most critical dilemmas de Gaulle faced as he pressed for the reform of the North Atlantic Alliance was the conflict between his campaign for tripartite management and his need to avoid offending West Germany and its chancellor, Konrad Adenauer. (He appeared to care little about the effect of the U.S.-U.K.-France inner directorate on the other members of NATO.) Charles de Gaulle was languishing in a German prisoner of war camp in 1917 when Adenauer became mayor (burgermeister) of the city of Cologne in the Rhineland. Like de Gaulle, Adenauer was a devout Catholic, a conservative, and a confirmed Francophile. In the early 1920s, he had toyed with the idea of pressing for the establishment of an autonomous Rhenish Republic in an economic union with France to counter the influence of Protestant Prussia.[98]

As we have seen, de Gaulle had called for the detachment of the Rhineland and the Ruhr from occupied Germany before his resignation in January 1946. On his return to power in 1958, those vindictive plans for Germany had gone by the wayside. The two leaders had met for the first time on September 14, 1958, three days before de Gaulle had dispatched his memoranda to Eisenhower and Macmillan proposing the tripartite "inner directorate" for NATO that would leave the Federal Republic out in the cold. In a cordial gathering with Adenauer at de Gaulle's country home in Colombey—the only foreign statesman ever to be invited there during de Gaulle's term in office—the two leaders found common ground on standing firm on the status of Berlin that Khrushchev had begun to challenge. The West German chancellor agreed with his French host that the two countries should join forces to promote cooperation of non-Communist Europe apart from the two superpowers.[99]

In a subsequent meeting with Adenauer on July 29 and 30, 1960, at Rambouillet, de Gaulle stressed that Western Europe—with France and West Germany playing the commanding role—must become "a real entity playing its own part in world affairs" and should lay the groundwork for such a global role by organizing the continent "in the realms of politics, economics, culture, and defense." In short, cooperation among the West European nation-states would replace integration in the defense sphere. This first hint at the idea of a Paris-Bonn Axis did not yet tempt the West German leader, even after de Gaulle speculated that eventually the Federal Republic might be permitted to possess nuclear weapons and that such cooperation among sovereign European states would replace supranational security integration in the Atlantic alliance. Though he listened respectfully to his host's proposal and fully accepted France's pledge to defend the Federal Republic in the event of war with the Eastern bloc, Adenauer remained committed to military integration in the alliance. But de Gaulle continued to press his case. At his press conference on September 5, 1960, the French president urged France's European allies to accept his proposal to explore the ways to achieve closer political and military cooperation. At the end of the year, he waxed lyrical about the future of the old continent freed from the domination of the new. Europe must be transformed into "the greatest political, economic, military power that ever existed," which should preside over a radical reform of the Atlantic Alliance "in order better to defend the free world and to act together in all parts of the earth."[100]

Joining the Nuclear Club

The Atomic Energy Act of 1946 (usually referred to as the McMahon Act after its sponsor in the U.S. Senate, Democratic Senator Brien McMahon of Connecticut) prohibited the transfer of nuclear technology to foreign powers.[101] During a visit to Washington in October 1957, Macmillan was pleased to learn that Eisenhower and Dulles planned to ask Congress to amend the McMahon Act to allow for American support for the British nuclear program, which had been operational since the early 1950s. On July 3, 1958, a month after de Gaulle assumed power in Paris, the Act was amended by the U.S.-U.K. Mutual Defense Agreement. This amendment allowed Great Britain, which had already conducted more than twenty nuclear tests since 1952, to receive U.S. nuclear technology.[102]

De Gaulle obviously regarded the amendment of the Atomic Energy Act as a blatant example of the special, exclusionary relationship between the two "Anglo-Saxon" powers. He was convinced that for his country to retain its status as a great power, it would have to join the nuclear club, which then consisted of the two superpowers with their enormous nuclear arsenals and Great Britain with its small nuclear weapons system. De Gaulle did not invent the assertion that France must acquire a nuclear capability. He merely accelerated plans for developing nuclear weapons that had been approved under the Fourth Republic. Inchoate plans had been drawn up in the first half of the 1950s. But they were accelerated after France's humiliation during the Suez crisis of the fall of 1956.[103] In fact, one of the last acts of the government of Prime Minister Félix Gaillard in April 1958 was to authorize an atomic bomb test within two years.[104]

Inheriting this policy, de Gaulle lost no time in bringing it to fruition. On July 22, 1958, he set a target date for a French nuclear test for the first quarter of 1960. The target date was met on February 13, 1960, when France conducted a successful nuclear test at Reggane in the Algerian Sahara, less than three months before the abortive Paris summit conference. De Gaulle's ambassador to Washington recalled the president's remark that he wanted "to make 'his' bomb burst" before the summit began.[105] In a meeting between General Norstad (the SACEUR) and French Minister of Armies Pierre Messmer in March 1960, the Frenchman explained that the test was essential to restore confidence of the French people and to "convince them that they need not always rely upon others for their defense."[106]

Two months after the test in the Sahara, during de Gaulle's visit to Washington, Eisenhower raised with the French leader a "matter that was really none of his [Eisenhower's] business." He had received a warning from nine African countries that France's attempts to suppress the rebellion in Algeria and its recent atmospheric atomic test "were driving the African nations out of the Western camp." De Gaulle reminded the American president that he had unveiled on September 16 of the previous year his offer to Algeria of independence, remaining part of France, or an Algerian government tied to France by treaty. He noted that a number of former French colonies in Africa had been granted independence within the so-called French Community and offered to study the American president's suggestion that future tests be conducted underground.[107]

Eisenhower had been painfully ambivalent on the subject of whether the United States should assist France in the development of a nuclear capability. In October 1957, while the Fourth Republic still held sway in France, he accepted the advice of his advisers and approved a policy statement seeking to "discourage production of nuclear weapons by a fourth country" and to "persuade France not to undertake independent production of such weapons."[108] After de Gaulle's accession in June 1958, Eisenhower had done what he could to dissuade him from pursuing nuclear independence for France. This remained the official policy of the administration in its final two years. In early September 1959, Eisenhower visited France for the first time since de Gaulle had taken power.[109] When he stepped off the airplane, with the ubiquitous General Vernon Walters present to interpret, de Gaulle greeted him with the words "Whatever may come in the future . . . you will for us forever be the generalissimo of the armies of freedom." After translating, Walters saw the American president's eyes fill with tears.[110]

Eisenhower argued that French nuclear weapons were unnecessary because of the United States' commitment—which it had demonstrated in the two World Wars—to defend France. De Gaulle's rejoinder captured the essence of why he thought France required its own national means of dissuading an enemy from attacking it. "In the course of two world wars, America was France's ally, and France has not forgotten what she owes to American help," he conceded. "But neither has she forgotten that during the First World War that help came [to France] only after three long years of struggle which nearly proved mortal for her, and that during the Second she had already been crushed before you intervened. . . . As for harmonizing the possible use of our nuclear bombs and yours insofar as this might be feasible, we could do so within the framework of direct cooperation of the three atomic powers, which I have already proposed to you. Until you accept this, we shall, like you, retain complete freedom of action."[111]

In a press conference on November 10, 1959, de Gaulle had pointedly reminded the world that "the Anglo-Saxons on the one hand, and the Soviet Union on the other, have invented, tested, and made colossal nuclear armaments for some twenty years." After the failure of the Baruch plan for the international control of nuclear weapons in 1946, the United Nations had never asked the two superpowers "to destroy the nuclear arms they have in their possession, nor even to stop making them. France therefore refuses to halt its plan to acquire such weapons" while Washington and Moscow possess such huge stockpiles.[112] An angry Eisenhower responded that he was "astonished" that the French president would question "the good faith of this government." He softened the blow with praise for de Gaulle's goals for Algeria as outlined in his September 16 statement and the pledge that the United States will "continue to support your Algerian policy."[113] De Gaulle's response was a repetition of his oft-stated argument that France needed its own nuclear arsenal to deter aggression.[114]

It had become clear throughout 1959 that the very vague American intentions to assist the French nuclear program would fall far short of de Gaulle's hopes. Negotiations had begun on the transfer to France of a nuclear submarine and its atomic fuel that Dulles had promised in the summer of 1958. An agreement between Under-Secretary of State Christian Herter (soon to replace the ailing Dulles) and Ambassador Alphand on May 7, 1959, omitted the submarine engine and ended up supplying only about a third of the promised enriched uranium. Frustrated, de Gaulle let Eisenhower know in their early September meeting of French plans to test an atomic device in the next year. The French president fully understood that Eisenhower was not opposed to nuclear sharing with France. On the contrary, he knew that the American president was embarrassed about the U.S. government's refusal to assist France in developing a nuclear capability because of legislative restrictions. Toward the end of his final term in August 25, 1960, Eisenhower made one last effort to rectify the situation. On August 25, 1960, he ordered the National Security Council to study "whether and under what circumstances it might be in the security interests of the United States to enhance the nuclear capability of France." But this effort failed to persuade the NSC and the Joint Committee on Atomic Energy to consider amending the McMahon Act.[115]

The Tripartite Scheme That Would Not Die

In the last year of Eisenhower's presidency, he tried but failed to persuade de Gaulle to give up his project for a three-power directorate for NATO. In August the American president brusquely dismissed de Gaulle's proposal for an Anglo-American-French summit meeting.[116] In response the French president reasserted his call for a tripartite directorate, specifically mentioning the deteriorating situation in the newly independent Belgium Congo as just the type of crisis outside of the NATO area that should be handled by what de Gaulle hoped would become the Big Three.[117] Eisenhower privately complained about the nonstop pressure from de Gaulle on the tripartite proposal.[118]

At a high-level meeting of the National Security Council on August 25, Eisenhower proposed that the body discuss the topic of nuclear sharing with allies, in light of the plan to deploy forty nuclear-armed Polaris submarines within three years. Acting Secretary of State Douglas Dillon warned that "the problem of nuclear sharing was really the problem of France and the effect of nuclear assistance to France on our other NATO allies." He asserted that "if such assistance to France would create jealousy in NATO, then we should be reluctant to give such assistance."[119] France signed an agreement with the United States on September 6, 1960, equipping the French forces in West Germany with tactical (short-range, or battlefield) nuclear weapons, but they would remain under American control until a crisis required a decision about their use.[120]

The Withdrawal of the
French Mediterranean Fleet from NATO

De Gaulle launched his gradual, step-by-step campaign for the removal of French military forces from the integrated command structure of the North Atlantic Treaty Organization by focusing on French naval forces in the Mediterranean Sea. The Mediterranean Command (AFMED) was headquartered in Malta under the command of a British admiral. The French fleet had become the largest NATO naval force in the region after the American Sixth Fleet following the drastic reduction of Britain's naval presence there. Since the French fleet was actively engaged in the conflict in Algeria, de Gaulle resented the subordination to a British admiral in wartime. When Prime Minister Debré met with SACEUR Norstad on January 30, 1959, he emphasized that the western Mediterranean was a "vital artery for France" (to Algeria) and proposed a consideration of "certain changes in the NATO command structure" in the region. Norstad replied that he would be "disposed to study" any proposal from the French government.[121]

On March 4, General André Demetz, representing General Paul Ely, chief of the French Defense Staff, met with General Norstad to inform the SACEUR that the French government was about to remove the French Mediterranean fleet from NATO. Norstad replied that the United States was willing to consider all sorts of modification of the status of the French fleet in order to avoid what he called the "catastrophe" of a withdrawal. Two days later the French representative to the Atlantic Council formally announced that the French Mediterranean fleet would be detached from the NATO integrated command. In a handwritten letter to Eisenhower on May 25, de Gaulle reaffirmed the message conveyed by French prime minister Michel Debré on May 1 to Secretary of State Herter: the withdrawal of the Mediterranean Fleet and the refusal to authorize American-controlled nuclear weapons on French territory were directly linked to the lack of progress in discussions on the tripartite memorandum.[122]

Continued Pressure on NATO Integration

Throughout the rest of Eisenhower's second term, de Gaulle continued his drumbeat of criticism of the policy of military integration in NATO. Eisenhower's and de Gaulle's periodic discussions about the issues of national security and nuclear weapons had become a dialogue of the deaf in the years 1959 and 1960. By the latter year, de Gaulle fully realized that Eisenhower would not be in the White House beyond January 1961. Concentrating on bringing the nightmare of the Algerian War to an end, he took little interest in the presidential campaign of 1960 between Ike's vice president Richard Nixon and the junior senator from Massachusetts, John F. Kennedy. But as Eisenhower prepared to vacate the White House, de Gaulle dispatched an emotional letter addressed to his "dear friend": "At our age, I do not know what the future will hold for you and me," he began. "But I know that everything that has passed between us for the last twenty years has only increased the esteem, the admiration, and the friendship that I bring to you."[123]

CHAPTER EIGHT

~

Kennedy and de Gaulle, 1961–1963
JFK's Grand Design Derailed

When John F. Kennedy entered the White House on January 30, 1961, he inherited an exasperating situation with regard to U.S.-French relations. An exceedingly well-informed American newspaper reporter in Paris, Don Cook, summarized the situation succinctly: "In American eyes there was no logic in preaching firmness against Khrushchev in Berlin and then pulling NATO apart. There was no logic in France building an expensive tiny independent nuclear force and at the same time asking for a veto over American weapons. There was no logic in de Gaulle repeatedly protesting about America having been late in coming to France's assistance in two world wars, and then wanting to do away with the American command in Europe that made it impossible for that ever to happen again."[1]

Before the 1960 presidential election in the United States, John F. Kennedy was probably best known in French governing circles for his widely publicized speech in the Senate on July 1, 1957, severely criticizing the Eisenhower administration's tacit support for France in the Algerian war and calling for American diplomatic intervention to bring about a negotiated peace leading to autonomy or independence to Algeria. The furious reaction from the French government to what it regarded as a foreign intrusion into a domestic affair left a bitter memory in Paris that did not dissipate with the advent of the Fifth Republic.[2] To add insult to injury, three months after his speech on the Senate floor, Senator Kennedy published an article in the Catholic journal *America* worrying about the effects of the French effort to suppress the Algerian rebellion on the "the newly independent states in Africa."[3]

But once in the White House, the new American president changed his tune about the evolving French policy toward Algeria. In a high-level meeting with French ambassador Alphand, Kennedy expressed his "admiration" for de Gaulle's skillful handling of the Algerian policy. The ambassador explained that the sticking point was the FLN's refusal to compromise on the question of the fate of the more than one million European (mainly French) citizens in the country. Alphand relayed de Gaulle's hope that he could meet with Kennedy soon to discuss this and other matters of pressing concern.[4]

In the early months of the new administration in Washington, several high-ranking officers in the French army in Algeria would make one final effort to preserve the privileged status of the million Europeans (mainly French) over the nine million Muslims. After retiring in 1960, General Raoul Salan had relocated to Spain, where he issued stinging attacks on de Gaulle's Algerian policy and conspired with an extremist fringe of the Organisation de l'Armée Secrète (OAS), a group of hard-line officers prepared to do anything to keep Algeria French.[5]

In March 1961, Salan secured the secret support of General Maurice Challe, whom de Gaulle had transferred from his Algerian command to a position in NATO. Together with two other dissident generals who had served in the Free French army during the Second World War, they planned a military coup. Amid this volatile situation, de Gaulle unleashed a strident warning to the Muslim rebels in a press conference on April 10 that *The New York Times* claimed had "the impact of an atomic bomb." He announced that if the Algerians voted to secede from France, he would immediately suspend all financial aid to the breakaway country, invite the million-odd Europeans to depart Algeria for France, and expel the four hundred thousand Algerians working in France (whose remittances were crucial to their families' welfare).[6]

But the rebel officers were not assuaged by this tough talk from Paris. After Salan and Challe had slipped into Algiers, a regiment of the Foreign Legion seized control of the government buildings on April 22 and incarcerated the loyal army commander and the delegate general. The four rebellious generals appeared on a balcony before a boisterous crowd of *pieds noirs* calling for resistance. With the prospect of civil war looming, de Gaulle ordered all the French airports closed and severed all communications between the metropole and Algeria. He designated a loyal general in Algeria to assume control of the army and a loyal political lieutenant to take the office of delegate general. In the late afternoon of the following day, de Gaulle's counselor on all things African, after meeting with the chief of state in his office, announced to a friend: "Guess what the General just told me. 'In three days, it will be all over.'"[7] On the evening of the day of the coup attempt, de

Gaulle, dressed in the uniform of a brigadier general, appeared on television to denounce the putschists and rally the rest of the army to the government. "The State is flouted, the nation defied, our power shaken, our international prestige reduced, our place and our role in Africa compromised," he angrily declared. And he blatantly encouraged loyal members of the military in Algeria to resist the plotters, with violence if necessary. "In the name of France, I order that all means—I repeat *all means*—be used to bar the way elsewhere to these men until they are brought down."[8]

This stern warning dissuaded those officers and recruits who might have been tempted to throw in their lot with Salan, Challe, and the others. Most mid-level officers in Algeria refused to join the putsch. The plot quickly collapsed, although Supreme NATO Commander General Lauris Norstad was reporting on April 24 about de Gaulle's concern that French NATO units in Germany would defect to the rebel officers and plunge the country into "civil war."[9] All of the top planners of the coup were arrested and jailed by de Gaulle's government until they were pardoned by him seven years later. The mutinous Foreign Legion regiment was disbanded and its members dispersed among other units. More than 200 officers and 160 civilian officials were arrested for supporting the coup.[10]

In the aftermath of the crisis, rumors circulated of an American hand in the events in the early months of the Kennedy administration. The Soviet news agency TASS reported the CIA's active support for the putsch.[11] The counselor of the French embassy in Washington informed Assistant Secretary of Defense William Bundy over dinner on May 5 that de Gaulle suspected Washington's encouragement of the rebellious generals to topple him in the hopes of a more pro-American successor. Challe in particular had been in touch with Allied officers in SHAPE before resigning a few months before the coup attempt.[12] Rumors of Washington's involvement with the OAS continued to swirl into the year 1962.[13] CIA director Allen Dulles confirmed that no one in the agency had been authorized to assist the rebellious generals. In fact, the CIA had placed agents near the leaders of the FLN in order to keep abreast of its activities.[14] The well informed *New York Times* journalist C. L. Sulzberger noted that the rumors were spread by the Kremlin and even reached the pages of *Le Monde*, which alleged U.S. agents were in touch with Challe.[15] Kennedy's well-known public support for Algerian independence did not quash the unsubstantiated rumors.[16]

In the meantime, the tortuous negotiations between the government, represented by the loyal Gaullist Louis Joxe, and the FLN, which had begun in January 1962, gradually moved forward. On March 18, a cease-fire agreement was signed in the old spa town of Evian-les-Bains on Lake Geneva, which specified that a referendum would be held on the question of Algerian independence.[17]

In April the French, and in June the Algerians, voted by huge majorities in favor of independence. On July 3, 1962, coincidentally the day before America's day of celebration for independence from Great Britain, the Republic of Algeria officially came into being after 132 years of French control. To further bolster his authority amid the escalating violence over the future political status of Algeria, de Gaulle organized a referendum for September 1962 to amend the constitution to arrange for the direct election of the president, which he had long favored but had left out of the original constitutional draft to avoid antagonizing the parliament. De Gaulle later told his minister of information Alain Peyrefitte that liberating France from what he liked to call the albatross of Algeria was perhaps the greatest service he had rendered to his country.[18]

Regarding Peyrefitte, it is worth noting that de Gaulle had an ambivalent attitude toward and relationship with the French press, both the major newspapers and the state-run television network, Office de Radiodiffusion-télévision française (ORTF). He used them for his own communication purposes to the general public while regarding them as his antagonists.[19]

The American historian Irwin Wall, who has written a comprehensive study of the relationship between Washington and Paris regarding the Algerian problem, blames de Gaulle for drawing out for so long the settlement in the spring and summer of 1962 that had nefarious consequences for France, such as the chaotic flight of the *pieds noirs* (French Algerians) and the massacre of thousands of *harkis* (Muslims who had worked with and fought alongside the French) who were denied refuge in France in recognition for their service.[20] In the end de Gaulle's war in Algeria lasted longer than that of the leaders of the Fourth Republic.[21]

Resumption of the Franco-American Debate on the Atlantic Alliance

At the end of January 1961, as the new administration settled into office in Washington, an unsigned memorandum, approved by de Gaulle, summarized for the French ambassador in Washington the principal concerns of the French government relating to the United States. At the top of the list was the tripartite memorandum of 1958, followed by Berlin, NATO, and the usual litany of disputes between Paris and Washington.[22] On April 21, four days after the Bay of Pigs debacle in Cuba, Kennedy approved a report drawn up by former secretary of state Dean Acheson the previous month calling for a strengthening of American leadership in the Atlantic Alliance while tightening the integration of the political, economic, and military components of the transatlantic relationship.[23]

This ambitious approach to transatlantic relations reflected the influence of former secretary of state Acheson and especially of the new undersecretary of state, George Ball. Ball had become an ardent admirer and friend of Jean Monnet, whose image of Europe's future was the polar opposite of de Gaulle's. From their first meeting in 1945, the two men worked hand-in-hand to promote the cause of European economic and political integration. When Ball became the Kennedy's number two in the State Department in 1961, he focused all of his attention on America's relationship with Europe while Rusk (who had served as assistant secretary of state for Far Eastern affairs in the early 1950s) became increasingly preoccupied with affairs in Southeast Asia. De Gaulle's hostility to European integration and his insistence on promoting what both Ball and Monnet denigrated as an anachronistic brand of French nationalism cemented this transatlantic personal relationship in opposition to the French president.[24] In his memoirs, Ball compares the two great Frenchmen Monnet and de Gaulle: "De Gaulle's great weakness is that he habitually faces backwards, seeing the centuries that are past, not the future that is to come," he lamented. "De Gaulle's obsession is to establish France on a par with the global powers in spite of implacable facts of population and resources. . . . His great tragedy is that he wasn't born in the time of Louis XIV, when France was indeed the most populous and richest nation in Europe."[25]

Soon after Kennedy's arrival at the White House, Ball's friend Monnet was denouncing de Gaulle to his high-level contacts in Washington, declaring that "it would be nonsense" to assist France's nuclear weapons program, which would prompt the Germans "to ask for the same and create a real mess."[26] Another close friend of Ball, the distinguished French philosopher, political scientist, and journalist Raymond Aron, would later weigh in on the debate about how to treat the French president. He had fled to London after the fall of France in 1940 and joined de Gaulle's Free French movement (for which he edited the newspaper France Libre). But after the war, Aron wrote a regular column for the Parisian newspaper Le Figaro in which he criticized de Gaulle throughout his presidency and praised American foreign policy. Ball later invited his French friend to meet with President Kennedy, Bundy, and presidential aide Arthur Schlesinger Jr. in the spring of 1963. Aron's advice to the president was to avoid all public criticism of de Gaulle on the grounds that it would merely serve to build him up.[27]

Secretary of State Dean Rusk noted in his memoirs that Ball "wanted to launch a frontal assault on de Gaulle" but insisted that "neither President

Kennedy nor later President Johnson allowed a high-profile response to de Gaulle's obstructionism."[28] They favored tighter links between the United States and an integrated Europe in which national ambitions would be thwarted. Along with the new secretary of defense, Robert McNamara, they favored the centralized control of the alliance's nuclear weapons in the hands of the president, opposed any assistance to national nuclear forces in Europe, and called for the strengthening of NATO's conventional forces to enable the adoption of what later became known as the "flexible response" doctrine to replace the "all or nothing" approach of Dulles's "massive retaliation" strategy.[29]

The latter strategy had been announced by Dulles on January 12, 1954, in a speech before the Council on Foreign Relations. It was often referred to as the "New Look," an allusion to the annual Parisian fashion display of women's clothing.[30] Ball's and McNamara's criticism of de Gaulle's nuclear strategy was fully endorsed by Averill Harriman, the elder statesman of the Democratic Party who became an ambassador-at-large under Kennedy. In response to Ball's request for his recollections of Franklin Roosevelt's difficulties with de Gaulle, Harriman painted a harsh portrait of the French leader (whom he had met several times during the war) as "stubborn" and "unrealistic."[31]

Soon after Kennedy entered the White House, de Gaulle had sent as his personal emissary Jacques Chaban-Delmas, president of the French National Assembly, to Washington. Chaban-Delmas promptly dusted off the moribund tripartite proposal for "the most complete coordination" among the three members of an American-British-French "inner directorate" within NATO to jointly handle problems across the globe.[32] De Gaulle's ambassador in Washington reaffirmed the French president's earnest desire that the new American chief executive would warm up to the idea that had fallen by the wayside under Eisenhower.[33]

Still smarting from the Bay of Pigs fiasco of April 1961, Kennedy undertook a state visit to France during a planned European tour, perhaps to divert public attention from the abject failure of his first foreign-policy undertaking by basking in the glow of a high-level meeting with the French president. Kennedy sent Acheson to confer with de Gaulle in late April to brief him on the new American president's thinking about the Atlantic Alliance in preparation for their forthcoming meeting. The former secretary of state assured the French president that the United States had no intention of removing its nuclear weapons from Europe and every intention of fulfilling its solemn commitment to use them in response to both a nuclear and conventional attack from the east. De Gaulle forcefully raised the old proposal for tripartite cooperation among Washington, London, and Paris to handle problems not only in Europe but in the non-Western world as well. He used as an example the deteriorating situation in the former Belgian Congo, which might have been prevented if the three powers could have consulted and exerted pressure on the Belgians to pursue a rational policy there. Acheson replied that such informal discussions outside of NATO were entirely possible.[34]

In mid-April the new president had confided to Ambassador Alphand and former prime minister Paul Reynaud, who was visiting Washington, his views on the developing French *force de frappe*: "It was not simply a question of France's having nuclear capability, but the next step would be for Germany to have this capability," a grave concern because "Adenauer might be leaving the scene some day."[35] McGeorge Bundy later recalled a meeting of the Council on Foreign Relations in 1965 where Reynaud, responding to a question about whether de Gaulle had become senile, replied that "they speak about it often in medical circles."[36]

The exceedingly warm personal relationship between the two presidents during the last three years of Eisenhower's second term helped to keep the transatlantic conflict within bounds. Kennedy tried to preserve the modicum of good relations between Washington and Paris—despite all the acrimony behind the scenes—by making Paris his first stop on his European tour that began on May 31, 1961. Having smashed the attempted putsch in Algeria, de Gaulle was exultant while the young American president was licking his wounds from the Bay of Pigs debacle.

The Kennedy visit to Paris at the end of May and early June was a public relations extravaganza that allowed de Gaulle to showcase the grandeur that was France. As the limousine transported the couple and the French president to the French Foreign Ministry, where the Kennedys were to reside on the third floor, de Gaulle remarked that at least a million Parisians were in the streets and exclaimed "how Paris is pleased to see you!" The president and Mrs. Kennedy were wined and dined by the French president and both guests received rave reviews in the French press. After a visit to the Hall of Mirrors in the Palace of Versailles, de Gaulle arranged for a dinner for five hundred guests, with Jackie seated next to the French president. He confided to the American president nearby that she knew more about the history of his country than most French women. Jacqueline Bouvier Kennedy, with her French heritage on her father's side, declaimed in impeccable French to her appreciative host. She had studied at the Sorbonne and had traced her ancestry to the emigration of Les Bouviers after the fall of Napoleon in 1815.[37]

De Gaulle also demonstrated the firm grip he had on power in the country. While Kennedy and Secretary of State Dean Rusk had arrived in de Gaulle's ornate office at the Elysée Palace, Rusk recalled that Michel Debré and Couve du Murville treated the French leader like royalty. "I watched with amazement as the prime minister walked up to de Gaulle, gave a little schoolboy bow, clicked his heels, and presented himself much like a cadet at Saint-Cyr [the French West Point]. The foreign minister did the same thing." From his own conversations with the French president, he concluded that "talking with de Gaulle was like crawling up a mountain on your knees, opening a little portal at the top, and waiting for the oracle to speak."[38]

When de Gaulle had greeted the first couple at the airport, he uncharacteristically welcomed them in English—"Have you made a good aerial voyage?" At a banquet he lavishly praised the American president's energy and intelligence. Not to be outdone, Kennedy quoted passages from de Gaulle's memoirs and presented him with the gift of a letter from George Washington to Lafayette.[39] Malraux was so taken with the first lady that he later dedicated one of his books to her.[40] At the dinner table, Mrs. Kennedy was again seated next to the French president, enabling them to discuss questions on the history of France. When the American president joined them, he wanted to address more recent history. What was Churchill like? What about Franklin Roosevelt? De Gaulle discreetly fended off the question about FDR with an anodyne assessment that the two leaders did not really establish a satisfactory relationship.[41]

But the personal rapport between the young man and the old man could not mitigate the real differences that separated the two governments in foreign policy. De Gaulle conceded to the new American president that when NATO was established in 1949, France "was no longer a great power and had no ambitions to become one again." But after the passage of eleven years, he declared (with a remarkable understatement) that "she has again some ambition as a nation." For his part Kennedy pressed de Gaulle to acknowledge the credibility of the U.S. security guarantee to Western Europe. The French president had got wind of the proposals for a new policy of "flexible response," which he believed would severely undermine that credibility. De Gaulle shared with Kennedy what was in fact a bit premature judgment that "the Soviets and Americans are more or less equal and each can destroy the other."[42]

He envisioned the disaster of a war fought in Western and Central Europe with tactical nuclear weapons that would leave the two superpowers unscathed.[43] When Kennedy questioned the credibility of the emerging French *force de frappe* in response to a Soviet attack, de Gaulle noted that "the Rhine is much narrower than the Atlantic, and therefore France might feel more intimately tied to [West] German defense than the United States might feel tied to French defense."[44] In addition to the value of the U.S. military commitment to defend Western Europe, Kennedy and de Gaulle covered all of the outstanding issues between the two countries—Vietnam, Laos, the crisis in the Congo—without coming to any agreement.[45]

The Kennedy–De Gaulle Agenda

At their first meeting on May 31, 1961, Kennedy (who was to confer with Khrushchev in Vienna soon afterward) hinted at the possibility of negotiating with the Soviet leader on the Berlin issue: Khrushchev's threat to sign a separate peace treaty with East Germany and turn control of the three Western powers' access routes to it was totally unacceptable to de Gaulle, who sternly replied that the Allies must remain united and refuse to negotiate on this issue. In their second meeting the next day, which lasted for three hours and twenty minutes with a break for lunch, Kennedy raised the subject of the volatile situation in Laos and Vietnam and hinted that it might require a Western military intervention to force the Communists to negotiate. De Gaulle replied with a heated rejoinder that he would repeat many times in later years to Kennedy's successors. According to his memoirs, the French president warned that "the more you become involved out there against the Communists, the more the Communists will appear as the champions of national independence, and the more support they will receive, if only from despair. We French have had experience of it. You Americans want to take our place. . . . I predict that you will sink step by step into a bottomless military and political quagmire, however much you spend in men and money."[46]

After Berlin and Southeast Asia, Kennedy and de Gaulle discussed the issue of NATO and nuclear weapons. De Gaulle reiterated his belief that the United States could never be trusted to make good on its pledge of nuclear retaliation against a conventional Soviet attack in Europe since its own territory was now within range of Soviet ICBMs. Knowing that Kennedy and his secretary of defense, Robert McNamara, were preparing to abandon the old Eisenhower-Dulles strategic doctrine of "massive retaliation" for the new strategy of "flexible response" (which the American representative had unveiled to the Atlantic Council earlier in the month), de Gaulle criticized the new strategy for undermining the entire doctrine of extended deterrence. To de Gaulle's surprise, Kennedy then raised the possibility of reopening negotiations without preconditions about the 1958 tripartite proposal. De Gaulle turned it aside. He had by then decided to focus his attention on developing a bilateral relationship with West Germany as the nucleus of a European Third Force.[47] At the formal dinner at the Elysée Palace on June 1, Kennedy abandoned the text of his prepared toast that had been distributed in such a way that alarmed the French press. He omitted the pledge that American troops would "remain in Europe as long as they are required, ready to meet any threat with whatever response is needed." He also left out a reference to France as "a full and equal partner in the great alliance."[48]

On his return to Washington from his European tour, Kennedy briefed the congressional leadership and the vice president on the trip. When the question of de Gaulle and his attitude toward U.S. foreign policy came up, the president simply stated the obvious: the French president deeply resented the United States' policy of assisting the British nuclear effort but refusing similar aid to the French. As for the credibility of NATO's deterrence, de Gaulle had doubted whether the United States would be "prepared to act by trading New York for Paris."[49] As de Gaulle put it in his memoirs, "Now the Americans acknowledged our independence and dealt with us directly. But for all that, they could not conceive of their policy ceasing to be predominant, or of ours diverging from it. What Kennedy offered me in every case was a share in his projects. What he heard from me in reply was that Paris was by all means disposed to collaborate closely with Washington, but that whatever France did, she did on her own accord."[50]

De Gaulle would occasionally return to the subject of Vietnam he privately raised in May–June 1961 for the remainder of the Kennedy presidency, during the period before the deployment of American military forces to that country. His first significant public statement about the situation in Southeast Asia came on August 29, 1963, when he had his minister of information, Alain Peyrefitte, put out a statement that he had drafted calling for the neutralization of both North and South Vietnam.[51] The French ambassador to Saigon, Roger Laloulette, was quietly pursuing a peace initiative based on neutralization with de Gaulle's approval.[52] The United States was not interested in this approach, regarding neutralization as the first step toward the North's defeat of the South.[53] On September 29, 1963, Drew Middleton of The New York Times remarked that while Washington's other allies "content themselves with stifled 'tut-tuts,'" the French president "takes pains to let the world know that France is in favor of uniting Vietnam, free from foreign influence, including that of the United States."[54]

De Gaulle's motivation for pressing the United States on its Vietnam policy was based on two critical considerations. First, it represented the French president's bold bid to win support from the nations of the developing world, which was facilitated by France's impending withdrawal from Algeria that he had engineered. Second, he believed that a settlement in Vietnam would enhance the prospects for détente between east and west in Europe, always a key goal of de Gaulle's policy because it would lessen France's dependence on the U.S. for its security.[55] Ironically, Rusk later claimed that "if we had done nothing" under the SEATO treaty to defend South Vietnam, "President de Gaulle would have been the first to shrug his shoulders in Europe and say, 'See, you cannot really rely on the Americans.'"[56] Couve de Murville displayed his exasperation at what he regarded as Rusk's unquestioned belief that "the United States was fighting the good war for the just cause in Indochina," to wit, "the struggle against world communism, against what he persisted in calling the Sino-Soviet bloc" in apparent ignorance of the emerging Sino-Soviet conflict.[57]

After his meetings with de Gaulle at the end of May and early June, JFK proceeded to Vienna, where he was browbeaten and humiliated by Khrushchev in their one-on-one meetings on June 3 and 4. The Soviet leader reiterated his original demands about Berlin and added a six-month ultimatum for an agreement from the three Western allies. From the very beginning of the Berlin crisis to the most recent ultimatum, de Gaulle took a hard line. He advised Kennedy on the best response to Khrushchev's intimidation, insisting that "only an attitude of firmness and solidarity" among the United States, Great Britain, and France on the issue of Berlin would deter the Soviets. He added the advice "to speak clearly, to take openly military precautions, and to show ourselves in total agreement."[58] In light of the disastrous meeting in Vienna, de Gaulle feared that Kennedy was too young and inexperienced to handle the seasoned Russian leader and might succumb to the temptation to negotiate away Allied rights in Berlin to avoid a showdown with the Kremlin. But when Kennedy gave a televised address on July 25 pledging to stand firm on Berlin, requesting congressional authorization for an increase in defense spending and a call-up of reservists, a relieved de Gaulle fully approved of this get-tough stance.[59]

Two months later, of course, the Soviet Union and its East German ally constructed the Berlin Wall, which stemmed the flow of German refugees to the West. De Gaulle was furious that the three Western allies with occupation rights in West Berlin did nothing in response to this action. A few months later, he told Alain Peyrefitte that when the Russians and East Germans began to install barbed wire at the border between West and East Berlin preparatory to the construction of the concrete wall, "we should have destroyed this barbed wire with tanks." He tried to reach Macmillan, but the British prime minister was on a hunting trip. He failed to connect with Kennedy on an August Sunday. The result was a fait acccompli. "If they had followed me," he said, with considerable exaggeration, "there would not have been a wall."[60] Macmillan noted in his diary that while the Americans "have kept their heads," the French (meaning de Gaulle) "seem to contemplate war with equanimity."[61]

In the meantime, de Gaulle was not at all pleased when Kennedy authorized Dean Rusk to explore with the Soviets the possibility of negotiations on Berlin.[62] This initiative on the diplomatic front, coupled with the continuing pressure from Washington on the Atlantic Council to review the American proposal for adopting the strategy of flexible response, only confirmed the French leader's determination to develop an independent French nuclear force to compensate for what he feared would be Washington's reluctance to exploit its nuclear superiority vis-à-vis Moscow to dissuade the Soviet from pursuing a an aggressive policy toward the West. In a personal letter to West German chancellor Konrad Adenauer, the French president reiterated his demand for firmness among the three Western allies at a time both Washington and especially London seemed intent on pursuing a diplomatic settlement of the ongoing Berlin crisis. Adenauer replied that he was "overwhelmed with confidence and joy by such unqualified support for [West] Germany in her hour of danger."[63] He later lauded the French leader as a "rock," the only foreign leader whom he could completely trust.[64]

Continuing U.S. Reluctance to Support the French Nuclear Weapons Program

After the first French atomic test in the Algerian Sahara on February 13, 1960, de Gaulle had authorized a crash program to develop a credible nuclear striking force (*force de frappe*), including an effective delivery system. On March 21, 1961, President Kennedy replaced Ambassador Amory Houghton with retired General James "Jumpin' Jim" Gavin, who had parachuted behind the German lines on D-Day in Normandy with the Eighty-Second Airborne Division and was well known in French government circles. Once in office, Gavin became a strong advocate of assisting the French nuclear weapons program (a position that, as we have seen, Eisenhower had adopted privately as well). He argued that France's "substantial progress" in its fledgling nuclear weapons program qualified it to receive American support under the provisions of the 1958 amendment to the McMahon Act. But the State Department was not prepared to execute a change in U.S. policy toward this controversial issue.[65]

Kennedy rejected his ambassador's advice and reaffirmed his opposition to nuclear weapons assistance to France.[66] By February 1962, National Security Adviser McGeorge Bundy was urging Kennedy to take the opportunity of a forthcoming visit by Gavin to the White House to "very gently" rein in the ambassador, "an enthusiast for the French position" on nuclear sharing, even suggesting that he be replaced.[67] Bundy's subtle pressure finally resulted in Gavin's removal, although the latter had requested his own retirement.[68] Ironically, the French government made known its preference for Charles Bohlen as American ambassador to Paris. Bohlen, as we shall see, would become a long-serving U.S. ambassador to France. Gavin, who (unlike Bohlen) had no diplomatic experience and a shaky command of the French language, had been a strong advocate of French security concerns.[69] Bohlen, fluent in French and a seasoned diplomat, would follow Washington's instructions to put the brakes on the French nuclear ambitions.

On May 5, 1961, Secretary of Defense Robert McNamara had unveiled for the first time the essence of the new American security strategy at a NATO ministerial session in Athens. In this landmark speech, he urged America's European allies to adopt two critical changes in allied strategy. First, he called for the adoption of the aforementioned strategy of "controlled and flexible response" to a Warsaw Pact attack. Second, he called for the replacement of nuclear targeting of the urban areas in the Soviet Union (which he warned could result in tens of millions of death on both sides) with the so-called counter-force approach, that is, to target the Soviet missile sites to disarm the enemy. This new strategy depended on the tight centralization of nuclear decision-making. In short, without naming them, he was clearly aiming at the independent British nuclear weapons arsenal and the not-yet deployed French *force de frappe*. "Limited nuclear capabilities, operating independently," he declared, "are dangerous, expensive, prone to obsolescence and lacking in credibility as a deterrent."[70] Philip Cerny has provided a perceptive assessment of that complicated issue of the political and strategic credibility of the French nuclear deterrent.[71]

On the same day of McNamara's Athens speech, Rusk cabled to the U.S. ambassador in Paris a full statement of the new administration's policy toward the fledgling French nuclear weapons program. He reaffirmed the U.S. government's refusal to assist the French program. He ventured the prediction that the absence of American aid would compel France to incur such enormous costs that it would eventually be discouraged from preserving the *force de frappe*. He ended with the familiar warning that if the French ever succeeded in their nuclear effort, the Germans would seek to follow in their footsteps.[72]

In the same month, General Charles Ailleret, who (as a young air force colonel) had formed a powerful lobby promoting nuclear weapons under the Fourth Republic, was named chief of the general staff, the highest-ranking military officer.[73] At the end of May, McGeorge Bundy composed a scathing memorandum for the president titled "One last attack on de Gaulle's obsession with nuclear weapons."[74] He belittled the undertaking "on which he is now embarked, of seeking, at great expense, and within tight limits of eventual capability, a wholly autonomous nuclear force which the Soviets could destroy in an afternoon." At a press conference in June, Kennedy publicly reaffirmed his total opposition to U.S. assistance to the French nuclear effort.[75]

For de Gaulle, McNamara's Athens speech confirmed his certainty that Europe could not depend on the American doctrine of extended deterrence and that France needed to develop its independent nuclear force. The CIA had already been taking note in mid-March 1961 of the "widespread belief at the highest levels in Paris that the United States would not use its strategic weapons against the Soviet Union in the event of a Soviet attack in Europe."[76]

This concern was not new nor was it confined to France. A month before de Gaulle came to power, Dulles, traveling in Europe, had reported that British foreign secretary Selwyn Lloyd shared with him on a confidential basis a paper presented to the British cabinet by Defense Secretary Duncan Sandys with this candid question: "When in a few years' time the American continent comes within range of heavy Russian rocket attack, can we be confident that the American people will be willing to provoke wholesale death and destruction in their midst to prevent Soviet aggression in Turkey or Western Europe?" The British defense secretary warned that such a prospect "coupled with traditional isolationism" might provoke a "retreat from the policy of the nuclear deterrent," proving that "we cannot rely indefinitely of the [American] nuclear deterrent." The anxious secretary of state worried that "our European friends will not in fact depend on our willingness to initiate general nuclear war if there is an attack even in Europe."[77]

The West German government was also dismayed by the proposed new American strategic doctrine, which prompted de Gaulle to intensify his bid for a bilateral security link with Bonn. He advertised the developing French nuclear deterrent as "the beginning of a European force," which was well received by Adenauer and his "Gaullist" defense minister, Franz-Josef Strauss (both of whom were deeply troubled by the new doctrine of flexible response as a fatal weakening of extended deterrence).[78]

The Movement toward Political Cooperation among the EEC Members

At a meeting on February 10–11, 1961, the six representatives of the European Economic Community (EEC) agreed to explore means of establishing a close *political* cooperation among the member states. De Gaulle arranged for a study group under the French ambassador to Denmark, Christian Fouchet, to initiate the process for examining the prospects of such cooperation. On July 18 in Bad Godesberg near Bonn, the six heads of government reaffirmed their commitment to seeking a system of political cooperation and initiated an intensive series of meetings to hammer out the details. On October 19, Fouchet presented the first of a number of drafts for a purely intergovernmental body to replace the EEC that would coordinate political and defense as well as economic policy. Strong resistance from the other five member states eventually doomed the project. West Germany opposed the concept of a common European defense policy as a threat to the Atlantic alliance. The three Benelux countries, with the Dutch taking the lead, worried that the de Gaulle/Fouchet initiative would eviscerate the EEC, shut the United States out of Europe, and lead to Franco-German domination of the continent. By the end of 1962, the other five members had presented so many roadblocks to the plan that it died a quiet death.[79]

West German chancellor Konrad Adenauer had hastened to Paris to discuss with de Gaulle the stalled plans for a European political confederation on July 3, 1962. In their two-hour conversation, the eighty-six-year-old German leader pressed hard for a resurrection of the movement toward the integration of West Germany with France and the rest of Europe for one overriding reason: to avoid a return to policies of the Rapallo Treaty of 1922 and the Molotov-Ribbentrop Treaty of 1939 whereby Germany tied its fortunes to the Soviet Union. At their dinner that evening, both leaders exchanged toasts celebrating the Franco-German relationship as the nucleus of the European political entity that had met so many roadblocks put in place by the other EEC members. Adenauer made it clear that he was anxious to witness significant progress toward the coordination of foreign and defense policies between the two governments. De Gaulle listened respectfully as the German chancellor insisted on the centrality of the Atlantic alliance to the security of Western Europe and the hope that Great Britain could be included in the West European grouping.[80] But the first seeds were sown for what would later become a bilateral relationship between the two countries.

In the meantime, President John F. Kennedy had developed a complex program for the future relations between the United States and the Common Market. On the Fourth of July, 1962, Kennedy delivered a speech in Philadelphia's Independence Hall, where the Declaration of Independence had been signed in 1776, calling for a declaration of interdependence between the United States and the emerging European Economic Community, which he hoped Great Britain would soon join.

The very same day as Kennedy's speech, de Gaulle and Adenauer met in Paris and made progress on their plan, first adumbrated two years earlier at

Rambouillet, for a tightening of ties between Paris and Bonn. The French leader worked hard to convince the West German chancellor that he should fear U.S. disengagement from Europe more than France's disengagement from the Alliance's integrated command and affirmed that France could be relied on to come to the defense of its eastern neighbor in case of war. In September 1962, de Gaulle toured West Germany in an energetic bid to woo German public opinion. It was clear that the French leader had completely abandoned his earlier hard-line position vis-à-vis Germany, when (as we have seen) he had called for the separation of the Ruhr and the Rhineland from Germany, and was eagerly seeking a rapprochement with France's historic adversary.[81] The motivation for this volte face was evident: to court Bonn in order to lay the groundwork for a privileged bilateral relationship between the continent's two most powerful countries that would become the nucleus of a Europe independent of Washington.[82] So much for Kennedy's speech on transatlantic interdependence that formed the basis of his proposed "Grand Design."

De Gaulle knew full well that Ambassador James Gavin's departure from the Paris embassy in the fall of 1962 was due in part to Gavin's strong advocacy of France's independent nuclear force in the making. The ambassador had sent a sharply worded letter to McGeorge Bundy in the summer of 1961 decrying the American policy of refusing to assist the French nuclear program. "The French cannot understand why we tell them to stand firm on Berlin," he observed, while we deny them help with their nuclear program.[83] Before the visit of French minister of defense Pierre Messmer to meet with McNamara in the Pentagon in the late fall of 1961, Gavin had written directly to Kennedy urging him to release funds for the French program. He reported that the French government had invested heavily in a gaseous diffusion plant for the production of Uranium 232, which the United States sold to Great Britain at a huge cost. John McCone had told Gavin that when he was chairman of the Atomic Energy Commission, Eisenhower's entire cabinet save Secretary of State Christian Herter had favored the sale of U-232 to France, but that the president vetoed it in deference to his secretary of state. Gavin informed Kennedy that both he and McCone firmly believed that he should have approved the sale. Bundy replied in the negative a few days later, as did Rusk after clearing it with the president.[84]

Gavin had followed up this admonition in the spring of 1962, after meeting with Kennedy in Washington, with a plea that the United States take a close look at France's nuclear program by the test of "substantial progress" in our Atomic Energy Act (implying that such progress justified American nuclear assistance to France).[85] On April 16, Kennedy assembled a group of his top advisers in the Oval Office to sort out the contrasting opinions about whether his government should assist France's emerging nuclear program. Secretary of State Rusk represented the opposition to such assistance, while Defense Secretary McNamara spoke for the Pentagon in supporting such aid. Rusk repeated the familiar warning that if Washington provided Paris with nuclear support, the West Germans would wonder why they should not receive the same consideration. He added that to do so would give "signal to the world that America accepts the proliferation of nuclear weapons." Mc-Namara's rejoinder was simple and straightforward: with or without American aid, France would develop its *force de frappe*.[86]

In the meantime, Kennedy had become alarmed at newspaper articles by eminent journalists criticizing Washington's refusal to accommodate France's nuclear needs. On May 7, the esteemed *New York Times* journalist Cyrus Sulzberger, the American reporter who would interview de Gaulle more times than any other American newsman, lamented that "French-American relations are at a low ebb and nothing is being done to improve them." Two days later Joseph Alsop decried the "ugly relationship" between Washington and Paris. Undersecretary of State George Ball sent a sharp message to Gavin expressing Kennedy's "deep concern" about the two articles.[87]

On May 11, 1962, French cultural minister André Malraux arrived at the White House for a carefully planned meeting with Kennedy amid the former's goodwill trip to the United States. As noted above, Malraux had been taken by Kennedy and especially his Francophone and Francophile wife during the president's visit to Paris in the spring of 1961. In the morning the president's wife accompanied the French guest on a tour of the National Gallery of Art. Jackie Kennedy described Malraux, who had written about art; had participated in the Spanish Civil War, the Chinese Revolution, and the French Resistance; and had written such memorable novels as *La Condition humaine* (*Man's Fate*) as "a veritable Renaissance man."[88]

At the Malraux-Kennedy meeting, the president unburdened himself about his frustrations with de Gaulle and the state of Franco-American relations, issuing some controversial statements in the presence of Ambassador Alphand and McGeorge Bundy, the latter of whom took copious notes. Kennedy launched into a broadside about de Gaulle's suspicion that the United States intended to dominate Western Europe through its control of NATO. "General de Gaulle should make no mistake: Americans would be glad to get out of Europe," he declared, recalling that Eisenhower had recommended to the president-elect, just before leaving office, the removal of two-thirds of the U.S. divisions on the continent. Knowing that the French emissary and the French ambassador would repeat the essence of their conversation to de

Gaulle, JFK again declared that the United States would be perfectly willing to bring the GIs home "if that was what the Europeans wanted." He bluntly reminded Malraux that the U.S. tradition had historically been "fundamentally isolationist." But since World War II, "we have carried heavy burdens" that have been a drain on the country's balance of payments. "If it is desired that we should cease to carry the load in Europe, nothing could be better from our point of view."[89]

A New American Ambassador in Paris

"Jumpin' Jim" Gavin would be replaced by the experienced diplomat Charles F. Bohlen, known by his friends as Chip, on October 27, 1962. Bohlen had served in the Moscow embassy before World War II and acquired fluency in the Russian language, which enabled him to serve as Roosevelt's translator at the Yalta Conference from which de Gaulle had been excluded and which he constantly blamed for the postwar division of Europe. He became the State Department's chief Soviet specialist during the war before being named ambassador to the Soviet Union in 1953 and then to the Philippines during the Eisenhower administration. A close confidant of Kennedy, a longtime friend of French foreign minister Couve de Murville, and fluent in French, Chip Bohlen seemed an ideal choice to represent the United States in France. When Kennedy informed de Gaulle on July 26 that Gavin would be retiring soon and solicited the French president's approval of Bohlen as his successor, de Gaulle replied that he had no objection whatsoever to the appointment.[90] Kennedy's special adviser Arthur Schlesinger had earlier relayed the observation from *New York Times* correspondent Cyrus Sulzberger, "who has probably seen more of de Gaulle than any other living American," that the French president considered Bohlen the only American diplomat he really liked.[91]

But de Gaulle would have had good reason to be apprehensive about the appointment of a man who had served as Roosevelt's interpreter at Yalta.[92] He would have been even more concerned about the new American envoy had he known that Bohlen had described de Gaulle to Roosevelt as "one of the biggest sons of bitches who had ever straddled a pot." In any case, Bohlen expressed to an old friend an attitude of resignation at taking up his post: "I know there is not much I can do to deflect the current course of French policy, but at the least I shall do my best to try and minimize the consequences and live with it."[93] Bohlen would serve for almost six years in the Paris embassy and meet with the French president thirty-five times. In his memoirs, Couve de Murville lavished praise on Bohlen as "best intentioned and the most efficacious interlocutor during this entire difficult period."[94]

De Gaulle and the Missiles of October:
Support but Resentment

The eruption of the Cuban missile crisis in October 1962 interrupted de Gaulle's mounting criticism of American foreign policy. When push came to shove, the French leader demonstrated that he could be counted on to support the United States in its Cold War rivalry with the Kremlin. At the height of the crisis, Kennedy dispatched former secretary of state Dean Acheson on November 22—just before Kennedy's public announcement of a naval "quarantine" around the Caribbean island—to brief de Gaulle on the U-2 photographic evidence of the missile sites and to secure France's support in the impending high-level showdown with Khrushchev. The French president immediately asked the envoy, who had been escorted to the Elysée through a side door to preserve secrecy, if he had come to inform or consult him, to which Acheson bluntly replied "to inform you." De Gaulle interrupted Acheson's presentation with the remark that France would be at America's side if there were a war and at first declined to look at the photographic evidence. He expressed his utmost confidence that "a great nation like yours would not act if there were any doubt about the evidence." After assuring Acheson of unconditional French support, he glanced at the photos. He could not resist concluding the conversation with the acerbic declaration, "I must note that I have been advised, but not consulted."[95] When Bohlen, who was on an ocean liner headed for France when Kennedy gave his televised speech about the Cuban missiles, presented his credentials to de Gaulle at the Elysée, the French president repeated his solemn assurances to Acheson that France would be at the side of the United States in the event of war.[96]

The lesson that Kennedy, and much of the world, drew from the Cuban missile crisis was that the United States, with the total support of its NATO allies, was fully capable of deterring the Soviet Union from embarking on aggressive adventurism. He also concluded that, contrary to de Gaulle's oft-stated opposition, the power to deter was best centralized in the hands of the American president with full control of the decision-making process without having to worry about time-consuming consultation with allies. De Gaulle drew the opposite conclusion: the United States was capable of dragging his European allies into a war with the Soviet Union over issues—such as the deployment of Soviet missiles in Cuba—that (in his judgment) were peripheral to the interests of France and Europe.[97]

This apprehension was reinforced by what the French president regarded as Washington's increasingly dangerous involvement in Southeast Asia that might lead to a nuclear showdown with Moscow over another region far from Europe. The only alternative, in de Gaulle's eyes, was to construct a French-led West European defense capability that was separate from the United States. Also, Khrushchev's retreat in October ushered in the possibility of seeking a reduction of tensions in Europe that would enhance the possibility of freeing the continent from the dual embrace of the United States and the Soviet Union. But the bilateral negotiations between Washington and Moscow that resolved the crisis raised the specter of something that de Gaulle abhorred: the prospect of the two superpowers addressing critical issues over the heads of the Europeans and possibly to their determent.

In his July 4, 1962, speech in Philadelphia, as part of his call for a declaration of transatlantic interdependence, Kennedy had revived a bold plan that would, as we shall see, raise the hackles of de Gaulle in the following several years. First adumbrated by the Eisenhower administration, it proposed the upgrading of the Western alliance's nuclear deterrent by means of a "multilateral nuclear force (MLF)" in which NATO countries would participate as equals for the first time. In a long meeting with Couve de Murville on May 23, 1963, Kennedy explained to the French foreign minister his concern that France's deployment of nuclear weapons independently might serve as a pretext for West Germany to join the nuclear club as well. Couve had to concede that "it is possible that we are setting a bad example for the Germans."[98]

The next month in his commencement address at American University, Kennedy called for a partial nuclear test ban treaty that would prohibit testing in the atmosphere as a first step. The president hoped to inaugurate a process of strategic arms control negotiations that would reduce the risks of an all-out nuclear war that the world had come close to in the autumn of 1962. De Gaulle firmly opposed both proposals, which struck him as a ploy for tightening American control of NATO's nuclear deterrent while leaving open the possibility of direct negotiations between Washington and Moscow that would leave Europe in the lurch. He also thought the two proposals were directed against France's efforts to develop a credible nuclear deterrent independent of the United States.

Washington, Paris, London, and the Common Market

The issue of Great Britain's relationship with the European continent would become a major point of contention between de Gaulle and British prime minister Harold Macmillan. As we have seen, the two men had first met during the Second World War in North Africa, where Macmillan had been sent by Churchill to become the British minister resident in Algiers. While

there he became a strong supporter of de Gaulle and his Free French movement, while his American counterpart, Robert Murphy, tended to support
the Vichy officials in the region.

In 1951 Great Britain had declined to join the European Coal and Steel
Community that had been masterminded by the Frenchman Jean Monnet
and subsequently refused to be a part of the negotiations that resulted in
the signing of the Treaty of Rome in March 25, 1957, that established the
European Economic Community (EEC). Often referred to as the Common
Market, the EEC officially came into existence on January 1, 1958, only
five months before de Gaulle took power in France. In retirement he had
opposed French membership in the European Coal and Steel Community
(ECSC) for the same reason that he bristled at France's subordinate role in
NATO: *military* integration in NATO and *economic* integration in the ECSC
both encroached on French sovereignty and independence. After the Treaty
of Rome was approved, the British set up a rival group of the "outer seven"
(Austria, Britain, Denmark, Norway, Portugal, Sweden, and Switzerland),
called the European Free Trade Association, which promoted economic cooperation without the encroachments on national sovereignty in the Treaty
of Rome. Europe, as wags liked to put it, was at sixes and sevens.

In the summer of 1961, Harold Macmillan, who had succeeded Anthony
Eden as British prime minister in 1957 after the Suez fiasco the previous year,
recognized that Britain had, as he put it, "missed the bus" that was leading
the six members of the Common Market to greater productivity and prosperity. On July 31, he formally submitted Britain's application for membership
in the European Economic Community, breaking with the tradition of aloof-
ness toward the continent since the end of the Second World War. To be
precise, the British application was simply a request for discussions with the
six members of the EEC to explore the possibility of obtaining terms that
would be advantageous enough for him to sell the option of membership
to his Conservative Party and to the British public. Macmillan's accurate
comments that the British request had the full support of the Kennedy
administration were like pouring oil on the fire of de Gaulle's suspicions of
Anglo-Saxon conspiracies.[99] Indeed, Washington was increasingly curious
about de Gaulle's attitude toward the British candidacy. When Ambassador
Gavin had met with the French president on February 20, 1962, he was told
that the discussion "will be very delicate and will take a long time," adding
that the EEC "does not want the [British] Commonwealth in Europe."[100]

Faced with political opposition from the Labour Party but also within his
own Conservative party to joining Europe, Macmillan sought de Gaulle's assistance in navigating this treacherous political terrain. He underestimated

de Gaulle's deeply felt hostility to Great Britain and his equally strong belief that France could and should preside over a non-Communist Europe apart from the two Anglo-Saxon powers. In the course of the next fifteen months of tortuous negotiations, Macmillan was obliged to drive a hard bargain on all manner of issues in order to curry favor with his domestic opposition. This strategy merely confirmed de Gaulle's belief that the island kingdom did not belong in a continental bloc. Even before the British application was being considered, de Gaulle made it clear where he stood on the issue. During a visit to Bonn on May 20, 1961, de Gaulle had warned Adenauer and his foreign minister Heinrich von Brentano that "England was not cut from the same wood as France and Germany" and that it "was and remained an island," while those two countries were located on the Continent.[101]

Nevertheless, the British and French leaders met three times as the accession negotiations droned on in Brussels: at Macmillan's home in Sussex in November 1961; at the Château des Champs outside Paris in June 1962; and at a final stormy encounter at the Château de Rambouillet on December 15–16, 1962, in which de Gaulle lectured his British guest about the need for patience while the French president pondered the consequences of France's losing its preeminent place among the Six by allowing Britain into the club.[102] During the Rambouillet conversation, the two men discussed Macmillan's forthcoming trip to the Bahamas to discuss an unrelated American proposal to provide Britain with Polaris nuclear missiles to upgrade its nuclear deterrent. De Gaulle offered no objection to this projected "Anglo-Saxon" arrangement and included a vague but totally unserious suggestion that Britain and France—the only two members of the nuclear club in Western Europe—might combine their two forces.[103]

Macmillan met with Kennedy from December 28 to 31, 1962, amid the warmth of the British Caribbean island of Nassau. The topic of conversation was how to upgrade the British nuclear delivery system, the so-called V bombers, which had been rendered obsolete by advances in Soviet air defenses. Privately, Kennedy believed that the British nuclear deterrent was seriously deficient. The American president had already irritated the British by canceling for cost reasons a joint project for an airborne missile called Skybolt, which had been promised to them in 1960. Kennedy worried that if he didn't give the British something, they might be tempted to sign up with the French. So he agreed to deliver Polaris submarine-launched ballistic missiles (SLBM) to Britain as replacements for the Skybolt. But Kennedy imposed two conditions on the deal: Britain would have to pledge that the submarines would be assigned to NATO and to agree to join the vague American project for a multilateral nuclear force (MLF) for the European members of NATO that had been a topic of discussion for years. These two conditions were designed to ensure the centralized command and control of nuclear weapons that Kennedy and his secretary of defense, Robert McNamara, deemed essential. Macmillan reluctantly agreed to both of the conditions, in spite of his personal skepticism about the MLF, which he thought was full of ambiguities.[104]

Kennedy worried that when news of the Nassau agreement reached Paris, de Gaulle might demand American assistance to France's developing independent nuclear striking force. So he told Macmillan that he planned to make the same offer to France. American Polaris missiles would be provided to French submarines if France promised to assign its nuclear forces to NATO. Kennedy hoped that this offer would lure de Gaulle back into the NATO fold. On the last day of the conference, December 10, Kennedy wrote de Gaulle about his intention to extend the offer of Polaris missiles to France. In a separate letter dispatched on the same day, Macmillan assured the French president that the Nassau Accord had preserved the independence of the British nuclear deterrent, implying that the same would be true of the *force de frappe*. Kennedy officially extended the offer to de Gaulle through diplomatic channels on December 21. Foreign minister Couve de Murville acknowledged receipt of the message and replied that de Gaulle would study it carefully.[105]

Bohlen and Rusk had been working on a plan for de Gaulle to visit the United States for months, with the idea of Palm Beach, Florida, as the ideal venue away from the glare of publicity in Washington. It now seemed opportune for such a visit so that Kennedy could inform the French president in person what had transpired between him and Macmillan in Nassau. But before any headway could be made in that project, Bundy alerted Kennedy to a simmering dispute within the administration between McNamara at the Pentagon (who favored a prompt arrangement with France on nuclear matters) and the "multilateralists" in the State Department led by Ball who opposed cooperation with France on the Nassau model.[106]

As we have seen, Chip Bohlen had arrived in France on October 24, 1962, and presented his credentials to de Gaulle three days later at the height of the Cuban missile crisis. He was able to keep the French president fully informed about the negotiations that led to solution to the crisis in the Caribbean. Despite de Gaulle's assurances of support for Washington during the Cuban affair, Kennedy was anxious about what he saw as de Gaulle's systematic body blows to the United States and wondered if he intended to drive the U.S. out of Europe. Bohlen denied that that was de Gaulle's intention but admitted that the Europeans had good reason to anticipate an

American disengagement from Europe, which he characterized as inevitable in the long run.[107]

Officials in Paris did not conceal their disdain for the Nassau Accord. Couve de Murville remarked to the American chargé d'affaires before Bohlen's arrival that the agreement was a bad omen for Macmillan's application for membership in the Common Market because it proved that Britain "had not yet decided that she really wanted to be European." Bohlen had been briefed on the proposal by Kennedy in Palm Beach and instructed to discuss the offer with de Gaulle, which would be his first significant meeting with the French president since taking his post. After Bohlen filled in the details of the project to de Gaulle in early January 1963, the French president assured him that he would not be hasty in his reply and would give the offer serious consideration, which prompted Bohlen to report to Washington that there was a fifty-fifty chance that it would be accepted.[108]

But de Gaulle had already made up his mind and was totally noncommittal in his response to the American ambassador. He then held a news conference—one of two that he customarily allowed in each year—on January 14, 1963, coincidently on the same day Kennedy delivered his State of the Union address at the Capitol in Washington. De Gaulle planted the questions with the reporters and carefully prepared his response to them. The televised press conference revealed that he had decided to deliver two knockout blows to his Anglo-Saxon allies. Kennedy naively assumed that his olive branch to de Gaulle with the offer of Polaris would resolve the Franco-American dispute and cement the unity of the Alliance. Before addressing the nuclear issue, the French president brought up Britain's application for admission to the EEC. "England is insular, maritime, linked through its trade, markets, and food supplies to very diverse and often distant countries," he observed. "Its activities are essentially industrial and commercial and only slightly agricultural. . . . In short, the nature and structure and economic context of England differ profoundly from those of other states on the continent." If Britain were to join the EEC, he continued, the existing six member states would lose their cohesion and "in the end would appear a colossal Atlantic Community under American dependence and leadership which would soon completely swallow up the European Community." He called for the preservation of a "strictly European construction" and allowed that if, someday, the United Kingdom would accept membership with the EEC "without restrictions and without reservation," he could imagine France welcoming her in the future. But since "England is not yet prepared to do this," that day would have to be postponed.[109]

De Gaulle then turned to the American offer to provide France with Polaris missiles that had been discussed at Nassau. He noted American displeasure at the French decision to build an independent nuclear deterrent. "In politics and in strategy, as in the economy," he observed, "monopoly quite naturally appears to the person who holds it to be the best possible system." And in response to the Kennedy administration's claim that the fledgling French *force de frappe* was and always would be too small to deter potential aggressors, he summarized the doctrine of proportional deterrence that had been developed by his nuclear strategists, particularly General Pierre Gallois. As Gallois bluntly put it: "Making the most pessimistic assumptions, the French nuclear bombers could destroy ten Russian cities; and France is not a prize worthy of ten Russian cities."[110]

General Gallois later confessed to second thoughts about the effectiveness of the *force de frappe* when he visited the American embassy in a mood of "urgency and gloom" to plead for American nuclear assistance through an amendment of the McMahon Act. He described the French nuclear arsenal as "truly a mirage not a reality," noting that a Soviet preemptive strike could easily wipe out the twenty-five airbases where the French jets were located. He also remarked that the planned land-based missiles (IRBMs) would be armed with a "very heavy" warhead and a "quite primitive guidance system."[111] But de Gaulle had none of these second thoughts about the deterrent power of the planned *force de frappe*. He rejected the part of the Nassau Accords proposing an MLF. It would introduce complications that would prevent the immediate use of nuclear weapons that, de Gaulle believed, was essential for deterrence.[112] In short, by keeping Britain out of the EEC, he guaranteed that France remained the only power in the organization with an independent nuclear force.[113]

Two weeks after the explosive press conference, Ambassador Alphand visited McGeorge Bundy to try to smooth the ruffled feathers in Washington. He complained that the American press was overemphasizing the points of difference between the two governments and ignoring the "olive branches" included in de Gaulle's speech. The American national security adviser unleashed a torrent of recrimination against the French president in the presence of the shocked French ambassador. Bundy claimed that he had read de Gaulle's memoirs and other writings and concluded that he favored transforming Europe into a Third Force under French leadership, a sort of arbiter between the Anglo-Saxons and the Soviets that would seek to "eliminate the American presence from Europe." He ended with a not-so-veiled threat, declaring that "if French diplomacy should seek an American withdrawal of this sort, it would be foolhardy to suppose" that the guarantees of Article 5 of the North Atlantic Treaty could remain reliably in force.[114]

It is astonishing that officials in the White House, the State Department, and the Pentagon were so entirely caught off guard by de Gaulle's press conference. Even the exceedingly well informed Ambassador Bohlen professed to be "shocked" by the event.[115] The chargé d'affaires in the American embassy in Paris reported on December 24 that Couve de Murville had emphasized that France at present lacked the submarines, would probably be unable to miniaturize the warheads for the missiles, and could not obtain the necessary uranium to accommodate the Polaris.[116]

Two weeks later Couve de Murville went to Brussels to declare that the stalled negotiations with Britain for membership were pointless and should be suspended. A furious Macmillan recorded in his diary that "De Gaulle is trying to *dominate* Europe. His idea is not a partnership, but a Napoleonic or a Louis XIV hegemony."[117] Secretary of State Rusk was convinced that de Gaulle's veto of Britain's application to the Common Market after the Kennedy-Macmillan meeting in the Bahamas was disingenuous. "Nassau was only an excuse," he wrote in his memoirs. "De Gaulle's agenda aimed at establishing a European continental system led by France." Rusk later expressed a view that would seem to validate de Gaulle's dark suspicions of American policy toward the EEC: "We hoped that if Britain had joined the Common Market, it would take into Europe that special relationship with the United States," he recalled. "Perhaps our special relationship could be extended into Europe itself. We were rather miffed, therefore, when President de Gaulle used that special relationship as an excuse for vetoing British membership."[118]

De Gaulle's "double no" in his January 14 press conference destroyed Kennedy's Grand Design for transatlantic relations and dramatically signaled France's refusal to accept the two major components of American defense policy—flexible response and the multilateral nuclear force. Although the former would become official NATO policy during de Gaulle's term in office, the latter would die a slow death in 1963–64, as we will see. The French veto—the first in 1963 and a second one in 1967—kept Britain out of the Common Market for the rest of de Gaulle's presidency. Ambassador Bohlen interpreted the stunning move as nothing less than a "declaration of independence of revitalized France and rejection of 'Anglo-Saxon' political, economic, and military domination."[119] Kennedy complained that "De Gaulle is cooperating with us in none of our policies and might attempt to run us out of Europe by means of a deal with the Russians."[120]

In mid-February Bohlen responded to Kennedy's plaintive question: did de Gaulle really plan to remove American presence from Europe? The ambassador responded with a thoughtful assessment of the French president's goals, which he said were rooted in his unswerving belief that "the only permanent unit in international affairs is the nation." This opposition to supra-nationalism explained de Gaulle's opposition to military integration in NATO as well as his resolute insistence that the EEC be "a union of states." As for the MLF, Bohlen predicted total opposition from France. He reported that the "big question" was whether de Gaulle envisaged "a coordinated European economic capability of which his *force de frappe* would be the 'nucleus' or whether it would remain under exclusive French control."[121]

A Paris-Bonn Axis as an Alternative to Atlanticism

With these blows against "a colossal Atlantic Community under U.S. dependence and leadership that would soon completely swallow up the European Community," the French president turned his attention to the next item on his agenda: the solidification of the bilateral alliance between France and West Germany as a means of providing Europe with an alternative to Atlanticism. As we have seen, de Gaulle had pressed for the detachment of the Ruhr and the Rhineland from what would become West Germany before resigning in January 1946. He had confided to Dulles at their first meeting after de Gaulle's return to power on July 5, 1958, that he had originally preferred a "confederal state composed of several states," but added quickly that the current partition of Germany into two states "did not bother him."[122]

De Gaulle reinforced his bid for military independence from the United States with attempts to achieve political independence from the transatlantic superpower as well. He attempted to loosen the ties between West Germany and the United States while improving France's relations with the Communist world. On January 22, 1963, a week after de Gaulle's "double no" to Kennedy and Macmillan, the French president invited West German chancellor Konrad Adenauer to the Elysée Palace, where the two concluded a Franco-German friendship treaty (called thereafter the Elysée Treaty), which de Gaulle hoped would evolve into the nucleus of a reinvigorated Western Europe freed from what he regarded as Washington's domination of Western Europe. Since France enjoyed national unity and membership in the nuclear club whereas West Germany lacked both of these advantages, de Gaulle assumed that his country would be the senior partner in the projected Paris-Bonn Axis. The bilateral treaty stipulated that representatives of the two governments would meet at regular intervals and that the two governments would consult each other prior to any decision on all important questions of foreign policy.[123]

The Kennedy administration was anxious about the long-term consequences of this bilateral agreement. The president had first expressed his
concern about rumors of such an understanding between these two American allies in the spring of 1962, long before it was in the works.[124] George
Ball expressed the fear that it might expand into a Paris-Bonn-Moscow axis
that would reshape the geopolitical situation on the continent, leading to a
Soviet withdrawal from East Germany and a confederation between the two
Germanys that would lead to "the end of NATO and the neutralization of
Germany."[125] Despite his visceral antipathy to the French president, the undersecretary of state counseled an attitude of "impeccable politeness without
indulgence in recrimination or threats, while making clear the basic contrast
between our goals and those of de Gaulle."[126]

Washington staged what in basketball is called a "full-court press" to
weaken the provisions of the bilateral treaty (which made no mention of
NATO) by appealing to the West Germans. The effect of this U.S. diplomatic offensive was to force Adenauer to pull back from his enthusiastic and
unconditional advocacy of the treaty. He was compelled to accept a preamble to the treaty in the Bundestag on May 16, when the German parliament
ratified the treaty. The preamble was a painful blow to de Gaulle's policy of
separating Washington and Bonn. It stipulated that the Federal Republic
was totally committed to the common defense "within the framework of the
Atlantic Alliance" and, as a final blast at the French president, pressed for
the unification of Europe "by admitting Great Britain into it." Kennedy's trip
to West Berlin on June 23–26, during which he delivered his famous "Ich
bin ein Berliner" speech to a deliriously appreciative audience, was part of
the president's campaign to lure the West Germans away from the French.
He had snubbed de Gaulle by avoiding a stop in Paris on his way to the
beleaguered German city.[127] In any case, the French president worried that
Kennedy might make concessions on the subject of East Berlin to preserve
the status quo in West Berlin.[128]

In the autumn of 1963, Washington short-circuited the Elysée Treaty,
which had included a provision for Franco-German arms cooperation, with
agreements with the West Germans for the co-production of tanks and other
military hardware.[129] After Couve de Murville traveled to Washington and
complained to Rusk on October 7 that Kennedy was obliging Bonn to choose
between the United States and France, the president himself later in the
day shot back to the French foreign minister at the White House that the
bilateral treaty seemed to be more than "the healing of old wounds" but was
"outside of, and directed at, NATO." Kennedy acknowledged the oft-stated
French belief that the danger of war with the Eastern bloc in Europe had

declined significantly, but he asserted that it was very difficult to reduce U.S. forces on the continent "because of German nervousness."[130]

The De Gaulle Visit to Washington that Never Happened

In early 1963, de Gaulle had rebuffed Kennedy's attempt to lure him into a trip to Washington to hash out their differences, declaring that such a visit would produce no results.[131] The French president belatedly and reluctantly agreed to visit the United States despite his concern that the visit "would attract much publicity without the possibility of accomplishing anything, and would thus lead to serious repercussions for both of them."[132] But the matter dragged on for months. In mid-June 1963, Rusk informed Bohlen that Kennedy would like to see de Gaulle before the end of the year to press him to agree to terminate French nuclear testing in the atmosphere.[133] With the Americans pressing for a meeting between the two leaders, the French requested that the announcement be held up. With the president's approval, Ball instructed Bohlen in late September to inform de Gaulle that Kennedy "does indeed expect the General early in 1964."[134] As it turned out, the French president did visit Kennedy later in the month, but only to pay his last respects to his coffin.

~

CHAPTER NINE

Johnson and de Gaulle, 1963–1968

Distant Antagonists

Lyndon B. Johnson had been the master of the U.S. Senate, where he served as majority leader in the 1950s before being picked by Kennedy as his running mate in 1960, primarily to assure that his home state of Texas would vote Democratic. His focus had always been on domestic affairs, a preoccupation that would lead to such landmark institutions as Medicare (health insurance for the elderly) in 1965, the Civil Rights Act of 1964, and the Voting Rights Act of 1965, which set in motion the gradual improvement of the situation of America's African American citizens. In many ways his so-called Great Society was a continuation of the path-breaking domestic reforms initiated by Franklin Roosevelt's New Deal. But he knew little about foreign affairs and had not evinced a strong interest in the world outside. His biographer Eric Goldman cited LBJ's caustic remark that "foreigners are not like the folks I am used to."[1] On the other hand, George Ball notes in his memoir that Johnson had excellent relations with West German chancellor Ludwig Erhard, in part because the LBJ ranch in Texas along the Pedernales River was in the midst of a German American community.[2]

The first time that Lyndon B. Johnson met Charles de Gaulle was at the funeral for the slain Kennedy in November 1963. The Kennedy assassination had prompted an outpouring of grief in France and throughout the world. De Gaulle confided to a friend, "I am stunned. People are crying all over France. It was if he were a Frenchman, a member of their own family."[3] Ambassador Bohlen recalled that the French president did not commit to attending the funeral in Washington until he learned that other allied leaders had announced their intention to do so.[4] Once he decided to make the trip, Rusk met him at the airport and thanked him for coming. De Gaulle replied, "Don't thank me. The little people of France demanded that I come."[5]

The American secretary of state recalled urging that de Gaulle be driven to the funeral service in light of the threats to his personal safety in France and the many assassination attempts against him. The French president adamantly refused, announcing that "I shall walk with Mrs. Kennedy."[6] The scene of the six-feet-four-inch French president resplendent in full military regalia next to the diminutive emperor of Ethiopia, Haile Selassie, walking down Pennsylvania Avenue from the Capitol—where the body had lain in state—toward the White House and then to Saint Matthew's Cathedral was perhaps the most memorable photographic image of the solemn event.

During their brief encounter in Rusk's office in the State Department, the new American president remarked to de Gaulle that "we may have some problems" but expressed the optimistic faith that "we will find a solution to them." He added that de Gaulle's staunch support for the United States during the Cuban missile crisis had "proved that France would stand by the U.S." in an international crisis. Johnson expressed the hope that the French president could visit the United States the following February, a statement he repeated to de Gaulle on the way to the elevator in the State Department.[7] When de Gaulle responded evasively, Johnson later announced to the press that the general had accepted the invitation. "The first misunderstanding to clear up," Ambassador Alphand noted in his diary.[8] The state visit never would take place. The two men would meet only one more time, briefly, at Adenauer's funeral in 1967.

In his summary of his impressions of President de Gaulle after having served in Paris for one year, which he asked Secretary Rusk to pass on to President Johnson, Ambassador Bohlen attempted to strike a balance. On the psychological level, he asserted that the French president was "egocentric . . . with touches of megalomania" and relished the multitudinous conflicts between his government and Washington. On the positive side, he believed that de Gaulle did not wish the United States to withdraw its military forces from Western Europe and had shown "no sign of any concerted move to push us out."[9]

But the era of good feeling would not last very long. In his New Year's Day press conference on January 1, 1964, de Gaulle spoke out forcefully against American policy in Vietnam. A few days later, National Security Adviser McGeorge Bundy warned that any effort to work with de Gaulle would "inevitably stir talk of neutralization at the wrong time." He cautioned that any move to neutralize South Vietnam would lead to the toppling dominoes that Eisenhower had warned about in the 1950s. Malaysia would be next, followed by "a shift toward neutrality in Japan and the Philippines."[10] De Gaulle's ambassador to Washington asked the French president if he was eager to invite the new American president to confer with him in Paris about the multitude of issues responsible for the sorry state of Franco-American relations, including Vietnam and the French attitude toward the Atlantic alliance. De Gaulle responded defiantly: "Let him come! We will be happy to welcome him, but our choice has been made. In no case will we accept . . . any arrangement that would put our atomic force under American control. If such a project sees the light of day, that will give us a perfect occasion to withdraw from NATO."[11]

The next month Bohlen reported that the French press was full of stories about "the stubborn and bumbling Americans slowly being forced to acknowledge French clairvoyance" on the subject of Vietnam.[12] Johnson became agitated by information sent from Saigon by American ambassador Henry Cabot Lodge about "reports of intrigue by French agents" in South Vietnam against American interests. Lodge, who had been Nixon's vice presidential candidate in the 1960 presidential election, provided the Democratic president with some political cover for his policies in Southeast Asia. He was also, in the terminology of the day, a "hawk," advocating bringing the war to North Vietnam.[13] He complained bitterly about the French president's persistent campaign for neutralization of all Southeast Asia at a time when South Vietnam was experiencing great political instability.[14] When told by South Vietnamese leaders that de Gaulle's proposals were undermining morale, Lodge allayed their concerns with the remark that "De Gaulle had no real chips to play in SEA [Southeast Asia]—neither men, nor arms, nor money of any significance" and that "if anyone wanted to play in this poker game, one had to buy a seat at the table."[15]

The ambassador in Saigon urged the State Department to protest directly to de Gaulle that French money and agents were subverting the Saigon government, adding that "it is well for him to know that we know what is going on, and that we suspect a secret agreement between him and the Chicoms [familiar shorthand for the People's Republic of China]. We should give him a sense of pressure."[16] At a press conference on February 1, Johnson was asked if he ruled out the possibility of neutralization in Vietnam as de Gaulle had proposed. He replied he could "consider sympathetically" a proposal for the neutralization of both North and South Vietnam. When pressed to explain how his willingness to accept neutralization of both Vietnams differed from the proposal from the French president, he erroneously responded that de Gaulle's recommendation applied only to South Vietnam. When the French press called attention to this mistake, the Public Affairs Bureau of the State Department asked the White House for clarification but got only a statement that de Gaulle's proposal was ambiguous and lacking in specific details.[17]

An exasperated Johnson bluntly asked Ambassador Bohlen for suggestions for how to deal with the recalcitrant de Gaulle on the issue.[18] The ambassador replied that it would be impossible to pin down the French president on his views of how the Vietnam problem could be solved because he relishes "ambiguity" and has "no plan" for solving the issue. Bohlen speculated that de Gaulle's ultimate goal would be to get Washington to run to him for advice, giving him the satisfaction of demonstrating his success "in forcing the U.S., as it were to throw itself on his mercy."[19]

Johnson would not let the matter rest. He suggested that Lodge himself travel to Paris and sound out de Gaulle, a proposal that the ambassador to Saigon politely sidestepped on the grounds that if the South Vietnamese government got wind of the mission, it might conclude that the United States was about to "sell them down the river," which would be "a body blow to morale."[20] Lodge lamented that "France and the United States are headed for a collision course" on Vietnam because so many highly placed officials in the Khanh government in Saigon with whom he had spoken "sincerely believe that General de Gaulle wishes the destruction of the Republic of Vietnam" and that "French agents have worked with the Viet Cong in recent terrorism against Americans."[21]

A furious Johnson instructed Bohlen to meet with de Gaulle and let him know that "we expect France, as an ally, to adopt an attitude of cooperation rather than obstruction in this critical area of United States interest."[22] When the ambassador finally secured an appointment with the French president on April 2, he was confronted with the restatement of de Gaulle's earlier warning that "we could not possibly succeed in the course that we were on," which would "merely repeat the experience that the French had earlier." He added that "the quicker we came out for neutralization in Vietnam, possibly through the mechanism of a Geneva-type conference including the Chinese, the better it would be." A disappointed Bohlen cut short the interview with the remark that "there would be a considerable degree of disappointment in Washington" over his position on this matter.[23]

Johnson finally decided to make one last effort to bring the French president around to Washington's point of view on Vietnam by dispatching Under-Secretary of State George Ball to engage in a spirited discussion with de Gaulle on the matter during a trip to Paris in early June. Johnson had instructed him to inform the French president that "we must depend on you in Southeast Asia as we did in the Cuban Missile Crisis." The American special envoy should also ask him for "any new blueprint" for ending the conflict he had in mind as well as "clarification" of his oft-repeated suggestions for negotiation.[24] Before Ball's departure for France, he had attended a discussion among Secretary of Defense McNamara, National Security Adviser McGeorge Bundy, and the renowned journalist Walter Lippmann, which Johnson briefly attended. Lippmann issued a passionate plea for neutralization along the same lines advocated by de Gaulle, without mentioning him by name.[25]

In his meeting with de Gaulle in Paris on June 5, Ball was treated to a repetition of the French president's claim that the problem was "more political than military" in nature. "The more the U.S. becomes involved in the actual conduct of military operations," he declared, the more the Vietnamese people would turn against it since "they regard the United States as a foreign power." He closed with the mordant observation, probably reflecting his memory of the Franco-Vietnamese war from 1946 to 1954, that the area "is a rotten territory in which to fight." Ball, who himself was already developing a skeptical view of the American war effort that would increase in intensity as the military intervention grew in size, agreed with de Gaulle that the problem was more political than military. But he halfheartedly retorted with the standard argument that if Washington were to enter into negotiations, as the French president advised, the South Vietnamese regime might "lose the will to resist." When Ball returned to the American embassy, he and Bohlen surmised that de Gaulle was "merely waiting for events [in Vietnam] to come his way, after which he expects that Washington will ask France, Communist China, and North Vietnam to participate in another Geneva conference, as in 1954, to end the conflict."[26]

De Gaulle followed up this meeting with the State Department's number two with a somewhat patronizing letter to President Johnson reminding him once again that "France had a direct and in many ways sad experience" with the Southeast Asian country. He ended his letter with a proposal that the two leaders establish "personal contact" with one another to sort out this and other issues in dispute (a suggestion that fell on deaf ears in the White House).[27] Within a month, *Time* magazine was lamenting in a sharply worded editorial, "From NATO to the U.N., from Latin America to Red China, there is hardly an issue or an area in the world on which France has not taken a stance at variance with U.S. policy"—a bit of an exaggeration but indicative of American unease at de Gaulle's outlier status in the Western alliance.[28] In his July 23 press conference, the French president went beyond his earlier proposals for neutralization of the Indochinese peninsula. He specified that four powers—the United States, the Soviet Union,

Communist China, and France—should publicly pledge "no longer to be committed" there. To the State Department's intelligence office (repeating the warning from Lodge), such a statement would shatter the morale of the government in Saigon.[29]

The Quagmire Deepens as De Gaulle's Criticism Escalates

Within two weeks of de Gaulle's scolding the United States about its deepening involvement in Southeast Asia, a controversial event occurred off the coast of North Vietnam that would lead both to an expansion and intensification of the American war effort and to an increase in the French president's criticism of Washington's military campaign. On August 4, reports reached the Defense Department that two U.S. destroyers, the USS *Maddox* and the USS *Turner Joy*, that were engaged in electronic intelligence collection in the Gulf of Tonkin had come under attack by three North Vietnamese patrol boats. The only evidence that the attacks had taken place were initial reports citing radar and sonar signals, but those reports were promptly withdrawn. President Johnson used this incident, which subsequent evidence definitely demonstrated had never taken place, to dispatch a request to Congress for an authorization to conduct retaliatory air strikes against North Vietnam. The U.S. House of Representatives and the Senate passed a joint resolution on August 10 authorizing the president, without a formal declaration of war by Congress, to employ military force in Southeast Asia to defend America's allies in the region as the president deemed necessary.[30]

Even before the major consequence of this authorization, the unleashing of bombing attacks on North Vietnam for the first time in the war, word came from Paris of Gaullist France's fervent opposition to the campaign. De Gaulle was on his summer vacation in Colombey, but his top officials promptly declared that this crisis demonstrated yet again the wisdom of his suggestion at his July 23 news conference for a great power international conclave on Southeast Asia to arrange for the independence and neutralization of the region. When NATO headquarters learned of the crisis, France was the lonely outlier in the organization. Some of the diplomats from countries that had been overrun by Hitler's armies said that if Britain and France had taken this kind of "preventive action" after 1933 that the U.S. president proposed to take, it would have prevented World War II.[31]

After several months of fruitless give-and-take between the French president and his American interlocutors on the question of the war in Vietnam, de Gaulle summarized his unchanging position on the matter by expressing to Bohlen toward the end of 1964 the fervent hope that "we would find some way of disengaging ourselves from this situation, for the good of the world and the United States." He ended the conversation with his familiar refrain that "the longer it was postponed, the worse it would get."[32] When Secretary of State Rusk visited Paris in mid-December, he secured a one-hour meeting with de Gaulle. After hearing the American secretary of state's familiar refrain about the need to contain the spread of Communism in Southeast Asia, the French president repeated his oft-stated suggestion for a solution: "The best means of disengaging from this bad situation is to do what France . . . has proposed: sponsor a conference with the Asian countries, including China, to explore the possibilities of a Pacific *modus vivendi*," adding, "It will not be impossible to find it."[33]

Much earlier in the year, Rusk had complained to his staff at the State Department that de Gaulle's neutralization proposals had "greatly complicated our already difficult position in Vietnam."[34] The historian Fredrik Logevall speculates that the visceral reaction to the French leader's call for neutralization was "colored by his intense personal dislike of Charles de Gaulle, a disdain he maintained throughout his term as Secretary of State."[35] Thomas Schoenbaum quotes Rusk telling the journalist C. L. Sulzberger, who was interviewing him, "You have found me in a bad mood. I'm so goddamned sore at de Gaulle."[36]

As the U.S. campaign in Vietnam and the French criticism of it escalated in the first half of 1965, Johnson had finally had enough of the recriminations flowing from Paris.[37] At a high-level meeting in the White House on February 19, 1965, to which he had summoned the French foreign minister and French ambassador and his top foreign policy advisers, LBJ let loose his rage at the deteriorating situation in Vietnam and France's lack of sympathy with his plight. Johnson bristled as he learned from Foreign Minister Couve de Murville that the Chinese chargé d'affaires in Paris, just back from Beijing, had agreed with de Gaulle's proposal for a return to the 1954 Geneva Conference to seek a diplomatic settlement of the conflict. LBJ retorted that Hanoi had shown no willingness to negotiate. "We would leave tomorrow if anyone could provide effective guarantees of the independence of South Vietnam," he declared, adding the old domino theory that "if we were to abandon Vietnam, we would be forced to give up Laos, Thailand, Burma, and would be back to Hawaii and San Francisco."[38] The president still had the support of the American public for his war in Southeast Asia and would retain it for the rest of the year. The Gallup Poll would still find in late December that 52 percent of the public favored the American war effort versus 26 percent opposed.[39]

Several months later an angry Rusk instructed Bohlen to remind the French government that "we find objectionable both its public needling

212 ⟋ Chapter Nine

regarding Vietnam and its public posture of concerting with the Soviet Union on this problem."[40] On February 2, 1965, officials at the French Foreign Ministry had submitted to the American embassy a detailed report of the long list of meetings between French officials, on the one hand, and the Chinese chargé d'affaires in Paris and North Vietnamese delegates, on the other, in late December and early January 1965 in Paris.[41] Hanoi then sent the diplomat Mai Van Bo to explore the possible use of France as a mediator with Washington. Bohlen speculated that the North Vietnamese government hoped that "French influence would be helpful to its interests."[42] Rusk later informed him that if Hanoi wanted an indirect method of communication with Washington, "the choice of this channel raises serious problems." It would have to find a secret procedure "other than via the French."[43] At the end of March, the leaders of seventeen nonaligned nations meeting in Belgrade issued an appeal to the United States, North Vietnam, and South Vietnam and other interested governments to begin negotiations soon, to no avail.[44]

De Gaulle, America, and the People's Republic of China

In the winter and spring of 1964, de Gaulle had turned his attention to developments in East Asia, a region that had occupied his attention only sporadically. Since the end of the Chinese Civil War in 1949, Washington had done everything in its power to isolate the Communist regime in Beijing (then called Peking), blocking its entrance into the United Nations and pressuring America's allies to withhold recognition of Mao's government. On December 16, 1963, de Gaulle had hinted to Rusk that a change in French foreign policy was in the offing. Couve de Murville alerted Ambassador Bohlen on January 15, 1964, that de Gaulle had decided to recognize of the People's Republic. On the same day in Washington, Ambassador Alphand so informed the State Department.[45] When the journalist Cyrus Sulzberger got the news off the record from the American ambassador the next day, he fulminated to his diary, "The shit has hit the fan . . . and we are boiling mad" about the decision to recognize the PRC.[46]

De Gaulle believed that the Sino-Soviet split heralded the breakup of the two blocs and hoped that it would lead to the emancipation of Europe from the domination of the two superpowers. On February 28, the CIA speculated that the main motive for France's recognition of the People's Republic was the grandiose aspiration "to make France the chief Western spokesman in an Asia dominated by China."[47] It might even be said that France and China were playing a similar role in challenging the authority of their respective superpower masters. Both Mao and de Gaulle had bristled at the refusal of their supposed allies to assist in their countries' bid to join the nuclear club, which France did in 1960 and China did in 1964, both on their own. The French president's obsession with the geopolitical position of the PRC would continue after France's recognition. In early July 1965, he issued a solemn (and prescient) warning to the journalist Cyrus Sulzberger, which he knew would be forwarded to Washington: "China has 700 million people. It is not a great power today. But in twenty years it will be a great power and in fifty years it will be an enormous power." And he dismissed the ideological connection between Moscow and Beijing, repeating what he had often observed about the respective importance of ideology and nationalism: "Of course, being communists, they always put everything on an ideological basis. But the truth is the opposition between Russia and China has national origins."[48]

Emancipating Europe from the Two Superpowers

In his press conference on July 23, 1964, de Gaulle trotted out all the arguments in favor of a European security system independent of the United States: the two blocs were beginning to disintegrate, China was going its own way, and (in an extraordinary exaggeration based on wishful thinking) Eastern Europe was moving away from the Soviet Union. Earlier in the month, the CIA had emphasized that de Gaulle was absolutely convinced that because "national interests transcend ideological considerations" everywhere, "resurgent nationalism would eventually disrupt Communist bloc unity." The independent policies pursued by Romania heralded "the evolution of Eastern European states away from 'Russian' domination," while the threat from China will "force Moscow to seek its own place in a larger European context."[49]

In fact, between 1963 and 1965, France signed fifteen major trade agreements with Eastern European countries and the Soviet Union. Governments of all Eastern European countries except East Germany and Albania sent high-level officials to Paris.[50] All of this demonstrated the need to construct an independent Western Europe to defend itself. The American reading of this latest broadside from Paris was a somber one. It seemed that France was about to leave the Atlantic alliance in the near future.[51]

The Multilateral Force/Farce

We have seen how the U.S. proposal to create a multilateral nuclear force (MLF) for Western Europe had been in the planning stages for many years.

It is appropriate here to briefly summarize the historical background of this concept, which caused such tension between de Gaulle and a succession of American presidents, from Eisenhower to Johnson. The idea of creating a multilateral nuclear force was the brainchild of Harvard professor and former director of policy planning in the State Department Robert Bowie and had been debated as early as October 1959 in the National Security Council. But the plan had run into roadblocks that prevented progress on the project for the rest of Eisenhower's term in office. As Ike prepared to leave the White House, it was unveiled to America's European allies in December 1960 by Secretary of State Christian Herter at a NATO ministerial meeting in Paris. His justification for the multilateral force was based on assumptions that would animate U.S. policy toward France's plans to develop a national nuclear force for years to come. "We believe that creation of additional national nuclear weapons capabilities would have a marked divisive effect on the Alliance," the American secretary of state had insisted. "It would mean duplication of effort and diversion of resources, tend to stimulate competition within the Alliance in the nuclear weapons field, and increase the possibilities of nuclear war through miscalculation or accident."[52] For the new Kennedy administration, the main purpose of the proposed multilateral nuclear force for Europe was simple and straightforward: "to discourage separate nuclear capabilities such as the French and the Germans." Kennedy had admonished Alphand in April 1961 with the oft-repeated warning that "it was not simply a question of France's having nuclear capability, but the next step would be for Germany to have this capability."[53]

After many discussions and debates, the project was formally presented to the European allies in the spring of 1963 by the Kennedy administration. The concept found little enthusiasm among the European allies. It proposed a fleet of twenty-five surface ships, each armed with eight Polaris missiles, with mix-manned crews of Americans and West Europeans. It would be under the control of the Supreme Allied Commander (always an American general) until a crisis required a decision about whether to use the missiles that would require a unanimous approval of the participating states. The United States hinted that it might give up its right of veto if a joint European decision-making process were perfected and institutionalized. De Gaulle abhorred the project, not only because he saw it as a means of solidifying Washington's control over the alliance's nuclear policies, but also because it would for the first time allow West Germany to gain access to nuclear decision-making.[54]

The Kennedy State Department had regarded the MLF as a means of placating Bonn's insistent demands for a greater say in nuclear policy. McNamara and the Pentagon were not enthusiastic about nuclear sharing with the Germans but went along with the proposal.[55] In a recorded interview long after the demise of the project, the former defense secretary simply declared that the project "had no military value."[56] De Gaulle often hinted to American officials that it was inevitable that the Federal Republic would make a sustained bid to acquire nuclear weapons. Couve de Murville bolstered this warning, claiming that the MLF would only whet West German appetites for acquiring a national nuclear force.[57]

The French foreign minister informed his American interlocutors that the Paris-Bonn link enshrined in the Elysée Treaty was intended to eventually incorporate West Germany into a Europe-wide nuclear deterrent, which, of course, required a degree of political integration far beyond what the EEC had achieved at that point. Under-Secretary of State George Ball, the most ardent proponent of European economic and political union in the U.S. government, pointed out to Couve that de Gaulle's conception of a Europe based on separate sovereign nation-states, "Europe des Patries," made European decision-making in security matters impossible and, coupled with France's *force de frappe*, served as a justification for West Germany's case for its own national nuclear deterrent.[58]

That was precisely what the MLF was intended to prevent. The French foreign minister countered with the very optimistic prediction that within ten years Europe might well be able to move toward the kind of political unity that could absorb any German national nuclear weapons program in a West European deterrent. He even spoke of a European Council, an intergovernmental body, and an elected European parliament that would enable a single political authority to manage such a continent-wide deterrent.[59]

When the Kennedy administration had pressed for a nuclear test ban treaty, it had been met by ferocious opposition from de Gaulle. By prohibiting nuclear tests in the atmosphere, in space, and underwater but allowing them to be conducted underground, it struck the French president as another way of sidelining the French *force de frappe* since France was not yet capable of organizing such underground tests. When the Partial Test Ban Treaty was finally signed in Moscow on August 5, 1963, by the United States, the Soviet Union, and Great Britain, France was ostentatiously the odd-man out and would continue atmospheric tests in Algeria and, later, near its possessions in the South Pacific. The United States had tried to induce France to sign the treaty with the hint that some American assistance to the French nuclear weapons project was possible. De Gaulle declined this overture, knowing that even if the American president decided to provide such assistance, it would be hamstrung by the amended McMahon Act.[60]

The debate on the MLF had heated up in the autumn of 1963. A succession of French officials continued to insist that the French nuclear striking force (which was not yet fully operational) would not be restricted to France but would be the cornerstone of a Europe-wide nuclear deterrent. That claim encountered strong skepticism in Washington. Defense Secretary Robert McNamara told French ambassador Alphand on December 9 that the hope of a united Europe that could deploy a European nuclear force was a very distant prospect. Throughout the year 1964, the Johnson administration was increasingly leery of de Gaulle's efforts to court the Germans in his effort to reduce their enthusiasm for the proposed project. By assuring the government in Bonn that it could depend on France to defend it, with nuclear weapons if necessary, de Gaulle seemed to be maneuvering West German chancellor Ludwig Erhard into dropping his choice of the MLF over the *force de frappe*.[61]

The dilemma was a stark one: could the MLF eventually evolve into a European nuclear force independent of the United States not subject to an American veto, or would it merely represent a continuation of European dependence on Washington for its security under a cloak of multilateralism? The State Department, particularly Under-Secretary of State Ball, enthusiastically pressed for the MLF as an elegant solution to the dilemma of promoting European unification, preventing the emergence of national nuclear systems, and retaining an Atlantic identity. But Secretary of Defense Robert McNamara had serious doubts about the entire project. Johnson in the end sided with Ball and his allies in the State Department. He concluded that the project was essential to prevent de Gaulle from luring the Germans into some kind of bilateral nuclear partnership that would leave the United States in the lurch. He persuaded Chancellor Erhard at the end of his visit to Washington in June 1964 to join him in striving for an agreement by the end of the year.[62]

De Gaulle opened a public offensive in the fall of 1964 against the MLF, warning the Germans that if adopted by Bonn it would seriously jeopardize Franco-German relations. He had Prime Minister Georges Pompidou, who had replaced Michel Debré in 1962, publicly declare that the proposal would be "destructive for Europe, provocative to other countries, and in the end directed more or less against France."[63] Couve de Murville dismissed the MLF to C. L. Sulzberger as "an attempt to ensure U.S. control of France's nuclear force after de Gaulle disappears."[64] When it became clear that Great Britain was very lukewarm about the project, West Germany continued to be its only vocal champion in NATO. This led to speculation that if the MLF ever came to fruition, it would be mostly a U.S.–West German operation.[65]

At the end of November, de Gaulle delivered a broadside against the proposal in a speech in Strasbourg, asserting that the MLF debate demonstrated the critical importance of the development of a purely European defense system apart from the United States.[66] When Ambassador Bohlen lunched with de Gaulle after his Strasbourg speech, de Gaulle repeated his familiar claim that "no one could expect the U.S. to risk its cities for the defense of Europe." He complained that Washington's veto in the MLF would prevent Europe from relying on nuclear weapons in response to aggression.[67]

A few days later the CIA weighed in with an analysis of de Gaulle's war against the MLF which emphasized his ultimate goal of establishing "an autonomous military policy" for Western Europe based on the member states possessing nuclear weapons (i.e., France).[68] The French president's assault against the project began to take its toll in West Germany and other NATO countries by the late fall of 1964, and officials in Washington began to get the hint that de Gaulle was not alone in his opposition. By the end of the year, the debate in the White House, and to a lesser extent in the State Department, began to move in the direction of serious second thoughts about the MLF concept. But Johnson had already lost his interest in the project and allowed it to be put in deep freeze, though the idea lingered on for another year before its definitive demise.[69]

De Gaulle's Campaign against "Flexible Response" and the U.S. Reaction

In the last year of the Kennedy administration and the first year of the Johnson administration, Gaullist France unleashed an attack against the U.S. campaign to replace the nuclear strategy of "massive retaliation," which had been adopted during the Eisenhower administration in 1954, with the strategy of "flexible response." The bitter conflict between Paris and Washington over this concept dovetailed with the bilateral dispute over the multilateral force. It seemed as though everything that Washington proposed for the Atlantic alliance met with sharp opposition from Paris.[70] The suggestion that NATO should consider a graduated response to a conventional attack in Central Europe, which might or might not include a nuclear response, obliterated the metaphorical concept of the presence of American conventional forces along the Central Front as "trip wire" guaranteeing prompt nuclear retaliation.

In July 1964, the first Mirage IV nuclear-armed bombers entered into service, providing France with a credible deterrent force for the first time. The State Department thereupon floated a trial balloon about the possibility of working out a plan for joint targeting schedules between the MLF and the force de frappe, a suggestion that led to nothing. As early as October 1963, Couve de Murville had made it clear to Rusk that the very concept of flexible response would seriously undermine the assumption of both America's NATO allies and the Soviet Union that a conventional military attack from the east would result in a prompt nuclear response from the United States.[71]

Ambassador Bohlen was convinced that de Gaulle was exploiting the controversy over the flexible response proposal to undermine European faith in America's willingness to respond with nuclear weapons to a conventional attack from the Warsaw Pact.[72] In the summer of 1964, de Gaulle would take note at a press conference that the two superpowers had achieved an "automatic balance of deterrence" between them—a variant of McNamara's "mutual assured destruction" phrase—that "only covered themselves and not the other countries of the world." Three months later he again attempted to persuade the West Germans to accept the deterrent power of the French *force de frappe* as a more reliable guarantee than the flexible response doctrine Washington was pushing. He pointedly reminded the president of the West German Bundestag that "we are in Europe, whereas the Americans are not. . . . Germany and France can perfectly well be destroyed without the United States being so."[73]

Washington, Paris, Brussels, and International Economic Relations

De Gaulle was able to pursue his ambitious plan to restore to his country its long-lost grandeur in the world because he could depend on two critical sources of French power. The first was the extraordinary political stability of the Fifth Republic. The acute political *in*stability of the Third and Fourth Republics, with their revolving door governments, was a thing of the past. He was able to govern without interference from the other major political parties with a compliant parliament and a constitutional system that granted enormous powers to the executive in the area of foreign relations. The second was the impressive economic gains of France in the middle of the 1960s, the height of what was later labeled "Les Trente Glorieuses" (the Glorious Thirty Years since the end of the Second World War). France's rate of economic growth during part of this period exceeded that of the United States, Great Britain, and even West Germany.

Under the Fourth Republic, France had of course been at the forefront of the movement toward European integration. As we have seen, the Treaty of Rome establishing the European Economic Community (EEC) had come into force on January 1, 1958, five months before de Gaulle assumed power in France. In the earlier years of the Fifth Republic, the French president tolerated the activities of the EEC as long it did not move in the direction of the kind of supranational entity that this dyed-in-the-wool defender of national sovereignty abhorred. That attitude of tolerance would come to an end in the so-called empty chair crisis that began on July 1, 1965, a conflict that would drag on for another six months and severely weaken the Community and gravely disappoint those who wished to see it progress toward a federalist structure. It all began with a proposal authored by the president of the European Commission, Walter Hallstein, in 1965 to dilute the powers of the member states of the Community by allocating a greater role to the Commission. De Gaulle's specific fear was that if the concept of majority voting ever replaced the unanimity requirement in the Community, it would directly threaten the livelihood of France's politically powerful farmers. Whereas West Germany had overtaken France in most indices of industrial production, France remained the EEC's most efficient producer of agricultural products. De Gaulle pressed hard for what came to be called the EEC's Common Agricultural Policy (which greatly benefited French farmers).

But his most deeply held apprehension about the EEC remained the bogeyman of supra-nationalism or federalism, which directly clashed with his insistence on a confederal "Europe des Etats" or "Europe des Patries" controlled by the governments of the member states. So he ordered his representative to refuse to participate in the Council of Ministers—hence the term "empty chair"—the first time that the EEC had been prevented from operating by a boycott by a member state. Although the crisis was resolved several months later with the so-called Luxembourg Compromise, de Gaulle's non-negotiable insistence that the nation-state retain absolute sovereignty prevented significant movement toward the goal of economic (and ultimately political) integration that had been dear to the hearts of Jean Monnet and the founders of what would eventually become the European Union.[74]

While chastising the EEC for daring to replace the nation-states of Europe with a supranational conglomeration with headquarters in Brussels that might threaten French economic interests, de Gaulle took aim at what he disdained as the attempt of the United States to bring Western Europe under its economic domination through the use of its monetary power. At a February 4, 1964, press conference, he had railed against the privileged status of the dollar as the reserve currency, igniting a bitter transatlantic dispute about this monetary issue. He expressed the desire to return to the gold standard as a replacement of the international monetary system established at the Bretton Woods monetary conference in 1944, based on fixed exchange rates and the link between the dollar and gold. But in the twenty years since Bretton Woods, when the United States accounted for half of the world's economic output, the explosive economic growth of Japan and the major European countries brought into question the privileged position of the dollar as the world's reserve currency. The U.S. had run up large balance-of-payments deficits, which enabled it to borrow abroad much more cheaply than other nations because it could pay in its own currency. To set in motion this attack on the dollar, the French president proclaimed his decision to sell dollars for gold, a policy that would rattle international financial markets and directly threaten the role of the American currency as the foundation of the postwar international economic order.[75]

De Gaulle was admittedly not an expert on economics in general and international monetary issues in particular. Relying on the advice of the esteemed French economist Jacques Rueff, he was adamant in rejecting the dollar's unique status as the world's reserve currency. But the objective of this policy was not entirely economic: as Francis Gavin has noted, Gaullist France was "fully aware of America's balance-of-payments problems" and was perfectly willing to "use its monetary power in a political dispute."[76]

Another Minor Irritant: De Gaulle Denounces the U.S. Intervention in the Dominican Republic

In February 1963, the Dominican Republic in the Caribbean had held its first ever free elections, which were won by Juan Emilio Bosch Gaviño, a mild mannered short-story writer and reformist who embarked on an ambitious political and economic reform program until he was overthrown and expelled after seven months in office by a right-wing military coup. When his supporters in the military attempted to reinstate him in the last week of April 1965 after ousting the reigning junta, a civil war broke out in the little country. Fearing the emergence of a Communist regime in Santo Domingo on the model of Havana, President Johnson ordered a U.S. military intervention that expelled the fledging reformist military regime. De Gaulle did not conceal his displeasure at this apparent return to U.S. military interventionism in its hemisphere.[77]

In response to the French president's critique of the Dominican intervention as a sign that Washington "was coming to believe that force will solve everything," Ambassador Bohlen defended it on the spurious grounds that the leaders of the effort to reinstate Bosch had been "trained in Cuba" and were intent on launching "a Castro-type coup." This justification for the U.S. military action did not seem to impress de Gaulle.[78] When Vice President Hubert Humphrey met with de Gaulle during a trip to Paris in June, all the French president wanted to discuss was the Dominican intervention. Humphrey repeated Bohlen's earlier assertion, citing the fear of another

Cuba as justification for the intervention. De Gaulle noted the clear differences between the two situations—"the Dominican Republic is not Cuba"—and expressed his distress at what he described as this blatant attempt to deny the inhabitants the right to "self-determination." De Gaulle recalled meeting Bosch in Paris and found him a "calm, capable, and worthy man." The vice president warned darkly that "anarchy and chaos" had threatened the small Caribbean country and directly appealed for "support of friends in this difficult time."[79]

De Gaulle's comment to the journalist Walter Lippmann that the United States was the "greatest danger in the world today to peace"[80] was reflected in French public opinion polls, which found that almost two-thirds of the French public had "no confidence in the wisdom of U.S. leadership" and more than a half favored neutrality in the Cold War.[81] In his brief meeting with the American vice president, de Gaulle expressed his "sadness" about the American interventions in Vietnam and the Dominican Republic and found excessive Washington's reaction to his criticisms, "as if we were hostile and malevolent toward the United States," which was "not true."[82]

Anticipating NATO without France[83]

Since the beginning of the year 1965, Ambassador Bohlen had become convinced that the French president believed that the Soviet threat to Western Europe had significantly diminished and that his ultimate goal was nothing less than the replacement of military integration in NATO by cooperation among the military staffs of the member states in peacetime.[84] This perception had been confirmed by de Gaulle, who told his ambassador to Washington in early January that between then and the projected date for the renewal of the Washington Treaty in 1969, France would leave the NATO command and integration would be replaced by cooperation among national forces at all levels.[85] In the next couple of months, the simmering dispute over the future of France's relations with the Western alliance alarmed French ambassador to Washington Alphand. After traveling widely in the United States, speaking to various groups beyond the U.S. capital, what he discovered, and reported to the French foreign ministry, was "a deterioration of American public opinion with regard to France." In addition to the French attitude toward NATO, he cited de Gaulle's criticism of the war in Vietnam and the MLF as well as his recognition of the People's Republic of China as the major sources of concern.[86]

The French president had given more than enough warning to Washington that he intended to disengage France from the integrated military command of the North Atlantic Treaty Organization. As we have seen, de Gaulle had announced in June 1963 the removal of France's Mediterranean fleet from the alliance. He also ordered the withdrawal of French naval units under the Atlantic command (ACLANT) and the English Channel command (ACCHAN) by January 1, 1964. Another move in the direction of French disengagement was the redeployment of the two French divisions of the Second Army Corps in West Germany to the rear of NATO's forward line of defense, forming a kind of reserve force behind the Americans and West Germans. This switch was not a major concern of the United States military planners, who valued a strong reserve force. But it had the symbolic effect of highlighting French disengagement from NATO's integrated defense of Western Europe.[87]

By the end of 1964, the French president had unmistakably telegraphed his intention to press for a fundamental reorganization of the Atlantic alliance when the date for the renewal of the Washington Treaty arrived in 1969. He told C. L. Sulzberger bluntly that while the arrangement between the United States and France to support each other in case of war must be preserved, NATO "will not be maintained" after the renewal date of the alliance in 1969. He added that "before then we must decide on another kind of organization to replace it, or there will be none. France will not agree to keep NATO."[88] On December 31, 1964, he publicly announced that in the coming year France would resume its campaign to free itself of "Atlanticism," which would "keep us under the hegemony we know."[89]

In May 1965, de Gaulle launched trial balloons to determine what the American response to a full French disengagement would be. He told Bohlen that before 1969 integration would cease to exist and, for the first time, suggested that all foreign forces in France would have to depart from France.[90] He confided to Alphand that "NATO as far as we are concerned will disappear in 1969," to be replaced by a series of bilateral agreements. He added that the French decision to bail out would be announced in early 1966.[91] Ambassador Bohlen suggested in early June that Washington study means of coping with what he was certain would be de Gaulle's decision to leave NATO and demand the removal of its headquarters (SHAPE) from France after the French presidential election in December.[92]

By the end of the month, Rusk ordered a full-scale review of the alliance's future without France. Under-Secretary of State George Ball began actively exploring the possibility of discussions with the other NATO allies about the prospect of a French withdrawal. When asked by Sulzberger on July 1 if he intended to evict SHAPE from France by 1969, de Gaulle replied that "France cannot accept foreign forces on French soil except under French command. And SHAPE headquarters is part of the integration that France cannot accept."[93] Ball traveled to Europe in mid-July for intensive talks with British, German, Italian, Dutch, and Belgian officials about that anxiety-producing topic.[94]

McNamara's Alternative to the MLF and De Gaulle

During the spring Atlantic Council meeting in Paris, which took place from May 31 to June 1, 1965, Secretary of Defense McNamara tried to reassure the European members of NATO that the United States was a reliable strategic partner and protector, despite the French intimations that Washington intended to "denuclearize" Europe with its flexible response doctrine. He reminded the Europeans that the United States had significantly increased the number of tactical (short-range, or battlefield) nuclear weapons deployed in Europe and reaffirmed that the U.S. would not hesitate to use them if needed. To address the embarrassment of the slow death of the MLF (which continued its downward spiral despite Washington's refusal to publicly recognize its de facto demise), the defense secretary (who had never been a fan of the project) proposed the creation of a committee of allied defense ministers to study means of establishing close cooperation and consultation in nuclear planning.[95]

On July 5, de Gaulle rejected any French participation in such a committee but had no objection to that of the other defense ministers if they wished to do so. The other alliance members worked through the fall of 1965 to find a solution until November 17, when the defense ministers of ten alliance countries (without France) decided to establish a special committee to explore ways of establishing a firm platform for nuclear consultation. It was obviously McNamara's strategy to assuage the Germans' disappointment at the impending failure of the MLF by offering this consultative procedure in its place.[96] The MLF project swooned to its final death in the last four months of 1965. By then the Johnson administration had decided to press hard for a nuclear non-proliferation treaty (NPT). The preliminary negotiations with the Russians for the NPT that had begun in the summer had begun to bear fruit, so the MLF, which Moscow (and de Gaulle) detested, had to be sacrificed.

The speed of work in anticipation of a French exit increased in Washington. The State Department, the Defense Department, the CIA, and other executive agencies formed a high-level group under Rusk's chairmanship to study the matter and come up with remedial recommendations by September 1. At these high-level meetings, the State Department, represented by Ball, pushed for a hard line to let France know it could not be a free rider if outside the organization, while Under Secretary of Defense Cyrus Vance took a softer line. Interestingly, former president (and the first SACEUR) Eisenhower weighed in with the proposal that NATO be thoroughly overhauled, which was not far from de Gaulle's position: France and West Germany should be given joint responsibility in a revamped alliance, with France to be given command and West Germany to be given operational command of the forward-deployed forces.[97]

De Gaulle continued to take the hard line. In his September 9 press conference, he repeated for the umpteenth time that "by 1969 at the latest, the subordination called 'integration' that NATO entails and which puts our destiny under foreign authority, will cease as far as we are concerned." He also trotted out the familiar (and somewhat bizarre) mantra about the need for Europe to create a "constructive entente from the Atlantic to the Urals."[98] The puzzling concept "from the Atlantic to the Urals" had first been aired in a television speech in October 1961 and then quickly forgotten. Its revival four years later was intended as part of his long-term objective of liberating the old continent from what he regarded as the suffocating embrace of the two superpowers and reconstituting an independent "Europe balanced between the Atlantic and the Urals, once totalitarian imperialism has ceased to deploy its ambitions."[99]

The latter pronouncement, an obvious reference to Soviet domination of Eastern Europe, reflected de Gaulle's oft-repeated belief that nationalism was a much more powerful and lasting force than ideology. The Marxist-Leninist ideology, he believed, was little more than a ruse designed to conceal the pursuit of traditional Russian interests in Europe. As noted above, he always used the term "La Russie" rather than "L'Union Soviétique." But since the Eastern European countries were in no condition to emancipate themselves from the domination of the superpower to the east, Western Europe would have to take the lead in terminating the hegemony of the other superpower across the Atlantic. This development, de Gaulle apparently assumed, would remove the necessity for Moscow to maintain its iron grip on the East European satellites as buffers against American power in Western Europe. His preoccupation with removing the predominant role of Washington and Moscow in Europe had served as the defining characteristic of his foreign policy ever since his searing critique of the Yalta settlement, which, in his view, had split Europe in half. Reconciliation between the two halves would be the ultimate result. It was becoming clear that de Gaulle's tentative steps toward *Une Politique de l'Est* (a precursor of the *Ostpolitik* of West Germany's Willy Brandt) represented as serious a threat to NATO cohesion as de Gaulle's continuing threat to leave the alliance.

As if there was any doubt about Washington's wholesale rejection of the Gaullist proposals for a series of bilateral treaties to replace NATO's multilateral structure, Rusk demanded that Bohlen stress to Couve de Murville once again that Washington "has no interest in a bilateral treaty with France."[100] Johnson was apparently getting tired of de Gaulle's bluster about the Atlantic Alliance. At a White House luncheon, he erupted with the acerbic observation that the French president was "a grouchy old grandfather grumbling by the stove" and "a train that scatters people walking on the track. But as soon as the train has passed I am back again with my friend [Ludwig] Erhard walking arm in arm down the track."[101] Johnson had invited the German chancellor to spend the Christmas holidays in 1963. He gave Erhard a Texas cowboy hat and took him on a deer hunt. At the end of the visit, LBJ announced to the press that "I simply like everything about him." Erhard replied, "I love President Johnson and he loves me."[102]

On the last day of 1965, the well-informed journalist Cyrus Sulzberger speculated about the prospects of a face-to-face meeting between Johnson and de Gaulle amid this atmosphere of mutual recrimination, predicting that such a gathering was likely in the coming year. He recalled that when Senate Democratic Leader Mike Mansfield had visited de Gaulle the previous month to discuss the twin problems of NATO and Vietnam, the senator had pointedly suggested a meeting of the two presidents to clear the air. But de Gaulle's response was only "polite if vague agreement."[103]

The Withdrawal at Last

In late January 1966, de Gaulle hinted at a press conference that certain corrective measures would have to be taken with NATO's structure. When Bohlen asked him about his precise intentions, he assured the American ambassador that "I will do nothing precipitate. We shall take our time on this and examine everything very closely, but I shall certainly do nothing suddenly."[104] But things developed very quickly after these assurances. At a news conference on February 21, he telegraphed some of the precise details of his decision concerning France's role in NATO that he had been privately adumbrated to the State Department and Ambassador Bohlen: All foreign military forces would be required to vacate French territory, including all American service personnel. The French forces in West Germany, except those with occupation rights in Berlin, would be removed from integration in peacetime. But he again mentioned April 1969, when the North Atlantic Treaty came up for its twenty-year renewal, as the target date for his proposed transformation of the alliance.[105]

On March 7, 1966, French foreign minister Couve de Murville handed to American Ambassador Charles Bohlen a handwritten letter from de Gaulle to Johnson explaining precisely what he had done and why he had done it.[106] Since the contents of the letter were not revealed, the news media assumed that the matter would lead to negotiations in the course of the next three years, as implied in de Gaulle's February statement to the press.[107] But the written message to Johnson shortened the chronology by two years. It demanded that all foreign troops and NATO's headquarters located in the city of Rocquencourt near Versailles be gone by April 1, 1967. The French president was careful to reiterate his continued support for the Washington Treaty of April 4, 1949, before it had been transformed into the integrated military command system in 1950–51 that he abhorred.[108]

The behind-the-scenes reaction in Washington and the American embassy in Paris was an explosion of pent-up consternation and resentment. This reaction was disingenuous, since a secret informant at the Quai d'Orsay had been regularly passing along information about the impending announcement to the American embassy in Paris, which forwarded it to the State Department and President Johnson.[109] When Couve de Murville handed to Bohlen de Gaulle's letter to Johnson, even the American ambassador, who had himself called for a radical transformation of the alliance and had counseled patience with de Gaulle, blurted out that "Franco-American relations will be hurt for a long time. . . . I am saddened to have to transmit this message to my president."[110]

Under-Secretary of State George Ball escorted French ambassador Charles Lucet to the White House for an explanation to the president. Ball expressed his contempt for de Gaulle's ability to thumb his nose at the United States because he knew that his country's geographical situation to the west of the German Federal Republic would be protected if faced with a Warsaw Pact assault.[111] Johnson's NSC deputy Francis Bator agreed, noting that "if we are going to defend the Germans against the Russians, we cannot help but defend France too," an assessment echoed by Supreme Allied Commander General Lyman Lemnitzer.[112] Harlan Cleveland, the permanent U.S. representative to the Atlantic Council, later declared that the entire basis of America's willingness to defend Western Europe was the integrated command system and later attributed the withdrawal to an anachronistic French chauvinism.[113]

But reports had already begun to surface that Defense Secretary Robert McNamara had exercised a moderating influence on senior State Department officials who favored the imposition of tough economic sanctions on France in reprisal.[114] After considering his options, President Johnson sided with the Pentagon. His official response to de Gaulle's letter on March 22 was measured and diplomatic.[115]

He noted that "reliance in crisis on independent action by separate forces in accordance with national plans, only loosely coordinated with joint forces and plans, seems to me to be dangerous for all concerned." He expressed surprise that allied forces on French territory threatened French sovereignty, reminding de Gaulle that they were there at the request of the French government. He ended his letter with a wistful statement that a place for America's "old friend and ally" would await the country "whenever she decides to resume her leading role."[116] As Thomas Schwartz has observed, Johnson might well have exploited the public furor over the French withdrawal to divert attention from the growing public dissatisfaction in the United States with the war in Southeast Asia. But he chose not to do so.[117] A Gallup Poll revealed that well over 50 percent of all Americans, and almost two-thirds of college-educated Americans, did not believe that France was "a dependable ally of the United States."[118]

When the French Socialist Party introduced a motion of censure over de Gaulle's policy toward NATO in the National Assembly, Premier Georges Pompidou mounted the rostrum of the parliament to defend his president on April 23. Pompidou had replaced Michel Debré as prime minister in 1962 and was well on his way to becoming the longest-serving official in that office in the Fifth Republic, a record that still stands. He was regarded as a colorless politician compared to the grandiloquent president that he served. But he surprised his listeners with an animated address of an hour and a half that summarized the reasons for de Gaulle's withdrawal from the alliance's integrated command. Several times he referred to the fateful decision of Secretary of State McNamara to abandon the "Dulles doctrine" of instant nuclear retaliation in the event of a Soviet attack in Western Europe in favor of the doctrine of "flexible response," which "condemned Europe to destruction" in the next war. When the National Assembly took up the censure motion, it was soundly defeated by a vote of 345 to 137, a demonstration that de Gaulle had the country behind him in his defiance of the United States.[119] French public opinion was divided on the issue of withdrawal, but there were signs of remorse, particularly from French regions that had been liberated by U.S. troops. One woman from Alsace urged de Gaulle to "remember that without the American army Alsace would not have been returned to France."[120]

A tone of restraint similar to Johnson's respectful letter to de Gaulle on March 22 was expressed by Senator Frank Church, an influential member of the Senate Foreign Relations Committee who visited Paris for a lengthy meeting with de Gaulle on May 4. While most American officials were lambasting the French president for his withdrawal from the Alliance, Church agreed with most of what de Gaulle had to say to him about the current situation in Europe. The French president repeated his usual refrain that much had changed on the continent since the establishment of NATO in 1949 because "the Russian menace has diminished." He added that "Russia has China at its back," and with thousands of kilometers of a common border" with the People's Republic, Russia had "gradually turned away from its Western [European] ambitions." When the American senator agreed that "the permanent deployment of American forces in Europe is not natural," de Gaulle added the caveat that "because of Germany, it is normal that Americans should be in Europe, and I do not dream at all of kicking them out. . . . Let the alliance be maintained and let the American troops remain in Germany . . . but not in France."[121] This concern about keeping American forces in Europe as an insurance policy against a revival of a powerful threatening Germany recalled the oft-quoted declaration of the first secretary-general of NATO, General Hastings Ismay, that the purpose of the alliance was "to keep the Russians out, the Americans in, and the Germans down."

Hervé Alphand, the French ambassador to Washington from 1956 to 1965, had become secretary general of the French Foreign Ministry in October 1965. In a meeting with de Gaulle on March 31, 1966, the two men had discussed in detail the significance of the French withdrawal the previous March. De Gaulle declared that NATO in its present form had become useless. "In the case of aggression on the continent," two outcomes are guaranteed: either the fighting "will be localized in Europe, which will rapidly be submerged if not destroyed," or the outcome will be "massive reprisals," in which case the American armaments will "escape the control of [the other member states of] NATO."[122]

The Pentagon worked overtime to arrange for a smooth process of evacuating American combat units from France. By May 25, Secretary of Defense McNamara was assuring the president that the removal of American military personnel and installations could begin.[123] On June 15, McNamara announced that "virtually all" American air force units in France would be removed in "orderly stages" in the next few months.[124] An undated aide-memoire prepared by the Pentagon during the Eisenhower administration listed the number of U.S. service personnel in France as follows: 26,628 Army, 22,236 Air Force, 439 Navy, and a total of 37,863 American dependents.[125] At the end of December 1966, Supreme Allied Commander (SACEUR) General Lyman Lemnitzer opened up his morose thoughts to journalist C. L. Sulzberger about the collateral damage caused by de Gaulle's decision to evict American GIs from France. The United States had spent almost $2 billion in the course of two decades for military communications and infrastructure in the country, including airfields and 750,000 tons of equipment—from vehicles and tanks to spare parts and ammunition. He summarized the situation as one of "absolute disaster."[126]

The Long Burden Sharing Debate

Throughout 1966 and 1967, the United States suffered a serious financial crisis due in part by the continuing and mounting balance-of-payments deficits caused by the costs of financing American troops and their dependents in Western Europe while the costs of the war in Vietnam and the War on Poverty at home seemed to some observers a looming catastrophe. On August 31, 1966, Senator Mike Mansfield, the majority leader of Johnson's own Democratic Party in the upper body of Congress, introduced a resolution proposing a sharp reduction in American troop strength in Europe, perhaps up to half of the forces. In the autumn of 1966, the Johnson administration had pressed the British and West German governments to join in a trilateral negotiation in search of a solution. On April 28, 1967, an agreement provided for the reduction of British forces in West Germany—the so-called British Army of the Rhine (BAOR)—and thirty-five thousand GIs from the American army, removing (at least temporarily) the prospect of a much larger decrease in conventional American troop strength along the Central Front. An agreement was also reached to maintain the two non-integrated French divisions in West Germany.[127]

After almost a year of negotiations between the SACEUR, General Lyman Lemnitzer, and French General Charles Ailleret, the two officers reached an agreement on August 22, 1967, specifying the details of the role of the two French divisions in Germany in case of war. It in effect defined the French forces as a reserve force that would intervene behind the other NATO forces—meaning American and West German units—in response to Soviet aggression along the Central Front of the Cold War.

The concept of "burden sharing," which became increasing important in public discussion of the Atlantic alliance, was the flip side of the campaign pursued by the French president. De Gaulle's denunciation of Western Europe's dependence on its transatlantic "protector" and his call for Europe to develop its own security system was music to the ears of those in Congress who bristled at the huge expenditures required for the defense of Western Europe. The demand that the Europeans share more of the financial and manpower responsibilities of Western defense had begun in the Eisenhower administration, though never in public. The president had privately complained to friends about Europe's total dependence on the United States for its security. He suggested that the European pillar of NATO be given a much greater role in the defense of the continent. He wondered why the United States should continue to finance and provide manpower to defend a Western Europe that was enjoying unprecedented economic growth. Ike had frequently clashed with Dulles about the desirability of withdrawing most of America's troops from Europe because the Europeans were perfectly able financially to defend themselves.[128] "The United States lost $4.3 billion in gold last year," he had complained in 1959. "We are spending too many billions around the world without the Europeans taking a commensurate load."[129]

In a tense meeting with his secretary of state in December 1958, Eisenhower had recalled that when he arrived as the first SACEUR in 1951, "there had been talk that the United States assistance to the NATO countries' defense efforts would be for a 'maximum' of five years." It was high time, the president believed, to "wean" the Allies from this excessive dependence "and encourage them to make better efforts of their own." The American forces had been placed in Europe "on a stop-gap emergency basis," he argued, and were not meant to be "a permanent and definite commitment." He angrily concluded that the European Allies were close to "making a sucker out of Uncle Sam."[130] Ike's resentment at America's European allies continued to fester, but he realized that there was nothing he could do about it, so he kept his opinions private. If the West Europeans refused to bear their share of the burden for Western defense, he facetiously remarked, "then perhaps we had better rule the world."[131]

The mirage of West European defense cooperation continued to rear its head well into the Kennedy administration. After West German chancellor Konrad Adenauer had met with de Gaulle to discuss security issues on February 17, 1962, American ambassador James Gavin asked the French Foreign Ministry about the possibility of the European Economic Community's developing closer military cooperation. Foreign Minister Couve du Murville assured him that the leaders of the organization "definitely have in mind taking measures for their common defense" through such measures as joint production of military hardware and exchanges of military officers by the six member states. When Gavin asked about how these plans would affect relations with NATO, the French foreign minister replied that the thinking had not progressed that far.[132]

In a meeting with de Gaulle a few days later, Gavin pressed the French president about "the political union of the Six and the military significance of that union," expressing his government's keen interest in such an arrangement and its significance for NATO. Despite de Gaulle's confirmation of Couve's observation that a mutual defense pact was not yet under serious consideration, the American ambassador concluded that the United States might be able to anticipate "a military relationship [among the EEC six] that ultimately may come into being."[133] Needless to say, nothing ever came of this and other plans to provide for the Europeans' defense of their own continent.

Such concerns later emerged in the Johnson administration. Secretary of Defense McNamara had long complained about West Germany's failure to contribute sufficient manpower and funding to the Alliance. He also had begun to advocate a reduction of the U.S. troop strength in Europe and hoped that de Gaulle's policy would contribute to that result.[134] Indeed, the French president had often proposed such a radical downsizing of American troop strength on the continent. In a long talk with de Gaulle at the end of November 1964, Ambassador Bohlen had pointed out the enormous financial burden of maintaining the GIs and their dependents in Europe. De Gaulle was fully sympathetic, offering the comforting observation that with the decline of the Soviet threat on the continent, "it would be normal and logical" at some future date "for the United States to reduce progressively its forces in Europe."[135] In his meeting with de Gaulle in mid-December, Rusk speculated that "it was conceivable that at some date in the future Europe might be able to organize its own defense," but quickly added that there were as yet no signs of the continent's willingness to share the burden.[136]

When Senator Mansfield introduced a resolution in August 1966 calling for a significant reduction in U.S. military forces in Western Europe, he had acquired twelve cosponsors. The Senate majority leader declared that "fundamental changes had taken place" and that "the continued presence of so many American troops in Europe 20 years after the war was beginning to grate on the nerves" of Europeans.[137] As Mansfield sardonically complained, "The 250 million people of Western Europe, with its tremendous industrial resources and long military experience, are unable to organize an effective military coalition to defend themselves against 200 million Russians who are contending with 800 million Chinese, but must continue after 20 years to depend upon 200 million Americans for their defense."[138]

The American secretary of defense was becoming increasingly concerned about the inability or unwillingness of European allies, and particularly the West Germans, to pay the so-called offset costs, that is, the purchases of American weapons to "offset" the expense of keeping American troops in Europe. McNamara was considering reducing American spending in Western Europe by $200 million and even withdrawing a substantial number of GIs from the continent. But Johnson would not buy any of the arguments for such reductions.[139] To the claim that a draw down was possible because the Soviet threat had diminished, he complained to a sympathetic senator that "I'm not one of these folks that [have been] just sucked in by the Russians. . . . I don't believe in [Arkansas Senator J. William] Fulbright, Mansfield, [Missouri Senator Stuart] Symington whole goddamned theory that it's all over over there," he declared. "I think those sons of bitches [the Soviets] want to eat us any day they can."[140] He would privately refer to his antagonists as "milquetoast" (Mansfield) or a "crybaby" (Fulbright), leading Fredrik Logevall to emphasize the "machismo" feature of Johnson's reaction to those counseling moderation or caution.[141]

France Outside and Washington's Reaction

The negotiations concerning the means by which de Gaulle's policy of disengagement would be implemented began in the spring of 1966. As usual, there was a sharp split between the State Department and the Defense Department about how to deal with the de Gaulle challenge. The State Department—Rusk and Ball—took the hardest line, calling for a public denunciation of "the serious consequences of de Gaulle's unilateral decisions" for transatlantic relations as well as for congressional support for the alliance. Ball even proposed that the United States delay the withdrawal of GIs from French territory as a rear-guard gesture of contempt and speculated about repudiating the Article Five commitment in the North Atlantic Treaty to defend France. The Pentagon opposed an open break and pressed for a calming effort to strengthen the integrated defense arrangements without France and to proceed with plans to evacuate American military facilities from the country.[142]

In reply to Ball's demand for tough action, the president calmly insisted that he saw "no benefit to ourselves or our allies" in debating the position of the French government and concluded that "our task is to rebuild NATO outside of France as promptly, economically, and effectively as possible." To McNamara he simply declared that "when a man asks you to leave his house, you don't argue; you get your hat and go."[143] The deadline of April 1, 1967, for the removal of NATO bases was met with ease, and the headquarters of the Alliance was effortlessly transferred from Rocquencourt near Versailles to the village of Casteau, Belgium, outside of Brussels.

The final arrangements for the relationship between France and NATO had been carefully worked out in the autumn of 1966 in the form of a compromise by France that was accepted by the United States and the other allies and was ratified by the Atlantic Council on November 2. France would no longer participate in the Defense Planning Committee, which controlled military planning, but it would remain in the fourteen-member political institution of NATO, the North Atlantic Council.

It was clear that one of the primary motivations for de Gaulle's rejection of the integrated command structure of NATO was to pursue détente in Europe preparatory to a possible end to the Cold War. The partition of the old continent into two mutually hostile armed camps, what he tirelessly referred to as the "Yalta system," should become a thing of the past. But he was not only challenging non-Communist Europe's "Atlantic" link to Washington. He also increasingly came to believe in the possibility of a detachment of Communist Eastern Europe from the Soviet Union. The result would be a Europe liberated from the two superpowers that would become reunited after two decades of division.

The Trip to Moscow

De Gaulle had often emphasized to Ambassador Bohlen that he regarded the Soviet threat to Western Europe as a thing of the past, declaring that "the Russian attitude had ceased to be menacing."[144] In the spring of 1966, he decided to visit the Soviet Union in the last two weeks of June. When word leaked out of the proposed trip, an apprehensive Rusk implored Bohlen to see the French president before his departure to find out what he anticipated obtaining from the trip. De Gaulle's original plan was to visit Moscow for four days. His subsequent decision to expand the trip to twelve days and enlarge his itinerary raised serious concerns in Washington. The French foreign ministry had to deny reports that he was considering a non-aggression pact with NATO's eastern adversary.[145] As he prepared for his trip in the last two weeks of June 1966, de Gaulle assured the American ambassador that he would not respond favorably to Soviet pressure to recognize the German Democratic Republic if it were applied. He also said that he would press his hosts to recognize that German reunification should be embraced as a long-term goal, a position dear to the heart of many in West Germany.[146]

Bohlen had long been certain, as he had put it in a memorandum to Rusk at the end of 1963, that "there is no possibility that de Gaulle would try to double-cross the Alliance by a deal with the Soviet Union."[147] But a month before the trip, the CIA issued an analysis of the significance of the visit as a harbinger of a possible Franco-Soviet rapprochement. It concluded that relations between Paris and Moscow had improved considerably since the low point of 1963, when the Elysée Treaty seemed to herald a warming of relations between France and West Germany to the Soviet Union's detriment.

The American intelligence agency noted that there was "no other attitude shared more fully by Moscow and Paris than fear of a Europe under German domination." It predicted that the Kremlin "will move warily" in its courtship of de Gaulle to determine where his European policy was headed.[148]

During his sojourn in the Soviet Union from June 20 to June 30, de Gaulle told Leonid Brezhnev that Europe's problems should be addressed not by negotiations between the two superpowers but by the Europeans themselves. When Brezhnev dusted off the old Soviet proposal for a European Security Conference from which the United States would be excluded, de Gaulle replied that Washington would have to be included in any conference that discussed the German problem. He made good on his pledge to Ambassador Bohlen before departing for the Soviet Union that France favored the reunification of Germany in the distant future, which prevented his country from recognizing the German Democratic Republic. When the topic of France's relations with the two superpowers came up, de Gaulle had good news and bad news for his host. On the one hand, the French president informed Brezhnev that he was perfectly satisfied with the existence of Soviet military power "for without it, we would be exposed to the U.S.'s irresistible hegemony." The bad news was his assertion that "we see no inconvenience in U.S. power, without which we would probably be exposed to Soviet hegemony."[149]

An examination of the Soviet archives revealed Moscow's ambivalence about the French withdrawal from NATO's integrated military command: on the one hand, enthusiasm for the blow that it delivered to Western military cooperation; on the other, consternation about what was seen by the Kremlin as the ultimate Gaullist goal of transforming Europe—on both sides of the Iron Curtain—as a third force equidistant between the two superpowers.[150] When de Gaulle heard that Johnson suspected him of preparing a reversal of alliances, he exclaimed to his son, Philippe (who had accompanied him on the trip to Moscow), "How ridiculous! To see me associating with these oligarchs who succeed one another from revolution to revolution by [threats of] bullets."[151]

De Gaulle's visit to Moscow did not produce any lasting results. His advocacy of German unification in the long term and his refusal to recognize the DDR were anathema to the men in the Kremlin.[152] The CIA reported that concerns about a Franco-Soviet alliance were totally unfounded. So too were the anguished conclusions of the specialist in American affairs in the French foreign ministry, who described Soviet prime minister Alexei Kosygin's return visit to Paris in early December 1966 as "a turning point in history," a "deplorable" reversal of alliances. "France is now closer to Russia than to the United States," the Americanophile Quai official confidentially informed the American embassy. When de Gaulle says he will attempt to construct a new European order "from the Atlantic to the Urals, you should believe him."[153]

In a wide-ranging conversation with de Gaulle in Paris in mid-December, soon after the Soviet premier had departed, Rusk pressed the French president about what he had learned from the visit. De Gaulle reported that Kosygin had asserted that "were it not for Vietnam, there could be a real détente in the world." Berlin had receded to second place in Moscow's list of priorities. The Kremlin was willing to pursue détente with the Federal Republic on the condition that it accept its eastern frontiers, explicitly and publicly renounce "any pretentions to nuclear weapons," and accept the reality of two Germanies for the near future. De Gaulle replied that Paris had been pressing Bonn for some time to make "some gesture to show that they did not have any evil design on Eastern Europe." He expressed optimism that West German foreign minister Willy Brandt and West German chancellor Kurt Georg Kiesinger, who had just taken power in West Germany in December, "will produce something of this nature."[154]

Two months earlier Johnson had decided to unveil his own emerging intention to sound out the Soviet bloc about the possibility of seeking a relaxation of tensions in Europe. In a closely watched speech to the National Conference of Editorial Writers in New York City on October 7, the president called for the beginning of détente on the old continent. "We want the Soviet Union and the nations of Eastern Europe to know that we and our allies shall go step by step with them as far as they are willing to advance," he solemnly declared. "We must improve the East-West environment in order to achieve the unification of Germany in the context of a larger, peaceful, and prosperous Europe."[155] Although this gesture was also intended to obtain the Kremlin's support in leaning on North Vietnam to be more accommodating in the war in Southeast Asia, it also reflected Washington's hope of stealing the fire from Paris on this issue.

In fact, the cause of European détente was gaining momentum on both sides of the Iron Curtain in the second half of 1966 and 1967. In July 1966, the Warsaw Pact, meeting in Bucharest, had officially proposed the European Security Conference that Moscow had been calling for, and which Brezhnev had urged upon de Gaulle during his visit the preceding month. In West Germany, Willy Brandt, the new foreign minister in a Christian Democrat/Social Democrat "grand coalition," that took power in Bonn in December, began to make tentative steps in the direction of the relaxation of Cold War tensions in Europe. The time seemed ripe for an improvement in East-West relations on the continent, a cause that de Gaulle had been championing for years. De Gaulle and Brandt would develop a cordial personal relationship, perhaps based on their common experience of resistance to Nazism and exile during the Second World War.[156]

But the Johnson administration's interest in exploring détente was a double-edged sword from de Gaulle's perspective. On the one hand, it seemed to indicate that Washington was finally coming around to the French president's long-standing advocacy of a reduction of tensions on the European continent. On the other hand, it carried with it the danger that the two superpowers might resolve their differences between themselves and develop a cooperative relationship at Europe's expense.

The Resumption of De Gaulle's Critique of U.S. Policy in the Third World

Within six months of his withdrawal from NATO's integrated command and two months after his trip to Moscow, de Gaulle again raised the hackles of the Johnson administration by deepening his criticism of American policy in the Third World. In the previous year, he had consistently spoken out against the American bombing campaign against North Vietnam. When Johnson had temporarily suspended the bombing of North Vietnam on Christmas Day, 1965, he sent UN ambassador Arthur Goldberg on a special mission to explain to de Gaulle that the purpose of the brief bombing halt was to bring Hanoi to the conference table. De Gaulle replied that any such action was useless unless accompanied by the "assurance that in the end any negotiations would conclude with the departure of all foreign [military] forces."[157] The French president continued to pepper Johnson with his customary mantra that "only a political solution is possible."[158]

During de Gaulle's visit to Moscow in June 1966, he had secured the Soviet government's agreement that everything must be done to prevent the war in Southeast Asia from degenerating into a war between East and West in Europe.[159] The next month the Frenchman Jean Sainteny, who had negotiated with Ho Chi Minh before the outbreak of the Franco–Viet Minh war in 1946, was sounding out Beijing, Hanoi, and the National Liberation Front (including meetings with Ho Chi Minh and North Vietnamese prime minister Pham van Dong) about the prospects for peace. Sainteny shared with Ambassador Bohlen his belief that Hanoi was sincerely seeking a peaceful settlement, which Bohlen dutifully forwarded to Washington.[160]

In the course of the next two years, the U.S. government engaged in a periodic, top-secret effort to establish indirect contact with Hanoi. Under

the code name Marigold, a complex series of approaches through intermediaries included a bewildering cast of characters including Sainteny, Janusz
Lewandoski (Saigon-based Polish delegate to the International Control
Commission), Averill Harriman, Harvard professor Henry Kissinger, and
others. James G. Hershberg admirably untangled this abortive effort in indirect diplomacy to terminate the Vietnam War.[161]

In the meantime, de Gaulle had embarked on a trip to Southeast Asia
in the early fall of 1966 during which he unveiled his criticism of Washington's policy in the region. In a passionate speech to a cheering crowd of one
hundred thousand in Phnom Penh, Cambodia, on September 1, 1966, the
French president took Washington to task for its intervention in Vietnam
and its rejection of his suggestion to adopt a policy of neutrality in that
country—as Cambodia's Prince Sihanouk had done. He described the war
in South Vietnam as one of "national resistance" and repeated his familiar
claim that the United States "will not be able to bring about a military solution" to the conflict.[162]

The furious reaction of the Johnson administration to the speech was
simple and straightforward: "The French position has moved from an initial
critical but neutral attitude to one of open public opposition to us."[163] It is
worth noting that the United States' other European allies were very reticent
about publicly supporting Washington's war in Southeast Asia, although
West Germany was skeptical of the "domino theory" in Southeast Asia. As
Helga Haftendorn has noted, the Bonn government also "did regard the U.S.
engagement in Southeast Asia as an indication that Washington would also
meet its alliance commitments in any conflict over Berlin."[164]

But de Gaulle tirelessly tried to persuade Washington that he was merely
giving friendly advice to an ally in order to persuade it to cut its losses in
Southeast Asia. In early November, he urged Bohlen to convey the message
to Johnson that the United States "should unilaterally take the decision to
withdraw" from Vietnam or face "a long war."[165] Three months later, Senator Robert Kennedy (Dem.–New York), the brother of the slain president,
who was already beginning to have second thoughts about his support for the
U.S. effort in the war that would later inspire his candidacy against Johnson
a year later, visited Paris on a fact-finding mission. On January 31, 1967, he
spent more than an hour in an intimate conversation with de Gaulle about
the war. The next day he visited the Quai d'Orsay to speak with Etienne
Manac'h, director of Far East Affairs and a long-time specialist on Indochinese affairs. From Manac'h Kennedy learned that Mai Van Bo, chief of the
North Vietnamese diplomatic mission in Paris, had implied that Hanoi was
softening its position and that negotiations could follow an unconditional

cessation of bombing of the North. Two days after Kennedy returned to Washington from his ten-day European tour on February 4, he learned that the American news media were reporting that he had received a "peace feeler" from Hanoi. An enraged Johnson initially refused to respond to the senator's request for a meeting to clear the air. He eventually backed down and invited Kennedy to the Oval Office, where their increasing animosity toward one another was on full display. When the senator indicated that de Gaulle and other European leaders believed that only an American bombing halt could lead to peace talks, the president responded that he would never do such a thing and warned Kennedy that "if you keep talking like this, you won't have a political future within six months."[166]

Johnson woke up on the day after New Year's to read about the French president's denunciation in his New Year's Eve press conference of this "detestable war" that "leads a great nation to ravage a small one."[167] Three months later Vice President Hubert Humphrey traveled to Paris for a meeting with the French president. During a lunch at the Elysée Palace, he avoided the sensitive topic of Vietnam. But he issued a tribute to de Gaulle as "a man of courage" whom history would remember as a great leader, which elicited the response of "thank you" in English from the French president.[168]

De Gaulle's earlier critique of the U.S. intervention in the Dominican Republic and his frequent denunciation of the Vietnam policy had set the stage for this attempt to portray France as a spokesman for the smaller countries in the developing world. One of the key elements of this strategy was his relatively abrupt reversal of France's relations with Israel. France had been the major foreign supplier of military hardware to the Jewish state under the Fourth Republic. The two countries were united in their hostility to Egyptian president Gamal Abdel Nasser's brand of pan-Arabism, which had threatened the position of both the French in Algeria to the west and Israel to the east of Egypt. The perceived threat of Egypt to the Suez Canal had brought Britain into this bilateral relationship during the Suez affair of November 1956. After de Gaulle's accession to power two years later and his successful withdrawal from Algeria in 1962, he sought to repair France's tattered relations with the Arab world. During the crisis of the spring of 1967 leading up to Israel's preemptive strike against the neighboring Arab states on June 6, 1967, Ambassador Bohlen reported on de Gaulle's "disengagement from what he regards as the extreme position of support for Israel taken by the Fourth Republic" in favor of "a delicate balance between Israel and the Arabs."[169]

After Israel's stunning military victory against its Arab neighbors in the Six-Day War of June 1967, de Gaulle unleashed a torrent of invective against the Jewish state after its occupation of Egyptian territory in the Sinai

Peninsula and the Gaza Strip together with the West Bank of the Jordan River taken from Jordan. This French criticism of Israel occurred just as the United States was expanding its political and military ties to the Jewish state. He conveyed his bitter recriminations to the British ambassador, who dutifully passed them on to his American colleague. His major complaint was that Tel Aviv had rejected his advice to avoid war. He was convinced that Washington's distraction in Vietnam had kept it from taking "the necessary steps to stop Israel from attacking." He excoriated "Israeli intransigence" and demanded that Israel evacuate the territory it had conquered.[170] He soon followed up this about-face concerning Israel with a reference to Jews as "an elite people, sure of themselves and domineering."[171]

One of de Gaulle's most idiosyncratic, unexpected, and inexplicable forays into foreign policy occurred in the summer of 1967. When he was invited to attend the Expo 67 celebration in Montreal, he broke diplomatic protocol by traveling directly to the capital of the French-speaking province of Québec rather than coming first to Ottawa, Canada's capital. He sailed up the Saint Lawrence River on a French cruiser that he had boarded in Saint Pierre et Miquelon, the only remaining French possession in North America (which, as we have seen, his Free French forces had liberated from the Vichy regime's control in December 1941). Before leaving Paris, he told his son-in-law that he would make a symbolic gesture of regret at France's loss of its North American empire in 1783. "I will hit hard," he declared. "Hell will happen, but it has to be done." A small separatist movement in Québec had begun to develop a decade earlier. After delivering a stirring speech to an adoring crowd of ten thousand from the balcony of the Montreal City Hall on July 24, 1967, which was broadcast live on radio, he ended with the provocative declaration "Vive le Québec Libre, vive le Canada français, vive la France."[172]

Needless to say the Canadian government of Prime Minister Lester Pearson was outraged, and even de Gaulle's close associates, such as Couve de Murville, were horrified.[173] In the face of critical press reports about the Québec fiasco, de Gaulle delivered a televised speech from the Elysée on August 10 in which he issued an unpersuasive defense of the speech by comparing the aspirations of the "French Canadians" to those of the people of Vietnam and the Middle East.[174]

The Harmel Report: Détente and Flexible Response Adopted

At the instigation of the Belgian foreign minister, Pierre Harmel, and with the full support of Washington, the ministerial session of the Atlantic Council in December 1966 had begun to examine the question of the future goals of the alliance amid the new enthusiasm for a relaxation of East-West tensions in Europe. The speech by West German foreign minister Willy Brandt suggested that the new government in Bonn was about to move beyond the hard line of past German governments and would seek better relations with Eastern Europe, including East Germany. In January 1967, West German chancellor Kurt Georg Kiesinger asserted that Bonn and Paris were on the same wavelength. The French Foreign Ministry crowed that de Gaulle's ideas were finally catching hold, although Couve de Murville could not resist the mordant observation in his memoirs that "as soon as it was recommended by Washington" instead of Paris, détente became "respectable."[175]

The lengthy deliberations about the Harmel Report, which was designed to give the Alliance a new sense of purpose after the French withdrawal, progressed relatively smoothly until the autumn of 1967 when it ran up against stiff French opposition. It seemed to be designed to establish NATO as the main Western actor in the process of reconciliation with the East, in direct conflict with de Gaulle's entire policy of combating the two blocs in Europe. When the final version of the Harmel exercise, titled "Report on the Future Tasks of the Alliance," was presented to the Atlantic Council, it was unanimously adopted on December 14, 1967. By incorporating the goal of détente in the document, the Council had in effect adopted de Gaulle's policy as its own without giving him the credit that was due.

The Non-Proliferation Treaty: France vs. America

The other major controversy complicating Franco-American relations was the adoption in October 1966 by President Johnson of the proposal for a nuclear non-proliferation treaty (NPT) that had been under discussion between the United States and the Soviet Union. The Russians pressed for the NPT for two reasons. First, it would drive the final nail into the coffin of the MLF. Second, it would bury once and for all West Germany's aspiration to participate in nuclear sharing within NATO. On both counts the NPT seemed entirely consistent with de Gaulle's policy: terminate the MLF and insist that West Germany definitively renounce the acquisition of nuclear weapons to smooth the way toward East-West détente in Europe. The NPT would confer an extraordinary advantage on France by confirming its special status as one of the five declared nuclear states while prohibiting West Germany or any other country from ever joining that select nuclear club. Yet de Gaulle adamantly opposed the NPT because of its origins: a Soviet-American deal that could freeze the partition of the continent and preserve the bloc system he had long hoped to dissolve.[176]

"Defense in All Directions":
France's New Global Nuclear Strategy

With the development of a credible national nuclear deterrent force, de Gaulle decided to publicize his doctrine of deterrence by approving the contents of an article published by General Charles Ailleret in a widely read journal of defense affairs. Titled "Défense 'dirigée' ou défense 'tous azimuts'?"[177] (directed defense or defense in all directions?), it was the ultimate statement that the French nuclear deterrent would not be confined to the European continent. It was to consist of a mini-version of the American triad (Mirage IV bombers, land-based intermediate-range ballistic missiles [IRBMs], and submarine-launched ballistic missiles [SLBM]). It was not merely a supplement to the NATO deterrent force but would be directed at all possible threats to French security in the future from wherever they might emanate.[178] It was based on the assumption that the Cold War confrontation in Europe may dissipate in the future as a result of détente. The CIA had issued a top-secret report on the status of the French nuclear deterrent force in May 1967 that dismissed it as not credible. The first generation of the Mirage 4 supersonic jet bombers that had come on line posed little threat to the Soviet Union, which possessed jet fighters and surface-to-air missiles that could easily bring the planes down. The land-based IRBM system currently in the works would probably not be operational until 1970, while the project for a submarine-based nuclear strike force (SLBM) was still in the planning stages.[179]

1968: The Great Turning Point

In early February 1968, as Charles Bohlen prepared to vacate his position as ambassador to France that he had occupied since the fall of 1962, he let the State Department know of his ultimate evaluation of the current Franco-American situation: "Given the attitude of de Gaulle, there would seem to be very little chance of any real improvement in Franco-American relations," he declared. "I can offer little encouragement to any belief in a change in our relations with France until the departure of de Gaulle."[180] In the previous month, he had been informed of a provocative and puzzling statement de Gaulle had made to the American journalist Cyrus Sulzberger in which he identified only three people who were "under foreign oppression today—the French-speakers in Canada, the Arabs in Israel, and the Tibetans in China[!]." The American ambassador concluded that "the old boy is going off his rocker."[181]

At the end of 1967, the French press had given prominent coverage to a candid public remark Johnson had made about the situation: "I am sorry that my relations with him [de Gaulle] are not closer, and that we are not more often in agreement than in disagreement."[182] In his farewell message before returning to the United States, which did not hold much hope for the relations between the United States and France, Ambassador Bohlen reminded the State Department that "we should always continue to remember that France is eternal but de Gaulle is not."[183]

In fact, relations between the two countries would improve markedly in the following months. During a New Year's Eve televised address on December 31, 1967, the French president had inveighed once again against the "unjust" and "detestable" armed intervention of the United States "on the territory of Vietnam," a classic case of a "big nation attempting to destroy a small nation." As always, he offered the services of France to facilitate a negotiated settlement to the conflict.[184] At the beginning of February 1968, Johnson mulled over a pessimistic report from Secretary of Defense McNamara about the deteriorating situation in Vietnam and unloaded his frustration to a journalist as the so-called Tet offensive unfolded: "There's one of three things you can do. One is run and let the dominoes start fallin' over. . . . Or you can fight, or you can sit down and agree to neutralize all of it, but nobody's gonna neutralize North Vietnam. . . . So I think old man De Gaulle is puffin' through his hat."[185]

The situation in Vietnam deteriorated in the winter and spring of 1968. The Tet offensive in January–February was a military disaster for the North Vietnamese regulars and their Viet Cong allies in the south, with some twenty thousand casualties. It also failed to spark an uprising in South Vietnam against the government in Saigon, as had been intended. But the brief military success, which included the penetration of the heavily fortified U.S. embassy and the occupation of several cities in the south, had a devastating political effect in the United States, whose citizens had been assured that victory was just around the corner ("the light at the end of the tunnel," in the contemporary parlance).

Two senators from President Johnson's own party, first Senator Eugene McCarthy of Wisconsin and then Senator Robert F. Kennedy of New York, entered the Democratic Party presidential primary campaign on essentially a single platform: ending the war. Recognizing that public opinion had turned against him and his Vietnam policy, Johnson launched a veritable bombshell in a televised address on March 31: after announcing the suspension of bombing above the twentieth parallel in the war-torn country and offering to open negotiations with Hanoi immediately to seek a political settlement of the war, he announced his withdrawal from the forthcoming presidential election.

De Gaulle refrained from responding to this abrupt volte face in American military policy in the direction of a policy he had long advocated with a self-congratulating "I told you so" comment. On the contrary, he sent a gracious message praising the American president's "courageous political act" that elicited fulsome expressions of gratitude in Washington.[186] When the North Vietnamese government responded favorably to Johnson's proposal for negotiations, the immediate question was where they should take place.

Rusk later claimed that when Hanoi and Washington had begun discussions for the site of the proposed peace talks on Vietnam, the North Vietnamese rejected all of the Americans' suggestions, including Geneva and Vienna. The American secretary of state had deliberately left Paris off the list. Johnson was not in favor of Paris either "because he feared Charles de Gaulle's hostile attitude toward the war might negatively influence the talks." At one point a host of other cities were considered. Johnson turned down Hanoi's suggestions of Phnom Penh, Cambodia, and Warsaw, Poland. The North Vietnamese rejected Johnson's suggestions of Vientiane, Laos; Rangoon, Burma; Jakarta, Indonesia; and New Delhi, India. After a month of back-and-forth in which other sites were proposed, the two sides finally agreed in early May on Paris, at Rusk's suggestion.[187] The talks finally began on May 13. Rusk later admitted that "Paris proved a good choice; the French did everything possible to facilitate the talks."[188]

Meanwhile, the movement toward European détente gained momentum during the first half of 1968. Serious consideration was given to the goal of mutual and balanced force reductions (MBFR) in Europe. This move was partly intended to head off another resolution from Senator Mansfield, which he had promised in January to introduce again calling for a unilateral American force reduction in Europe. When the Atlantic Council adopted a resolution later in the spring calling for MBFR, the time seemed propitious for the advent of significant progress in the reduction in tensions between NATO and the Warsaw Pact. Despite his long campaign for détente in Europe, de Gaulle—always the outlier—opposed this proposal because it once again threatened to consign the European continent to a settlement reached and imposed by the two superpowers.

The May Crisis in France and Washington's Reaction

De Gaulle had long operated on the assumption that domestic affairs would not intrude on his foreign policy initiatives. With a legislative majority in the parliament, a relatively compliant media, and a constitution that vested full authority for foreign relations in the chief executive, he was free to act without having to devote much attention to political issues within the country. But in the first three weeks of May 1968, an explosion of social unrest severely shook that assumption. University students protesting antiquated educational facilities in Paris virtually shut down the capital, constructing barricades, scuffling with the riot police, and marching to the slogan "Adieu de Gaulle."[189] When the principal French labor organizations joined in the protests, which had spread to virtually every city and town in the country, the future for de Gaulle looked bleak. This political turmoil in turn generated severe financial problems in France, which further restricted de Gaulle's freedom to pursue bold initiatives in foreign policy.

Amid this acute crisis, de Gaulle slipped out of the country totally incognito on May 29 and arrived by helicopter in Baden-Baden, West Germany, at the home of the commander of French forces there, General Jacques Massu, to ensure the support of the officer corps in the current crisis. Massu was a much-decorated French officer who had fought in the Free French army of General Leclerc during World War II, with the French army that returned to Indochina in 1945, with the French paratroops that had landed along the Suez Canal in 1956, and finally in Algeria where he sought to suppress the National Liberation Front in what came to be known as the Battle of Algiers in 1955–57. [190] When Massu clashed with de Gaulle in 1960 over the future of Algeria, he had been relieved of his command, but six years later he was named head of the French forces in West Germany. After assuring himself of the support of his old comrade-in-arms, de Gaulle overcame his inclination to resign amid the political chaos in the country and retire to Colombey.

R. Sargent Shriver, the son-in-law of President Kennedy and founding director of the Peace Corps in the United States, had succeeded Bohlen as ambassador to France in the midst of the French domestic crisis and presented his credentials on May 25, four days before the general's secret trip to West Germany. The new American ambassador learned on the day of de Gaulle's disappearance that a well-connected journalist at Le Monde, André Fontaine, had been assured by Prime Minister Georges Pompidou that de Gaulle would be gone shortly. Shriver authorized a cable to Rusk, who transmitted it in a note to Johnson, that the resignation would be announced the following morning.[191]

But these predictions proved to be premature. De Gaulle abruptly returned to Paris, dissolved the parliament, and called a snap election, the first round on June 23 and the second on June 30. The election resulted in his party and its Independent Republican allies ending up with 354 of 487 seats in the National Assembly. The election was a de facto referendum on his reign, and his victory suggested that he was back where he was at the beginning of the Fifth Republic. He promptly reshuffled his cabinet by reaching back to his old loyal supporters. He replaced Pompidou at the prime minister's residence, the Hôtel Matignon, with Couve de Murville, who took office on July 11. In naming his longtime acolyte Michel Debré minister of foreign affairs, he exclaimed, "I need someone unshakable and it's necessary for France. The United States will also want to take advantage of the situation. You will know how to handle their diplomacy."[192] It seemed that, after the crises of the summer and fall of 1968, he was back in the saddle with the approbation of the public and a ministry of the old guard that had helped him to gain power a decade earlier.

The Czechoslovak Blow to De Gaulle's Dream of Détente

In the meantime, the Warsaw Pact's invasion of Czechoslovakia on August 21, 1968, to snuff out its liberalizing government delivered a mortal blow to de Gaulle's project of liberating both sides of the Iron Curtain from the domination by the two superpowers. His earlier pronouncements about the increasing independence of the Soviet satellites in Eastern Europe were contradicted by the crushing of the political and economic reforms of the so-called Prague Spring by Soviet tanks.[193]

De Gaulle and his spokespersons could not resist the temptation to blame the Soviet invasion on the division of Europe between the two superpowers. The government-controlled French television broadcast documentaries of the Yalta Conference (with photographs and commentaries), reminding its viewers that de Gaulle had not been invited to the conclave in February 1945 that divided the continent and pointing out that no nation could rely on its superpower protector to respect its independence. (One official even went so far as the compare the occupation of Prague to the American intervention in Santo Domingo three years earlier!) Perhaps to demonstrate that he remained fully in charge, he ordered the detonation of the first French hydrogen bomb at the Pacific testing site on August 24, 1968, in the midst of the Czechoslovak drama and one month after the opening to signatures of the NPT to which France had refused to adhere. The thermonuclear blast signified de Gaulle's intention to assert his country's determination to pursue its own defense policy without regard to its transatlantic superpower protector. In a news conference, France's defense minister, Pierre Messmer, declared that the country would be able to tip its existing intermediate-range-ballistic missiles with thermonuclear warheads "in a few years."[194]

Some in Washington, especially analysts in the CIA, were hopeful that the Soviet intervention in Prague might induce de Gaulle to become more moderate in his policies toward the European situation, especially since the financial crisis in France that followed the May events might give Washington some leverage in providing financial assistance.[195] The Americans continued throughout the fall of 1968 to hope that Gaullist France would repair its relations with the United States and take a strong stand against the new aggressiveness of Moscow. Walt Rostow, who had replaced McGeorge Bundy as Johnson's national security adviser, met with Foreign Minister Michel Debré in Washington on October 11 and bluntly asked him if, in light of recent events, France was "willing to work closer in security and other matters with the West." When the French franc came under intense pressure in the summer and fall, the U.S. treasury department, at the request of President Johnson, rushed to the defense of the French currency.[196] The West Germans refused to lend a helping hand.

When the new American ambassador had his first substantive talk with de Gaulle on September 23, the French president immediately raised the issue of Moscow's intervention in Czechoslovakia the previous month. Shriver ridiculed the Soviet attempt to justify the invasion on the grounds that West Germany had been meddling in Czechoslovakia. De Gaulle replied that in his judgment the Soviets were worried about the threat of a revitalized West Germany joining with Czechoslovakia and perhaps even East Germany and China in "joint actions against the Soviet Union." In short, it was "the specter of Germany and China [!] working together against Russia in the next five to ten years" that had prompted the action. After this bizarre analysis, de Gaulle pressed a perplexed Shriver about what the U.S. response to a Soviet invasion of West Germany would be. When the ambassador reiterated Washington's commitment to defend its allies, de Gaulle repeated his long-standing belief that the United States would not risk nuclear retaliation against its own territory by responding with nuclear weapons to a Soviet attack against the Federal Republic. He then added that France, like the United States, would also fail to act in such a circumstance since "an invasion of Germany was not an invasion of France," which must "look to its own life and death and to its own future.[197]

A month before the American presidential election in November 1968, President Johnson gave an interview to French foreign minister Debré at the White House. The president was in a very affable mood. He asked Debré to convey his deep gratitude to de Gaulle for his support for the Vietnam negotiations under way in Paris. He finished by declaring, with what appeared to be some emotion, "I must admit that I have not done much personally to improve that situation [between our two countries], but I believe that I have not contributed to their deterioration." He concluded by expressing his "great admiration" for the country and its people and the firm belief that "France and the United States will stand together if there be an international crisis."[198]

But the two leaders had no connection whatsoever to the very end of Johnson's tenure. When Johnson had suggested to de Gaulle that the two leaders have regular telephone contact, de Gaulle (who seldom used the telephone) expressed his doubts that "the telephone can bring that human contact that you are talking about."[199] Within a month of the U.S. elections in November that would be won by the Republican candidate, Richard Nixon, officials in the State Department predicted that notwithstanding the May events in France, the Soviet intervention in Prague in August, and the U.S. monetary support for the French currency in November, the new president would face a de Gaulle who might well renew his critique of American policy in Europe and the world.[200]

CHAPTER TEN

~

Nixon and de Gaulle, 1969

Realism Triumphant and Mutual Admiration

Soon after the election in November 1968 that brought Richard Nixon to the White House, de Gaulle dispatched two warm letters of appreciation to Lyndon Johnson for his time as president. On January 3 of the new year, he expressed the hope that the United States and France could get together "to help in the solution of grave problems that weighed on the world's future."[1] A few weeks later he said that he was "convinced that there existed between our two peoples a deep esteem and friendship that is always manifest in the decisive moments of History."[2] These were the last comments from de Gaulle about a U.S. president with whom he had never developed a working relationship, let alone a personal rapport, during the almost five years they had governed their respective countries.

The relationship between the man in the White House and the man in the Elysée Palace would dramatically change in course of the next four months. Governor William Scranton of Pennsylvania had arrived in Paris in September 1968 as an unofficial representative of Republican presidential candidate Richard Nixon. "I have very friendly relations with Mr. Nixon, whom I hold in very high esteem," de Gaulle told the governor in their hour-long meeting in his office. "If he is elected President of the United States, I would not be upset. On the contrary."[3] Charles de Gaulle and Richard Nixon had met three times before the latter's accession to the American presidency. Nixon recalled a lunch with the French leader on the outdoor patio of the Elysée Palace in 1962 after the American politician's embarrassing defeat in the California gubernatorial election, two years after Kennedy's victory over him for the presidency. The French president, who had suffered many defeats in his own career, offered a toast to his guest, predicting that "at some time in the future I [Nixon] would be serving my nation in a very high capacity."[4] At a lunch de Gaulle gave for Nixon during his brief trip to Paris on July 30, 1963, the host complained about the Kennedy administration's refusal to agree to nuclear cooperation with France. Nixon replied that many in the U.S. Congress agreed with de Gaulle's position—he mentioned Senators Everett Dirksen, Richard Russell, and Barry Goldwater—and expressed the hope that a procedure for sharing nuclear weapons information could be worked out.[5] The two met again on June 8, 1967, when the American politician had already begun to lay the groundwork for the presidential campaign that would bring him to the White House.[6] After the 1968 election, de Gaulle retained a high opinion of the American president-elect based on those fleeting encounters. Nixon was absolutely taken with the French president, whom he described, after his forced resignation in 1974, as "a genuine hero, one of the towering figures of the twentieth century."[7]

Nixon's national security adviser, Henry Kissinger, had praised de Gaulle in his writings as a realist who saw the world as it is rather than how it should be.[8] The references to "realism" popped up across the Atlantic after Nixon entered the White House. Officials at the French foreign ministry were telling Shriver of their expectation the president-elect was "likely to prove more realistic" than his Democratic predecessors.[9] De Gaulle wrote to Nixon that he would be delighted to meet with him to discuss international issues of interest to both countries as soon as the new American president was able to travel to Europe.[10]

In the meantime, relations between France and the Federal Republic of Germany had undergone a notable decline. De Gaulle partially blamed the West Germans for their economic and political support of the reformist government in Czechoslovakia as providing Moscow with a pretext to intervene in Prague. The failure of Bonn to support Paris during the monetary crisis in the fall of 1968 did not help matters. This cooling of Franco-German relations led to a French attempt to improve relations with Great Britain. De Gaulle had briefly hinted about the possibility of resurrecting the old tripartite proposal of 1958, though it was met with little enthusiasm in Washington and London.[11]

On February 4, 1969, less than a month after Nixon entered the White House, the new British ambassador to France, Christopher Soames, and his wife, Mary (Winston Churchill's daughter), attended a private lunch with de Gaulle in the Elysée Palace, with the ambition to mend the tattered relations between the two countries. De Gaulle reciprocated this démarche with an off-the-cuff suggestion: a modification of the EEC's Treaty of Rome in such a way as to enable this purely economic grouping to cooperate on political and security issues in a loose-knit coalition of European states. Once European security cooperation among the six member states had been established, it could replace NATO. The implication was that if London went along with the proposal, France would finally lift its veto of its application for membership in the organization de Gaulle had proposed to radically transform. When the British government leaked the ambassador's record of the meeting to the *London Times* on February 21, it precipitated an explosion of anti-French sentiment among the smaller countries in the EEC as well as in the United States (because de Gaulle also seemed to be suggesting that London and Paris cooperate in orchestrating a radical restructuring of the EEC and possibly a system of European defense cooperation that would replace NATO, all without Washington's participation). De Gaulle in turn was irritated with British prime minister Harold Wilson for having publicized what was supposed to be a top-secret conversation.[12]

As Anglo-French relations were reaching their lowest point in years, the new occupant of the White House decided to reach out to the French president. While still president-elect, Nixon had arranged for the submission of a sealed letter to French Ambassador Lucet a week before his inauguration with instructions to tell de Gaulle of his "strong desire" that the incoming administration would enjoy "the best relations with France." He added the expression of his "fervent hope" that the two leaders could "exchange views" in the near future.[13]

Throughout the month of February, a veritable wave of positive sentiments flowed between the White House and the Elysée Palace. On February 1, Kissinger phoned the French ambassador to confirm that the new president would be making his first transatlantic trip toward the end of the month, adding that the conversations he would hold with de Gaulle would be "by far the most important." Eleven days later Nixon wrote the French president personally to express his hope that their forthcoming encounters "will be but the first in a series of personal meetings" with world leaders and that "the traditional hallmark of relations between our two peoples must be reflected in the close contact of their leaders."[14]

Even Eisenhower, gravely ill with the malady that would take his life at the end of March, managed to send a letter to de Gaulle from Walter Reed Hospital, which elicited a warm response from the French president in his last communication with his old friend.[15] Nixon's decision to stop off in Paris for several days to confer with de Gaulle set in motion a flurry of friendly exchanges between the two leaders. While the French president laid out the red carpet for him, Nixon remained in the French capital from February 28 to March 2, 1969, and conducted a total of ten hours of discussions. In their three meetings, twice at the Elysée Palace and once at the Grand Trianon Palace in Versailles, the new American president bonded with the French chief executive in ways unimaginable in the days of Roosevelt, Truman, Kennedy, Johnson, and even Eisenhower. Couve du Murville and Kissinger attended some of the encounters, along with other officials on both sides.[16]

In their first meeting on February 28, a dinner at the Elysée Palace, de Gaulle made it abundantly clear that he was prepared to discuss all of the hot-button issues between Washington and Paris that had caused such consternation in both capitals. The American president gave a laudatory toast to his host, hailing de Gaulle as "a leader who has become a giant among men," because he had the courage and wisdom "which the world needs so much today" to resolve the problems of the world.[17] Nixon began by indicating his interest in exploring a meeting with the Soviet leaders and asking for the French president's views about that. De Gaulle strongly advised the American president to pursue a genuine rapprochement with the Soviet Union, reiterating his familiar refrain that Moscow no longer had any intention of committing aggression against Western Europe. The leaders in the Kremlin, he insisted, were obsessed about the threat from the Chinese, who "have long detested the Russians." This anxiety about the threat from the East, he believed, would oblige Moscow to seek a rapprochement with the West. He predicted that "in a world of détente, liberty would be the gainer" in Eastern Europe and possibly Russia as well. He forcefully expressed his oft-stated views about the ephemeral nature of ideology and the eternal power of nationalism: "There is Russia and there is Communism and . . . they were not always the same thing." When Nixon sought de Gaulle's advice about how to end the war in Vietnam, the French president restated what he had emphasized many times to Johnson. De Gaulle remarked that while the Algerian War and the Vietnam War were "similar," there was one major difference: unlike Algeria, where France had a million European settlers and had occupied the country for 130 years, the United States had limited involvement in Vietnam, no settlers there, and that country, unlike Algeria, "is not on your doorstep."[18]

If President Nixon "wanted to get rid of this bad affair and make peace," the French president advised, there were two interrelated steps to take: the first was to make genuine progress in the "political negotiations" that had been taking place in Paris since the spring of 1968; the second was to "establish a calendar for the departure of U.S. troops." He warned that if no deadline for withdrawal were set, the political negotiations were doomed to fail, adding that he had heard from the NLF delegate in the Paris talks, who knew that Nixon would be meeting with de Gaulle. The delegate complained that the talks were stalled and warned that if no progress was made, there might well be a new North Vietnamese/Viet Cong offensive in the future. The winding down of the American presence in Vietnam, de Gaulle concluded, would have the advantage of freeing Washington to pursue better relations with Moscow and Beijing. "The West should get to know China," the French president insisted. "We should try to get them to the table with us and offer them an opening." Nixon wondered if "it might be wise to open lines of communication with the Soviets and Chinese and so to speak not put all our eggs in one basket." The American president agreed with his host that the United States must acknowledge that the Soviet Union and China "were two great powers" and it made sense to "pursue parallel relationships with them." At the end of their final meeting in Paris, Nixon indicated his desire to set up means of communication with his French counterpart that would bypass normal diplomatic channels, with the proviso that all messages below the heads-of-state level should be routed through Kissinger rather than the state department.[19]

Kissinger met de Gaulle for the first time during the first conversation between Nixon and de Gaulle at the Elysée Palace. When an aide ushered the national adviser for a one-on-one conversation with the French president, de Gaulle immediately asked him, "Why don't you get out of Indochina?" De Gaulle was unimpressed with Kissinger's reply that a precipitate departure would severely weaken the credibility of U.S. pledges to defend its allies.[20] But in spite of his disagreement, Nixon and de Gaulle got along famously during the president's visit. The renowned journalist at Le Monde André Fontaine remarked that "General de Gaulle has [finally] found the American interlocutor that he had sought for a long time."[21] The French president attended a farewell dinner organized by Nixon at the American Embassy and then accompanied the American president to Orly airport for his departure, a gesture that protocol did not require. At a press conference on March 4 after his return to Washington, Nixon lavished praise on de Gaulle and expressed the hope that Western Europe would assume its appropriate responsibility in matters of defense. This extraordinary statement prompted Couve de Murville to declare that "such an evolution was what France had always hoped for."[22]

Nixon and Kissinger had on their own decided to launch an effort toward rapprochement with Moscow and Beijing on precisely the realist grounds that de Gaulle was advocating. They also had recognized the futility of continuing the American war effort in Vietnam and the need for a negotiated settlement, precisely the solution that de Gaulle had been unsuccessfully

254 ⁓ Chapter Ten

urging on Johnson until the latter threw in the towel in March 1968. Also on quintessential Gaullist realist grounds, he would simultaneously pursue détente with Moscow and Beijing in 1972.

A few days after the Nixon–de Gaulle tête-à-tête at the end of February and early March, Ambassador Shriver celebrated the "sweet smell of success" surrounding the visit and the "joy in official Paris circles" about the abrupt and unexpected improvement in Franco-American relations. He gloated about the "anxiety" of Washington's other loyal European allies (citing Britain in particular) and even their "disgust and dismay" at Nixon's "capitulation to the one man who has wrecked everyone's dreams (except his own)" about the future of Europe. The American ambassador added that the other allies hoped that the United States would reaffirm its commitment to "existing multilateral enterprises in Europe" and avoid "kowtowing to de Gaulle" and vigorously oppose the French when they threatened "to go their merry way without regard to the U.S. or Allied position."[23]

A week later Shriver reported that the Gaullists were "euphoric" at Nixon's very complimentary words about the French president and presumed that they would bolster his chances in the national referendum he had announced on February 2 for April 27 to secure public endorsement of his presidency. But in retirement de Gaulle shared with his old collaborator André Malraux the prediction that while Nixon was receiving applause for his efforts to end the war in Southeast Asia, "he hasn't seen the end of that Pandora's box. Every great plan is long-term. Despite its power, I don't believe the United States has a long-term policy."[24] Nixon, of course, would prolong the American military presence in Vietnam for the rest of his first term, before bowing to the inevitable and executing a full American withdrawal in 1973.

The last time de Gaulle and Nixon met was at the funeral for Eisenhower at the end of March. After paying his respects to the deceased American president's coffin, de Gaulle conveyed his condolences to the widow, Mamie Eisenhower.[25] When the two leaders met for an hour in the Oval Office on that solemn occasion, they exchanged emotional comments about their memories of the departed leader. According to his son, de Gaulle's solemn observation that "I have lost a great friend" elicited from Nixon the reply (pointing to himself), "You have another one."[26] They then got down to business. The American president, replying to de Gaulle's repeated plea to withdraw from Vietnam to free the United States to pursue other initiatives, shared with the French president his plan to organize a progressive withdrawal and to deepen the contacts with Hanoi's representatives.[27]

On the flight back to Paris, de Gaulle mentioned to Alphand, who had accompanied him on the transatlantic trip, that he expected to lose the nationwide referendum he had scheduled for April 27 and would be "very happy with the outcome."[28] The referendum was based on relatively trivial issues involving the Senate and the regions that could easily have been presented to the National Assembly for approval rather than to the country at large. He repeated this prediction several times as the day of the referendum approached. On April 24 he poignantly remarked to Michel Debré, his former premier and current foreign minister, "The dice have been rolled. I can do nothing more. The French people don't want me anymore. So I have nothing else to do but leave."[29] The day after the referendum was rejected by French voters by the slim margin of 52.41 percent against vs. 47.58 percent in favor, de Gaulle resigned and promptly returned to his country home in Colombey-Les-Deux-Eglises for good.[30]

Georges Pompidou had served as prime minister of France from 1962 to 1968. He had been long thought to be the dauphin before de Gaulle unceremoniously cast him aside in July 1968. But he retained his close ties to the Gaullist movement and was elected de Gaulle's successor to the presidency on June 15, 1969, with 58 percent of the vote. De Gaulle the private citizen visited Ireland to pay his respects to the country whence his ancestors on his mother's side came and took a brief trip to Spain. Nixon had sent General Walters to deliver a handwritten letter to Colombey with a formal invitation to visit Washington. De Gaulle was deeply touched by the letter and replied in his own handwritten letter leaving open the possibility of such a visit.[31] But he never took up Nixon on his invitation to come to the United States as a revered private citizen.[32] Instead, he settled down to work at Colombey on the last volume of his memoirs. They were intended to cover the period from 1958 to 1969. But he completed only the period 1958–1962 and a fragment covering the next four years.[33]

He died on November 9, 1970, two weeks before what would have been his eightieth birthday, of a ruptured blood vessel leading to the heart in the presence of his wife. Three days later more than eighty current or former heads of state or government, including Harold Macmillan, Anthony Eden, and Richard Nixon, attended the mass at Notre-Dame Cathedral in his honor. The funeral that same afternoon was held in the small church at Colombey. Malraux recalled seeing two enormous wreaths lying beside the open tomb sent by Mao and Zhou-enlai.[34]

~

CHAPTER ELEVEN

De Gaulle and the United States

A Long and Contentious Relationship

Long after de Gaulle's death in 1970, his former collaborator René Pleven told Jean Lacouture that "the reason that General de Gaulle misunderstood the United States is that he was a man for whom history counted more than anything else. In order to understand states and policies his natural and unvarying tendency was to resort to history. That is why he was so successful in dealing with Britain [?], Germany, or China. But where the United States was concerned, he was at a loss; he found no historical keys. Not that the United States possessed no history. But de Gaulle was not acquainted with it . . . and did not think it could be compared to that of 'real' nations."[1]

As he sought a privileged, dominant relationship with West Germany and détente with the Communist bloc, de Gaulle pursued a number of policies that antagonized the United States and its closest ally, Great Britain, two countries that (as we have seen) he so often lumped together as the "Anglo-Saxons."[2] His vetoes of London's application for admission to the European Economic Community in 1963 and 1967 were based on the assumption that it would act as a "Trojan horse" for American penetration of the emerging continental common market. His vocal criticism of Lyndon Johnson's military interventions in Vietnam and the Dominican Republic in the mid-1960s contrasted with the response of America's other NATO allies, who maintained either a supportive posture or a discreet silence.[3] In short, he was forever an outlier in the Western alliance on so many global issues.

Dean Rusk's final judgment was kinder than his exasperated comments while he butted heads with de Gaulle. He confided to the journalist Cyrus

Sulzberger a mordant reflection on the yawning gap between de Gaulle's aspirations and the reality of his policies. "Had he thrown France into the leadership of an authentic [West] European movement will full cooperation with the other side of the Atlantic, French prestige would be soaring. But the trend he has chosen may turn out to be tragic, especially for the dream he has himself desired to accomplish."[4] That comment perfectly summarized the dilemma that de Gaulle confronted when he thought about the United States. The only means by which he might have been able to loosen what he deemed to be the stranglehold of the transatlantic superpower on the non-Communist half of Europe would have been by fully embracing the political, military, and economic integration of Western Europe. But his ardent French nationalism prevented him from making the necessary sacrifices of French sovereignty for such a realignment to take place.[5] The European Union, successor to the EEC, has tried and failed miserably to develop an independent security force apart from NATO to this day.

Above all, as we have seen so often, de Gaulle's most salient and unwavering belief was that all political ideologies were transitory and that the only permanent political unit in the world was the nation-state. His own nation-state, France, held a special place in his thinking. How to resurrect it from the depths of military defeat and national humiliation after the summer of 1940 became his obsession for the rest of his life.

The poisonous relationship between de Gaulle and Franklin D. Roosevelt was inspired originally by the American president's disdain for the French political system of the Third Republic and for the country's ignominious collapse in 1940. Once de Gaulle appeared on the scene, protected and subsidized by Churchill, FDR adamantly refused to acquiesce in de Gaulle's seemingly quixotic bid to restore his country to its former position in the top ranks of the world's powers. Roosevelt's decision to play ball with the Vichy regime was motivated, as we have seen, by the twin goals of keeping the French fleet out of German and/or Italian hands and preserving a listening post for intelligence in the occupied country as America prepared for its eventual involvement in the war. De Gaulle in London, then in North Africa, and finally in liberated France represented an irritant to the American president's ambition to become what one of his biographers called "the soldier of freedom."[6]

FDR's antipathy for de Gaulle was shared by several key members of his administration, including Secretary of State Hull and his ambassador to Vichy France and later chief of staff, William Leahy. France's foremost expert on de Gaulle's foreign policies in general and toward the United States in particular has summarized the long-term effects of his treatment by Roos-

evelt: "The Second World War played a primeval role in fashioning the foreign policy of the Fifth Republic," Maurice Vaïsse observes, which consisted
of "preserving its freedom of action vis-à-vis American power."[7]

As Harry Truman began to lay the groundwork for what would become
his country's leadership in the Western world during the Cold War, he was
annoyed by the minor roadblocks that de Gaulle placed in his path in the
year after his accession to the presidency. He did not hesitate to exclude de
Gaulle from the Potsdam Conference in the summer of 1944 as FDR had
kept him from Yalta. He had never been a Francophile since his unpleasant
experience while on leave in Paris during the First World War, where he
shared his fellow soldiers' annoyance with overcharging shopkeepers and
reacted sharply to what he viewed as the immorality of the free-wheeling
displays in the cabarets in Montmartre. They met only once and never developed any rapport before de Gaulle resigned in early 1946.

After Charles de Gaulle returned from the political wilderness to take
control of France in 1958, President Dwight D. Eisenhower profited from the
two soldiers' cooperation during the Second World War to develop a decent
working relationship with de Gaulle in the two and a half years that their
presidencies overlapped. The disputes that divided them were manageable
and kept within bounds. Eisenhower's belief that France deserved to construct nuclear weapons of its own and his cooperation with de Gaulle on the
issue of Berlin (in opposition to British prime minister Harold Macmillan)
were the two high points of the relationship between these two leaders. It is
also certain that de Gaulle recalled with gratitude and nostalgia the support
he had received in his continual conflict with Roosevelt from the American
commanding general in the Second World War. There was also the fact that
both leaders were convinced, as Marc Trachtenberg put it, that "at the most
basic level, Eisenhower and de Gaulle wanted the same thing. Both wanted
the Europeans to stand on their own, to move away from a situation characterized by excessive dependence on the United States."[8]

The Kennedy presidency was obviously cut short by the assassination in
Dallas in November 1963. But, as we have seen, de Gaulle was enamored
of the American president and his elegant French-speaking wife during the
couple's visit to France. The return visit that was not to take place would
probably have resulted in tension between the two chief executives because
of de Gaulle's strident criticism of the American war in Vietnam and his
continuing barbs against the Atlantic Alliance. Some have argued that had
Kennedy been elected to a second term, he would have reversed America's
course in the Southeast Asian War and avoided the gradual buildup of U.S.
forces there that would be undertaken by his successor. But no evidence is

forthcoming to justify that assertion. In any case, de Gaulle and Kennedy continually sparred over the twin issues that separated Washington: the Multilateral Nuclear Force and the new doctrine of "flexible response." What seemed to have been de Gaulle's authentic grief in response to the assassination of the young American president belied their sharp policy differences. Kennedy's secretary of state, Dean Rusk, who remained in office during the term of his successor, failed to contain his disdain for the French president.

Lyndon Johnson and Charles de Gaulle had no personal relationship whatsoever and repeatedly clashed on all manner of issues. Johnson deeply resented the periodic transatlantic lectures he would have to endure from de Gaulle. They were all delivered through the good offices of his ambassador in Paris, Charles Bohlen. The two heads of state never sat down for a long review of the multitude of issues that separated France from the United States. Indeed, it is an astonishing fact that, apart from a few minutes together at the funerals of Kennedy in 1963 and Adenauer in 1967, de Gaulle had no direct contact with Johnson for eight years. The two salient problems were, of course, the French president's public denunciation of Johnson's intervention in Vietnam and de Gaulle's persistent criticism of the North Atlantic Treaty Organization that eventually led to France's withdrawal from its integrated command system. Directly related to that disagreement was de Gaulle's frequent declaration that France in particular and Western Europe in general could not and should not count on the United States to intervene to defend its allies in a war on the continent.

In his brilliant assessment of de Gaulle's foreign policy after his accession to power, Edward Kolodziej divides the story into three periods. From 1958 to 1962, the French president temporarily acquiesced in America's predominant power in the Atlantic alliance because of continuing pressures by Moscow on Western Europe and the burdensome war in Algeria. From 1962 to 1968, de Gaulle's goal was to liberate France from Washington's control of the West's strategic and diplomatic policies while enticing West Germany to abandon Washington in favor of Paris. In 1968 the internal rebellion against the Gaullist government, the ensuing financial disaster, the growing assertion of West German economic power, and the Warsaw Pact invasion of Czechoslovakia unraveled (temporarily, as it turned out) de Gaulle's hope for West-East détente in Europe and the loosening hold of the two superpowers on their respective halves of the continent.[9]

Perhaps the last word should belong to the late Stanley Hoffmann, the wisest and most perceptive analyst of French foreign policy and de Gaulle's relationship with the United States: "Americans were prompt to point out the contradictions of Gaullism in Europe," he observed. "Gaullism, they said, was using the European idea and West European institutions as a kind of smokescreen to flush out American predominance, but behind this screen purely French interests were being pursued without external interference—'Europe' meant a bar to the United States but no leash on France."[10] Or, as Ronald Steel put it in his devastating critique of American foreign policy toward the end of de Gaulle's time in office, the French president's "great failure has been his inability to realize that the independent Europe he wants to create can be forged only if France herself is willing to accept certain limitations on her national sovereignty." And he continued: "France does not have the power to take over America's role by herself. Only Europe as a whole could hope to exercise that power, and such a Europe does not yet exist."[11]

The love affair between Charles de Gaulle and Richard Nixon was an unexpected denouement of the relations between de Gaulle and the five previous occupants of the White House. The fact that they were together in office for less than four months leads to this counterfactual speculation: would the two have established a rapport that might have removed the long list of irritants that had exasperated every American president before the advent of the Nixon/Kissinger administration? Nixon's most daring, and surprising, initiatives in foreign policy in the year 1972—three years after de Gaulle's retirement and two years after his death—the trip to Moscow in pursuit of détente in Europe and the trip to Beijing to launch the process that eventually led to the reciprocal recognition of the United States and the People's Republic of China, were all policies advocated by the French president during his time in office. Nixon, in his early political career, had established a reputation as a hard-line anti-Communist, as a member of the "China Lobby" that supported the regime of Chiang Kai-Shek on Taiwan and opposed all suggestions for the admission of the People's Republic to the United Nations and for diplomatic recognition. Together with Kissinger he eventually affirmed what the French president had long insisted—that ideology is transient and that national interests are paramount. Of course, Nixon's decision to pull the remaining U.S. troops out of Vietnam took much longer than anyone expected. In fact, it took longer than the entire period during which Johnson had kept them there.

~

A Note on Sources

I have consulted a wide range of primary sources from presidential libraries, other repositories of private papers, memoirs, and contemporary newspaper and magazine articles. For the secondary sources on which this book relies, I have profited from many works in French and English on various aspects of de Gaulle's life. I have chosen to use English translations of works in French when they are available, since this book is intended primarily for an English-speaking audience. The English translation of Jean Lacouture's three-volume study *Charles de Gaulle* (condensed from the French version into two volumes: *The Rebel, 1890–1944* [New York: Norton, 1993] and *The Ruler, 1945–1970* [New York: Norton, 1993]) is one of the dozens of works on the French statesman that I have found most useful in preparing this study. It should be noted, however, that Lacouture's work, despite its criticism of de Gaulle's policies, runs the risk of approaching hagiography.

Two other biographies, not translated into English, are worth mentioning: Paul-Marie de La Gorce's *De Gaulle* (Paris: Perrin, 1999), which is even more uncritically laudatory than Lacouture's, and Eric Roussel's *De Gaulle* (Paris: Gallimard, 2002), which goes to the opposite extreme in its picayune criticism of many of its subject's policies. Among the many other secondary sources in English on the subject, a few are especially worth noting: Don Cook, *Charles de Gaulle: A Biography* (New York: G.P. Putnam's Sons, 1983); Brian Crozier, *De Gaulle: The First Complete Biography* (New York: Scribners, 1973); Charles Williams, *The Last Great Frenchman: A Life of General De Gaulle* (New York: Wiley, 1993); Jonathan Fenby, *The General:*

Charles De Gaulle and the France He Saved (New York: Skyhorse, 2012). By far, the most even-handed, lucidly written, exhaustively researched work on the subject is Julian Jackson, *De Gaulle* (Cambridge, MA: Harvard University Press, 2018), which arrived on my desk as I was well along in my research and writing for this book.

While, in my view, the aforementioned books provide an excellent treatment of the French leader's entire career, the indispensable scholarly studies of de Gaulle's *foreign policies* have been written by two distinguished French historians of international relations. Maurice Vaisse is the author of numerous works on almost every aspect of de Gaulle's relations with foreign leaders and governments during his tenure as French president. Among the many books he has published, my favorite is *La Grandeur: Politique étrangère du général de Gaulle, 1958–1969* (Paris: Fayard, 1998). The second master expositor of de Gaulle's foreign policies as president, particularly his relationship with the United States, is Frédéric Bozo, *De Gaulle, the United States, and the Atlantic Alliance*, trans. Susan Emanuel (Lanham, MD: Rowman & Littlefield, 2001). Finally, for the period of the Second World War, I have made extensive use of André Béziat's tour de force *Franklin Roosevelt et la France* (Paris: Harmattan, 1997), a model of careful research and eloquent exposition. There are many other excellent works in English and French on the subject. I shall refrain from listing them all here. I have carefully credited them in the footnotes in this work. Finally, although this book focuses on the relations between Charles de Gaulle and the six American presidents mentioned above, I have found it necessary to provide the historical context of the man's career before he entered the historical scene after France's military defeat in June 1940.

~

Notes

Chapter One

1. Jean Lacouture, *De Gaulle, The Rebel 1890–1944*, trans. Alan Sheridan (New York: Norton, 1993), 6.

2. Charles de Gaulle, *The Complete War Memoirs*, trans. Jonathan Griffin (New York: Simon & Schuster, 1972); Charles de Gaulle, *Memoirs of Hope: Renewal and Endeavor*, trans. Terence Kilmartin (New York: Simon & Schuster, 1971).

3. Eugen Weber, *The Nationalist Revival in France, 1905–1914* (Berkeley: University of California Press, 1968).

4. De Gaulle later sent his first book to Maurras, with a personal dedication to his "respectful homage," and a second book to the leader of the royalist, extreme-right organization *Action Française*. Julian Jackson, *De Gaulle* (Cambridge, MA: Harvard University Press, 2018), 79. Nora Beloff suggests, in a chapter titled "De Gaulle: Man and Monarch," that de Gaulle (a devout Catholic) abandoned Maurras when the Vatican denounced him in 1926 for his agnostic views. Nora Beloff, *The General Says No: Britain's Exclusion from Europe* (Harmondsworth: Penguin Books, 1963), 21–22.

5. His foreign minister Georges Bidault claims in his memoirs that de Gaulle's thinking "showed strong traces of Jacques Bainville." Georges Bidault, *Resistance: The Political Autobiography of Georges Bidault*, trans. Marianne Sinclair (London: Weidenfeld and Nicolson, 1967), 88. Richard Vinen includes de Gaulle as a Maurrasian "to some extent." Richard Vinen, *The Unfree French: Life under the Occupation* (New Haven, CT: Yale University Press, 2006), 74–75. Édmond Michelet, *Le Gaullisme, passionnante aventure* (Paris: Fayard, 1962), 20–26. William R. Keylor, *Jacques Bainville and the Renaissance of Royalist History in Twentieth-Century France* (Baton Rouge: Louisiana State University Press, 1979).

6. Philippe de Gaulle, *De Gaulle Mon Père: Entretiens avec Michel Tauriac* (Paris: Plon, 2005), 570.

7. Jonathan Fenby, *The General: Charles De Gaulle and the France He Saved* (New York: Skyhorse, 2012), 52.

8. De Gaulle, *War Memoirs*, 5.

9. Charles Williams, *The Last Great Frenchman: A Life of Charles de Gaulle* (New York: Wiley, 1993), 34.

10. Jean Pouget, *Un certain capitaine de Gaulle* (Paris: Aubéron, 2000), 125–127; Lacouture, *De Gaulle, The Rebel*, 50.

11. Lacouture, *De Gaulle, The Rebel*, 58–59; Brian Crozier, *De Gaulle: The First Complete Biography* (New York, Scribner's, 1973), 31.

12. Lacouture, *De Gaulle, The Rebel*, 64–65.

13. Jean-Raymond Tournoux, *Pétain et de Gaulle: Un Demi-Siècle d'Histoire Non Officielle* (Paris: Plon, 1964), 88; Bernard Ledwidge, *De Gaulle* (New York: St. Martin's Press, 1982), 30–31.

14. Pétain's election to the Academy in 1931 had nothing to do with his literary merits. He replaced Ferdinand Foch and managed a decent reference to his predecessor despite the fact that the two military leaders had long detested each other.

15. Georges Cattui, *L'Homme et son Destin* (Paris: Fayard, 1960), 44–45.

16. Ledwidge, *De Gaulle*, 34–35. She died at the age of twenty in 1948.

17. As we shall see, this attitude would inspire him to grant independence to most of the remaining territories of the French empire in 1960 in order to concentrate on France's position in Europe.

18. Charles de Gaulle, *Le Fil de l'epée* (Paris: Berger-Levrault, 1932), dedication.

19. Developed in total secrecy, the machine was originally called a water carrier, but since the British government tended to abbreviate everything, the term "WC" was unsuitable since it was short for water closet, or toilet. The new contraption was called a "water tank" and was eventually shortened to "tank," and the name stuck. Major General Sir Ernest D. Swinton, *Eye Witness, and the Origin of the Tanks* (New York: Doubleday, Doran & Co.,1933), 161.

20. Cited in Lacouture, *De Gaulle, The Rebel*, 160.

21. Robert A. Doughty, "De Gaulle's Concept of a Mobile Professional Army," *Parameters*, no. 4 (1974): 23–34.

22. The two British advocates of mechanized warfare took a different trajectory from de Gaulle's. Liddell Hart became an enthusiastic advocate of appeasement of Nazi Germany during the 1930s. Fuller became an ardent admirer of Hitler, joined the British Union of Fascists, and served as an influential adviser of its leader, Sir Oswald Moseley. www.oswaldmosley.com/j-f-c-fuller/.

23. In his memoirs, Guderian acknowledges the influence of the two British writers. Heinz Guderian, *Panzer Leader*, trans. Constantine Fitzgibben (London: Michael Joseph, 1952). This influence on the German strategist has been challenged in R. L. DiNardo, "German Armour Doctrine: Correcting the Myths," *War in History* 3, no. 4 (1996): 384–397.

24. Jackson, *De Gaulle*, 74.

25. Cited in Lacouture, *De Gaulle, The Rebel*, 128.

26. See, for example, de Gaulle letters to Reynaud, May 6, May 8, May 10, 1935, in Admiral Philippe de Gaulle, ed., *Charles de Gaulle, Lettres, Notes, et Carnets* (hereafter *LNC*), *1905–1941* (Paris: Laffont, 2010), 775–778.

27. Cited in Lacouture, *De Gaulle, The Rebel*, 144.

28. J.-R. Tournoux, *Pétain and de Gaulle* [English translation] (London: Heinemann, 1966), 88.

29. Fréréric Salat-Baroux, *De Gaulle-Pétain: Le destin, la blessure, la leçon* (Paris: Robert Laffont, 2010), 55–59.

30. See his critique of an article by Weygand, which omitted any reference to the necessity of more armored divisions. De Gaulle, "Note sur un écrit du général Weygand," December 27, 1938, *LNC, 1905–1941*, 877–879.

31. De Gaulle letter to Reynaud, January 30, 1940, *LNC, 1905–1941*, 915–916.

32. De Gaulle, *War Memoirs*, 53. A day after learning of his political appointment, he was still beseeching Weygand to authorize three additional armored divisions. De Gaulle letter to Weygand, June 2, 1940, *LNC, 1905–1941*, 936–937.

33. Bullitt cable to Roosevelt, June 5, 1940, Orville Bullitt, ed., *For the President Personal & Secret: Correspondence between Franklin D. Roosevelt and William C. Bullitt* (Boston: Houghton Mifflin, 1972), 452.

34. De Gaulle, *War Memoirs*, 55.

35. As the British prime minister prepared for the first wave of German bombers from occupied France in August 1940, Churchill muttered to de Gaulle, "You see, I was right to refuse it [the British fighter air force] at the end of the Battle of France. If today it was destroyed, all would be lost for you, as well as for us." De Gaulle, *War Memoirs*, 104.

36. Paul Reynaud, Mémoires, vol. II (Paris: Flammarion, 1963), 393–394.

37. De Gaulle, *War Memoirs*, 64–66 ; Lacouture, *De Gaulle, The Rebel*, 198.

38. Crozier, *De Gaulle*, 102–103.

39. *LNC, 1905–1941*, 941–942. De Gaulle was persuaded by the French minister of the interior, Georges Mandel, who was one of those who opposed a surrender, to withhold the letter.

40. Lacouture, *De Gaulle, The Rebel*, 200. In his memoirs, de Gaulle denies ever having heard those words.

41. De Gaulle, *War Memoirs*, 71.

42. De Gaulle, *War Memoirs*, 72–74.

43. De Gaulle, *War Memoirs*, 74–77; Richard Mayne, "Jean Monnet: A Biographical Essay," in *Monnet and the Americans: The Father of a United Europe and His U.S. Supporters*, ed. Clifford P. Hackett (Washington, DC: Jean Monnet Council, 2001), 13. In 1950 Monnet would draft the Schuman Plan for the European Steel and Coal Community, the forerunner of the European Union. Later in the same year, Pleven, then prime minister of France, would present a plan (also drafted by Monnet) for the creation of a West European army—The European Defense Community.

44. Major General Sir Edward Spears, *Two Men Who Saved France: Pétain and De Gaulle* (New York: Stein & Day, 1966), 131–132.

45. Of the dozens of translations of the speech, this one is from Jackson, *De Gaulle*, 128.

46. Jackson, *De Gaulle*, 126–127; Ebouche de l'appel du 18 juin 1940, De Gaulle, *LNC, 1905–1942*, 943. J.-L. Crémieux-Brilhac, *De Gaulle, la République, et la France Libre* (Paris: Perrin, 2014), 48–53.

47. Blake Ehrlich, *Resistance: France, 1940–1945* (Boston: Little, Brown, 1965), 51.

48. Robert O. Paxton, *Vichy France: Old Guard and New Order, 1940–1944* (New York: Knopf, 1972), 6–7.

49. De Gaulle, *War Memoirs*, 85–87.

Chapter Two

1. *Washington Post*, July 10, 1940.

2. *New York Times*, July 14, 1940.

3. Raoul Aglion, *Roosevelt and de Gaulle, Allies in Conflict: A Personal Memoir* (New York: The Free Press, 1988), 48.

4. André Gillois, *Histoire Secrète des Français à Londres, de 1940 à 1944* (Paris: Hachette, 1973), 250.

5. Cassin would later draft the Declaration of Human Rights for the United Nations in 1948 and win the Nobel Peace Prize in 1968. On his role in the Gaullist movement, see J.-L. Crémieux-Brilhac, *De Gaulle, la République, et la France Libre* (Paris: Perrin, 2014), 195–219.

6. Jean Lacouture, *De Gaulle, The Rebel 1890–1944*, trans. Alan Sheridan (New York : Norton, 1993) 262.

7. Julian Jackson, *De Gaulle* (Cambridge, MA : Harvard University Press, 2018), 157.

8. Charles de Gaulle, *The Complete War Memoirs*, trans. Jonathan Griffin (New York: Simon & Schuster, 1972), 88–90.

9. Christiane Rimbaud, *L'Affaire du Massiglia* (Paris: Seuil, 1984), 25–26.

10. Jackson, *De Gaulle*, 142, 152–153; Charles Williams, *The Last Great Frenchman: A Life of Charles de Gaulle* (New York: Wiley, 1993), 143.

11. Philippe Lasterle, "Could Admiral Gensoul Have Averted the Tragedy of Mers el-Kebir?" *Journal of Military History* 67, no. 3 (2003): 835–844.

12. Major General Sir Edward Spears, *Two Men Who Saved France: Pétain and De Gaulle* (New York: Stein & Day, 1966), 164–165.

13. "In spite of the pain and anger into which I and my companions were plunged," he decided, "I considered that the saving of France ranked above everything, even above the fate of her ships, and that our duty was still to go on with the fight." De Gaulle, *War Memoirs*, 92–93.

14. Jackson, *De Gaulle*, 139.

15. De Gaulle, *War Memoirs*, 151.

16. American General Vernon "Dick" Walters, who would later serve as the interpreter for discussions between several American presidents and de Gaulle and became friendly with the French president, heard de Gaulle assert that the British government intentionally gave him space in this venue because it was located on a dead end, with the only way in and out through Waterloo Place. Vernon Walters, *Silent Missions* (New York: Doubleday & Company, 1978), 483.

17. Bernard Ledwidge, *De Gaulle* (New York: St. Martin's Press, 1982), 76; Jackson, *De Gaulle*, 135.

18. De Gaulle, *War Memoirs*, 93.

19. Jonathan Fenby, *The General: Charles De Gaulle and the France He Saved* (New York: Skyhorse, 2012), 151.

20. Philip Farwell Bankwitz, "Defeat and Reversal," in *The French Defeat of 1940: Reassessments*, ed. Joel Blatt (Providence, RI: Berghahn Books, 1998), 335.

21. Lacouture, *De Gaulle, The Rebel*, 271–272.

22. Julian G. Hurstfield, *America and the French Nation, 1939–1945* (Chapel Hill: University of North Carolina Press, 1986), 18–20; André Béziat, *Franklin Roosevelt et la France* (Paris: Harmattan, 1997), 185.

23. Cited in Aglion, *Roosevelt and de Gaulle*, 58–59.

24. Cited in Eric T. Jennings, *Vichy in the Tropics: Pétain's National Revolution in Madagascar, Guadeloupe, and Indochina, 1940–1944* (Stanford, CA: Stanford University Press, 2001), 121–122.

25. See his fervent advocacy of the operation in his message to Churchill from one of the ships in the flotilla. De Gaulle cable to Churchill, September 17, 1940, De Gaulle, *LNC*, 1905–1942, 1034.

26. De Gaulle, *War Memoirs*, 119–126.

27. The *Nation* magazine, which would become one of de Gaulle's strongest supporters in the United States, castigated the operation as a "blunder." *The New York Times*, another pro-Gaullist newspaper in the United States, lamented that de Gaulle's "authority as the spokesman of 'Free France' has been discredited." *The Nation*, October 5, 1940, 245. *New York Times*, September 26, 1940.

28. De Gaulle, *War Memoirs*, 109–112.

Chapter Three

"I am a pigheaded Dutchman, Bill, and I have made up my mind about it. We are going ahead with it, and you cannot change my mind." Admiral William Leahy, Roosevelt's ambassador to Vichy France and then his chief of staff in the White House, recorded this declaration in his memoirs. The words prompted André Béziat to subtitle his superb study *Franklin Roosevelt et la France (1939–1945)* "La Diplomatie de L'Entêtement" ("The Diplomacy of Stubbornness").

1. Christopher Thompson, "Prologue to Conflict: De Gaulle and the United States, From First Impressions Through 1940," in *De Gaulle and the United States: A*

Centennial Appraisal, ed. Robert O. Paxton and Nicholas Wahl (Oxford: Berg, 1994), 22–25; Ladislas Farago, *Patton: Ordeal and Triumph* (New York: Ivan Obolensky, 1963), 120–122.

2. François Kersaudy, *De Gaulle et Roosevelt: Le Duel au Sommit* (Paris: Perrin, 2006), 7.

3. Cited in Mario Rossi, *Roosevelt and the French* (Westport, CT: Praeger, 1993), 79.

4. J. Kim Munholland, "The United States and the Free French," in *De Gaulle and the United States: A Centennial Reappraisal*, ed. Robert O. Paxton and Nicholas Wahl (Oxford: Berg, 1994), 67, Leopoldville to State Department, October 27, 1940, in *Papers Relating to the Foreign Relations of the United States* (hereafter *FRUS*), 1940, II, 504–505. In September 1941 the Empire Defense Council would be replaced by the French National Committee as the administrative authority of the Free French movement.

5. Anonymous, *Le Général Leclerc vu par ses compagnons de Combat* (Paris: Editions Alsatia, 1948), 25.

6. Jean Lacouture, *De Gaulle, The Rebel 1890–1944*, trans. Alan Sheridan (New York: Norton, 1993), 292.

7. The myth that Pétain's regime had been compelled by the Germans to enact anti-Semitic legislation during the occupation of France was first punctured by Robert Paxton's path-breaking book *Vichy France: Old Guard and New Order (1940–1944)* (New York: Knopf, 1972). Since then many studies have corroborated that revision of the standard histories of Vichy.

8. William R. Keylor, "France and the Illusion of American Support, 1919–1939," in *The French Defeat of 1940: Reassessments*, ed. Joel Blatt (Providence, RI: Berghahn, 1998), 241–244; John McVickar Haight, *American Aid to France, 1938–1940* (New York: Atheneum, 1970), 232, 238–239.

9. Cited in Will Brownell and Richard N. Billings, *So Close to Greatness: A Biography of William C. Bullitt* (New York, Macmillan, 1987), 257.

10. Orville Bullitt, ed., *For the President: Personal and Secret: Correspondence between Franklin D. Roosevelt and William C. Bullitt* (Boston: Houghton Mifflin, 1972), 275–276.

11. National Archives and Records Administration (hereafter NARA), General Records of the Department of State, Matthews-Hickerson File, Microfilm Reel 13, August 14, 1940.

12. Hull to Bullitt, May 22, 1940, in the Cordell Hull Papers, Library of Congress Manuscript Division, (hereafter CHP, LCMD), Reel 20.

13. These were all the justifications for the U.S. government's recognition of the Pétain regime, which formed the basis of the postwar book by William R. Langer, *Our Vichy Gamble* (New York: Norton, 1966).

14. Memorandum of Conversation between Hull and Henry-Haye, September 11, 1940. CHP, LCMD, Reel 29.

15. Memorandum of Conversation between Hull and Henry-Haye, September 11, 1940. CHP, LCMD, Reel 29.

16. *FRUS*, 1940, I, 246–247.

17. *FRUS*, 1940, II, 641.

18. Dorothy Shipley White, *Seeds of Discord: De Gaulle, Free France, and the Allies* (Syracuse, NY: Syracuse University Press, 1964), 202.

19. *FRUS*, 1940, II, 591–592, 911–912; *FRUS*, 1940, III, 48–49.

20. *New York Times*, June 7, 1940.

21. *Time*, June 17, 1940, 31; *Newsweek*, June 17, 1940, 20.

22. *Time* July 8, 1940, 32; *Newsweek*, July 8, 1940, 24.

23. *Time*, July 22, 1940, 24; Paxton and Wahl, *De Gaulle and the United States*, 29.

24. *Life*, August 26, 1940, 75.

25. *New York Times*, September 26, 1940.

26. *Newsweek*, Oct. 7, 1940, 24–25.

27. *Time*, Nov. 25, 1940, 26.

28. Munholland, "The United States and the Free French," 58; *FRUS*, 1940, II, 636–645.

29. Raoul Aglion, "The Free French Movement and the United States, from 1940 to 1944," in Paxton and Wahl, *De Gaulle and the United States*, 33. For a summary of the evolving relationship between the Gaullist movement and the French residing in the United States during the war, see Rossi, *Roosevelt and the French*, 57–68.

30. Raoul Aglion, *Roosevelt and de Gaulle: Allies in Conflict. A Personal Memoir* (New York: The Free Press, 1988), 121.

31. White, *Seeds of Discord*, 114–121.

32. *New York Herald Tribune*, November 14, 1940.

33. Aglion, "The Free French Movement," 34. In the late summer of 1940 De Gaulle had cabled his old Saint-Cyr classmate Jacques de Sieyès, who was located in New York City, to request detailed information about the personnel on the France Forever committee, adding that he "strongly wishes to bring together all the French energies in the United States." De Gaulle cable to Sieyès, July 31, 1940, De Gaulle, *Charles de Gaulle, Lettres, Notes, et Carnets* (hereafter *LNC*), *1905–1941* (Paris: Lafont, 2010), 988.

34. See, for example, the report in the *New York Times*, June 27, 1943.

35. Reproduced in Aglion, *Roosevelt and De Gaulle*, 33–34.

36. Julian G. Hurstfield, *America and the French Nation, 1939–1945* (Chapel Hill: University of North Carolina Press, 1986), 112.

37. Julian Jackson, *France, The Dark Years (1940–1944)* (New York: Oxford University Press, 2001), 43.

38. Clifford Hackett, "Jean Monnet and the Roosevelt Administration," in *Monnet and the Americans: The Father of a United Europe and his U.S. Supporters*, ed. Clifford P. Hackett (Washington, DC: Jean Monnet Council, 2001), 26–29. Marie and Tony Shannon, "Jacques Maritain," Catholic Truth Society, maritain.nd.edu/jmc/etext/lives.htm.

39. Raoul de Roussy de Sales, *The Making of Yesterday: Diaries, 1938–1942* (New York: Raynal and Hitchcock, 1947), 226. Roussy de Sales was a descendent of Saint Francis de Sales (1567–1622), a revered Catholic saint. Kersaudy, *De Gaulle et Roosevelt*, 90.

40. Aglion, *Roosevelt and de Gaulle*, 24–25.

41. De Gaulle cable to Pleven, September 23, 1941, De Gaulle, *LNC, 1905–1941*, 1307.

42. Wahl comment, in Paxton and Wahl, eds., *De Gaulle and the United States*, 96. Wahl wondered whether the "career interests" of these two Third Republic politicians prompted them to promote FDR's opposition to de Gaulle. On the allegations of Cot's spying, see John Earl Haynes and Harvey Klehr, VENONA. Decoding the Soviet Espionage in America (New Haven, CT: Yale University Press, 1999), 211; Harvey Klehr, John Earl Haynes, and Fridrikh Igorevich Firsov, The Secret World of American Communism (New Haven, CT: Yale University Press, 1995), 235–237, and Herbert Romerstein and Eric Breidel, *The Venona Secrets: Expanding Soviet Espionage and America's Traitors* (Washington, DC: Regnery History, 2001), 56–57.

43. Aglion, "The Free French Movement," 39.

44. Biddle to Roosevelt, May 9, 1941, President's Secretary's File (hereafter PSF), Diplomatic, Box 34, Franklin D. Roosevelt Library (hereafter FDRL). See Ben Lucien Burman, *The Generals Wore Cork Hats* (New York: Taplinger, 1963), for an account of his tour in the part of French Africa that had rallied to de Gaulle.

45. Biddle to Roosevelt with enclosures, May 12, 15, and 26, 1941, PSF, Diplomatic, Box 34, FDRL.

46. Cited in Munholland, "The United States and the Free French," 70.

47. Sumner Welles, *The Time for Decision* (New York: Harper & Brothers, 1944), 156, 159, 165, and 167.

48. On the relations between the French exiles in the United States and de Gaulle, see Rossi, *Roosevelt and the French*, 58–68.

49. Saint Exupéry would become well known to American parents as the author of *The Little Prince* novella and bedtime story, which was published in 1943. It has been translated into some three hundred languages and is one of the best-selling books of all time.

50. As one of the few female journalists in France, she had been a strong opponent of appeasement during the 1930s. After arriving in New York on July 26, 1940, she was greeted by President Roosevelt and his wife, Eleanor, at Hyde Park. The president's wife contributed a strong message of support to the first issue of a French language newspaper in America that Madame Tabouis helped to found, *Pour la Victoire*, which appeared on January 10, 1942. Aglion, *Roosevelt and de Gaulle*, 94–96.

51. Aglion, "The Free French," 41. On the long list of French exiles who came to the United States, see Colin Nettlebeck, *Forever France: Exile in the United States, 1939–1945* (London: Bloomsbury Academic, 1991).

52. Aglion, *Roosevelt and de Gaulle*, 83–84. Saint-Exupéry would eventually join the Free French air force in April 1943. On a reconnaissance mission after the D-Day landing on July 31, 1944, his plane disappeared in the Mediterranean.

53. De Gaulle cable to Pleven, August 9, 1941, in Maurice Ferro, *De Gaulle et L'Amérique: Une Amitié Tumulteuse* (Paris: Plon, 1973), 40.

54. James J. Dougherty, *The Politics of Wartime Aid: American Assistance to France and Northwest Africa, 1940–1946* (Westport, CT: Greenwood Press, 1978), 55.

55. Oscar Cox letter to Hopkins, July 7, 1941, Harry Hopkins Papers, Box 326, Book 7, Lend-Lease Operations in France, FDRL.

56. Harry Hopkins Papers, Box 326, Book 7, Lend-Lease in Operation: France, FDRL.

57. Harry Hopkins Papers, Box 326, Book 7, Lend-Lease in Operation: France, FDRL.

58. Cited in Aglion, *Roosevelt and de Gaulle*, 110.

59. Cited in Aglion, *Roosevelt and de Gaulle*, 46.

60. *FRUS*, 1942, I, 509.

61. Aglion, *Roosevelt and de Gaulle*, 47–48.

62. Nerin Gun, *Les Secrets des archives américaines: Pétain, Laval, De Gaulle* (Paris: Albin Michel, 1979), 103; Lacouture, *De Gaulle, The Rebel*, 529; André Béziat, *Franklin Roosevelt et la France* (Paris: Harmattan, 1997), 64. He passionately defended the activities of his father-in-law during the German occupation in the iconic film *Le Chagrin et la Pitié* (*The Sorrow and the Pity*) brought out in 1969 by Marcel Ophuls.

63. Aglion, "The Free French," 97–98.

64. For the close relationship between Leger and Welles, see the correspondence between them in Welles Papers, Box 89, folder 09, FDRL. For Roosevelt's relationship with Leger, see Leger letter to Roosevelt, November 8, 1943, in which he flatters the president as the "guarantor of democracy" for the French people"; Roosevelt letter to Leger, November 29, 1943, President's Personal File, folder 8339 Leger, Alexis, FDRL. For Leger's fawning over FDR, see Leger letters to Mrs. Francis Biddle, September 13, November 6, 1940, Alexis Leger (Saint Jean Perse), *Oeuvres Complètes* (Paris: Gallimard, 1972), 898–900.

65. *New York Times*, October 17, 1941.

66. Ferro, *De Gaulle et L'Amérique*, 41.

67. Milton Viorst, *Hostile Allies: FDR and De Gaulle* (New York: Macmillan, 1965), 70–71; Kersaudy, *De Gaulle et Roosevelt*, 96, 99.

68. Béziat, *Franklin Roosevelt et la France*, 174.

69. Charles Bohlen, *Witness to History, 1929–1969* (New York: W.W. Norton, 1973), 206.

70. William D. Leahy, *I Was There: The Personal Story of the Chief of Staff to Presidents Roosevelt and Truman* (London: Gollancz, 1950), 43.

71. Leahy, *I Was There*, 42.

72. Robert Murphy, *Diplomat Among Warriors* (Garden City, NY: Doubleday, 1964), 128–130.

73. Leahy, *I Was There*, 94, 100.

74. Murphy, *Diplomat Among Warriors*, 119.

75. Leahy letter to Welles, April 14, 1941, Sumner Welles Papers, Box 70, folder Leahy, William, FDRL.

76. Leahy, *I Was There*, 42.

77. Béziat, *Franklin Roosevelt et la France*, 136–137.

78. Leahy letter to Welles, February 24, 1941, Sumner Welles Papers, Box 70, folder Leahy, William, FDRL.

79. Memorandum of Conversation between Hull and Halifax, May 21, 1941, CHP, LCMD, Reel 30.

80. Memorandum of Conversation between Hull and Henry-Haye, June 20, 1941, CHP, LCMD, Reel 29.

81. Roosevelt letter to Pétain, August 21, 1941, PSF, Diplomatic Correspondence, France, 1941, Box 29, FDRL. Pétain letter to Roosevelt, September 17, 1941, PSF, Diplomatic Correspondence, France, 1941, Box 29, FDRL.

82. Hervé Coutau-Bégarie and Claude Huan, *Darlan* (Paris: Fayard, 1989), 460.

83. Béziat, *Franklin Roosevelt et la France*, 156–158.

84. There are actually three islands in the group: Saint Pierre, Grande Miquelon, and Petite Miquelon.

85. Leahy, *I Was There*, 84.

86. Douglas G. Anglin, *The St. Pierre and Miquelon Affair of 1941: A Study in Diplomacy in the North Atlantic Triangle* (Toronto: University of Toronto Press, 1966), 51–53.

87. *FRUS*, 1941, II, 542–544; David Woolner, "Canada, Mackenzie King and the St. Pierre and Miquelon Crisis of 1941," *London Journal of Canadian Studies* 24 (2008–2009): 42–84.

88. Aglion, *Roosevelt and de Gaulle*, 59.

89. Charles De Gaulle, *The Complete War Memoirs*, trans. Jonathan Griffin (New York: Simon & Schuster, 1972), 214.

90. De Gaulle, *War Memoirs*, 214–215; Winston S. Churchill, *The Second World War* (Boston: Houghton Mifflin, 1948), 590–591; Cordell Hull, *The Memoirs of Cordell Hull* (New York: Macmillan, 1948), II: 1129; Anglin, *The St. Pierre and Miquelon Affair*, 82–83.

91. For a report on Wolpert's antics, see *Newsweek*, January 5, 1942, 49–50.

92. De Gaulle, *War Memoirs*, 114.

93. *New York Times*, December 25, 1941.

94. Anglin, *The St. Pierre and Miquelon Affair*, 85.

95. There is no evidence that Hull knew of the term used by Vichy.

96. Memorandum of Conversation between Hull and Halifax, December 26, 1941, CHP, LCMD, Reel 30. On Christmas Day the secretary of state had filled in the president on the details of the operation and Britain's acquiescence in it. Hull letter to Roosevelt, December 25, 1944. PSF, Box 30, folder France 1944–1945, FDRL.

97. Lacouture, *De Gaulle, The Rebel*, 316.

98. Memorandum of Conversation between Hull and Henry-Haye, January 6, 1942, CHP, LCMD, Reel 29.

99. Dorothy Thompson, *New York Herald Tribune*, December 30, 1941. That exact phrase as well as the term "blunder" were used by Walter Lippmann in a column on January 2 that was syndicated in more than a hundred papers throughout the United States.

100. *New York Times*, December 26, 1941.

101. *Christian Science Monitor*, December 26, 1941.

102. Aglion, *Roosevelt and De Gaulle*, 65. Hull later claimed he had referred to "so-called Free French ships" because he was uncertain that the vessels in question did in fact belong to de Gaulle's movement. Hull to American consul in Saint-Pierre, January 10, 1942, PSF, Diplomatic Correspondence: France, Box 31, FDRL.

103. Cited in Aglion, *Roosevelt and De Gaulle*, 67. Irwin F. Gellmann, *Secret Affairs: Franklin Roosevelt, Cordell Hull, and Sumner Welles* (Baltimore: Johns Hopkins University Press, 1995), 271–274.

104. Hull, *Memoirs*, 1133–1134.

105. Memorandum of Conversation between Hull and Halifax, December 29, 1941, CHP, LCMD, Reel 3.

106. Memorandum of Conversation between Hull and Henry-Haye, January 6, 1942, CHP, LCMD, Reel 29.

107. Hull letter to Roosevelt, January 8, 1942, PSF, "Safe File," Box 2, folder France, FDRL.

108. Hull, *Memoirs*, II: 1137. See Waverly Root in *The Nation*, January 17, 1942, noting that while de Gaulle was fighting the Axis, Pétain was the prisoner of the Axis.

109. The definitive account of this contentious relationship so far from Europe is J. Kim Munholland, *Rock of Contention: Free French and Americans and Americans at War in New Caledonia, 1940–1945* (New York: Berghahn, 2005).

110. Munholland, "The United States and the Free French," 72–74.

111. J. Kim Munholland, "The Trials of the Free French in New Caledonia, 1940–1942," *French Historical Studies* 14, no. 4 (Fall 1986): 547–579. When Argenlieu returned from the Pacific and passed through Washington en route to London, he informed Hull that he retained "the most happy impressions of his cooperation with the American forces in the Far East." He claimed that the "friction" with the American GIs had been dispelled after two or three days. Memorandum of Conversation between Hull, Tixier, and d'Argenlieu. December 8, 1942, CHP, LCMD, Reel 29.

112. Munholland, *Rock of Contention*, 178–179.

113. The conference was attended by Churchill, Roosevelt, Soviet foreign minister Maxim Litvinov, and the Nationalist Chinese foreign minister T. V. Soong. The occupied countries Belgium, Czechoslovakia, Greece, the Netherlands, and Poland were there as well. "1942: La Déclaration de Nations Unis," www.un.org/fr/sections//history-united-nations-/charter/1942-declaration-united-nations/. Andrew Williams, "France and the Origins of the United Nations, 1944–1945: Si la France ne compte plus, qu'on nous le dise," *Diplomacy and Statecraft* 28, no. 3 (June 2017): 216–217.

114. Robert E. Sherwood, *Roosevelt and Hopkins: An Intimate History* (New York: Bantam Books, 1948), 17–18; Aglion, "The Free French and the United States," 40.

115. For the long, drawn-out dispute about the Free French movement's exclusion from the January 1 Declaration on United Nations, which came to a head in the autumn of 1944, see *Documents Diplomatiques Français* (hereafter *DDF*), 1944, Vol. II, 163–165, 315, 331–332.

116. Béziat, *Franklin Roosevelt et la France*, 203.

117. Welles cable to Leahy, March 27, 1942, Welles Papers, Box 80, folder Leahy, FDRL.

118. Leahy, *I Was There*, 110.

119. Cited in Blake Ehrlich, *Resistance: France, 1940–1945* (Boston: Little, Brown, 1965), 68.

120. Béziat, *Franklin Roosevelt et la France*, 219–220.

121. *Life*, August 24, 1942, 87. Several of those named were well known in the United States, such as the former boxer Georges Carpentier, the stage and film actor Sacha Guitry, the actress Mistinguette, and the crooner Maurice Chevalier. In addition to Chevalier, other popular French singers who went to Germany not at the invitation of the Germans but to sing for French prisoners of war or volunteer workers in Germany included Edith Piaf and Charles Trenet. Jackson, *France: The Dark Years*, 313. On Chevalier see Edward Behr, *Thank Heaven for Little Girls: The True Story of Maurice Chevalier's Life and Times* (New York: Hitchinson, 1993). The crooner makes an insipid appearance in the film *Le Chagrin et la Pitié* (*The Sorrow and the Pity*), by Marcel Ophuls.

122. De Gaulle, *War Memoirs*, 294.

123. After the end of the war, a bridge over the Seine was renamed Pont de Bir Hakeim alongside the Pont d'Austerlitz (for France's defeat of the Austrians in 1805) and the Pont d'Iena (for the defeat of the Prussians in 1806).

124. He kept his promise. This unlikely feminist granted French women the right to vote in 1944.

125. Béziat, *Franklin Roosevelt de la France*, 243.

126. De Gaulle cable to Roosevelt, July 10, 1942, De Gaulle, *LNC, 1905–1942*, 111.

127. Rick Atkinson, *An Army at Dawn: The War in North Africa, 1942–1943* (New York: Henry Holt and Company, 2002), 26–27.

128. Albert Kammerer, *Du débarguement africain au meutre de Darlan* (Paris: Flammarion, 1949), 106.

129. Béziat, *Franklin Roosevelt et la France*, 250–251.

130. Quoted in Sherwood, *Roosevelt and Hopkins*, 222–223.

131. Hopkins to Roosevelt, September 21, 1942, enclosing cable from Halifax to Hull, September 17, 1942, DSF, Diplomatic Correspondence, folder France 1942, FDRL.

132. Atkinson, *An Army at Dawn*, 44–46.

133. De Gaulle letter to Roosevelt, October 6, 1942, PSF, Diplomatic Correspondence, folder France 1942, FDRL.

134. Tixier to Welles with enclosures, October 31, 1942, PSF, Diplomatic Correspondence, folder France 1942, FDRL.

135. Aglion, *Roosevelt and de Gaulle*, 134–135.

136. Pierre Billotte, *Le Temps des Armes* (Paris: Plon, 1972), 239.

137. Jacques Soustelle, *Envers et contre tout*, vol. I (Paris: Lafont, 1947), 452.

138. De Gaulle, *War Memoirs*, 349–350. In his memoirs Murphy bemoaned the injustice of blaming the secretary of state, who was merely following the orders of his president.

139. Robert Sherwood, *White House Papers* (London: Eyre & Spottiswoode, 1949), II: 662.

140. The appearance of the German major was pure poetic license. There were no uniformed German officers in French North Africa.

141. *Casablanca* won several Academy Awards in the year it appeared and has been one of the world's most-viewed films in the past seven decades. See Charles Francisco, *You Must Remember This: The Filming of Casablanca* (Englewood Cliffs, NJ: Prentice Hall, 1980); Aljean Harmetz, *Round Up the Usual Suspects: The Making of Casablanca: Bogart, Bergman, and World War II* (New York: Hyperion, 2017); Noah Eisenberg, *The Life, Legend, and Afterlife of Hollywood's Most Beloved Movie* (New York: W.W. Norton, 2017).

142. Frédérique Dufour, "Charles de Gaulle dans les actualités cinématographiques amércaines durant le Second Guerre mondiale," *Espoir* (Revue de la Fondation et de l'Institut Charles de Gaulle), no. 136 (September 2003): 57–61.

143. See Arthur L. Funk, "Negotiating the Deal with Darlan," *Journal of Contemporary History* 8, no. 2 (April 1973): 81ff.

144. At the request of Darlan's widow, Roosevelt arranged for the son, Ensign Alain Darlan, to be admitted to the president's favorite retreat in the spa town of Warm Springs, Georgia. Ensign Alain Darlan letter to Roosevelt, July 29, 1943; Roosevelt letter to Alain Darlan, August 16, 1943; President's Personal File, folder 8405, FDRL.

145. Donovan cable to Roosevelt, April 21, 1942, PSF, Box 163, FDRL.

146. Béziat, *Franklin Roosevelt et la France*, 280–281.

147. Churchill letter to Eisenhower, November 13, 1942, Pre-Presidential Series, Principal File, folder "Churchill," Box 23, Dwight D. Eisenhower Library (hereafter DDEL).

148. Claude Collot and Jean-Robert Henry, *Le Mouvement Nationale Algérien: Textes 1912–1954* (Algiers: Office des Publications Universitaire, 1981), 66–67; Martin Evans, "Algeria and the Liberation: Hope and Betrayal," in *The Liberation of France: Image and Event*, ed. H. R. Kedward and Nancy Wood (Oxford: Berg, 1995), 260–265.

149. Cited in Charles Kaiser, *The Cost of Courage* (New York: Other Press, 2015), 96; Lacouture, *De Gaulle, The Rebel*, 406–407.

150. De Gaulle, *War Memoirs*, 351.

151. Aglion, "The Free French," 43.

152. De Gaulle cable to General Catroux (Beirut), Governor-General Eboué and General Leclerc (Brazzaville), and the Free French delegation in Washington, November 10, 1942, De Gaulle, *LNC, 1942–1958*, 209–210.

153. Note from Noguès to Patton, November 18, 1942, Pre-Presidential Series, Principal File, Folder "Patton, George, Box 91, DDEL. In his memoirs Leahy claimed that Darlan's switch saved thousands of American soldiers' lives while Churchill "seemed to be doing everything possible to inject de Gaulle into the picture." Leahy, *I Was There*, 135–136.

154. *The Nation*, November 21, 1942.

155. *New York Times*, November 15, 1942; *New York Herald Tribune*, November 13, 1942.

156. Cited in Atkinson, *An Army at Dawn*, 198.

157. John Morton Blum, *From the Morgenthau Diaries: Years of War, 1941–1945* (Boston: Houghton Mifflin Company, 1967), 149–151. On the same day, Roosevelt cabled to Churchill his repeated claim that "the present temporary arrangement in North and West Africa is only a temporary expedient, justified solely by the stress of battle." He praised Darlan for making a "mopping up" campaign unnecessary, thereby saving American, British, and French lives. Warren Kimball, ed., *Churchill and Roosevelt: The Complete Correspondence, Vol. II, Alliance Forged* (London: Collins, 1984), 9.

158. Sherwood, *Roosevelt and Hopkins*, 252–254.

159. Milton Eisenhower, *The President Is Calling* (New York: Doubleday, 1974), 141.

160. *New York Times*, November 17, 1942.

161. De Gaulle note to Allied governments, November 19, 1942, De Gaulle, *LNC, 1942–1958*, 219.

162. De Gaulle, *War Memoirs*, 357–358. Lacouture, *De Gaulle, The Rebel*, 349. In fact, Darlan *had* given FDR Algiers. His orders to French troops in French North Africa "in the name of Marshal Pétain" to cease opposition to the landing were largely followed. Aglion, "The Free French and the United States," 43.

163. J. J. McCloy, Memorandum for the Chief of Staff, November 25, 1942, NARA, RG 165, Records of the War Department, OPD 336 France; J.-L. Crémieux-Brilhac, *De Gaulle, La République, et la France Libre, 1940–1945* (Paris: Perrin, 2014), 375.

164. Béziat, *Franklin Roosevelt et la France*, 296–297.

165. Bedell Smith cable (for Eisenhower) to War Department, November 25, 1942, Pre-Presidential Series, Principal File, Box 2, folder cable log November 1942, DDEL. Eisenhower letter to Marshall, December 7, 1942, Pre-Presidential Series, Principal File, Box 80, folder "Marshall," DDEL.

166. Bedell Smith cable (for Eisenhower), November 30, 1942, Pre-Presidential Series, Principal File, Box 2, folder "Cable Log November 1942," DDEL.

167. The matter was finally settled on October 21, 1943, when the French National Committee reinstated the Cremieux law.

168. Announcement reprinted in Leahy, *I Was There*, 560–561. The Allies with French participation in the fighting would eventually receive the German surrender in Tunisia, thereby liberating all of French North Africa.

169. Patton Memorandum to Eisenhower, January 2, 1943, Pre-Presidential Series, Principal File, folder "Patton, George," DDEL. Bedell Smith cable, January 6, 1943, Smith Papers, Cable Log January 1943, Box 43, folder cable logs (January 1943), DDEL. The possibility of a vast conspiracy involving all the key players in Algiers (the British Secret Service, the American Office of Secret Services, and de Gaulle), without any definitive proof, is examined in Anthony Verrier, *Assassination in Algiers: Roosevelt, Churchill, de Gaulle, and the Murder of Admiral Darlan* (New York: Norton, 1990).

170. Cited in Atkinson, *An Army at Dawn*, 252–253.

171. Memorandum of Conversation, Adrien Tixier and Under-Secretary of State Welles, December 28, 1942, Sumner Welles Papers, Box 85, folder Adrian [sic] Tixier, FDRL; Sherwood, *Roosevelt and Hopkins*, 263.

172. De Gaulle, *War Memoirs*, 382–385.

173. Leahy, *I Was There*, 145–146.

174. Memorandum of Conversation between Hull and Halifax, January 5, 1943, CDP, LCMD, Reel 30.

175. Roosevelt referred to Giraud as "a rather simple minded soldier." Robert Dallek, "Roosevelt and De Gaulle," 51.

176. Cited in Simon Berthon, *Allies at War: The Bitter Rivalry Among Churchill, Roosevelt, and De Gaulle* (New York: Carroll and Graf, 2001), 234. FDR would frequently refer to de Gaulle as "the bride" in his exchanges with Churchill throughout the rest of the war.

177. FRUS, 1943, II, 23ff; Anthony Eden, *The Memoirs of Anthony Eden, Earl of Avon: The Reckoning* (Boston: Houghton Mifflin, 1965), 416–421. De Gaulle, *War Memoirs*, 78–84.

178. Murphy, *Diplomat Among Warriors*, 213; Kersaudy, *De Gaulle et Roosevelt*, 210–211.

179. Harry Hopkins noticed the surreptitious presence of the Secret Service officers armed with Tommy guns. "One could not risk the possibility of an accident happening to the president," he observed, but added that "none of this transpired when Giraud saw Roosevelt." He also noted that the Free French leader "was covered by guns" (by the Secret Service) through his whole visit. Sherwood, *Roosevelt and Hopkins*, 685.

180. De Gaulle, *War Memoirs*, 391–393. Béziat, *Franklin Roosevelt et la France*, 316–317.

181. De Gaulle, *War Memoirs*, 398.

182. Dallek, "Roosevelt and De Gaulle," 53; Hopkins Notes, January 24, 1943, Hopkins Papers, FDRL.

183. De Gaulle, *War Memoirs*, 399.

184. Kimball, *Churchill and Roosevelt*, 209.

185. Justus D. Doenecke and Mark A. Stoler, *Debating Franklin D. Roosevelt's Foreign Policies, 1933–1945* (Lanham, MD: Rowman & Littlefield, 2005), 55.

186. Aglion, "The Free French and the United States," 43–47. Aglion, *Roosevelt and de Gaulle*, 156–164.

187. Hackett, "Jean Monnet and the Roosevelt Administration," 56; François Duchêne, *Jean Monnet: The First Statesman of Interdependence* (New York: Norton, 1994), 103–110.

188. André Kaspi, *La Mission de Jean Monnet à Alger, Mars–Octobre 1943* (Paris: Publications de la Sorbonne, 1971); Murphy, *Diplomat Among Warriors*, 181; Jean Monnet, *Mémoires* (Paris: Fayard, 1976), 199; Sherwood, *Roosevelt and Hopkins*, 330.

189. "Résumé d'un entretien avec le Cardinal Francis Joseph Spellman, Achevêque de New York à Londres," March 23, 1943, De Gaulle, *LNC, 1942–1958*, 302–308.

190. Duchêne, *Jean Monnet*, 119–123.

191. Cited in Don Cook, *Charles de Gaulle: A Biography* (New York: G.P. Putnam's Sons, 1983), 187.

192. Robert Sherwood Memorandum for the President, June 6, 1943, the President to Stephen Early for Hull, June 8, 1943, PSF, Box 29, folder France, FDRL.

193. Henri Giraud, *Un seul but la victoire* (Paris: Juillard, 1949), 195–196.

194. *New York Times*, July 10, 1943.

195. Three years after de Gaulle had returned to power in France in 1958, President Kennedy sent Dean Acheson to meet with the French president to discuss matters in dispute between Washington and Paris. The former secretary of state opened the meeting by recalling that as a junior officer in the State Department during World War II, he had drafted speeches for Hull that included favorable references to the Free French, only to have them struck out by the secretary. American Embassy, Paris, cable from Acheson to State Department for the President, April 21, 1961, National Security Files (hereafter NSF), France, Box 70A, folder 1–20 to 3–15, 1961, John F. Kennedy Library (hereafter JFKL).

196. Giraud, *Un seul but la victoire*, 196–197.

197. Berthon, *Allies at War*, 271.

198. Kimball, *Churchill and Roosevelt*, 593.

199. Béziat, *Franklin Roosevelt et la France*, 369.

200. *FRUS*, 1944, III, France, January 24, 1944, 773.

201. Harold Macmillan, *War Diaries: Politics and War in the Mediterranean, January 1943–May 1945* (London: Macmillan, 1984), 318.

202. Walter LaFeber, "Roosevelt, Churchill, and Indochina, 1942–1945," *American Historical Review*, no. 80 (December 1975): 1277–1295.

203. Béziat, *Franklin Roosevelt et la France*, 361.

204. François Kersaudy, *De Gaulle et Churchill: Le mésentente cordial* (Paris: Perrin, 2010), 339.

205. NARA, Matthews-Hickerson File, Microfilm Reel 13, January 1944. Irwin Wall, *The United States and the Making of Postwar France, 1945–1954* (Cambridge: Cambridge University Press, 1991), 25–26.

206. Henry L. Stimson and McGeorge Bundy, *On Active Service in Peace and War* (New York: Harper & Brothers, 1947), 545.

207. Béziat, *Franklin Roosevelt et la France*, 364.

208. Roosevelt cable to Churchill, January 12, 1944, Harry Hopkins Papers, Box 334, folder Civil Affairs in France, FDRL.

209. *New York Times*, Feb. 12, 1944.

210. Eden, *The Reckoning*, 519.

211. Stimson and Bundy, *On Active Service in Peace and War*, 546–547. Thomas M. Campbell and George C. Herring, eds., *The Diaries of Edward R. Stettinius, 1943–1946* (New York: New Viewpoints, 1975), 61–62. Roosevelt's directive is printed in Harry L. Coles and Albert K. Weinberg, *Civil Affairs: Soldiers Become Governors* (Washington, DC: Center of Military History, 1964), 667–668.

212. For the development of the AMGOT policy from the perspective of Treasury Secretary Henry Morganthau, see Blum, *The Morgenthau Diaries*, 166–173.

213. *FRUS*, 1943, II (France), 111–112.

214. Hull, *Memoirs*, 1245.

215. Eric Roussel, *Jean Monnet, 1888–1979* (Paris: Fayard, 1996), 407.

216. McCloy Memoranda to Secretary of War, January 13 and 20, February 29, 1944, NARA, RG 107 Records of the Office of the Secretary of War, ASW 370.8, France. Munholland, "The United States and the Free French," 90.

217. Stimson recorded in his diary that Hull hated de Gaulle so fiercely that he was "incoherent on the subject." Cited in Blum, *The Morgenthau Diaries*, 173.

218. CBS Radio speech by Hull. April 9, 1944, Hopkins Papers, FDRL. A large section of the Hull address is reprinted in Arthur L. Funk, *Charles de Gaulle: The Crucial Years, 1943–1944,* (Norman: University of Oklahoma Press, 1959), 240.

219. Hull, *Memoirs*, 1429–1430.

220. Murphy to Hull, April 6, 1944; Hull to Murphy April 8, 1944, *FRUS*, 1944, III, 670–673.

221. Roosevelt letter to Hull, April 15, 1944, NARA, 851.01/3711; Leahy, *I Was There*, 236.

222. Winant (U.S. ambassador to the United Kingdom) to Hull, May 4, 1944, *FRUS*, 1944, III, 681.

223. Cited in Funk, *Charles de Gaulle*, 247.

224. See, for example, Harriman cable to Hull, July 9, 1944, *FRUS*, 1944, III, 723.

225. F. S. V. Donnison, *History of the Second World War, UK Military Series, Civil Affairs and Military Government: Central Organization and Planning* (London: Her Majesty's Stationery Office, 1966), 69.

226. Eisenhower cable to War Department, May 11, 1944; Roosevelt cable to Eisenhower, May 12, 1944, MRF, FDRL.

227. Philippe de Gaulle, *De Gaulle Mon Père: Entretiens avec Michel Tauriac* (Paris: Plon, 2005), 502.

228. Robert H. Ferrell, ed., *The Eisenhower Diaries* (New York: W.W. Norton, 1981), entry of May 22, 1944, 117.

229. Wall, *The United States and the Making of Postwar France*, 28.

230. Roosevelt cable to Churchill, May 27, 1944, FRUS, 1944, III, 692.

231. Funk, *Charles de Gaulle*, 256.

232. De Gaulle, *War Memoirs*, 556–557.

233. Eisenhower note to Churchill, June 1, 1944, Pre-Presidential Series, Principal File, Box 22, Folder Churchill (5), DDEL.

234. Rick Atkinson, *The Guns at Last Light: The War in Western Europe, 1944–1945* (New York: Henry Holt, 2013), 35.

235. Forest C. Pogue, *George Marshall, Organizer of Victory* (New York: Viking, 1973), III: 400–401.

236. Alfred Duff Cooper, *Old Men Forget* (London: Rupert Hart-Davis, 1953), 332; Claude Hertier de Boislambert, *Les Fers de l'espoir* (Paris: Plon, 1978), 436–437.

237. Dwight D. Eisenhower, *Crusade in Europe* (New York: Doubleday, 1948), 248; De Gaulle, *War Memoirs*, 558–560.

238. Berthon, *Allies at War*, 311.

239. State Department memorandum for Roosevelt, June 16, 1944, PSF, Diplomatic, Box 31, folder De Gaulle, FDRL.

240. Hull Memorandum for the President, June 26, 1944, enclosing message from de Gaulle, PSF, Diplomatic, Box 31, folder De Gaulle. FDRL.

241. *New York Times*, June 13, 1944. For earlier editorials calling for U.S. recognition of the French National Committee, see *New York Times*, February 4 and March 3, 1943.

242. De Gaulle, *War Memoirs*, 563–564.

243. The most judicious assessment of the aborted plans for AMGOT and the circulation of the U.S.-printed currency is Charles L. Robertson, *When Roosevelt Planned to Govern France* (Amherst: University of Massachusetts Press, 2011).

244. Ray Argyle, *The Paris Game: Charles de Gaulle, the Liberation of Paris, and the Gamble that Won France* (Toronto: Dundurn, 2014), 217.

245. The entire speech is reprinted in de Gaulle, *LNC, 1942–1958*, 517–518.

246. Stimson and Bundy, *On Active Service in Peace and War*, 550–551.

247. Campbell and Herring, *The Diaries of Edward R. Stettinius*, 35–36.

248. Beatrice Bishop Berle and Travis Beal Jacobs, eds., *Navigating the Rapids. 1918–1971, From the Papers of Adolf A. Berle* (New York: Harcourt Brace Jovanovich, 1973), entry of June 13, 1944, 453.

249. Chapin (Algiers) cable to State Department, June 8, 1944, PSF, Diplomatic Correspondence, Box 31, FDRL; McCloy Memorandum for the President, June 10, 1944, PSF, folder De Gaulle, FDRL.

250. Roosevelt cable to Churchill, June 12, 1944, FRUS, 1944, III, 707–708.

251. De Gaulle, *War Memoirs*, 565.

252. Elmer Davis letter to President, June 22, 1944, PSF, Diplomatic Correspondence, Box 31, folder De Gaulle, FDRL.

253. For a comprehensive assessment of that support, see Charles Foulon, *Le Pouvoir en province à la liberation* (Paris: Colin, 1975).

254. De Gaulle cable to Roosevelt, July 3, 1944; De Gaulle Public Declaration in Algiers, July 5, 1944, in De Gaulle, *LNC, 1942–1958*, 526–527.

255. Aglion, *Roosevelt and de Gaulle*, 175.

256. Cited in Kersaudy, *De Gaulle et Roosevelt*, 415.

257. Cook, *Charles de Gaulle*, 229.

258. De Gaulle, *War Memoirs*, 571–573.

259. "Instructions for the Arrival of General de Gaulle: A 17-gun salute," July 5, 1944, OF, FDRL; De Gaulle, *War Memoirs*, 572–575.

260. *New York Times*, July 7, 1944.

261. vastarrayofthevaguelyinteresting.blogspot.com/2011/8/unfortunate tete-a -tete-de-gaulle meets-html. Roy Jenkins, *Churchill: A Biography* (New York: Farrar, Straus & Giroux, 2002), 743. A slightly different version of the encounter is provided by Raoul Aglion: "It's been a long time since I've seen him." Aglion, *Roosevelt and de Gaulle*, 179.

262. Cable from de Gaulle to Henri Hoppenot, July 2, 1944, De Gaulle, *LNC, 1942–1958*, 326.

263. Cited in Aglion, *Roosevelt and de Gaulle*, 117.

264. De Gaulle letter to Roosevelt, July 10, 1944; Roosevelt letter to de Gaulle, July 13, 1944, PSF, Diplomatic Correspondence, Box 31, folder De Gaulle, FDRL. Roosevelt cable to Churchill, July 10, 1944, *FRUS, 1944*, III, 723–724.

265. De Gaulle, *War Memoirs*, 578–579.

266. Eisenhower cable to War Department, August 15, 1944; War Department cable to Eisenhower, August 16, 1944, MRF, FDRL.

267. A. W. DePorte, *De Gaulle's Foreign Policy, 1944–1946* (Cambridge, MA: Harvard University Press, 1968), 63.

268. Ehrlich, *Resistance: France 1940–1945*, 212.

269. Michael Neiberg, *The Blood of Free Men: The Liberation of Paris, 1944* (New York: Basic Books, 2012), 128–129.

270. Matthews letter to Leahy, October 5, 1944, enclosing memo from Douglas MacArthur II dated September 19, reporting on a lengthy interview with Herriot's secretary about the affair, PSF, Diplomatic Correspondence, Box 30, folder France 1944-1945, FDRL.

271. Eisenhower, *Crusade in Europe*, 296; De Gaulle, *War Memoirs*, 636–637.

272. Kaiser, *The Cost of Courage*, 171; Ehrlich, *Resistance: France 1940–1945*, 215. The German commander's decision to disobey Hitler was graphically portrayed in the blockbuster film *Is Paris Burning?* (1966), with a script by Gore Vidal and Francis Ford Coppola and an all-star cast including Kirk Douglas, Glenn Ford, Alain Delon, Yves Montand, and Jean-Paul Belmondo.

273. On March 18, 1871, a left-wing municipal government was established in Paris as German military forces surrounded the city, enacting several radical socio-economic reforms. Known as the Paris Commune, it was crushed on May 28 by French troops sent by the French government headquartered in Versailles.

274. De Gaulle, *War Memoirs*, 643–644. De Gaulle's son, Philippe, then in the French navy, recalls his father telling him that he expected "that the 2nd armored division of General Leclerc to move across Normandy and head toward Paris." Philippe De Gaulle, *De Gaulle Mon Père*, 500.

275. De Gaulle told a different story to his son, Philippe, claiming that "I had nothing against this resistant [Rol-Tanguy]. The fact that he was a communist was of no interest to me." Philippe de Gaulle, *De Gaulle Mon Père*, 506.

276. Neiberg, *The Blood of Free Men*, 233–235.

277. Georges Bidault, *Resistance: The Political Autobiography of Georges Bidault*, trans. Marianne Sinclair (London: Weidenfeld and Nicolson, 1967), 47–53. On Moulin, see Adam Clinton, *Jean Moulin, 1899–1943: The French Resistance and the Republic* (London: Macmillan, 2002), especially 203–216.

278. De Gaulle, *War Memoirs*, 650.

279. De Gaulle, *Discours et messages (1940–1946)* (Paris: Poche, 1970), 397–398.

280. Neiberg, *The Blood of Free Men*, 236–237.

281. Bidault, *Resistance*, 54–55.

282. Bidault, *Resistance*, 54–55.

283. Cited in Cook, *Charles de Gaulle*, 251.

284. De Gaulle, *War Memoirs*, 673.

Chapter Four

1. The Dumbarton Oaks mansion, originally the home of a diplomat, had been donated to Harvard University in 1940. A junior State Department official named Alger Hiss suggested it as a comfortable venue for the first meeting to lay the groundwork for what would come to be called the United Nations.

2. Andrew Williams, "France and the Origins of the United Nations, 1944–1945: Si la France ne compte plus, qu'on nous le dise," *Diplomacy and Statecraft* 28, no. 3 (June 2017): 218.

3. Thomas M. Campbell and George C. Herring, eds., *The Diaries of Edward R. Stettinius, 1943–1946* (New York: New Viewpoints, 1975), 113, 118; David L. Bosco, *Five to Rule Them All: The UN Security Council and the Making of the Modern World* (New York: Oxford University Press, 2009), 24–28.

4. A. W. DePorte, *De Gaulle's Foreign Policy, 1944–1946* (Cambridge, MA: Harvard University Press, 1968), 64–65. Robert C. Hildebrand, *Dumbarton Oaks: The Origins of the United Nations and the Search for Postwar Security* (Chapel Hill: University of North Carolina Press, 1990); Stephen Schlesinger, *Act of Creation: The Founding of the United Nations* (Boulder, CO: Oxford, 2003).

5. Cordell Hull, *The Memoirs of Cordell Hull* (New York: Macmillan, 1948), II: 1673ff. Memorandum of Conversation between Hull and Hoppenot, September 19, 1944. CHP, LOCMD, Reel 29. Hopkins personal and secret memorandum for the president, October 13, 1944, Harry Hopkins Papers, Box 334, folder Civil Affairs in France, FDRL.

6. David Mayers, *FDR's Ambassadors and the Diplomacy of Crisis* (Cambridge: Cambridge University Press, 2013), 163–164. See also Steven Sapp, "Jefferson Caffery, Cold War Diplomat: American-French Relations 1944–1949," *Louisiana History*, no. 23 (1982): 180–181; "Careerist to Paris," *Time*, October 2, 1944, 20.

7. *New York Times*, September 21, 1944.

8. Hull Memorandum to Roosevelt, September 7, 1944, Roosevelt Response to Hull, September 19 and 22, 1944, PSF, Diplomatic Correspondence, Box 30, folder France 1944-1945, FDRL.

9. Hull Memorandum to the President, September 17, 1944, Hopkins Papers, Box 334, folder Civil Affairs in France, FDRL.

10. FDR cable to Churchill, October 18, 1944, Hopkins Papers, Box 334, folder Civil Affairs in France, FDRL.

11. Declaration of Acting Secretary of State Edward Stettinius, October 23, 1944, Hopkins Papers, Book 9, Civil Affairs in France, FDRL. *New York Times*, October 24, 1944; James J. Dougherty, *The Politics of Wartime Aid: American Assistance to France and Northwest Africa, 1940–1946* (Westport, CT: Greenwood Press, 1978), 180. The Paris embassy was reopened on December 1 and Caffrey presented his credentials on December 30.

12. Campbell and Herring, *Stettinius Diaries*, 35–36.

13. Cited in Anthony Beever and Artemis Cooper, *Paris after the Liberation* (London: Penguin, 1995), 122.

14. Caffrey cable to Secretary of State, October 24, 1944; H. Freeman Matthews to Hopkins, October 26, 1944, Hopkins Papers, Box 334, folder Civil Affairs in France, FDRL.

15. Monnet to Stettinius, January 2, 1945, Stettinius to Monnet, January 13, 1945, Hopkins Papers, Box 334, folder Civil Affairs in France, FDRL.

16. Caffrey cable to State Department, November 3, 1944, *FRUS*, 1944, III, 890–891; Caffrey cable to State Department, December 8, 1944, *FRUS*, 1944, III, 919. Michael Creswell, *A Question of Balance: How France and the United States Created Cold War Europe* (Cambridge, MA: Harvard University Press, 2006), 9.

17. Caffrey cables to State Department, November 13 and 14, 1944, PSF, Diplomatic Correspondence, France, FDRL.

18. André Béziat, *Franklin Roosevelt et la France* (Paris: Harmattan, 1997), 423–424.

19. De Gaulle letter to Eisenhower, September 31, 1944, Pre-Presidential Series, Principle File, Box 34, folder "Charles de Gaulle," DDEL.

20. Leclerc to Devers, December 14, 1944; Devers to Leclerc, December 18, 1944, Devers to War Minister A. Diethelm, December 18, 1944, Pre-Presidential Series, Principal File, Box 34, folder De Lattre de Tassigny, DDEL.

21. See de Gaulle's letter to Eisenhower, January 3, 1945, De Gaulle, *Charles de Gaulle, Lettres, Notes, et Carnets* (hereafter *LNC*), *1942–1958* (Paris: Lafont, 2010), 605–606.

22. Quoted in Rick Atkinson, *The Guns at Last Light: The War in Western Europe, 1944–1945* (New York: Henry Holt, 2013), 480.

23. Dwight D. Eisenhower, *Crusade in Europe* (New York: Doubleday, 1948), 362–363; Charles De Gaulle, *The Complete War Memoirs*, trans. Jonathan Griffin (New York: Simon & Schuster, 1972), 836–839; Lord Alanbrooke, *War Diaries 1939–1945* (London: Weidenfeld & Nicolson, 2001), 642. Milton Viorst, *Hostile Allies: FDR and De Gaulle* (New York: Macmillan, 1965), 227–229.

24. Hoppenot letter to Bidault, December 20, 1944, *Documents Diplomatiques Français* (hereafter *DDF*), 1944, Vol. II, 467–474.

25. De Gaulle letter to Eisenhower, September 6, 1944, Pre-Presidential Series, Principal File, Box 34, folder Charles de Gaulle, DDEL.

26. Stettinius memorandum to Roosevelt, January 4, 1945, PSF, Diplomatic Correspondence, Box 30, folder France 1944-1945, FDRL.

27. Robert E. Sherwood, *Roosevelt and Hopkins: An Intimate History* (New York: Bantam Books, 1948), 485.

28. Julian Jackson, *France, The Dark Years (1940–1944)* (New York: Oxford University Press, 2001), 427.

29. For an in-depth description of his entire career, see Clinton, *Jean Moulin*. Moulin's memoir, *Premier Combat*, was published posthumously by his sister Laure (Paris: Les Editions du Minuit, 1965). See also Ray Argyle, *The Paris Game: Charles de Gaulle, the Liberation of Paris, and the Gamble that Won France* (Toronto: Dundurn, 2014), 161–163, 185–186.

30. Blake Ehrlich, *Resistance: France, 1940–1945* (Boston: Little, Brown, 1965), 58.

31. See Gilbert Renault (Rémy), *Dix Ans Avec De Gaulle, 1940–1950* (Paris: France-Empire, 1971), chapter 1.

32. Jean Lacouture, *De Gaulle, The Rebel 1890–1944*, trans. Alan Sheridan (New York: Norton, 1993), 370. On Dewavrin, see his memoirs: *Colonel Passy, Souvenirs*, 2 volumes (Monte Carlo: R. Solar, 1947). The best study of the social, political, and economic context of the French collaboration and resistance is Jackson, *France: The Dark Years*.

33. Stephen Kinzer, *The Brothers: John Foster Dulles, Allen Dulles, and Their Secret World War* (New York: Henry Holt, 2013), 65–66.

34. See Robert Belot and Gilbert Karpman, *L'Affaire Suisse: La Résistance a-t-elle trahi de Gaulle? (1943–1944)* (Paris: Armand Colin, 2009). See also Belot's *La Résistance sans de Gaulle* (Paris: Fayard, 2006).

35. Matthews (London) to Ray Atherton (head of the European Desk of the State Department), February 26, March 4, March 5, March 26, April 5, June 25, 1943, NARA, RG 59, Box General Records of the State Department, Miscellaneous Office Files, 1910-1944, Box 18.

36. J. Edgar Hoover letter to Attorney General, December 13, 1944, PSF, Diplomatic Correspondence, Box 30, folder France 1944-1945, FDRL.

37. Lacouture, *De Gaulle, The Rebel*, 373.

38. Will Brownell and Richard N. Billings, *So Close to Greatness: A Biography of William C. Bullitt* (New York, Macmillan, 1987), 294–297.

39. Brownell and Billings, *So Close to Greatness*, 302–304; Bullitt, *For the President*, 604–605. As an honorary French citizen, he was able to accept the commission and retain his American citizenship. Irwin F. Gellman, *Secret Affairs: Franklin Roosevelt, Cordell Hull, and Sumner Welles* (Baltimore: Johns Hopkins University Press, 1995), 345.

40. An American colonel witnessed several of these shavings, noting that the spectacle "delighted the crowd, which roared its laughter, mingled with loud boos." Brenton G. Wallace, *Patton and his Third Army* (Harrisburg, PA: Military Service Publishing Company, 1946), 74–75.

41. Michael Neiberg, *The Blood of Free Men: The Liberation of Paris, 1944* (New York: Basic Books, 2012), 253. See Hal Vaughn, *Sleeping with the Enemy: Coco Chanel's Secret War* (New York: Knopf, 2011), and Fabrice Virgili, *Shorn Women: Gender and Punishment in Liberated France* (Oxford: Berg, 2002).

42. See Peter Novick, The Resistance Versus Vichy: The Purge of Collaborators in Liberated France (London: Chatto & Windus, 1968).

43. J. R. Tournoux, *Pétain et de Gaulle: Un Demi-Siècle d'Histoire Non Officielle* (Paris: Plon, 1964), 345–347.

44. Thomas R. Christofferson with Michael S. Christofferson, *France During World War II: From Defeat to Liberation* (New York: Fordham University Press, 2006), 193. Peter Novick, The Resistance Versus Vichy: The Purge of Collaborators in Liberated France (London: Chatto & Windus, 1968), 169–174.

45. Jean-Paul Cointet, *Pierre Laval* (Paris: Fayard, 1993), 511–533.

46. Cited in Don Cook, *Charles de Gaulle: A Biography* (New York: G.P. Putnam's Sons, 1983), 260.

47. Caffrey to Secretary of State, November 3, 1944; Hoppenot letter to Hull, November 4, 1944; PSF, Diplomatic Correspondence, Box 30, folder France 1944–1945, FDRL.

48. François Lévêque, "Les relations entre l'Union soviétique et la France Libre," in *De Gaulle et la Russie*, ed. Maurice Vaisse (Paris: CNRS Editions, 2012), 27–29.

49. De Gaulle, *War Memoirs*, 729–735.

50. "Compte Rendu de l'Entretien du Général de Gaulle avec le Maréchal Staline," December 2, 1944, *DDF*, (1944), vol. II, 350–353.

51. "Conversation entre M. Bidault et M. Molotov," Kremlin, December 5, 1944, *DDF* (1944), vol. II, 375–383.

52. "Entrevue entre Le Général de Gaulle et Le Maréchal Staline," December 8, 1944, *DDF* (1944), vol. II, 419–422.

53. Harriman cable to State Department, December 8, 1944, PSF, FDRL; De Gaulle, *War Memoirs*, 756–757.

54. *FRUS, 1944, The Conferences of Malta and Yalta* (1945), 288–290; DePorte, *De Gaulle's Foreign Policy, 1944–1946*, 77.

55. *Le Monde*, January 12, 14, and 19, 1945.

56. De Gaulle, *War Memoirs*, 759.

57. The reference to "last time" must have been to the premature withdrawal of American troops from their occupation zone in the Rhineland in 1923. Roosevelt cable to Churchill, November 18, 1944; Churchill cable to Roosevelt, November 19, 1944, *FRUS, The Conferences at Malta and Yalta* (1945), 286–287.

58. Stettinius Memorandum for the President, January 4, 1945, *FRUS, The Conferences at Malta and Yalta* (1945), 293–294.

59. Roosevelt cable to Churchill, December 6, 1944, *FRUS, The Conferences at Malta and Yalta* (1945), 291.

60. Grew (Acting) memorandum for Roosevelt, January 16, 1945, enclosing cable from Caffrey reporting the French foreign ministry's formal request that the French government be invited to the Yalta Conference. PSF, Diplomatic Correspondence, Box 30, folder France 1944-1945, FDRL. In his message Caffrey repeated Bidault's statement that France "could not consider itself bound by any decisions taken without it" and warned that such decisions might "lose some of their value." Caffrey cable to Secretary of State, January 16, 1945, *FRUS, The Conferences at Malta and Yalta* (1945), 296–297.

61. Sherwood, *Roosevelt and Hopkins*, 487–488.

62. De Gaulle, *War Memoirs*, 762.

63. Cited in Cook, *Charles de Gaulle*, 274.

64. *FRUS, The Conferences at Malta and Yalta* (1945), 252–253.

65. *FRUS, The Conferences at Malta and Yalta* (1945), 628.

66. Russell D. Buhite, *Decisions at Yalta: An Appraisal of Summit Diplomacy* (Wilmington, DE: Scholarly Resources, 1986), 9, 29; Viorst, *Hostile Allies*, 230–231.

67. Buhite, *Decisions at Yalta*, 29. *FRUS, The Conferences of Malta and Yalta* (1945), 618.

68. Churchill, *The Second World War*, Vol. 6, 308; Sherwood, *Roosevelt and Hopkins*, 492.

69. Bohlen, *Witness to History*, 184–185.

70. Interview of H. Freeman Matthews, June 7, 1973, by Richard D. McKinzie. www.trumanlibrary.org/oralhist/matthewh.htm.

71. Charles Bohlen, *Witness to History, 1929–1969* (New York: W.W. Norton, 1973), 185.

72. Buhite, *Decisions at Yalta*, 51; *FRUS, The Conferences at Malta and Yalta* (1945), 679–681.

73. Georges Bidault, *Resistance: The Political Autobiography of Georges Bidault*, trans. Marianne Sinclair (London: Weidenfeld and Nicolson, 1967), 78–79.

74. Roosevelt Note to Caffrey, February 11, 1945, MRF, FDRL.

75. De Gaulle, *War Memoirs*, 766–768.

76. Sherwood, *Roosevelt and Hopkins*, 504.

77. Bohlen, *Witness to History*, 204–205.

78. Nowhere in de Gaulle's description of the Crimea Conference does he recognize the enormous gains that his country had obtained despite his absence from the gathering. De Gaulle, *War Memoirs*, 763–769.

79. Diane Shaver Clemens, *Yalta* (New York: Oxford University Press, 1970), 223.

80. De Gaulle letter to Roosevelt, January 1, 1945, PSF, Diplomatic Correspondence, Box 30, folder France 1944–1945, FDRL.

81. Roosevelt letter to de Gaulle, March 24, 1945, PSF, Diplomatic Correspondence, Box 30, folder France 1944-1945, FDRL. On FDR's last months before his death, see Joseph Lelyveld, *His Final Battle: The Last Months of Franklin Roosevelt* (New York: Vintage, 2017).

82. Raoul Aglion, *Roosevelt and de Gaulle: Allies in Conflict. A Personal Memoir* (New York: The Free Press, 1988), 199.

Chapter Five

1. Harry S. Truman letters to Bess Wallace, April 14, October 11, 1918. Family, Business, and Personal Affairs File, Harry S. Truman Library (hereafter HSTL).

2. Harry S. Truman, *The Autobiography of Harry S. Truman* (Boulder: University Press of Colorado, 1980), 50–51.

3. David McCullough, *Truman* (New York: Simon & Schuster, 1992), 425.

4. Charles de Gaulle, *The Complete War Memoirs*, trans. Jonathan Griffin (New York: Simon & Schuster, 1972), 845.

5. Cited in Rick Atkinson, *The Guns at Last Light: The War in Western Europe, 1944–1945* (New York: Henry Holt and Company, 2013), 610.

6. De Lattre noted the significance of the city of Ulm as the battlefield where Napoleon had defeated the Austrian army in 1805.

7. Harry S. Truman, *Year of Decisions* (New York: Doubleday, 1955), 237–239; Jean de Lattre de Tassigny, *Histoire de la Première Armée Francaise* (Paris: Plon, 1949), 567–571.

8. Robert J. Donovan, *Conflict and Compromise: The Presidency of Harry S. Truman, 1945–1948* (New York: Norton, 1977), 58.

9. Irwin Wall, "Harry Truman and Charles de Gaulle," in *De Gaulle and the United States*, ed. Robert O. Paxton and Nicholas Wahl (Oxford: Berg, 1994), 119. Stimson to Truman, May 1, 1945, Naval Aide to President Files, HSTL; *Papers Relating to the Foreign Relations of the United States* (hereafter FRUS), 1945, IV, France, May 1, 1945,

682; Charles Williams, *The Last Great Frenchman: A Life of Charles de Gaulle* (New York: Wiley, 1993), 299.

10. De Gaulle cable to Doyen May 4, 1945, De Gaulle, *Charles de Gaulle, Lettres, Notes, et Carnets* (hereafter *LNC*), *1942–1958* (Paris: Lafont, 2010), 660.

11. Caffrey cable to State Department, May 6, 1945. President's Personal File (hereafter PPF), Box 166, folder Telegrams, Paris-Caffrey, HSTL.

12. *FRUS*, 1945, IV, France, May 17, 19, and 20, 729–732.

13. De Gaulle Message to Truman, May 15, 1945, *LNC*, *1942–1958*, 667–668.

14. Churchill cables to Truman, June 4 and June 6, 1945; Truman cable to Churchill, June 11, 1945; Naval Aide to the President's Files, Box 8, folder Churchill-Truman, June–July 1945. HSTL.

15. Caffrey to Secretary of State, June 10, 1945, President's Secretary's File (hereafter PSF), Box 166, folder Telegrams, Paris, Caffrey, HSTL; Georges Bidault, *Resistance: The Political Autobiography of Georges Bidault*, trans. Marianne Sinclair (London: Weidenfeld and Nicolson, 1967), 76–77; *FRUS*, 1945, IV, France, June 6, 1945, 735. Irwin Wall, *The United States and the Making of Postwar France, 1944–1954* (Cambridge: Cambridge University Press), 31–32.

16. *FRUS*, 1945, IV, France, June 9, 1945, 420; Wall, "Harry Truman and Charles de Gaulle," 121. Truman, *Year of Decisions*, 239–240.

17. Churchill Cable to Roosevelt, November 13, 1943, Warren Kimball, ed., *Churchill and Roosevelt; The Complete Correspondence, Vol. II, Alliance Forged* (London: Collins, 1984), 599–600.

18. For de Gaulle's version of the dispute, see De Gaulle, *War Memoirs*, 878–888.

19. De Gaulle, *War Memoirs*, 889.

20. Caffrey cables to Secretary of State, June 1, 4, and 6, 1945, PSF, Box 166, folder Telegrams, Paris, Caffrey, HSTL.

21. Cited in Donovan, *Conflict and Crisis*, 58.

22. Thomas M. Campbell and George C. Herring, eds, *The Diaries of Edward R. Stettinius, 1943–1946* (New York: New Viewpoints, 1975), 302.

23. "French Protest Omission of Language at Parley," *New York Times*, March 27, 1945.

24. "Instructions du government à la delegation à la conference de San Francisco," (no date), De Gaulle, *LNC*, *1942–1958*, 644–650. The American planners decided not to translate the opening speeches at the conference. When Secretary of State Stettinius opened his address, a voice in the audience began loudly to translate his remarks into French. When Stettinius paused and asked the secretary general of the conference, Alger Hiss, for assistance, Hiss simply responded, "We've been outsmarted." The loud translation continued to the end of Stettinius's address. David L. Bosco, *Five to Rule Them All: The UN Security Council and the Making of the Modern World* (New York: Oxford University Press, 2009), 35.

25. Harold Callender, "Bidault Suspects that U.S. Eyes Colonies," *New York Times*, March 28, 1945. He specifically mentioned French Indochina. Harold Callender, "Allies Bid France to Territory Talks," *New York Times*, March 29, 1945.

26. *New York Times*, March 31, 1945.

27. *New York Times*, April 28, 1945.

28. Statement by the President, May 18, 1945, Official File (hereafter OF), 201B, Box 911, HSTL; "Memoranda of Truman-Bidault Conversations," NARA, Record Group5 59, State Department Main Decimal File, 711.51/5-2045, 20 May, 1945; 711.51/5-2145. 21 May 1945. Wall, "Harry Truman and Charles de Gaulle," 122. "Memoranda of Truman-Bidault conversations," May 19, 1945, *op. cit. New York Times*, May 19, 1945.

29. See, for example, the editorial in the *New York Herald Tribune* titled "America's Stake in France." *New York Herald Tribune*, July 2, 1945.

30. Admiral Wilson Brown Memorandum for Miss Tully (Secretary to the President), March 24, 1945; Elsey Memorandum for Admiral Brown, March 24, 1945, Elsey letter to Langer, June 19, 1945, Elsey Papers, Box 3, folder W.L. Langer's History; HSTL. Wilson Brown to Dorothy Brady (secretary) March 26, 1945, PSF, 82, Navy, Wilson Brown, Franklin Delano Roosevelt Library (hereafter FDRL). Julian G. Hurstfield, *America and the French Nation, 1939–1945* (Chapel Hill: University of North Carolina Press, 1986), 225.

31. George M. Elsey, "President Roosevelt's Policy Towards De Gaulle," June 21, 1945; Elsey Papers, Box 3, folder W.L. Langer's history, HSTL.

32. William L. Langer, *Our Vichy Gamble* (New York: Norton, 1966). The original edition appeared in 1947. For a brilliant critique of the book, see Louis R. Gottschalk, "Our Vichy Fumble," *The Journal of Modern History* 20, no. 1 (March 1948): 47–56.

33. On the topic of reparations, de Gaulle complained through the official French news agency that he had not been invited to participate in the Reparation Commission that had been planned at the Yalta Conference whereas the Polish government had been. *New York Times*, May 29, 1945.

34. Unsigned memorandum of press conference, April 17, 1945; Conference with Association of Radio News Analysis, June 16, 1945, Papers of Eben A. Ayers, Box 6, folder De Gaulle, Charles, HSTL.

35. Caffrey cable to Secretary of State, August 16, 1945; PSF, Box 166, folder Telegrams, Paris, Caffrey, HSTL.

36. *New York Times*, August 23, 1945.

37. Memorandum of Conversations at the White House on August 22, 1945, between the President and General de Gaulle, PSF, Box 156, folder France-General, HSTL.

38. *New York Times*, August 27, 1945.

39. David G. Marr, *Vietnam, 1945: The Quest for Power* (Berkeley: University of California Press, 1995), 54–69.

40. André Béziat, *Franklin Roosevelt et la France* (Paris: Harmattan, 1997), 433–434.

41. Caffrey (Paris) cable to Secretary of State, March 13, 1945, *FRUS*, 1945, VI, 300. Caffrey cable to Secretary of State, April 11, 1945, NARA, II, RG59, Decimal File 1945-49, 711.5121/11-48, Box 3318.

42. Robert Dallek, *Franklin D. Roosevelt and American Foreign Policy* (New York: Oxford University Press, 1979), 511–513.

43. For a summary of this debate, see Stein Tonnesson, "Franklin Roosevelt, Trusteeship, and Indochina: A Reassessment," in *The First Vietnam War: Colonial Conflict and Cold War Crisis*, ed. Mark Attwood Lawrence and Frederik Logevall (Cambridge, MA: Harvard University Press, 2007), 57–60. See also his brilliant *The Vietnamese Revolution of 1945: Roosevelt, Ho Chi Minh, and de Gaulle in a World at War* (London: Sage Publications, 1991).

44. Bernard Fall, *Last Reflections on a War* (New York: Doubleday, 1967), 133; Arthur M. Schlesinger Jr., *The Bitter Heritage: Vietnam and American Democracy, 1941–1966* (London: André Deutsch, 1967), 11.

45. Senator Mike Gravel, ed., *The Pentagon Papers: The Defense Department History of United States Decision-making on Vietnam* (Boston: Beacon Press, 1971), I: 2.

46. Edward R. Drachman, *United States Policy Toward Vietnam, 1940–1945* (Cranbury, NJ: Fairleigh Dickinson University Press, 1970), 93–94, 161–162.

47. Walter LaFeber, "Roosevelt, Churchill, and Indochina, 1942–1945," *American Historical Review* 80 (December 1975): 1288–1291.

48. Irwin Wall, *The United States and the Making of Postwar France, 1945–1954* (Cambridge: Cambridge University Press, 1991), 235; Gravel, *The Pentagon Papers*, I: 14–15.

49. Wall, "Harry Truman and Charles de Gaulle," 124; *New York Times*, August 24, 1945.

50. Mark Atwood Lawrence, *Assuming the Burden: Europe and the American Commitment to War in Vietnam* (Berkeley: University of California Press, 2005), 74–75.

51. Pierre Journaud, *De Gaulle et le Vietnam, 1945–1969* (Paris: Tallendier, 2011), 28.

52. Mark Atwood Lawrence, "Forging the 'Great Combination': Britain and the Indochina Problem, 1945–1950," in *The First Vietnam War: Colonial Conflict and Cold War Crisis*, ed. Mark Atwood Lawrence and Fredrik Logevall (Cambridge, MA: Harvard University Press, 2007), 105–117.

53. Ronald H. Spector, *Advice and Support: The Early Years of the U.S. Army in Vietnam, 1941–1960* (New York: The Free Press, 1985), 37.

54. See the memoir by Archimedes Patti, *Why Vietnam? Prelude to America's Albatross* (Berkeley: University of California Press, 1980); Marr, *Vietnam, 1945*, 279–291; Mark P. Bradley, *Imagining Vietnam and America: The Making of Postcolonial Vietnam* (Chapel Hill: University of North Carolina Press, 2000), 125–128. The activities of the OSS in northern Vietnam raised the suspicions that Washington was plotting to replace France in the country. With no hard evidence to substantiate this claim, the newly appointed French high commissioner, Admiral Thierry d'Argenlieu, peddled this dubious assertion thereafter. Lawrence, *Assuming the Burden*, 94.

55. Fredrik Logevall, *Embers of War: The Fall of an Empire and the Making of America's Vietnam* (New York: Random House, 2013), 101.

56. Jean Lacouture, *Ho Chi Minh*, trans. Peter Wiles (Harmondsworth, UK: Penguin Books, 1968), 26–31.

57. The speech is reprinted in Gareth Porter, ed., *Vietnam: The Definitive Documentation of Human Decisions, Vol. I, The First Indochina War and the Geneva Agreements, 1941–1954* (Stanfordville, NY: Coleman Enterprises, 1979), 64–66.

58. Philippe Devillers, *Histoire du Viet-Nam de 1940 à 1952* (Paris: Le Seuil, 1952), 144; Martin Shipway, *The Road to War: France and Vietnam, 1944–1947* (Providence, RI: Berghahn, 1966), 59–62.

59. On Gracey's role in facilitating the return of the French soldiers and administrators, see Logevall, *Embers of War*, 113–118.

60. Lawrence, *Assuming the Burden*, 104–105. Stein Tonnesson, *Vietnam 1946: How the War Began* (Berkeley: University of California Press, 2010), 30–31.

61. Tonnesson, *Vietnam 1946*, 83–85.

62. Ho's letters are conveniently assembled on www.historyisaweapon.com /defcon2/hochiminh/. See also "Annamese Independence Committee" cable from Shanghai addressed to Truman, forwarded by the Embassy in Chungking to State Department, November 10, 1945, Naval Aid to President files, folder Communication to Truman, 1945, HSTL. *United States–Vietnam Relations, 1945–1967. Study Prepared by the Department of Defense*, 12 vols. (Washington, D.C.: US Government Printing Office, 1971), 1: 20–33, 8: May 9, 23, 1945). This series was later leaked by the researcher Daniel Ellsberg as the famous (or infamous) "Pentagon Papers."

63. Charles de Gaulle, *Discours et messages* (hereafter *DM*), *1940–1946* (Paris: Poche, 1970), 450; Andrew Shennan, *Rethinking France: Plans for Renewal, 1940–1946* (New York: Oxford University Press, 1989), 250–251.

64. Julian Jackson, *De Gaulle* (Cambridge, MA: Harvard University Press, 2018), 378–380.

65. Jonathan Fenby, *The General: Charles De Gaulle and the France He Saved* (New York: Skyhorse, 2012), 308.

66. De Gaulle, *LNC, 1942–1958*, 771.

67. De Gaulle, *War Memoirs*, 989.

68. Philippe Mioche, *Le Plan Monnet: Genesis et elaboration, 1941–1947* (Paris: Publications de la Sorbonne, 1987), 82–84.

69. François Duchêne, *Jean Monnet: The First Statesman of Interdependence* (New York: Norton, 1994), 143. James J. Dougherty, *The Politics of Wartime Aid: American Assistance to France and Northwest Africa, 1940–1946* (Westport, CT: Greenwood Press, 1978), 201–202.

70. John S. Hill, "De Gaulle's Strategy for Economic Reconstruction," in *De Gaulle and the United States: A Centennial Reappraisal*, ed. Robert O. Paxton and Nicholas Wahl (Oxford: Berg, 1994), 106–109.

71. Cited in Don Cook, *Charles de Gaulle: A Biography* (New York: G.P. Putnam's Sons, 1983), 292.

72. Barry Eichengreen, *The European Economy Since 1945* (Princeton, NJ: Princeton University Press, 2007), 105–106.

73. Edward L. Morse, *Foreign Policy and Interdependence in Gaullist France* (Princeton, NJ: Princeton University Press, 1973), 283–285.

74. Simon L. Millner, "Current Conditions in France," October 9, 1944, PSF, Diplomatic Correspondence, Box 30, folder France 1944-1945, FDRL.

75. Hill, "De Gaulle's Strategy for Economic Reconstruction," 109. "Control and Administration of Germany," Memorandum by the French Delegation to the Council of Foreign Ministers, September 13, 1945, *FRUS*, 1945, III, 869–871.

76. De Gaulle, *DM, 1940-1946*, 627ff. John W. Young, *France, the Cold War, and the Western Alliance,1944–1949* (Leicester, UK: Leicester University Press, 1990), 84.

77. Murphy to Secretary of State, September 23, 1945, *FRUS*, 1945, III, 871–873.

78. John W. Young, *Britain, France, and the Unity of Europe* (London: Salem House Publishers, 1984), 28.

79. Francis M. B. Lynch, "Resolving the Paradox of the Monnet Plan: National and International Planning in French Reconstruction," *Economic History Review* 37, no. 2 (May 1984): 236.

80. Hill, "De Gaulle's Strategy for Economic Reconstruction," 112.

81. Report on Franco-American conversations held in Washington, 13–20 November 1945, concerning the future status of the Rhineland and the Ruhr, November 20, 21, 1945, *FRUS*, 1945, III, 907–908.

82. A. W. DePorte, *De Gaulle's Foreign Policy, 1944-1946* (Cambridge, MA: Harvard University Press, 1968), 266–268.

83. Wall, "Harry Truman and Charles de Gaulle," 128.

84. See Irwin Wall, "Les Accords Blum-Brynes, la Modernisation de la France at la guerre froide," *Vingtieme Siecle*, no. 13 (January–March 1987): 45–63. Wall, *The United States and the Making of Postwar France*, 49–62.

85. De Gaulle, *LNC, 1942–1958*, 771.

86. De Gaulle, *War Memoirs*, 993. Resignation letter of General de Gaulle to M. Félix Gouin, January 21, 1946, De Gaulle, *LNC, 1942–1958*, 784.

87. Cited in Cook, *Charles de Gaulle*, 300.

Chapter Six

1. The English version of the town's name is "Colombey with two churches." But there was (and is) only one church in the village.

2. Anne O'Hare McCormick, "A Familiar Voice Is Heard Again in France," *New York Times*, June 17, 1946.

3. *New York Times*, January 24, 1946.

4. *New York Times*, May 11, 1946.

5. Gilbert Renault (Rémy), *Dix Ans avec de Gaulle, 1940–1950* (Paris: France-Empire, 1971), chapter 3.

6. Cited in Don Cook, *De Gaulle: A Biography* (New York: G.P. Putnam's Sons, 1983), 305. General Georges Boulanger had won widespread public support in 1889 with his criticism of the Third Republic and was suspected of planning a coup to as-

sume power. Paul von Hindenburg was the president of Germany's Weimar Republic who named Hitler chancellor in 1933.

7. Irwin Wall, *The United States and the Making of Postwar France, 1945–1954* (Cambridge: Cambridge University Press, 1991), 81–84, 136.

8. Frank Giles, *The Locust Years, 1946–1958* (London: Secker and Warburg, 1991), 78–79.

9. Cited in Cook, *Charles de Gaulle*, 308.

10. Pierre Sainderichin, *De Gaulle et le Monde* (Paris: Le Monde, 1990), 34; Jonathan Fenby, *The General: Charles De Gaulle and the France He Saved* (New York: Skyhorse, 2012), 327–332.

11. U.S. State Department, *Papers Relating to the Foreign Relations of the United States* (hereafter *FRUS*), 1948, III, France, January 14, March 17, and May 8, 1948, 374, 392, and 397.

12. *FRUS*, 1948, III, December 10, 1948, 419.

13. Frédéric Bozo, *Two Strategies for Europe: De Gaulle, the United States, and the Atlantic Alliance*, trans. Susan Emanuel (Lanham, MD: Rowman & Littlefield, 2001), 7–8.

14. De Gaulle's position on the European Defense Community (EDC) was prescient. The Pleven Plan for the EDC was rejected by the French government in 1954, and West Germany was permitted to rearm and join NATO in 1955.

15. Cited in Wall, *The United States and the Making of Postwar France*, 211.

16. De Gaulle, *Discours et messages, 1946–1958* (hereafter *DM*) (Paris: Poche, 1970) 609; De Gaulle, "Commentaires aux délégués du Rassemblement du peuple français," June 13, 1953, *Charles de Gaulle, Lettres, Notes, et Carnets* (hereafter *LNC*), *1942–1958* (Paris: Lafont, 2010), 1116–1122. Julian Jackson, *De Gaulle* (Cambridge, MA: Harvard University Press, 2018), 427.

17. Most of the profits were used to fund a foundation for children with Down syndrome in memory of his beloved daughter Anne.

18. De Gaulle, *DM, 1946–1958*, 647. On the other hand, he supported Mendès-France's decision to grant autonomy to Tunisia. A year later he told an interviewer that "we are in the presence of a wave that is carrying peoples toward emancipation. There are some imbeciles who do not want to understand this." Michael Kettle, *De Gaulle and Algeria, 1940–1960: From Mers El-Kébir to the Algiers Barricades* (London: Quartet Books, 1993), 59; Irwin Wall, *France, the United States, and the Algerian War* (Berkeley: University of California Press, 2001), 199.

19. Brian Duchin, "The 'Agonizing Reappraisal': Eisenhower, Dulles, and the European Defense Community," *Diplomatic History* 16, no. 2 (April 1, 1992): 201–221; François David, "John Foster Dulles, Sécretaire d'Etat, et la France," Doctoral Dissertation, Université de la Sorbonne, Paris IV (2006), II: 627–635; Daniel Lerner, *France Defeats EDC* (New York: Praeger, 1957).

20. *New York Times*, November 11, 1953.

21. Jackson, *De Gaulle*, 432.

22. In my opinion, the best studies of the complicated relationship between de Gaulle and the situation in Algeria are Maurice Vaïsse, *De Gaulle et l'Algérie, 1943–1969* (Paris: Armand Colin, 2012), and Benjamin Stora, *De Gaulle et l'Algérie* (Paris: Fayard, 2010).

23. The term means "black feet," reportedly referring to the tall black boots worn by French colonial soldiers. It became a standard reference to all European settlers in Algeria.

24. For an estimate of the total number of French soldiers stationed in Algeria until that country's independence compared to those stationed elsewhere, see Lothar Ruehl, *La politique militaire de la Ve République* (Paris: Presses de la Fondation Nationale des Sciences Politiques, 1976), 328.

25. J. K. Emmerson (U.S. Embassy in Paris) cable to State Department, June 21, 1957, *FRUS, 1955–1957*, XXVII, 127–128. Allesandro Brogi, *A Question of Self-Esteem: The United States and the Cold War Choices in France and Italy, 1944–1958* (Westport, CT: Praeger, 2002), 228.

26. Jackson, *De Gaulle*, 449.

27. Of the dozens of books about this fascinating writer, my favorite is David Sherman, *Camus* (New York: John Wiley, 2009).

28. Albert Camus, *Carnets, Vol. III, Mars 1951–Décembre 1959* (Paris: Gallimard, 1989), 216.

29. Jackson, *De Gaulle*, 458–459.

30. Wall, *France, the United States, and the Algerian War*, 138–139.

31. Cited in Fenby, *The General*, 385. On the machinations of de Gaulle's agents and their connections with the military plotters in Algiers, see Charles Maier and Dan S. White, *The Thirteenth of May: The Advent of de Gaulle's Republic* (New York: Oxford University Press, 1968), 236–259.

32. De Gaulle letter to Bidault, May 20, 1958, *LNC, 1942–1958*, 1277.

33. Michel Debré, *Trois Républiques pour une France*, vol. I (Paris: Albin Michel, 1988), 308.

34. Vincent Nouzelle, *Des Secrets Si Bien Gardé* (Paris: Fayard, 2009), 24–26. Fenby, *The General*, 390.

35. Cook, *Charles de Gaulle*, 321.

36. Fenby, *The General*, 396.

37. The Elysée Palace, originally a mansion occupied by Madame de Pompadour, the favorite mistress of King Louis XV, had become the official residence of French presidents in 1871.

38. Sudhir Hazareesingh, *In the Shadow of the General: Modern France and the Myth of De Gaulle* (New York: Oxford University Press, 2012), 9.

Chapter Seven

1. Couve's ten-year term as French foreign minister broke all records for consecutive service in this post since the eighteenth century.

2. Cited in Raoul Aglion, *Roosevelt and de Gaulle, Allies in Conflict: A Personal Memoir* (New York: The Free Press, 1988), 124–125.

3. Several years later the Paris bureau chief of *The New York Times* suggested that he must have meant, "I have understood you—and I do not agree with you at all." Robert C. Doty, "The Man, the Monument Called de Gaulle," *New York Times*, May 8, 1961.

4. Irwin Wall, *France, the United States, and the Algerian War* (Berkeley: University of California Press, 2001), 159.

5. Michèle Cointet, *De Gaulle et l'Algérie française, 1958–1962* (Paris, Librairie Académique Perrin, 2012), 21–25. Massu had served in Leclerc's Free French forces in the African desert, fought in Indochina, and was a loyal Gaullist.

6. The best study of the process of French decolonization in French West Africa, which is based on extensive interviews with surviving policymakers as well as an exhaustive review of primary and secondary sources, happens to be in English: Tony Chafer, *The End of Empire in French West Africa: France's Successful Decolonization?* (Oxford: Berg, 2002). On de Gaulle's role, see pages 172–185.

7. George Lichtheim, *Europe and America: The Future of the Atlantic Community* (London: Thames and Hudson, 1963), 179.

8. For the evolution of the French Community in its brief years of existence, see Yves Guéna, *Historique de la Communauté* (Paris: Fayard, 1962), and Alfred Grosser, *French Foreign Policy under De Gaulle*, trans. Lois Ames Pattison (Boston: Little, Brown and Company, 1967), 56–58.

9. Several years later the Intelligence and Research Branch of the U.S. State Department prepared a comprehensive assessment of de Gaulle's financial and commercial policies toward France's former African colonies, attributing them to his goal of buttressing France's claims to be a world power. It also noted that de Gaulle vigorously opposed any effort by foreign countries (and particularly the U.S.) to impinge on France's special bilateral economic relationship with these countries through foreign aid projects provided to them. "French Aid to Less Developed Countries," Department of State, Bureau of Intelligence and Research, Director Thomas L. Hughes Memorandum to Rusk, April 24, 1963, NSF, France, Box 72, folder 4/4 to 4/8 1963, John F. Kennedy Library (hereafter JFKL).

10. *New York Times*, October 1, 1958.

11. Eisenhower cable to de Gaulle, December 23, 1958, Ann Whitman File, Presidential Series, Box 13, folder De Gaulle June '58-Oct.59, Dwight D. Eisenhower Library (hereafter DDEL).

12. Eisenhower letter to de Gaulle, January 8, 1959, Ann Whitman File, Presidential Series, Box 13, folder June '58-Oct. 59, DDEL.

13. De Gaulle letters to Eisenhower, January 8, 12, 1959; Ann Whitman File, Presidential Series, Box 13, folder De Gaulle June '58-Oct. '59, DDEL.

14. Cited in Allesandro Brogi, *A Question of Self-Esteem: The United States and the Cold War Choices in France and Italy, 1944–1958* (Westport, CT: Praeger, 2002), 236.

15. Gaulle letter (personal and secret) to General Challe, January 3, 1959, de Gaulle, *Charles de Gaulle, Lettres, Notes, et Carnets* (hereafter *LNC*), *1958–1970* (Paris: Lafont, 2010), 112–113.

16. Julian Jackson, *De Gaulle* (Cambridge, MA: Harvard University Press, 2018), 523–524.

17. Pierre Démaret and Christian Plume count thirty-one attempts on de Gaulle's life: the first during the Second World War and the rest during his presidency. Pierre Démaret and Christian Plume, *Target de Gaulle: The True Story of the 31 Attempts on the Life of the French President*, trans. Richard Barry (New York: The Dial Press, 1975).

18. Jean-Raymond Tournoux, *La Tragédie du Géneral* (Paris: Plon, 1967), cited in Maurice Vaisse and Jean Doise, *Politique étrangère de la France: Diplomatie et outil militaire, 1871–1991* (Paris: Seuil, 1987), 588.

19. Jack Raymond, "Pentagon Weighing Shift of NATO Bases," *New York Times*, May 19, 1958.

20. Truman to Eisenhower letter, March 20, 1952, with attached letter from Eisenhower, March 11, 1952, Student Research File (B file), no. 34A, North Atlantic Treaty Organization, Box 1, folder 3, Harry S. Truman Library (hereafter HSTL).

21. Sebastian Reyn, *Atlantis Lost: The American Experience with De Gaulle, 1958–1969* (Amsterdam: Amsterdam University Press, 2009), 33.

22. Vernon Walters, *Silent Missions* (New York: Doubleday & Company, 1978), 188.

23. Discussion at the 366th Meeting of the National Security Council (NSC), May 22, 1958, Ann Whitman File, NSC Series, Box 10, folder of meeting of May 22, 1958, DDEL.

24. Discussion at the 368th Meeting of the National Security Council, June 3, 1958, Ann Whitman File, NSC Series, Box 10, folder of meeting of June 3, 1958, DDEL.

25. De Gaulle letter to Eisenhower, June 3, 1958, Ann Whitman File, International Series, Box 13, folder De Gaulle June 1958-October 1959, DDEL.

26. *New York Times*, June 2, 1958.

27. "The Tide for De Gaulle Rises," *Life Magazine*, June 2, 1958, 15–21.

28. Frédéric Bozo and Pierre Mélandri, "La France devant l'opinion américaine, Le retour de De Gaulle, debut 1958-printemps 1959," *Relations internationales*, no. 58 (Summer 1989): 195–215.

29. When Eisenhower's old friend C. D. Jackson published an editorial in *Time* magazine very critical of de Gaulle in early June 1958, Eisenhower complained to his secretary, Ann Whitman, and authorized her to pass the conversation on to Jackson, about his negative reaction to the editorial. He recalled that "there is no one that has had more satisfying and revealing conversations than with General de Gaulle." She added that both the president and Dulles "believe that de Gaulle has got a tremendous opportunity to further the interests of France and the Free World." Ann C. Whitman to C. D., June 5, 1958, Ann Whitman File, Dulles-Herter Series, Box 10, DDEL.

30. Cited in Don Cook, *Charles de Gaulle: A Biography* (New York: G.P. Putnam's Sons, 1983), 333.

31. Houghton to Dulles, June 4, 1958; Ann Whitman File, Dulles-Herter Series, Box 10, folder "Dulles 1958," DDEL.

32. Memorandum of Conversation," Anglo-American Relations with General de Gaulle's Government," June 9, 1958, Ann Whitman File, International Subseries, Box 24, folder Macmillan, DDEL.

33. "Points for Conversation with General de Gaulle," June 28, 1958, Box 127, Reel 50, John Foster Dulles Papers, Seely Mudd Manuscript Library, Princeton University (hereafter JFDP—Seeley Mudd).

34. Bernard Ledwidge, *De Gaulle et les Américans: Conversations avec Dulles, Eisenhower, Kennedy, Rusk: 1958–1964* (Paris: Flammarion, 1984), 11. From 1965 to 1969, Ledwidge served as counselor to the British embassy in Paris.

35. William R. Keylor, "Versailles and International Diplomacy," in *The Treaty of Versailles: A Reassessment After 75 Years*, ed. Manfred Boemeke, Gerald Feldman, and Elizabeth Glaser, 469–505 (Cambridge: Cambridge University Press, 1998); François David, "John Foster Dulles, Secretaire d'Etat et la France: Les Relations Franco-Américaines entre Idéalisme Politique et Réalités Militaires," Doctoral Dissertation, Université de la Sorbonne, Paris IV (2006), 24–27.

36. Dulles to Eisenhower, July 2, 1958, Ann Whitman File, Dulles-Herter Series, Box 10, folder Dulles July 1958. Eisenhower letter to de Gaulle, July 3, 1958, Ann Whitman File, International Series, Box 13, folder De Gaulle, Jan. '58-Oct. '59, DDEL.

37. John Foster Dulles, "Memorandum of Private After-Luncheon Conversation with General de Gaulle," July 5, 1958, Ann Whitman File, International Series, Box 13, folder De Gaulle June '58-October '59, DDEL. Ledwidge, *De Gaulle et les Américains*, 14–23.

38. "Dulles Denies Nuclear Aid to France, "*New York Herald Tribune*, July 6, 1958; "Dulles Issues a Denial," *New York Times*, July 8, 1958. The *Herald Tribune* quoted French officials indicating that de Gaulle had told Dulles France would join the nuclear club "with or without access to American nuclear secrets."

39. Dulles, "Memorandum of Private After-Luncheon Conversation with General de Gaulle," July 5, 1958, Ann Whitman File, International Series, Box 13, folder De Gaulle June '58-October '59, DDEL.

40. Wall, *France, the United States, and the Algerian War*, 9–32.

41. Michael M. Harrison, *The Reluctant Ally: France and Atlantic Security* (Baltimore: Johns Hopkins University Press, 1981), 87.

42. Enunciated by the American president in a message to Congress on January 5, 1957, the Eisenhower Doctrine authorized a U.S. military intervention in the Middle East "to secure and protect the territorial integrity and political independence of such nations, requesting such aid against overt armed aggression from any nation controlled by international communism."

43. Wall, *France, the United States, and the Algerian War*, 165.

44. Pascaline Winand, *Eisenhower, Kennedy, and the United States of Europe* (New York: St. Martin's Press, 1996), 209–210; Maurice Couve de Murville, *Une Politique Etrangère, 1958–1969,* (Paris: Plon, 1971), 33.

45. Hervé Alphand, *L'Etonnement d'être: Journal 1939–1973* (Paris: Fayard, 1977), 291.

46. The memorandum was first published in Jean-Raymond Tournoux, *Jamais dit* (Paris: Plon, 1971), 191–192. Macmillan met de Gaulle for the first time in many years on the weekend of June 29–30. The British prime minister found de Gaulle "just as obstinate as ever." Peter Catterall, ed., *The Macmillan Diaries, Vol. II: Prime Minister and After, 1957–1966* (London: Macmillan, 2011), entry for June 30, 1958, 130.

47. De Gaulle letter to Eisenhower, September 17, 1958, Ann Whitman File, International Series, Box 13, folder De Gaulle June 1958–October 1959, DDEL. See the excellent analyses of the memorandum in Wilfred L. Kohl, *French Nuclear Diplomacy* (Princeton, NJ: Princeton University Press, 1971), 70–81, and Harrison, *The Reluctant Ally,* 86–101.

48. Maurice Vaisse, "Aux origins du memorandum de September 1958," *Relations internationales* 38 (Summer 1989): 253–262; William Hitchcock, *France Restored: Cold War Diplomacy and the Quest for Leadership in Europe* (Chapel Hill: University of North Carolina Press, 1998), 122.

49. Dulles and Spaak Memorandum of Conversation, September 27, 1958, *Papers Relating to the Foreign Relations of the United States* (hereafter FRUS), 1958–1960, VII, part 1, Western Europe, 359–360. Although Spaak rejected the idea of an inner directorate, he agreed with de Gaulle (without naming him) that "the concept of a military Atlantic Alliance restricted to a specific geographical area" was no longer adequate and needed to be provided with a "worldwide scope." Spaak speech to the Atlantic Treaty Association in Boston, September 27, 1958, published in Department of State Bulletin, October 20, 1958, 607–611.

50. Memorandum of Conversation, September 27, 1958, National Archives and Records Administration (hereafter NARA), Department of State (D/S) Secretary's Mem Com, Lot 64 D199.

51. Carolyne Davidson, "Dealing with de Gaulle: The United States and France," in *Globalizing de Gaulle: International Perspectives on French Foreign Policies, 1958–1969,* ed. Christian Nuenlist, Anna Locher, and Garret Martin (Plymouth: UK: Lexington Books, 2010), 114.

52. Frédéric Bozo, *Two Strategies for Europe: De Gaulle, the United States, and the Atlantic Alliance,* trans. Susan Emanuel (Lanham, MD: Rowman & Littlefield, 2001), 20.

53. Macmillan lamented the "incredible folly" of de Gaulle's forwarding to Spaak a memorandum that was supposed to be top secret, which complicated his forthcoming meeting with Adenauer on October 8. At that meeting the West German chancellor expressed his "disgust and resentment" at this campaign to relegate his country

to second-class status in the alliance. Catterall, *The Macmillan Diaries*, October 8, 1958, 162–163.

54. Hubert Beuve-Méry, *Onze Ans de Regne, 1958–1969* (Paris: Flammarion, 1974), 12.

55. Eisenhower to de Gaulle, October 20, 1958, Ann Whitman File, International Series, Box 12, DDEL; *FRUS*, 1958–1960, VII (2), 99ff; Jack Raymond, "U.S. Won't Oppose Changes in NATO," *New York Times*, October 29, 1958.

56. Bohlen later reported that the journalist Cyrus Sulzberger (a frequent interviewer of de Gaulle) swore that the French president had told him three times that he had never received an acknowledgment from Eisenhower of his tripartite proposal. Bohlen cable to Rusk, March 6, 1963, NSF, France, Box 72, folder 3/1 to 3/9 1963, JFKL.

57. Bohlen cable to Rusk, July 12, 1964, National Security File (hereafter NSF), France, Box 169, Lyndon B. Johnson Presidential Library (hereafter LBJL). Eisenhower's response was finally made public by Senator Henry M. Jackson's Subcommittee on National Security and International Operations in the summer of 1966. Francis Bator Memorandum for the President, July 26, 1966, NSF, France, Box 170, LBJL.

58. "Big Three Survey Firmer Alliance," *New York Times*, December 5, 1958.

59. Cook, *Charles de Gaulle*, 337.

60. Alphand, *L'Etonnement d'être*, 317.

61. Michel Gamrasni, "France/Etats-Unis: le grand malentendu," in *De Gaulle et l'Algérie, 1943–1969*, ed. Maurice Vaisse (Paris: Armand Colin, 2012), 99.

62. Dulles to Acting Secretary of State from Paris, December 18, 1958, Ann Whitman File, International Series, Box 10, folder Dulles, December 1958, DDEL.

63. Murphy and Joint Chiefs of Staff, Memorandum of Conversation, January 30, 1959, *FRUS* 1958–1960, VII (2), 168–169; Reyn, *Atlantis Lost*, 52.

64. Macmillan to Eisenhower, March 11, 1959, Ann Whitman File, International Series, Box 24, folder Macmillan, 1958–1959, DDEL.

65. Eisenhower to Macmillan, March 11, 1959, Ann Whitman File, International Series, Box 24, folder Macmillan, 1958–1959, DDEL. Early in the year Macmillan had become convinced that "De Gaulle is determined to break up NATO." Catterall, *The Macmillan Diaries*, entry for January 31, 1959, 187.

66. Harold Callender, "A Consistent de Gaulle," *New York Times*, March 27, 1959.

67. Memorandum of Conversation, Camp David, March 22, 1959, Ann Whitman File, International Series, Box 4, folder Macmillan, 1958–1959, DDEL.

68. Memorandum of Conversation, Camp David, March 22, 1959.

69. President's trip to Europe, September 1959, Palais de l'Elysée, 2 September 1959, Ann Whitman File, International Meetings, Box 3, Paris Visit, September 2–4, 1958, 4–5, DDEL

70. Harold Macmillan, *Pointing the Way*, vol. 5 of Macmillan's memoirs (London: Macmillan, 1972), 101.

71. Eisenhower, Memorandum for the Files, August 10, 1960, Ann Whitman File, International Series, Box 13, folder De Gaulle, DDEL.

72. French prime minister Michel Debré would later continually emphasize the need to extend the coverage of NATO to the Middle East and Africa. Luncheon at Hôtel Matignon with Norstad and Debré, September 7, 1960, Norstad Papers, Box 48, France, '60-'62, DDEL.

73. Cited in Ledwidge, *De Gaulle et les Américains*, 46–50, 58.

74. De Gaulle letters to Eisenhower, March 11, 26, 1959, Ann Whitman File, International Series, Box 13, folder "De Gaulle June 1958–October 1959," DDEL

75. Catterral, *Macmillan Diaries*, entries of March 9, March 10, 1959, 204.

76. Bozo, *Two Strategies for Europe*, 31–33.

77. When news of the forthcoming Khrushchev-Eisenhower meeting broke, de Gaulle's prime minister, Michel Debré, warned publicly about the possibility that France could be "crushed" between the two superpowers. *New York Times*, August 23, 1959.

78. "Memorandum: President Eisenhower's talks with Chairman Khrushchev at Camp David," Sent to de Gaulle October 30, 1959, Ann Whitman File, International Series, Box 13, folder De Gaulle, DDEL.

79. De Gaulle letters to Eisenhower, October 20 and 26, 1959, Ann Whitman File, International Series, Box 13, folder De Gaulle June 1958–October 1959, DDEL. Dwight D. Eisenhower, *The White House Years: A Personal Account. Waging Peace, 1956–1961* (Garden City, NY: Doubleday, 1965), 413. For de Gaulle's lingering anxiety about the plans for the summit, see Herter to Eisenhower, April 14, 1960, Ann Whitman File, International Series, Box 12, folder Herter April 1960, DDEL.

80. Philippe de Gaulle, *De Gaulle Mon Père: Entretiens avec Michel Tauriac* (Paris: Plon, 2005), 583.

81. Memorandum of Conversation, President's Office, April, 22, 1960, Ann Whitman File, International Series, Box 14, folder "De Gaulle Visit to the U.S.," DDEL. For Ambassador Alphand's record of the trip, see Alphand, *L'Etonnement d'être*, 326–329.

82. Bozo, *Two Strategies for Europe*, 42.

83. Memorandum of Conversation, President's Office, April 22, 1960, Ann Whitman File, International Series, Box 14, folder "De Gaulle Visit to the U.S.," DDEL.

84. Memorandum of Conversation, April 25, 1960, President's Office, Ann Whitman File, International Series, Box 14, folder "De Gaulle Visit to the U.S.," DDEL.

85. Translation of Mr. Khrushchev's message to Prime Minister Macmillan of May 10, text of Prime Minister Macmillan's message to Mr. Khrushchev of May 11, translation of Khrushchev's letter to Macmillan and de Gaulle, May 15; Ann Whitman file, Presidential Papers, folder Herter, May 1960, DDEL. Catterall, *The Macmillan Diaries*, entries for May 9, 15, 1960, 293, 296–297.

86. Memorandum of Conversation with the President, 4:30pm, May 15, 1960, Ann Whitman File, International Series, Box 44, folder Paris Meetings, May 1960.

87. Meeting at Elysée Palace, 10:00 a.m., May 16, 1960, Eisenhower, de Gaulle, Macmillan, Ann Whitman File, International Series, Box 44, folder Paris Meetings, May 1960, DDEL.

88. Macmillan, *Pointing the Way*, 204.

89. Press conference by U.S. press secretary James Hagerty, May 16, 1960, Ann Whitman File, International Series, Box 44; folder Paris Meetings May 1960. Meeting of Chiefs of State and Heads of Government, Paris, May 16, 1960, Elysée Palace, 11:00 am-2:10 pm, DDEL; *FRUS*, 1958–1960, IX, 438–452. Eisenhower, *The White House Years*, 555–556; Catterall, *The Macmillan Diaries*, entry of May 21, 1960, 297–299.

90. Walters, *Secret Missions*, 346.

91. Memorandum of Conversation, May 16, 1960, Ann Whitman File, Eisenhower's Office Files, part 2, International Series, Box 39, DDEL.

92. Former ambassador to France C. Douglas Dillon complained to *New York Times* correspondent Cyrus Sulzberger that "the trouble with de Gaulle was that he always returned to his September 1958 letter on the *directoire*." C. L. Sulzberger, The *Last of the Giants* (New York: Macmillan, 1970), 707–708.

93. Memorandum of Conversation, May 18, 1960, Elysée Palace, Ann Whitman File, International Series, Box 44, folder Paris Meetings, May 1960; De Gaulle letter to Eisenhower, June 10, 1960, Ann Whitman File, International Series, Box 13, folder De Gaulle, DDEL. The best treatment of the failed summit is still Michael Beschloss, *May Day: Eisenhower, Khruschev, and the U-2 Affair* (New York: Harper & Row, 1968).

94. Memorandum of Conversation, May 15, 1960, Elysée Palace, Ann Whitman File, International Series, folder Paris Meetings, Box 44, DDEL.

95. Herter cable to State Department, May 16, 1960, Ann Whitman File, International Series, Box 44, folder Paris Meetings May 1960, DDEL.

96. Memorandum of Conversation between de Gaulle, Eisenhower, and Macmillan, May 16, 1960, 2:30 pm, Ann Whitman File, International Series, Box 44, folder Paris Meetings May 1960, DDEL.

97. De Gaulle-Macmillan meeting, March 10, 1959, *Documents Diplomatiques Français* (hereafter *DDF*) (1959), Vol. I, 317.

98. Klaus Epstein, "Adenauer and Rhenish Separatism," *The Review of Politics* 4 (October 1967): 536–545.

99. De Gaulle-Adenauer Conversations, Sept. 14, 1958, *DDF*, Vol. XIII, 754–763. Jeffrey Glen Giauque, *Grand Designs and Visions of Unity: The Atlantic Powers and the Reorganization of Western Europe, 1955–1963* (Chapel Hill: University of North Carolina Press, 2002), 85.

100. Cited in Bozo, *Two Strategies for Europe*, 49. Pierre Maillard, *De Gaulle et l'Allemagne: Le Rêve inachevé* (Paris: Plon, 1990), 187, 191.

101. The language of the Act could not be more explicit: "Until Congress declares by joint resolution that effective and enforceable international safeguards against the use of atomic energy for destructive purposes have been established, there shall be

no exchange of information with any other nations with respect to the use of atomic energy for industrial purposes." Public Laws, 79th Congress, Chapter 724, Atomic Energy Act of 1946, 766.

102. John Baylis, "The 1958 Anglo-American Mutual Defence Agreement: The Search for Nuclear Interdependence," The Journal of Strategic Studies 31 (June 2008): 425–466.

103. The defense planners of the Fourth Republic also recognized the close connection between nuclear weapons and industrial development. Wolf Mendl, *Deterrence and Persuasion: French Nuclear Armament in the Context of National Policy, 1945–1969* (London: Faber & Faber, 1970), 178.

104. Colette Barbier, "The French Decision to Develop a Military Nuclear Program in the 1950s," *Diplomacy and Statecraft* 4, no. 1 (1993): 105–113; Maurice Vaisse and Jean Doise, *Politique étrangère de la France: Diplomatie et outil militaire, 1871–1991* (Paris: Seuil, 1987), 597–601.

105. Alphand, *L'Etonnement d'être*, 316.

106. Conversation between General Norstad and Mr. Messmer, March 24, 1960, Norstad Papers, Box 48, folder France, 1960-62, DDEL. On Norstad's service as SACEUR, see Robert S. Jordan, *Norstad: Cold War NATO Supreme Commander* (New York: St. Martin's Press, 2000).

107. Memorandum of Conversation, President's Office, April 22, 1960, Ann Whitman File, International Series, Box 14, folder "De Gaulle Visit to the U.S.," DDEL.

108. NSC5721/ U.S. Policy on France, October 19, 1957, NSC Series, Policy Paper Subseries, Box 22, DDEL. Winand, *Eisenhower, Kennedy, and the United States of Europe*, 212.

109. Earlier de Gaulle had said of his old wartime associate, "I would like to see the President. He has been my friend since always." Cited in C. L. Sulzberger, *The Test: De Gaulle and Algeria* (New York: Harcourt, 1962), 115.

110. Walters, *Silent Missions*, 489.

111. Cited in Cook, *Charles de Gaulle*, 345–346.

112. Text of De Gaulle press conference, November 10, 1959, Ann Whitman File, International Series, Box 13, folder De Gaulle, DDEL.

113. Eisenhower letter to de Gaulle, November 17, 1959, Ann Whitman File, International Series, Box 13, folder De Gaulle, DDEL.

114. De Gaulle letter to Eisenhower, November 24, 1959, Ann Whitman File, International Series, Box 13, folder De Gaulle, DDEL.

115. *FRUS*, 1958–1960, VII, West European Integration and Security, NATO, NSC 457, August 15, 1960, 627.

116. Eisenhower letter to de Gaulle, August 2, 1960, Ann Whitman File, International Series, Box 13, folder De Gaulle, DDEL.

117. De Gaulle letter to Eisenhower, August 9, 1960, Ann Whitman File, International Series, Box 13, folder De Gaulle Sept. 15 1959 on, DDEL.

118. Eisenhower Memorandum for the files, August 10, 1960, International Series, Box 13, folder De Gaulle, Sept. 15 1959 on, DDEL.

119. Ann Whitman File, NSC Series, Box 13, folder "457th Meeting of the National Security Council," August 25, 1960, DDEL.

120. Bozo, *Two Strategies for Europe*, 43.

121. M. Debré-General Norstad Meeting, January 30, 1959, Norstad Papers, Box 47, folder France, 55'59. DDEL.

122. General Lauris Norstad, "Memorandum for the Record, March 5, 1959, DDEL. De Gaulle to Eisenhower, May 25, 1959, France, Vol.1, International Series, White House Office, Office of the Staff Secretary, Box 5, DDEL. Reyn, *Atlantis Lost*, 53–54.

123. De Gaulle letter to Eisenhower, January 18, 1961, de Gaulle, *LNC, 1958–1970*, 317–318.

Chapter Eight

1. Don Cook, *Charles de Gaulle: A Biography* (New York: G.P. Putnam's Sons, 1983), 347.

2. Irwin Wall, *France, the United States, and the Algerian War* (Berkeley: University of California Press, 2001), 85–86; Michael Kettle, *De Gaulle and Algeria, 1940–1960: From Mers El-Kébir to the Algiers Barricades* (London: Quartet Books, 1993), 83.

3. Senator John F. Kennedy, "The Algerian Crisis: A New Phase?" *America* 101 (October 5, 1957): 15–17. Benjamin Stora, *De Gaulle et Algérie* (Paris: Fayard, 2010), 85–86. There were hardly any "independent states in Africa" at this time.

4. Memorandum of Conversation, March 10, 1961, Kennedy, Rusk, Acheson, Bundy, Alphand, *et al*, Box 70A, folder 1/20 to 3/15, 1961, John F. Kennedy Library (hereafter JFKL).

5. Michel Tauric, *Vivre avec De Gaulle: Les derniers témoins raconte l'homme* (Paris: Plon, 2008), 301–302.

6. "De Gaulle's Thunderbolt," *New York Times*, April 12, 1961.

7. Tauriac, *Vivre avec De Gaulle*, 497.

8. Cook, *Charles de Gaulle*, 331.

9. General Norstad (SACEUR) to Admiral Arleigh Burke (Chairman, Joint Chiefs of Staff), April 24, 1961, Norstad Papers, Box 48, folder France, 1960–1962, Dwight D. Eisenhower Library (hereafter DDEL).

10. On the trial and the punishment of the conspirators, see Julian Jackson, *De Gaulle* (Cambridge, MA: Harvard University Press, 2018), 553–556.

11. Gavin cable to State Department, May 3, 1961, NSF, France, Box 70A, folder "excerpts from Paris briefing books," JFKL.

12. William Bundy memorandum for McNamara et al., May 6, 1961, NSF, France, Box 70A, folder "excerpts from Paris briefing books," JFKL.

13. Gavin cable to State Department, February 10, 1962, NSF, France, Box 71, folder 2/10 to 2/16, 1962, JFKL.

14. Wall, *France, the United States, and the Algerian War*, 240.

15. C. L. Sulzberger, *The Test: De Gaulle and Algeria* (New York: Harcourt, 1962), 168–169.

16. Maurice Vaisse, *Alger: Le Putsch* (Brussels: Editions Complex, 1983), 124–125. The rumors of CIA involvement in and support for the attempted coup d'état in the spring of 1961 is exhaustively reviewed in Vincent Jauvert, *L'Amérique Contre De Gaulle: Histoire Secrèt, 1961–1969* (Paris: Seuil, 2000), 187–202. See also Wall, *France, the United States, and the Algerian War*, 240–241. Constantin Melnick, a young adviser on security and intelligence at the prime minister's office, notes that Foreign Minister Couve de Murville was regularly suspecting the U.S. intelligence services of secretly intervening in the Algerian situation but was confused about which Algerian forces it was backing: "The CIA supports the FLN. . . . The CIA pressed [General] Challe to execute the putsch. . . . The CIA secretly pulling the strings of the OAS." Constantin Melnick, *De Gaulle, les services secrets, et l'Algérie* (Paris: Nouveau Monde Editions, 2012), 184.

17. On the Evian meetings, see Maurice Vaisse, *Vers la paix en Algérie: Les négociations d'Evian dans les archives diplomatiques françaises 15 janvier–26 juin 1962* (Brussels: Bruylant, 2003).

18. Alain Peyrefitte, *C'était de Gaulle*, Vol. II (Paris: Fayard, 1997), 56, 74, 89. Wall, *France, the United States, and the Algerian War*, 195; Edward L. Morse, *Foreign Policy and Interdependence in Gaullist France* (Princeton, NJ: Princeton University Press, 1973), 106. William G. Andrews, *French Politics and Algeria* (New York: Appleton-Century-Crofts, 1962), 189ff.

19. Jean K. Chalaby, *The de Gaulle Presidency and the Media: Statism and Public Communications* (New York: Palgrave-Macmillan, 2002).

20. The role of the Harkis and their fate after the FLN victory is covered from a variety of perspectives in Fatima Besnaci-Lancou and Gilles Manceron, eds., *Les Harkis dans la colonisation et ses suites* (Ivry-sur-Seine: Editions de l'Atelier, 2008); François-Xavier Hautreux," De Gaulle face au problème des harkis," in Maurice Vaisse, ed., *De Gaulle et l'Algérie, 1943–1969* (Paris: Armand Colin/Ministère de la Défense, 2012), 264–275; Martin Evans, "Reprisal Violence and the Harkis in French Algeria, 1962," *International History Review* 39, no. 1 (2017): 89–106; Barnett Singer, *The Americanization of France: Searching for Happiness After the Algerian War* (Lanham, MD: Rowman & Littlefield, 2013), 42–43, 60–61.

21. Wall, *France, the United States, and the Algerian War*, 252–253. This interpretation is in sharp contrast with that of the French historian Maurice Vaisse, who tends to depict the French president's withdrawal from Algeria as a masterful solution to a very difficult problem. Vaisse, *De Gaulle et l'Algérie, 1943–1969*. I count both of these superb scholars as friends.

22. "Projet pour l'ambassade de France à Washington," end of January 1961, in De Gaulle, *Charles de Gaulle, Lettres, Notes, et Carnets* (hereafter *LNC*), *1958–1970* (Paris: Lafont, 2010), 321–325.

23. Unsigned memorandum, "A Review of North Atlantic Problems for the Future," March 1961, NSF, Regional Security (RS), NATO, Box 220, JFKL.

24. In a legislative hearing on transatlantic trade policy, one annoyed senator reminded the undersecretary of State "that he was in the pay, not of M. Monnet, but of the United States." David L. DiLeo, "Catch the Night Train for Paris: George Ball and Jean Monnet," in *Monnet and the Americans: The Father of a United Europe and his U.S. Supporters*, ed. Clifford P. Hackett (Washington, DC: Jean Monnet Council, 2001), 161–166.

25. George W. Ball, *The Past Has Another Pattern: Memoirs* (New York: W. W. Norton, 1982), 96.

26. Robert W. Komer [member of National Security Council] Memorandum for the President, March 6, 1961, NSF, France, Box 60A, folder 1/30 to 3/15, 1961, JFKL.

27. McGeorge Bundy memorandum to Kennedy, April 30, 1963, NSF, France, Box 72, folder 4/23 to 4/30 1963, JFKL.

28. Dean Rusk, *As I Saw It: A Secretary of State's Memoirs* (New York: W. W. Norton, 1990), 268.

29. Frédéric Bozo, *Two Strategies for Europe: De Gaulle, the United States, and the Atlantic Alliance*, trans. Susan Emanuel (Lanham, MD: Rowman & Littlefield, 2001), 61.

30. Georges-Henri Soutou, *La Guerre de Cinquante Ans: Les Relations Est-Ouest, 1943–1990* (Paris: Fayard, 2001), 280–283. Saki Dockrill, *Eisenhower's New-Look National Security Policy, 1953–1961* (London: Macmillan, 1996).

31. Harriman Memorandum to Ball, May 28, 1962, NSF, Country Series France, Box 71, folder 5/27 to 5/31 1962, JFKL.

32. Memorandum of Conversation between President Kennedy and Jacques Chaban-Delmas, "Tripartite Consultation between France, the United States, and the United Kingdom," March 10, 1961, NSF, France, Box 70A, folder 1/30 to 3/15 1961, JFKL.

33. Memorandum of Conversation among Bundy, Paul Nitze, and Alphand, May 8, 1961, NSF, France, Box 70A, folder 5/1 to 5/10 1961, JFKL.

34. De Gaulle letter to Kennedy, February 6, 1961, De Gaulle, *LNC, 1958–1970*, 326–329; American Embassy, Paris, cable from Acheson to State Department for the President, April 21, 1961, NSF, France, Box 70A, folder 3/16 to 4/21 1961, JFKL.

35. Department of State Memorandum of Conversation, April 14, 1961, NSF, France, Box 70, folder 3/16/ to 4/21, 1961, JFKL.

36. Cited in Maurice Vaïsse, *La Grandeur: Politique étrangère du Général de Gaulle* (Paris: CNRS, 2013), 367.

37. Jauvert, *L'Amérique Contre de Gaulle*, 29.

38. Rusk, *As I Saw It*, 240, 271.

39. Jonathan Fenby, *The General: Charles De Gaulle and the France He Saved* (New York: Skyhorse, 2012), 471.

40. She returned the compliment. In a recorded interview after her husband's assassination that was published long after own her death, Jacqueline Kennedy described Malraux as "the most fascinating man I have ever talked to." Janny Scott, "In Tapes, Candid Talk by Young Kennedy Widow," *New York Times*, September 11, 2011.

41. Jauvert, *L'Amérique Contre de Gaulle*, 22.

42. *Papers Relating to the Foreign Relations of the United States* (hereafter FRUS), 1961–1963, XIII, 310.

43. Jackson, *De Gaulle*, 582.

44. *FRUS, 1961–1963*, XIII, 310–311.

45. Bernard Ledwidge, *De Gaulle et les Américains: Conversations avec Dulles, Eisenhower, Kennedy, Rusk: 1958–1964* (Paris: Flammarion, 1984), 100–115.

46. Charles de Gaulle, *Memoirs of Hope: Renewal and Endeavor*, trans. Terence Kilmartin (New York: Simon & Schuster, 1971), 256.

47. Cook, *Charles de Gaulle*, 351.

48. Robert C. Doty, "Kennedy Studies Defense Issues with de Gaulle," *New York Times*, June 2, 1961.

49. Memorandum of Conversation with Congressional Leadership and Vice President Johnson, June 5, 1961, NSF, France, Box 70A, folder 6/61, JFKL.

50. De Gaulle, *Memoirs of Hope*, 255.

51. Peyrefitte, *C'était de Gaulle*, II: 649. *Le Monde*, August 31, 1963.

52. *Documents Diplomatiques Français* (hereafter *DDF*) (1963), Vol. II, 255–256.

53. *FRUS, 1961–1963*, IV, 93–94.

54. Drew Middleton, "De Gaulle's France: His Independent Stand is Aimed to Elevate Country's Stature," *New York Times*, September 29, 1963.

55. Yuko Torikata, "The U.S. Escalation in Vietnam and de Gaulle's Secret Search for Peace," in *Globalizing de Gaulle: International Perspectives on French Foreign Policies, 1958–1969*, ed. Christian Nuenlist, Anna Locher, and Garret Martin (Plymouth, UK: Lexington Books, 2010), 158; Maurice Vaisse, "De Gaulle et la Guerre de Vietnam," in *La Guerre du Vietnam et l'Europe*, ed. Christopher Goscha and Maurice Vaisse, 169–178 (Brussels: Bruylant, 2003).

56. Dean Rusk Oral History Collection, Series Rusk C, Interview by Richard Rusk and Thomas J. Schoenbaum, September 11, 1984. DROHC, Series Rusk QQQ.

57. Maurice Couve de Murville, *Une Politique Etrangère, 1958–1969* (Paris: Plon, 1971), 128.

58. De Gaulle letter to Kennedy, July 6, 1961, in de Gaulle, *LNC, 1958–1970*, 378–379.

59. De Gaulle letter to Kennedy, July 27, 1961, in de Gaulle, *LNC, 1958–1970*, 388–389.

60. Peyrefitte, *C'était de Gaulle*, II: 19.

61. Harold Macmillan, *Pointing the Way*, vol. 5 of Macmillan's memoirs (London: Macmillan, 1972), diary entry of August 25, 1961, 394.

62. Rusk never forgave de Gaulle for his obstinate refusal to accept any direct negotiations with the Kremlin over Berlin. Interview with Richard Rusk and Thomas J. Schoenbrun, June 1986. DROHC, Series Rusk QQQ.

63. Cook, *Charles de Gaulle*, 351.

64. Hans Peter Schwartz, *Konrad Adenauer: A German Politician and Statesman in a Period of War*, Vol. II, *The Statesman (1952–1967)* (Providence, RI: Berghahn Books, 1997), 403–404.

65. Gavin letter to Kennedy, March 9, 1962; "Balance Sheet of U.S. and French Requests in Military Field," *FRUS*, 1961–1963, XIII, France; State Department (Ball) cable to Gavin, March 14, 1962, 683–690. Jauvert, *L'Amérique Contre De Gaulle*, 47.

66. McGeorge Bundy, *Danger and Survival: Choices About the Bomb in the First Fifty Years* (New York: Random House, 1988), 484–486.

67. McGeorge Bundy Memorandum for the President, February 28, 1962, NSF, France, Box 61, folder 2/17 to 3/4 1962, JFKL.

68. Bundy letter to Gavin, May 10, 1962, Gavin letter to Bundy, May 23, 1962, Bundy Memorandum to the President, July 4, 1962, NSF, France, Box 71A, Gavin Resignation Folder, JFKL.

69. John Newhouse, *De Gaulle and the Anglo-Saxons* (New York: The Viking Press, 1970), 121–122.

70. Quoted in Pascaline Winand, *Eisenhower, Kennedy, and the United States of Europe* (London: Salem House Publishers, 1984), 233–234. See also Jane E. Stromseth, *The Origins of Flexible Response: NATO's Debate over Strategy in the 1960s* (London, Macmillan, 1988), 44. The McNamara speech was finally leaked to *The New York Times*, which published it on June 7, 1962. Two years later French defense minister Pierre Messmer would insist that the counter-force strategy was an "absurdity. . . . The only objectives that have deterrent value are demographic," that is, an unmistakable commitment to devastate Soviet cities in response to an attack. Pierre Messmer, "Notre Politique Militaire," in *Revue de Défense Nationale*, May 1963, cited in Carl H. Amme Jr., *NATO Without France: A Strategic Appraisal* (Stanford, CA: Hoover Institution Press, 1967), 36.

71. Philip Cerny, *Politics of Grandeur: Ideological Aspects of de Gaulle's Foreign Policy* (Cambridge: Cambridge University Press, 1980), 194–197.

72. Rusk cable to Gavin, May 5, 1961, NSF, France, Box 70A, folder 5/1 to 5/10 1961, JFKL. On the issue of the costs of the *force de frappe*, Rusk's prediction was borne out once the French deterrent was developed. Over a quarter of the French defense budget after the mid-1960s would go to the nuclear program, diverting funds for other military purposes. Edward A. Kolodziej, *French International Policy under de Gaulle and Pompidou* (Ithaca, NY: Cornell University Press, 1974), 105.

73. The nuclear delivery force would be placed under the direct command of the president in January 1964. Michael M. Harrison, *The Reluctant Ally: France and Atlantic Security* (Baltimore: Johns Hopkins University Press, 1981), 118–120.

74. McGeorge Bundy Memorandum for the President, "One last attack on de Gaulle's obsession with nuclear weapons," May 31, 1961, NSF, France, Box 70A, folder 5/30 to 5/31 1961, JFKL.

75. Bozo, *Two Strategies for Europe*, 77.

76. NSC, France, Box 70A, folder CIA Briefing Packet, March 18, 1961, JFKL.

77. Dulles to Acting Secretary of State, May 9, 1958; copy of paper by Duncan Sandys handed to Secretary Dulles by Selwyn Lloyd in May 1958, Ann Whitman File, Series Dulles-Herter, Box 12, folder Herter, DDEL.

78. American Embassy, Paris cable to State Department, May 18, 1962, NSF, France, Box 71A, JFKL.

79. Winand, *Eisenhower, Kennedy, and the United States of Europe*, 258–259.The best full-length study of this topic is Alessandro Silj, *Europe's Political Puzzle: A Study of the Fouchet Negotiations* (Cambridge, MA: Harvard University Press, 1967). See also Georges-Henri Soutou, *L'Alliance Incertain: Les rapports politico-stratégiques franco-allemands, 1954–1996* (Paris: Fayard, 1996), chapter 6, and Jeffrey Glen Giauque, *Grand Designs and Visions of Unity: The Atlantic Powers and the Reorganization of Western Europe, 1955–1963* (Chapel Hill: University of North Carolina Press, 2002), 138–148.

80. Robert C. Doty, "De Gaulle Meets Adenauer Two Hours," *New York Times*, July 4, 1962.

81. On February 5, 1945, de Gaulle had publicly called for the detachment of the Ruhr and the Rhineland from a future German state, a policy that was pressed vigorously by his foreign minister, Georges Bidault, at the foreign ministers' conference in London the following September. See Raymond Poidevin, "Frankreich und die Ruhrfrage 1945–1951," *Historische Zeitschrift* 228, no. 2 (April 1979): 317–334.

82. The renowned defense analyst of *The New York Times*, Drew Middleton, had once referred to Adenauer as the "continent's leading non-French Gaullist." Drew Middleton, "The Key to Western Unity is France, and France is de Gaulle," *New York Times*, March 18, 1961.

83. Gavin letter to Bundy, June 30, 1961 NSF, France, Box 601A, folder 7/1 to 8/20 1961, JFKL.

84. Gavin letter to Kennedy November 12, 1961, NSF, France, Box 70A, folder 11/61 to 12/61, JFKL. Bundy letter to Gavin, November 16, 1961, NSF, France, Box 70A, folder 11/61 to 12/61, JFKL.

85. Gavin letter to Kennedy, March 9, 1962, NSF, France, Box 71, folder 3/5 to 3/10 1962, JFKL.

86. Jauvert, *L'Amérique contre De Gaulle*, 54–55.

87. Ball cable to Gavin, May 9, 1962, NSF, France, Box 71, folder 4/30 to 5/9 1962, JFKL.

88. Jauvert, *L'Amérique Contre De Gaulle*, 56–57.

89. Bundy Notes of Meeting in the Cabinet Room, May 11, 1962; Participants: Kennedy, Alphand, Malraux, Bundy, NSF, France, Box 71, folder 5/10 to 5/11 1962, JFKL.

90. Kennedy letter to de Gaulle, July 26, 1962; De Gaulle letter to Kennedy, July 29, 1962, NSF, Country File France, Box 70A, Gavin resignation folder, JFKL.

91. Arthur M. Schlesinger memorandum to McGeorge Bundy, May 8, 1961, NSF, France, Box 70A, folder 3/16 to 4/21 1961, JFKL.

92. Bohlen would finally tire of de Gaulle's frequent public denunciations of the Yalta Conference for dividing up the world, reminding Couve de Murville years later that he was at Yalta and de Gaulle's allegation was totally untrue. Bohlen cable to Secretary of State, June 3, 1965, NSC, France, Box 170, LBJL.

93. Bohlen to Josiah Child, September 6, 1962. Charles E. Bohlen Papers, MDLC, Box 29, folder "Correspondence on Appointment to Paris."

94. Couve de Murville, *Une Politique Etrangère, 1958–1969*, 82.

95. Quoted in Douglas Brinkley, *Dean Acheson: The Cold War Years, 1953–1971* (New Haven, CT: Yale University Press, 1994), 167; David L. Bosco, *Five to Rule Them All: The UN Security Council and the Making of the Modern World* (New York: Oxford University Press, 2009), 97.

96. Charles Bohlen, *Witness to History, 1929–1969* (New York: W.W. Norton Company, 1973), 494. For a lucid discussion of America's European allies' response to the Cuban missile crisis by several French historians, see Maurice Vaisse, ed., *L'Europe et la crise de Cuba* (Paris: Colin, 1993).

97. Kennedy was warned by his advisers about this negative consequence of the Cuban crisis, which "increased the fear that by our own local action [in Cuba] we might quite literally bring an end to Europe. These questions are only *spoken* by our opponent de Gaulle, but they are *felt* by our friends." Memorandum for the President, January 30, 1963, President's Office Files, Box 116A (italics in original), JFKL.

98. Couve de Murville, *Une Politique Etrangère, 1958–1969*, 97.

99. Cook, *Charles de Gaulle*, 356.

100. Gavin cable to Secretary of State, February 20, 1962, NSF, France, Box 71, folder 2/17 to 3/4 1961, JFKL.

101. Konrad Adenauer, *Erinnerungen 1959–63. Fragmente* (Stuttgart: Deutsche Verlags-Anstalt, 1968), 109–110, quoted in Winand, *Eisenhower, Kennedy, and the United States of Europe*, 261–262.

102. Peter Catterall, ed., *The Macmillan Diaries, Vol. II: Prime Minister and After, 1957–1966* (London: Macmillan, 2011), entry for December 16, 1962, 526–527.

103. Macmillan was reportedly on the verge of tears when he briefed the British embassy on the discussions. Jackson, *De Gaulle*, 591.

104. Winant, *Eisenhower, Kennedy, and the United States of Europe*, 320; Marc Trachtenberg, *A Constructed Peace: The Making of the European Settlement, 1945–1963* (Princeton, NJ: Princeton University Press, 1999), 154–157.

105. Bohlen cable to State Department, December 21, 1962, NSF, France, Box 71A, folder 12/17 to 12/26, JFKL.

106. Bohlen cable to Rusk for the President, November 10, 1962; Rusk draft to the President, December 24, 1962; Bundy memorandum to president, December

29, 1962, NSF, France, Box 71A, folders 12/18 to 12/26 1962, 12/27 to 12/31 1962, JFKL.

107. Bohlen cable to State Department, February 16, 1963, NSF, France, Box 72A, JFKL.

108. Bohlen, *Witness to History*, 500–501.

109. Cook, *Charles de Gaulle*, 361. Ferro, *De Gaulle et l'Amérique: Une Amitié Tumultueuse* (Paris: Plon, 1973), 303–305.

110. Quoted in Bill Gunston, *Bombers of the West* (New York: Scribner's, 1973), 105. De Gaulle would often return to the defense of the doctrine of proportional deterrence in his press conferences. See, for example, the one on July 23, 1964, where he praised the *force de frappe* as "an incomparable guarantee" of French security and hailed its relatively low cost for enabling France to reduce its conventional forces, a claim reminiscent of Eisenhower's defense secretary Charles Wilson's defense of the doctrine of massive retaliation: "bigger bang for the buck."

111. Bohlen cable to Rusk, April 2, 1963, NSF, France, Box 72, folder 4/1 to 4/3 1963, JFKL.

112. Rusk privately denounced the French doctrine of proportional deterrence. "What does de Gaulle mean when he talks of a trip-wire strategy and immediate use of nuclear weapons?" he asked rhetorically in a wide-ranging talk with C. L. Sulzberger on December 13, 1963. "Does that mean that France would use its atomic weapons immediately if Russia attacked Norway or Turkey? I rather doubt that. . . . When it comes down to targeting, de Gaulle will find out how many Soviet missiles are aimed at France and will have to think about that." C. L. Sulzberger, *An Age of Mediocrity: Memoirs and Diaries, 1963–1972* (New York: Macmillan, 1973), entry of December 13, 1963, 52–53.

113. Garrett Joseph Martin, *General de Gaulle's Cold War: Challenging American Hegemony. 1963–1968* (Providence, RI: Berghahn Books, 2013), 18.

114. McGeorge Bundy, Memorandum for the Record, January 28, 1963, NSF, France, Box 72, folder 1/24 to 1/31 1962, JFKL.

115. Bohlen, *Witness to History*, 201.

116. Lyon to Secretary of State, December 26 1962, NSF France, Box 71A, folder 12/20 to 12/26/62, JFKL.

117. Catterall, *The Macmillan Diaries*, Vol. II, entry for January 28, 1963, 536.

118. Rusk, *As I Saw It*, 267–268.

119. Bohlen cable to Secretary of State, January 21, 1963, NSF, France, Box 73A-74, "France" Subjects 1/14/ to 1/22 1963. JFKL. Winand, *Eisenhower, Kennedy, and the United States of Europe*, 331.

120. Record of NSC Executive Meeting, No. 38, Part II, January 25, 1963, *FRUS, 1961–1963*, XIII, Western Europe, 487–489.

121. Bohlen cable to Rusk for the President, February 16, 1963, NSF, France, Box 72, folder 2/16 to 3/9 1963, JFKL. On the short-term consequences of the veto, see Giauque, *Grand Designs and Visions of Unity*, 185–192.

122. John Foster Dulles, "Memorandum of Private After-Luncheon Conversation with General de Gaulle," July 5, 1958, Ann Whitman File, International Series, Box 13, folder De Gaulle June '58-October '59, DDEL.

123. Soutou, *L'Alliance incertaine*, 241–252. Jacques Bariéty, "De Gaulle, Adenauer, et la genèse du traité de l'Elysée du 22 janvier, 1963," in *De Gaulle et son siècle*, Vol. V (Paris: Institute Charles de Gaulle, 1992).

124. Kennedy message to Gavin via Bundy, May 18, 1962. NSF, France, Box 71, folder 5/16 to 5/18, 1962, JFKL.

125. Ball, *The Past Has Another Pattern*, 271.

126. Unsigned [but Ball author] Secret Report, February 9, 1963, NSF Meetings, 1963, No. 510, 5/18/62-8/3/62, Box 314, JFKL. Winand, *Eisenhower, Kennedy, and the United States of Europe*, 339.

127. Bozo, *Two Strategies for Europe*, 106.

128. Marvin R. Zahniser, *Uncertain Friendship: American-French Relations through the Cold War* (New York: John Wiley & Sons, 1975), 283–284.

129. "De Gaulle Backs into a Corner?" CIA, Office of National Estimates: Memorandum, October 10, 1963, NSF, France, Box 72A, JFKL.

130. David Klein memorandum to the President, Memorandum of Conversation at the White House, Kennedy, Couve de Murville, and others, October 7, 1963, NSF, France, Box 72, JFKL.

131. Bohlen cable to Rusk for the president, January 4, 1963, NSF, France, Box 72, folder 1/1 to1/23 1963, JFKL.

132. Bohlen, *Witness to History*, 504.

133. Rusk cable to Bohlen, June 14, 1963, NSF, France, Box 74, folder "Proposed de Gaulle Visit," JFKL.

134. Ball cable to Bohlen, September 25, 1964, NSF, France, Box 72a, folder 9/24 to 9/30 1963, JFKL.

Chapter Nine

1. Eric F. Goldman, *The Tragedy of Lyndon Johnson* (New York: Knopf, 1968), 378.

2. George W. Ball, *The Past Has Another Pattern: Memoirs* (New York: W. W. Norton, 1982), 335.

3. Thurston Clark, *JFK's Last Hundred Days* (New York: The Penguin Press, 2013), 349.

4. Charles Bohlen, *Witness to History, 1929–1969* (New York: W. W. Norton, 1973), 504. A different version is supplied by Ambassador Alphand; Couve had telephoned him to lay out three possibilities: either de Gaulle comes with Couve; Couve comes by himself, or Alphand would represent the government of France. After considerable discussion, the first option was chosen. Hervé Alphand, *L'Etonnement d'être: Journal 1939–1973* (Paris: Fayard, 1977), 413.

5. Interview with Richard Rusk and Thomas J. Schoenbaum, June 1986, DRP, Richard B. Russell Library, Athens, Georgia, DROHC, Rusk QQQ, part 1 of 2.

6. Dean Rusk, *As I Saw It: A Secretary of State's Memoirs* (New York: W. W. Norton, 1990), 321. There was considerable anxiety among law enforcement officers about the French president's decision to walk down Pennsylvania Avenue in light of the many assassination attempts on him. "Security for de Gaulle Is Tightest in Big Four," *The Washington Post*, November 26, 1963.

7. Memorandum of Conversation Among Johnson, Rusk, de Gaulle, and Couve de Murville, November 25, 1963, NSF, Country File, France, Box 169, Lyndon B. Johnson Library (hereafter LBJL). Rusk took the French foreign minister aside and warned him: "Don't be deceived, it is he who will govern. He will conduct foreign policy as personally as his predecessor and he will make decisions." Maurice Couve de Murville, *Une Politique Etrangère, 1958–1969* (Paris: Plon 1971), 121. Johnson writes in his memoirs that when de Gaulle indicated that French people were certain that the U.S. would intervene to defend France if attacked, he "stared hard at the French president, suppressing a smile" in light of de Gaulle's frequent references to the un-reliability of Washington in response to Soviet aggression. Lyndon B. Johnson, *The Vantage Point: Perspectives of the Presidency, 1963–1969* (New York: Holt, Rinehart and Winston, 1971), 23.

8. Alphand, *L'Etonnement d'être*, 416.

9. Bohlen Memorandum for Rusk, December 13, 1963; NSF, Country File France, Box 169, LBJL.

10. Bundy memorandum to the President, January 6, 1964, *Papers Relating to the Foreign Relations of the United States* (hereafter *FRUS*), 1964–1968, I, 1964, Vietnam, 14–15.

11. Alphand, *L'Etonnement d'être*, 442.

12. Bohlen cable to State Department, February 4, 1964, NSF, Country File France, Box 169, LBJL. Allegations of French meddling in South Vietnam had surfaced toward the end of the Kennedy administration and were vehemently denied by Couve de Murville. Bohlen cable to Rusk, September 25, 1963, NSF, France, Box 72A, folder9/24 to 9/30 1963, John F. Kennedy Library (hereafter JFKL).

13. For Lodge's role in denouncing de Gaulle's proposals about neutralization as well as his advocacy of greater pressure on North Vietnam, see Fredrik Logevall, *Choosing War: The Last Chance for Peace and the Escalation of War in Vietnam* (Berkeley: University of California Press, 1999), 118–120.

14. Rusk cable to Bohlen, February 25, 1964, NSF, France, Box 169, LBJL. Couve de Murville denied these most recent allegations, insisting to Bohlen that France had no "network of agents" and "no form of operations" in the country. Bohlen cable to Rusk for Bundy, March 4, 1964, NSF, France, Box 169, LBJL.

15. Lodge Cable to State Department, January 21, 1964, *FRUS*, 1964–1968, I, Vietnam 1964, 32–33.

16. Lodge cable to State Department, January 29, 1964, NSF, Country File Viet Nam, Box 1, LBJL.

17. Memorandum of Telephone Conversations Between the Assistant Secretary of State for Public Affairs (Manning) and the Secretary of State, February 1, 1964, *FRUS, 1964–1968*, I, Vietnam 1964, 57ff.

18. Rusk cable to Bohlen from the President, February 25, 1964, *FRUS, 1964–1968*, I, Vietnam 1964.

19. Bohlen cable to State Department for the President, February 26, 1964, *FRUS, 1964–1968*, I, Vietnam 1964.

20. Message from the President to the Ambassador in Vietnam (Lodge), March 17, 1964; Lodge Message to the President, March 19, 1964, *FRUS, 1964–1968*, I, Vietnam 1964, 167–169, 182–184.

21. Lodge cable to State Department, March 23, 1964, *FRUS, 1964–1968*, I, Vietnam 1964, 186–187. On the role of Lodge in this dispute, see Pierre Journoud, *De Gaulle et le Vietnam, 1945–1969* (Paris: Tallendier, 2011), 163–170.

22. Message from the President to the Ambassador in France, March 24, 1964, *FRUS 1964–1968*, I, Vietnam 1964, 191–193.

23. Bohlen Message to the President, April 2, 1964, *FRUS 1964–1968*, I, Vietnam 1964, 216–219. Couve de Murville insisted that his own discussions with the Chinese ambassador led him to believe that Beijing would not object to a Geneva-type conference on Vietnam. Couve de Murville, *Une Politique Etrangère, 1958–1969*, 131.

24. Johnson Memorandum to Ball, undated (but early June 1964), NSF, France, Box 170, LBJL.

25. Ronald Steel, *Walter Lippmann and the American Century* (Boston: Little, Brown-Atlantic Press, 1980), 549. Letter from the Undersecretary of State (Ball) to the Secretary of State, May 31, 1964, *FRUS 1964–1968*, I, Vietnam 1964, 400–402. Ball recalled that when he would meet with the French president, de Gaulle welcomed him with the bittersweet greeting "Ah, Monsieur Ball, c'est vous encore [Ah, Mr. Ball, it's you again]." Ball, *The Past Has Another Pattern*, 331.

26. Bohlen cable to State Department for the President, June 6, 1964, NSF, France, Box 170, LBJL; Ball cable to Secretary of State, June 6, 1964, *FRUS, 1964–1968*, 465–470. De Gaulle had made the same point to Kennedy at a time that there were (as yet) no American combat troops in the country. Couve de Murville, *Une Politique Etrangère, 1958–1969*, 113.

27. De Gaulle letter to Johnson, June 10, 1964, De Gaulle, *Charles de Gaulle, Lettres, Notes, et Carnets* (hereafter *LNC*), *1958–1970* (Paris: Lafont, 2010), 650–651.

28. *Time*, June 12, 1964, 42.

29. Research Memorandum from the Director of the Bureau of Intelligence and Research (Hughes) to the Secretary of State, July 25, 1964, *FRUS, 1964–1968*, I, Vietnam 1964, 573–574.

30. See Edwin E. Moise, *Tonkin Gulf and the Escalation of the Vietnam War* (Chapel Hill: University of North Carolina Press, 1966).

31. Drew Middleton, "France Withholds Support for U.S. Air Attack But Most in NATO Back It," *New York Times*, August 6, 1964.

32. Bohlen cable to State Department, November 30, 1964, NSF, France, Box 170, LBJL.

33. Meeting between Rusk and de Gaulle, December 16, 1944, *Documents Diplomatiques Français* (hereafter DDF), 1964, Vol. II, 568–574.

34. See, for example, State Department Circular, February 8, 1964 NSF, Country File Vietnam, Box 236, LBJL.

35. Logevall, *Choosing War*, 118.

36. Thomas J. Schoenbaum, *Waging Peace and War: Dean Rusk in the Truman, Kennedy, and Johnson Years* (New York: Simon and Schuster, 1988), 359.

37. De Gaulle's son recalled that his father often exclaimed, "Ah! If only Kennedy were still here." Philippe de Gaulle, *De Gaulle Mon Père: Entretiens avec Michel Tauriac* (Paris: Plon, 2005), 591.

38. Memorandum of Conversation in the White House, February 19, 1965; President Johnson, George Ball, Charles Bohlen, McGeorge Bundy, Foreign Minister Maurice Couve de Murville, and Ambassador Alphand, NSF, France, Box 170, LBJL. Couve de Murville, *Une Politique Etrangère, 1958–1969*, 132–134.

39. Gallup Poll, *Public Opinion, Vol. III, 1959–1971* (New York: Random House, 1972), 1982.

40. Rusk cable to Bohlen, March 7, 1965, NSF, Country File France, Box 170, LBJL.

41. Bohlen cable to Rusk, February 3, 1965, NSF, Country File France, Box 170, LBJL.

42. Bohlen cable to Rusk, March 25, 1965, NSF, Country File France, Box 170, LBJL.

43. Rusk cable to Bohlen, May 22, 1965, NSF, Country File France, Box 170, LBJL.

44. Maurice Ferro, *De Gaulle et l'Amérique: Une Amitié Tumulteuse* (Paris: Plon, 1973), 367.

45. Alphand, *L'Etonnement d'être*, 421–422.

46. C. L. Sulzberger, *An Age of Mediocrity: Memoirs and Diaries, 1963–1972* (New York: Macmillan, 1973), entry of January 16, 1964, 59. Great Britain had recognized the PRC in January 1950 in order to preserve its position in Hong Kong.

47. Central Intelligence Agency, "Special Report: New Emphasis in French Foreign Policy," February 28, 1964, NSF, France, Box 169, LBJL.

48. Sulzberger, *An Age of Mediocrity*, entry of July 1, 1965, 188.

49. Central Intelligence Agency, "Special Report: De Gaulle's Eastern European Policy," July 17, 1964, NSF, France, Box 170, LBJL.

50. Robert L. Pfaltzgraff Jr., *The Atlantic Community: A Complex Imbalance* (New York: Van Nostrand Reinhold Co., 1969), 150–151.

51. Frédéric Bozo, *Two Strategies for Europe: De Gaulle, the United States, and the Atlantic Alliance*, trans. Susan Emanuel (Lanham, MD: Rowman & Littlefield, 2001), 110.

52. Christian A. Herter Papers, Box 18, NATO, December 1960, Herter Statement at NATO Ministerial Meeting, political-military section, 2–3, Dwight D. Eisenhower Library (hereafter DDEL).

53. State Department Memorandum of Conversation, 14 April 1961, NSF, France, Box 70, "5/1/61" 2, JFKL. Winand, Eisenhower, Kennedy, and the United States of Europe, 219.

54. André Fontaine described it as "a modest reprise of the European Defense Community of the 1950s." André Fontaine, Un seul lit pour deux rêves: Histoire de la "détente" 1962–1981 (Paris: Fayard, 1982), 73.

55. Bozo, Two Strategies for Europe, 111–112.

56. Robert McNamara, Recorded Interview, February 26, 1970, 2, Oral History Project, JFKL.

57. "Brief of President's Talk with Couve de Murville on May 25, 1963, NSF, France, Box 72, folder 5/25 to 5/25 to 5/29, JFKL.

58. Ball, The Past Has Another Pattern, 261–262.

59. Memorandum of Conversation, Ball-Couve de Murville, May 25, 1963, NSF, Country File France, Box 72, folder 5/25 to 5/29 1963, JFKL.

60. July 30, 1963, NSF, France, Box 72, JFKL.

61. Bozo, Two Strategies for Europe, 116–117.

62. "Memorandum of Discussion of the MLF at the White House at 5:30 p.m. on April 10, 1964," and "Briefing for the President. Notes on the MLF Status and Needed Decisions," NSF, Folder Multilateral Force (hereafter MLF), Box 22, LBJL; Colette Barbier, "La Force multilatérale," Relations internationales, no. 69 (Spring 1992): 3–18.

63. Le Monde, November 5, 1964.

64. Sulzberger, An Age of Mediocrity, entry of November 24, 1964, 137.

65. "Strains in the West: Focus on de Gaulle," New York Times, November 15, 1964.

66. Speech in Strasbourg, November 22, 1964, in de Gaulle, Discours et messages (hereafter DM) (1962–1964) (Paris: Poche, 1970), 312–316.

67. Bohlen cable to Secretary of State, November 23, 1964, NSF, France, Box 169, LBJL.

68. CIA, Office of Current Intelligence, Special Report, "De Gaulle, Europe, and the MLF," November 27, 1964, France, Box 170, LBJL.

69. Charles Cogan, Oldest Allies, Guarded Friends: The United States and France since 1940 (New York: Praeger, 1994), 143–144; Manlio Brosio, who became NATO secretary-general in August, described to the journalist Cyrus Sulzberger a long talk that he and Johnson had during an airplane ride in which the president "showed very little understanding" of the MLF. Sulzberger, An Age of Mediocrity, entry of October 9, 1964, 109.

70. See Jane E. Stromseth, The Origins of Flexible Response: NATO's Debate over Strategy in the 1960s (New York: Palgrave-Macmillan, 1988).

71. Memorandum of Conversation, Rusk-Couve de Murville, October 8, 1963, NSF, France, Box 72A, JFKL.

72. Bohlen Cable to Secretary of State, November 25, 1963; Bohlen Memorandum to Secretary of State, December 13, 1963, NSF, France, Box 169, LBJL.

73. Bozo, *Two Strategies for Europe*, 127.

74. Jean-Marie Polayret, Helen Wallace, and Pascaline Winand, eds., *Victims, Votes, and Vetoes: The Empty Chair Crisis and the Luxembourg Compromise Forty Years On* (Berne: Peter Lang, 2006); Piers Ludlow, *The European Community and the Crises of the 1960s: Negotiating the Gaullist Challenge* (New York: Routledge, 2006), 71–93; Barry Eichengreen, *The European Economy Since 1945* (Princeton, NJ: Princeton University Press, 2007), 185–187.

75. Thomas Alan Schwartz, *Lyndon Johnson and Europe: In The Shadow of Vietnam* (Cambridge, MA: Harvard University Press, 2003), 71.

76. Francis J. Gavin, *Gold, Dollars, and Power: The Politics of International Monetary Relations, 1958-1971* (Chapel Hill: University of North Carolina Press, 2004), 75.

77. Drew Middleton, "De Gaulle Condemns U.S. on Dominican Intervention," *New York Times*, May 7, 1965.

78. Bohlen cable to Rusk, May 4, 1965, NSF, France, Box 170, LBJL.

79. "Humphrey Briefed de Gaulle on Latin Crisis," *New York Times*, June 22, 1965; Bohlen cable to Rusk, June 20, 1965, NSF, France, Box 170, LBJL. Rusk reminded Ambassador Alphand that Washington had the full support of the Organization of American States (OAS) in the intervention. Alphand cable to Couve de Murville, June 15, 1965, *DDF*, 1965, Vol. I, 747–748.

80. Bohlen cable to Rusk, June 3, 1965, NSF, France, Box 170, LBJL.

81. Frank Costigliola, *France and the United States: The Cold Alliance since World War II* (New York: Twayne, 1992), 142; Schwartz, *Lyndon Johnson and Europe*, 93.

82. Cited in Vaisse, *La Grandeur: Politique Etrangère du Général de Gaulle* (Paris: CNRS, 2013), 166–167.

83. For a succinct summary of the background of the French withdrawal from the alliance, see Vaisse, *La Grandeur*, 381–386.

84. Bohlen cable to State Department, January 5, 1965, NSF, France, Box 170, LBJL.

85. Alphand, *L'Etonnement d'être*, 444.

86. Alphand cable to Couve de Murville, April 22, 1965, *DDF*, 1965, Vol. I, 477–480.

87. Bozo, *Two Strategies for Europe*, 131–132.

88. Sulzberger, *An Age of Mediocrity*, entry for December 21, 1964, 143.

89. Radio and television broadcast, December 31, 1964, in De Gaulle, *DM (1964–1964)*, 317–319.

90. *FRUS*, 1964–1968, XIII, 206ff.

91. Alphand, *L'Etonemenent d'être*, 452–453.

92. Bohlen cable to State Department, June 3, 1965, NSF, France, Box 171, LBJL.

93. Sulzberger, *The Age of Mediocrity*, entry of July 1, 1965, 185–186.

94. Ball, *The Past Has Another Pattern*, 332ff.

95. Remarks by Secretary McNamara, Defense Secretaries Meeting, Paris, France, May 31, 1965, NSF, Agency File, DoD., Box 11, 11–13, LBJL.

96. Paul Buteux, *The Politics of Nuclear Consultation in NATO, 1965–1980* (Cambridge: Cambridge University Press, 1983), 44–45.

97. "Memorandum to the President," "Meeting with General Eisenhower," General Goodpaster, September 14, 1965, National Security Council (hereafter NSC), Memos to the President, Box 7, LBJL.

98. When asked by C. F. Sulzberger what the strange term referred to, he replied: "I recognize that the phrase irritates the Russians, but that is their affair, not mine. The real Russia stops at the Urals. All the rest . . . are all colonies. Colonies colonized by the Russians." *Sulzberger, An Age of Mediocrity*, entry of July 1, 1965, 188.

99. See Alain Larcan, "L'Europe de l'Atlantique à l'Oural," in *De Gaulle et la Russie*, ed. Maurice Vaisse, 285–313 (Paris: CNRS Editions, 2006). See also Hélène Carrère d' Encausse, *Le Général de Gaulle et la Russie* (Paris: Fayard, 2017).

100. Rusk cable to Bohlen, October 19, 1965, NSF, France, Box 172, LBJL.

101. *Newsweek*, December 13, 1965, 42; Schwartz, *Lyndon Johnson and Europe*, 94.

102. Richard J. Barnet, *The Alliance: America, Europe, and Japan: Makers of the Postwar World* (New York: Simon & Schuster, 1983), 240. Thomas A. Schwartz, "The De Gaulle Challenge: The Johnson Administration and the NATO Crisis of 1966–1967," in *The Strategic Triangle: France, Germany, and the United States in the Shaping of the New Europe*, ed. Helga Harftendorn et al. (Baltimore: Johns Hopkins University Press, 2006), 129.

103. C. L. Sulzberger, "A Two Man Summit in Paris?" *New York Times*, December 31, 1965.

104. Bohlen, *Witness to History*, 506.

105. Henry Tanner, "De Gaulle: Anti-American or Only Pro-French?" *New York Times*, February 27, 1966.

106. De Gaulle letter to Johnson, English translation, March 6, 1966, NSF, Special Head of State Series, Country France, Box 16, LBJL.

107. Henry Tanner, "De Gaulle Writes Johnson on Control of Bases: Couve Handed Letter to Bohlen on March 7," *New York Times*, March 8, 1966.

108. Bohlen surmised that de Gaulle short-circuited his plan for an extensive analysis of the NATO situation before dispatching the letter because he had already scheduled a trip to Moscow in June and worried that if he waited too long it might seem that the NATO withdrawal had been promoted by the Kremlin. Bohlen, *Witness to History*, 507.

109. Jauvert, *L'Amérique Contre de Gaulle*, 144ff.

110. Bohlen, *Witness to History*, 506. The American ambassador had good reason to feel betrayed. At a diplomatic dinner at the Elysée Palace on February 10 (less than a month before the withdrawal announcement), de Gaulle assured Bohlen that he "did not propose any changes in the treaty itself" and was "in no hurry" to suggest

modifications in the alliances organizational structure." Bohlen cable to Rusk, February 11, 1966, NSF, France, Box 172, LBJL.

111. Bozo, *Two Strategies for Europe*, 168. Bohlen cable to Washington, March 8, 1966, Bohlen-Couve de Murville Meeting, MAE, Pactes 1961–1970, Box 261. Ball claims in his memoirs that several months before the withdrawal announcement he had heard de Gaulle indicate, in a private conversation at the Elysée Palace, that he intended to withdraw from NATO and expel the organization from French territory. When he reported this to Washington "few of my colleagues believed that de Gaulle would do exactly what he stated." Ball, *The Past Has Another Pattern*, 333.

112. FRUS, 1964–1968, XIII, 327. Schwartz, *Lyndon Johnson and Europe*, 102. Lemnizer wondered if he could rely on the two French divisions stationed in Germany to participate in forward defense once they we removed from his command. Sulzberger, *An Age of Mediocrity*, entry for June 21, 1966, 274.

113. Harlan Cleveland, *NATO: The Transatlantic Bargain* (New York: Harper & Row, 1970), 104. The previous year Cleveland had poured out his vitriolic attitude toward de Gaulle to C. L. Sulzberger: "France simply doesn't have the influence in the world to which it aspires, so there is no reality to de Gaulle's policy." Sulzberger, *An Age of Mediocrity*, entry for November 1, 1965, 218.

114. Benjamin Welles, "Reply by Johnson to de Gaulle Firm," *New York Times*, March 23, 1966.

115. In his memoirs Johnson indicated that he had "long since decided that the only way to deal with de Gaulle's fervent nationalism was by restraint and patience," adding that his French antagonist "would not remain in power forever. Johnson, *The Vantage Point*, 305.

116. Johnson letter to de Gaulle, March 22, 1966, NSF, Special Head of State Series, France, Box 16, LBJL.

117. Schwartz, "The De Gaulle Challenge," 133.

118. Gallup Poll, *Public Opinion, Vol. III*, 2017.

119. Henry Tanner, "France Explains the Whys," *New York Times*, April 24, 1966.

120. A Swiss cartoon by Jean Leffell portrays the French president turning his back on an American warship on whose deck a sailor yells to de Gaulle, "Remember, if you're in trouble and need us again, the number is 14-18-39-45," referring to the two world wars. Sudhir Hazareesingh, *In the Shadow of the General: Modern France and the Myth of De Gaulle* (New York: Oxford University Press, 2012), 107.

121. "Transcript of Senator Church Meeting with President de Gaulle," May 4, 1966, NSF, France, Box 172, LBJL. The French record of the meeting may be found in "Procès-verbal de l'audience à l'Elysée de Mr. Church, sénateur des Etats-Unis d'Amérique," May 4, 1966, De Gaulle, *LNC, 1958–1970*, 813–817.

122. Alphand, *L'Etonnement d'être*, 476.

123. McNamara memorandum for the President, "Disposition of U.S. Facilities and Forces in France," May 25, 1966, NSF, France, Box 172, LBJL. Frank Costigliola cites the number of 26,000 military personnel and 37,000 dependents that were

evacuated within a year of de Gaulle decision. Costigliola, *France and the United States*, 144–145.

124. Benjamin Welles, "U.S. To Pull Out All Air Force Units from France: Shift Is Due Soon," *New York Times*, June 16, 1966.

125. Aide-Memoire: US Contribution in French Economy. No date, unsigned, Norstad Papers, Box 42, folder France '55 to '59. DDEL.

126. Sulzberger, *An Age of Mediocrity*, entry of December 5, 1966, 295–296.

127. Bozo, *Two Strategies for Europe*, 210–211.

128. Ike's dispute with Dulles on this matter was ironic, since (as we have seen) it was his secretary of state who famously threatened an "agonizing reappraisal" of America's commitment to defend Western Europe if the Europeans declined to approve the European Defense Community (EDC) project for a West European military force, which they did after France rejected the EDC in 1954.

129. Cited in Costigliola, *France and the United States*, 119.

130. Memorandum for Smith, Merchant, and Reinhardt, December 14, 1958, John Foster Dulles Memos, Box 8, July-December Meetings with the President, DDEL. Winand, *Eisenhower, Kennedy, and the United States of Europe*, 208.

131. NSC meeting, November 12, 1959, *FRUS*, 1958–1960, VII, no. 1, 508–509, cited in Marc Trachtenberg, *A Constructed Peace: The Making of the European Settlement, 1945–1963* (Princeton, NJ: Princeton University Press, 1999), 153–154.

132. Gavin cable to Secretary of State, February 17, 1962, NSF, France, Box 71, folder 2/10 to 2/16 1962, JFKL.

133. Gavin cable to Secretary of State, February 21, 1962, NSF, France, Box 71, folder 2/10 to 2/16 1962, JFKL.

134. *FRUS*, 1964–1968, XIII, 304; Schwartz, *Lyndon Johnson and Europe*, 98.

135. Bohlen cable to Rusk, November 30, 1964, NSF, France, Box 170, LBJL.

136. Bohlen cable to Rusk, November 30, 1964, NSF, France, Box 170, LBJL.

137. See Peter Lázár, "The Mansfield Amendment and the U.S. Commitment in Europe, 1966–1975," MA Thesis, Naval Postgraduate School, Monterey, Calif. (2003).

138. Senator Mike Mansfield guest column for Andrew Tully, August 7, 1970, "The Case for the Europeanization of NATO," cited in William R. Keylor, "Leading from Behind When No One is in Front: Eight Years of Frustration with the International Community's Failure to Share the Burden of Preserving World Order," in Maud Quessard and Maya Kandel, eds., *Les Etats-Unis à la Fin de la Grande Stratégie: Un Bilan de la Politique Étrangère d'Obama*, (Poitiers: Étude de l'Institut de recherché stratégigue de l'École militaire, 2017).

139. McNamara to the President, September 19, 1966, NSF, NSC history, TNN, Box 50, LBJL.

140. *FRUS*, 1964–1968, XV, 417; Schwartz, *Lyndon Johnson and Europe*, 122–123.

141. Logevall, *Choosing War*, 393.

142. Carolyn Davidson, "Dealing with de Gaulle: The United States and France," in *Globalizing de Gaulle: International Perspectives on French Foreign Policies*,

1958–1969, ed. Christian Nuenlist, Anna Locher, and Garret Martin, 111–134 (Plymouth, UK: Lexington Books, 2010), 127.

143. *FRUS, 1964–1968*, XIII, 376; Johnson, *The Vantage Point*, 305; Schwartz, *Lyndon Johnson and Europe*, 105.

144. Bohlen to Secretary of State, October 28, 1965, NSF, France, Box 172, LBJL.

145. Benjamin Welles, "Reply by Johnson to de Gaulle Firm," *New York Times*, March 23, 1966.

146. Bozo, *Two Strategies for Europe*, 177. The previous year de Gaulle had confided to C .L. Sulzberger that "we should perhaps try and unify Germany but we cannot do this until all of Germany's neighbors agree. . . . This cannot come about by peaceful methods for a long, long time." C. L. Sulzberger, *An Age of Mediocrity*, entry of July 1, 1965, 188.

147. Bohlen memorandum to Rusk, December 13, 1963, NSF, France, Box 169, LBJL.

148. CIA, "Problems and Prospects for Soviet-French Rapprochement," May 20, 1966, NSF, France, Box 172, LBJL.

149. Cited in Peyrefitte, *C'était de Gaulle*, Vol. III (Paris: Fayard, 2000), 200.

150. Mikhail Narinsky, "Le retrait de la France de l'organisation militaire de l'OTAN vu de Moscou," in *De Gaulle et la Russie*, ed. Maurice Vaisse, 258–269 (Paris: CNRS Editions, 2012).

151. Philippe de Gaulle, *De Gaulle Mon Père*, 592.

152. Pierre Maillard, *De Gaulle et l'Allemagne: Le rêve inachevé* (Paris: Plon, 1990), 250. De Gaulle's private views about German unification were revealed when he asked Bohlen, "Why are you Americans so interested in the unification of Germany?" When the American ambassador replied that the division of Germany represented a danger to the peace of the world, de Gaulle replied, "So would a united Germany." Bohlen, *Witness to History*, 514.

153. Bohlen cable to Rusk, December 9, 1966, NSF, France, Box 173, LBJL.

154. Rusk cable to the president, December 15, 1966, NSF, France, LBJL.

155. Speech to editorial writers, October 7, 1966, NSF, Speech File, Box 5, LBJL; Schwartz, *Lyndon Johnson and Europe*, 135.

156. Maurice Vaisse, "De Gaulle et Willy Brandt: Deux non-conformistes au pouvoir," in *Willy Brandt und Frankreich*, ed. Horst Muller and Maurice Vaisse (Munich: Oldenberg, 2005), 103ff.

157. Rusk cable to Paris Embassy, enclosing letter from Johnson to de Gaulle, December 29, 1965; McGeorge Bundy Memorandum for the President, January 5, 1966, enclosing de Gaulle's reply; NSF, Special Head of State Series, France, Box 16, LBJL.

158. De Gaulle letter to Johnson, February 5, 1966, NSF, Special Head of State Series, France, Box 16, LBJL. Couve de Murville, *Une Politique Etrangère, 1958–1969*, 137.

159. Yuko Torikata, "The U.S. Escalation in Vietnam and de Gaulle's Secret Search for Peace," in *Globalizing de Gaulle: International Perspectives on French Foreign*

Policies, 1958–1969, ed. Christian Nuenlist, Anna Locher, and Garret Martin (Plymouth, UK: Lexington Books, 2010), 169.

160. Torikata, "The U.S. Escalation, 170. Bohlen cable to Rusk for the President, July 22, 1966, NSF, France, Box 170, LBJL.

161. James G. Hershberg, *Marigold: The Last Chance for Peace in Vietnam* (Stanford, CA: Stanford University Press, 2012). For a brief summary, see James G. Hershberg, "'Marigold': Franco-American Relations, and Secret Vietnam Peace Diplomacy, 1966–1967," *Diplomacy and Statecraft* 28, no. 3 (2017): 403–430.

162. State Department text of De Gaulle's speech in Phnom Penh, Cambodia, September 1, 1966, NSF, France, Box 172, LBJL. The French version appears in Charles de Gaulle, *Discours d'Etat* (Paris: Perrin, 1970), 151–158.

163. "Memorandum for the President, Call by the French Foreign Minister, October 1, 1966," NSF, France, Box 172, LBJL.

164. Helga Haftendorn, "The NATO Crisis of 1966–1967: Confronting Germany with a Conflict of Priorities," in *The Strategic Triangle: France, Germany, and the United States in the Shaping of the New Europe*, ed. Helga Haftendorn et al. (Baltimore: The Johns Hopkins University Press, 2006), 82.

165. Bohlen cable to Rusk, November 11, 1966, NSF, France, Box 173, LBJL.

166. David Kraslow and Stuart H. Loory, *The Secret Search for Peace in Vietnam* (New York: Random House, 1968), 174–178, 201–203.

167. *New York Times*, January 2, 1967.

168. *New York Times*, April 8, 1967; Arnold A. Offner, *Hubert Humphrey: The Conscience of the Country* (New Haven, CT: Yale University Press, 2018), 254.

169. Bohlen cable to Rusk, May 26, 1967, NSF, France, Box 173, LBJL.

170. Bohlen cable to Rusk, July 13, 1967, NSF, France, Box 173, LBJL.

171. Cited in Irwin Wall, *France, the United States, and the Algerian War* (Berkeley: University of California Press), 205.

172. "De Gaulle Fiasco in Quebec," New York Times, July 30, 1967.

173. For the causes and consequences of the speech, see Dale C. Thompson, Vive le Québec Libre (Toronto: Deneau Publishers, 1988). See also Alain Ripaux, *Charles de Gaulle: Une certain idée du Québec* (Appilly: Ripaux, 2017).

174. De Gaulle, *Discours d'Etat*, 159–168. On the Quebec speech and its domestic and international repercussions, see Vaisse, *La Grandeur*, 648–670.

175. Couve de Murville, *Une Politique Etrangère, 1958–1969*, 227.

176. Bohlen cabled memorandum to Rusk, February 22, 1967, "French Position on a non-proliferation treaty," NSF, France, Box 173, LBJL. France and China, the only declared nuclear states, did not join the NPT until 1992. Vaisse, *La Grandeur*, 378–379.

177. General Charles Ailleret, "Défense 'dirigé' ou defense tous azimuts,'" *Revue de Défense Nationale* (December 1967): 192ff.

178. On the "all-azimuth strategy," see Pfaltzgraff, *The Atlantic Community*, 38–40.

179. Central Intelligence Agency, "The French Advanced Weapons Program— A Status Report," May 26, 1967, NSF, France, Box 173, LBJL. A year earlier the

CIA had predicted that the surface-to-surface missiles would become operational in August 1966 and the SLBM in spring 1968. Central Intelligence Agency, Intelligence Information Cable, "French Strategic Weapons Program," July 20, 1966, NSF, France, Box 172. LBJL.

180. Bohlen cable to Rusk, February 9, 1968, quoted in Bohlen, *Witness to History*, 520.

181. Sulzberger, *The Age of Mediocrity*, entry of January 23, 1968, 404.

182. Bohlen to Rusk, December 22, 1967, NSF, France, Box 172, LBJL.

183. "De Gaulle and Franco-American Relations," Bohlen cable to State Department, February 9, 1968, reprinted in Jauvert, *L'Amérique Contre De Gaulle*, 253.

184. Henry Tanner, "De Gaulle Again Attacks U.S. as Prolonging the Vietnam War," *New York Times*, January 2, 1968.

185. Cited in Robert Dallek, *Flawed Giant: Lyndon Johnson and His Times* (New York: Oxford University Press, 1998), 101–102.

186. Alphand, *L'Etonnement d'être*, 501.

187. Pierre Journoud, *De Gaulle et Vietnam, 1945–1969* (Paris: Tallandier, 2011), 324–328. Dallek, *Flawed Giant*, 538.

188. Rusk, *As I Saw It*, 485.

189. In his bitter reflection on the student-led explosion, De Gaulle's son, Philippe, who was with his parents during these events, blamed the mounting unrest on the student leader Daniel Cohn-Bendit (Danny-le Rouge), "a German anarchist, who frequented terrorist groups in his country and whose inspiration was Herbert Marcuse, who lived in the United States." Philippe de Gaulle, *De Gaulle Mon Père*, 298.

190. The French paratroop commander Lieutenant Colonel Mathieu, the swashbuckling leader of the French soldiers in Gillo Pontecorvo's epic film *The Battle of Algiers*, was loosely based on Massu.

191. Jonathan Fenby, *The General: Charles De Gaulle and the France He Saved* (New York: Skyhorse, 2012), 601.

192. De Gaulle letter to Michel Debré, quoted in Bernard Ledwidge, *De Gaulle* (New York: St. Martin's Press, 1982), 387.

193. Edward L. Morse, *Foreign Policy and Interdependence in Gaullist France* (Princeton, NJ: Princeton University Press, 1973), 95.

194. Henry Tanner, "De Gaulle Gets His H-Bomb," *New York Times*, September 1, 1968.

195. Central Intelligence Agency, Memorandum, "Possibilities for Accommodation between the U.S. and France," August 28, 1968, NSF, France, Boxes 173–174, LBJL.

196. In his memoirs Johnson noted that while De Gaulle's government "had been uncooperative" in previous international monetary difficulties," he magnanimously declared that the international monetary system "is not a field for pettiness or retribution." Johnson, *The Vantage Point*, 319.

197. Shriver cable to Rusk, September 23, 1968, NSF, France, Box 174, LBJL. The French minutes of the meeting may be found in *DDF*, 1968, Vol. II, 483–489.

198. Meeting of President Johnson and Foreign Minister Debré in Washington, October 10, 1968, *DDF*, 1968, Vol. II, 626–629.

199. Vaisse, *La Grandeur*, 290.

200. Department of State research memorandum, Thomas L. Hughes, "De Gaulle's Foreign Policy: 1969 Version," December 30, 1968, NSF, France, Box 174, LBJL.

Chapter Ten

1. De Gaulle letter to Johnson, 3 January 1969, in de Gaulle, *Charles de Gaulle, Lettres, Notes, et Carnets* (hereafter *LNC*), *1958–1970* (Paris: Lafont, 2010), 273–274. The French version appears in *Documents Diplomatiques Français* (hereafter *DDF*) (1969), Vol. I, 21.

2. De Gaulle letter to Johnson, January 29, 1969, *LNC*, *1958–1970*, 287.

3. Minutes of a Meeting between General de Gaulle and Governor Scranton, September 20, 1968, *DDF*, 1968, Vol. II, 462–468.

4. Richard M. Nixon, *RN: The Memoirs of Richard Nixon* (New York: Grosset & Dunlap, 1978), 348.

5. Bohlen cable to Rusk, July 30, 1963, NSF, France, Box 72A, folder 7/16 to 7/31 1963, John F. Kennedy Library (hereafter JFKL).

6. Bohlen cable to Rusk, June 8, 1967, NSF, France, Box 173, Lyndon B. Johnson Library (hereafter LBJL).

7. Richard M. Nixon, *Leaders* (New York: Warner, 1982), 41.

8. See Henry Kissinger, "Dealing with De Gaulle," in *De Gaulle and the United States: A Centennial Reappraisal*, ed. Robert Paxton and Nicholas Wahl (Oxford: Berg, 1994), 331–341.

9. Shriver cable to State Department, January 25, 1969, NSC, France, Vol. I, Richard M. Nixon Library (hereafter RMNL).

10. Translation of letter from de Gaulle to Nixon, January 17, 1969, President's Personal File, Name/Subject File. 1969-1974, Box 3, Folder de Gaulle, RMNL.

11. Thomas L. Hughes, Department of State research memorandum, "De Gaulle's Foreign Policy: 1969 Version," December 30, 1968, LBJL, NSF, France, Box 174.

12. Shriver cable to State Department, March 7, 1969, NSC Files, Presidential/ HAK Mem Coms, Box 1023, RMNL. Julian Jackson, *De Gaulle* (Cambridge, MA: Harvard University Press), 742–744.

13. Lucet cable to Foreign Minister Debré, January 13, 1969, *DDF* (1969), Vol. I, 71.

14. Lucet cable to Foreign Ministry, February 1, 1969, 205–206; Nixon's letter of February 15 (in English) handed to Ambassador Lucet for transmission to de Gaulle, *DDF* (1969) Vol. I, 262.

15. De Gaulle letter to Eisenhower, February 13, 1969, *DDF* (1969) Vol. I, 285.

16. Maurice Couve de Murville, *Une Politique Etrangère, 1958–1969* (Paris: Plon 1971), 155.

17. Cited in Yves-Henri Nouailhat, "Richard Nixon et Charles de Gaulle," in *Le Général De Gaulle et Les Presidents des Etats-Unis* (Paris: Fondation Charles de Gaulle, Cahiers no. 6, 2006), 109.

18. See also the commentary in Robert Dallek, *Nixon and Kissinger: Partners in Power* (New York: Harper/Collins, 2007), 114.

19. Memorandum of Conversation, Nixon, de Gaulle, and translators, Elysée Palace, March 2, 1969, NSC Files, Presidential/HAK Mem Coms, The President and General de Gaulle, February 28–March 2, 1969, Box 1023, RMNL. Nixon extemporaneously added that he thought it was "useful" for the U.S. to have "another power like France with a nuclear capability." The complete transcripts of all three meetings between Nixon and de Gaulle may be found in *DDF* (1969), Vol. I, 396–406, 409–430, and 431–436.

20. Kissinger, "Dealing with De Gaulle," 331–332.

21. *Le Monde*, March 4, 1969.

22. Couve de Murville, *Une Politique etrangère*, 155. On the entire visit, see Yves-Henri Nouailhat, "Nixon-De Gaulle: Un épisode original des relations franco-américains," *Revue Française d'Etudes Américanes*, no. 32 (April 1987): 310–318.

23. Shriver cable to Secretary of State, March 7, 1969, NSC Files, Country Files, France, Vol. 1, RMNL.

24. André Malraux, *Felled Oaks: Conversations with de Gaulle*, trans. Irene Clephane (New York: Holt, Rinehart and Winston, 1971), 30.

25. Michel Tauriac, *Vivre avec De Gaulle: Les derniers témoins raconte l'homme* (Paris: Plon, 2008), 712.

26. Philippe de Gaulle, *De Gaulle Mon Père: Entretiens avec Michel Tauriac* (Paris: Plon, 2005), 597.

27. Yves-Henri Nouailhat, "Nixon-De Gaulle," 31.

28. Hervé Alphand, *L'Etonnement d'être: Journal 1939–1973* (Paris: Fayard, 1977), 519.

29. Cited in Jonathan Fenby, *The General: Charles De Gaulle and the France He Saved* (New York: Skyhorse, 2012), 621.

30. Henry Tanner, "De Gaulle Quits After Losing Referendum," *New York Times*, April 28, 1969.

31. Vernon Walters, *Silent Missions* (New York: Doubleday & Company, 1978), 501.

32. Peter Grose, "Nixon Praises de Gaulle," *New York Times*, April 29, 1969.

33. Charles de Gaulle, *Memoirs of Hope: Renewal and Endeavor*, trans. Terence Kilmartin, (New York: Simon & Schuster, 1971).

34. Malraux, *Felled Oaks*, 10.

Chapter Eleven

1. Interview with Pleven, March 15, 1983, Jean Lacouture, *De Gaulle, The Rebel 1890–1944*, trans. Alan Sheridan (New York: Norton, 1993), 334–335.

2. John Newhouse, *De Gaulle and the Anglo-Saxons* (New York: The Viking Press, 1970).

3. Rusk noted caustically that while blasting the United States for its military intervention in the Dominican Republic in the spring of 1965, de Gaulle privately asked that American marines be deployed to protect the French Embassy in Santo Domingo. After the Marines were redeployed to protect the embassy, "he never thanked us. In fact, he continued to berate us publicly." Dean Rusk, *As I Saw It: A Secretary of State's Memoirs* (New York: W.W. Norton, 1990), 270.

4. C. L. Sulzberger, *An Age of Mediocrity: Memoirs and Diaries, 1963–1972* (New York: Macmillan, 1973), entry of December 15, 1963, 54.

5. For a brilliant assessment of the conflict between de Gaulle's vision for Western Europe and his narrow brand of French nationalism, see Philip H. Gordon, *A Certain Idea of France: French Security Policy and the Gaullist Legacy* (Princeton, NJ: Princeton University Press, 1993), especially 31–52.

6. James Macgregor Burns, *Roosevelt: The Soldier of Freedom, 1940–1945* (New York: History Book Club, 2006).

7. Maurice Vaisse, *La Puissance ou L'Influence?: La France dans le monde depuis 1958* (Paris: Fayard, 2009), 170.

8. Marc Trachtenberg, *A Constructed Peace: The Making of the European Settlement, 1945–1963* (Princeton, NJ: Princeton University Press, 1999), 227.

9. Edward A. Kolodziej, *French International Policy under De Gaulle and Pompidou* (Ithaca, NY: Cornell University Press, 1974), 70–71.

10. Stanley Hoffmann, *Decline or Renewal? France Since the 1930s* (New York: The Viking Press, 1974), 343.

11. Ronald Steel, *Pax Americana* (New York: The Viking Press, 1968), 83.

~

Bibliography

Primary Sources

Presidential Libraries

Franklin D. Roosevelt Library, Hyde Park, New York.
  Map Room File
  Official File
  President's Personal File
  President's Secretary's File
  Adolf Berle Papers
  Harry Hopkins Papers
  Henry Morgenthau Papers
  Sumner Welles Papers

Harry S. Truman Library, Independence, Missouri.
  Student Research File
  Office Files
  Eben A. Ayers Papers
  George Elsey Papers

Dwight D. Eisenhower Library, Abilene, Kansas.
  Pre-Presidential Papers
  Presidential File, 1953–1961 (Ann Whitman File)
  Dulles-Herter Series
  International Series
  International Meetings Series

International Security Council Series
Christian A. Herter Papers
Lauris Norstad Papers
Walter Bedell Smith Papers

John F. Kennedy Library, Boston, Massachusetts.
Countries Series
Departments and Agencies Series
Meetings and Memoranda Series
George W. Ball Papers
McGeorge Bundy Papers

Lyndon B. Johnson Library, Austin, Texas.
National Security Files
Country Files
George W. Ball Papers
McGeorge Bundy Papers
Walt A. Rostow Papers
Dean Rusk Papers

Richard M. Nixon Library, Yorba Linda, California.
Country Files
President's Meetings Files

Private Papers Collections
Cordell Hull Papers, Manuscript Division of the Library of Congress, Washington, D.C.
Charles E. Bohlen Papers, Manuscript Division of the Library of Congress, Washington, D.C.
John Foster Dulles Papers, Seely Mudd Manuscript Library, Princeton University, Princeton, New Jersey.

Government Archives
Archives du Ministère des Affaires Etrangères (MAE), Courneuve, France.
Department of State Bulletin.
Documents Diplomatiques Français.
General Records of the Department of State, National Archives and Records Administration (hereafter NARA), College Park, Maryland.
NARA, RG 59, General Records of the State Department, Miscellaneous Office Files.
NARA, RG 107, Records of the Office of the Secretary of War (ASW).
NARA, RG 165, General Records of the War Department.

NARA, Matthews-Hickerson File, Microfilm Reel 13.
Papers Relating to the Foreign Relations of the United States, U.S. State Department.

Published Correspondence of Charles de Gaulle
De Gaulle, Admiral Philippe, ed., *Charles de Gaulle, Lettres, Notes, et Carnets,*
    1905–1941. Paris: Lafont, 2010.
———, ed. *Charles de Gaulle, Lettres, Notes, et Carnets, 1942–1958.* Paris: Lafont,
    2010.
———, ed. *Charles de Gaulle, Lettres, Notes, et Carnets, 1958–1970.* Paris: Lafont,
    2010.
De Gaulle, Charles. *Discours d'Etat.* Paris: Perrin, 1970.
———. *Discours et messages (1940–1946).* Paris: Poche, 1970.
———. *Discours et messages (1946–1958).* Paris: Poche, 1970.
———. *Discours et messages (1962–1964).* Paris: Poche, 1970.

Newspapers Cited
New York Times
New York Herald Tribune
Christian Science Monitor
Le Monde
Le Figaro
New York Post

Magazines Cited
The New Republic
Time
Newsweek
Life
The Nation

Memoirs, Diaries, and Correspondence of Participants and Contemporary Witnesses Cited
Aglion, Raoul. *Roosevelt and de Gaulle, Allies in Conflict: A Personal Memoir.* New
    York: The Free Press, 1988.
———. "The Free French Movement and the United States, from 1940 to 1944."
    In *De Gaulle and the United States: A Centennial Appraisal*, ed. Robert Paxton and
    Nicholas Wahl, 33–48. Oxford: Berg Publishers, 1994.
Alanbrooke, Lord. *War Diaries 1939–1945.* London: Weidenfeld & Nicolson, 2001.
Alphand, Hervé. *L'Etonnement d'être: Journal 1939–1973.* Paris: Fayard, 1977.
Ball, George W. *The Past Has Another Pattern: Memoirs.* New York: W. W. Norton,
    1982.

Bankwitz, Philip Farwell. "Defeat and Reversal." In *The French Defeat of 1940: Reassessments*, ed. Joel Blatt, 327–353. Providence, RI: Berghahn Books, 1998.

Berle, Beatrice Bishop, and Travis Beal Jacobs, eds., *Navigating the Rapids. 1918–1971: From the Papers of Adolf A. Berle*. New York: Harcourt Brace Jovanovich, 1973.

Bidault, Georges. *Resistance: The Political Autobiography of Georges Bidault*. Trans. Marianne Sinclair. London: Weidenfeld and Nicolson, 1967.

Blum, John Morton. *From the Morgenthau Diaries: Years of War, 1941–1945*. Boston: Houghton Mifflin Company, 1967.

Bohlen, Charles. *Witness to History, 1929–1969*. New York: W. W. Norton, 1973.

Bullitt, Orville, ed. *For the President Personal and Secret: Correspondence between Franklin D. Roosevelt and William C. Bullitt*. Boston: Houghton Mifflin, 1972.

Burman, Ben Lucien. *The Generals Wore Cork Hats*. New York: Taplinger, 1963.

Campbell, Thomas M., and George C. Herring, eds. *The Diaries of Edward R. Stettinius, 1943–1946*. New York: New Viewpoints, 1975.

Camus, Albert. *Carnets, Vol. III, Mars 1951–Décembre 1959*. Paris: Gallimard, 1989.

Catterall, Peter, ed. *The Macmillan Diaries, Vol. II: Prime Minister and After, 1957–1966*. London: Macmillan, 2011.

Churchill, Winston S. *The Second World War*. Boston: Houghton Mifflin, 1948.

Couve de Murville, Maurice. *Une Politique Etrangère, 1958–1969*. Paris: Plon, 1971.

De Gaulle, Charles. *The Complete War Memoirs*. Trans. Jonathan Griffin. New York: Simon & Schuster, 1972.

———. *Memoirs of Hope: Renewal and Endeavor*. Trans. Terence Kilmartin. New York: Simon & Schuster, 1971.

De Gaulle, Philippe. *De Gaulle Mon Père: Entretiens avec Michel Tauriac*. Paris: Plon, 2005.

———. *Mémoires accessoires 1946–1982*. Paris: Perrin, 2010.

De Lattre de Tassigny, Jean. *Histoire de la Première Armée Francaise*. Paris: Plon, 1949.

De Roussy de Sales, Raoul. *The Making of Yesterday: Diaries, 1938–1942*. New York: Raynal and Hitchcock, 1947.

Debré, Michel. *Trois Républiques pour une France*, vol. I. Paris: Albin Michel, 1988.

Dewavrin, André (Passy). *Colonel Passy, Souvenirs*, 2 volumes. Monte Carlo: R. Solar, 1947.

Duff Cooper, Alfred. *Old Men Forget*. London: Rupert Hart-Davis, 1953.

Eden, Anthony. *The Memoirs of Anthony Eden, Earl of Avon: The Reckoning*. Boston: Houghton Mifflin, 1965.

Eisenhower, Dwight D. *Crusade in Europe*. New York: Doubleday, 1948.

———. *The White House Years: A Personal Account. Waging Peace, 1956–1961*. Garden City, NY: Doubleday, 1965.

Eisenhower, Milton. *The President Is Calling*. New York: Doubleday, 1974.

Fall, Bernard. *Last Reflections on a War*. New York: Doubleday, 1967.

Ferrell, Robert H., ed. *The Eisenhower Diaries*. New York: W.W. Norton, 1981.

Giraud, Henri. *Un seul but la victoire*. Paris: Juillard, 1949.

Hertier de Boislambert, Claude. *Les Fers de l'espoir*. Paris: Plon, 1978.

Ho Chi Minh. Letters to Truman. www.historyisaweapon.com/defcon2/hochiminh.

Hull, Cordell. *The Memoirs of Cordell Hull*. New York: Macmillan, 1948.

Johnson, Lyndon B. *The Vantage Point: Perspectives of the Presidency, 1963–1969*. New York: Holt, Rinehart and Winston, 1971.

Kimball, Warren, ed. *Churchill and Roosevelt: The Complete Correspondence, Vol. II, Alliance Forged*. London: Collins, 1984.

Kissinger, Henry. "Dealing with De Gaulle." In *De Gaulle and the United States: A Centennial Appraisal*, ed. Robert O. Paxton and Nicholas Wahl. Oxford: Berg, 1994.

Leahy, William D. *I Was There: The Personal Story of the Chief of Staff to Presidents Roosevelt and Truman*. London: Gollancz, 1950.

Ledwidge, Bernard. *De Gaulle et les Américans: Conversations avec Dulles, Eisenhower, Kennedy, Rusk: 1958–1964*. Paris: Flammarion, 1984.

Leger, Alexis (Saint Jean Perse). *Oeuvres Complètes*. Paris: Gallimard,1972.

Macmillan, Harold. *Pointing the Way*. Vol. 5 of Macmillan's memoirs. London: Macmillan, 1972.

———. *War Diaries: Politics and War in the Mediterranean, January 1943–May 1945*. London: Macmillan, 1984.

Monnet, Jean. *Mémoires*. Paris: Fayard, 1976.

Moulin, Laure. *Premier Combat*. Paris: Les Editions du Minuit, 1965. Posthumous. Memoir published by Moulin's sister.

Murphy, Robert. *Diplomat Among Warriors*. Garden City, NY: Doubleday, 1964.

Nixon, Richard M. *RN: The Memoirs of Richard Nixon*. New York: Grosset & Dunlap, 1978.

———. *Leaders*. New York: Warner, 1982.

Patti, Archimedes. *Why Vietnam? Prelude to America's Albatross*. Berkeley: University of California Press, 1980.

Peyrefitte, Alain. *C'était de Gaulle*, Vols. II and III. Paris: Fayard, 1997, 2000.

Renault, Gilbert (Rémy). *Dix Ans avec de Gaulle, 1940–1950*. Paris: France-Empire, 1971.

Reynaud, Paul. *Mémoires*, vol. II. Paris: Flammarion, 1963.

Rusk, Dean. *As I Saw It: A Secretary of State's Memoirs*. New York: W. W. Norton, 1990.

———. Oral History Collection, Series Rusk C, Interview by Richard Rusk and Thomas J. Schoenbaum, September 11, 1984. DROHC, Series Rusk QQQ.

Sherwood, Robert. *White House Papers*, vol. II. London: Eyre & Spottiswoode, 1949.

Soustelle, Jacques. *Envers et contre tout*, vol. I. Paris: Lafont, 1947.

Stimson, Henry L., and McGeorge Bundy. *On Active Service in Peace and War*. New York: Harper & Brothers, 1947.

Sulzberger, C. L. *An Age of Mediocrity: Memoirs and Diaries, 1963–1972*. New York: Macmillan, 1973.

Swinton, Major General Sir Ernest D. *Eye Witness, and the Origin of the Tanks*. New York: Doubleday, Doran & Co., 1933.

Tauriac, Michel. *Vivre avec De Gaulle: Les derniers témoins raconte l'homme*. Paris: Plon, 2008.

Truman, Harry S. *The Autobiography of Harry S. Truman*. Boulder: University Press of Colorado, 1980.

———. *Year of Decisions*. New York: Doubleday, 1955.

Walters, Vernon. *Silent Missions*. New York: Doubleday & Company, 1978.

Welles, Sumner. *The Time for Decision*. New York: Harper & Brothers, 1944.

Secondary Sources Cited

I have decided to list only the secondary works that I have cited in the foot-notes. The most complete bibliography of the hundreds of works about de Gaulle is provided by Julian Jackson, *De Gaulle* (Cambridge, MA: Harvard University Press, 2018). Most (but not all) of my citations pertain to the relations between de Gaulle and the U.S. government since the defeat of France in the spring of 1940.

Ailleret, General Charles. "Défense 'dirigé ou defense tous azimuts.'" *Revue de Défense Nationale* (December 1967).

Amme, Carl H. Jr. *NATO Without France: A Strategic Appraisal*. Stanford, CA: Hoover Institution Press, 1967.

Andrews, William G. *French Politics and Algeria*. New York: Appleton-Century-Crofts, 1962.

Anglin, Douglas G. *The St. Pierre and Miquelon Affair of 1941: A Study in Diplomacy in the North Atlantic Triangle*. Toronto: University of Toronto Press, 1966.

Anonymous. *Le Général Leclerc vu par ses compagnons de Combat*. Paris: Editions Alsatia, 1948.

Argyle, Ray. *The Paris Game: Charles de Gaulle, the Liberation of Paris, and the Gamble that Won France*. Toronto: Dundurn, 2014.

Arzakanian, Marina. "De Gaulle pendant la Second Guerre mondiale à travers les archives soviétiques," in *De Gaulle et la Russie*, ed. Maurice Vaisse. Paris: CNRS Editions, 2012.

Atkinson, Rick. *An Army at Dawn: The War in North Africa, 1942–1943*. New York: Henry Holt and Company, 2002.

———. *The Guns at Last Light: The War in Western Europe, 1944–1945*. New York: Henry Holt, 2013.

Barbier, Colette. "La Force multilatérale." *Relations internationales*, no. 69 (Spring 1992): 3–18.

———. "The French Decision to Develop a Military Nuclear Program in the 1950s." *Diplomacy and Statecraft* 4, no. 1 (1993): 105–113.

Bariéty, Jacques. "De Gaulle, Adenauer, et la genèse du traité de l'Elysée du 22 janvier, 1963." In *De Gaulle et son siècle*, Vol. V. Paris: Institute Charles de Gaulle, 1992.

Barnet, Richard J. *The Alliance: America, Europe, and Japan: Makers of the Postwar World*. New York: Simon & Schuster, 1983.

Baylis, John. "The 1958 Anglo-American Mutual Defence Agreement: The Search for Nuclear Interdependence." The Journal of Strategic Studies 31 (June 2008): 425–466.

Beever, Anthony, and Artemis Cooper. *Paris after the Liberation*. London: Penguin, 1995.

Behr, Edward. *Thank Heaven for Little Girls: The True Story of Maurice Chevalier's Life and Times*. New York: Hitchinson, 1993.

Beloff, Nora. *The General Says No: Britain's Exclusion from Europe*. Harmondsworth, UK: Penguin Books, 1963.

Belot, Robert. *La Résistance sans de Gaulle*. Paris: Fayard, 2006.

Belot, Robert, and Gilbert Karpman. *L'Affaire Suisse: La Résistance a-t-elle trahi de Gaulle? (1943–1944)*. Paris: Armand Colin, 2009.

Berthon, Simon. *Allies at War: The Bitter Rivalry Among Churchill, Roosevelt, and De Gaulle*. New York: Carroll and Graf, 2001.

Beschloss, Michael. *May Day: Eisenhower, Khruschev, and the U-2 Affair*. New York: Harper & Row, 1968.

Besnaci-Lancou, Fatima, and Gilles Manceron, eds. *Les Harkis dans la colonization et ses suites*. Ivry-sur-Seine: Editions de l'Atelier, 2008.

Beuve-Méry, Hubert. *Onze Ans de Regne, 1958–1969*. Paris: Flammarion, 1974.

Béziat, André. *Franklin Roosevelt et la France*. Paris: Harmattan, 1997.

Billotte, Pierre. *Le Temps des Armes*. Paris: Plon, 1972.

Blatt, Joel, ed. *The French Defeat of 1940: Reassessments*. Providence, RI: Berghahn Books, 1998.

Bosco, David L. *Five to Rule Them All: The UN Security Council and the Making of the Modern World*. New York: Oxford University Press, 2009.

Bozo, Frédéric. *Two Strategies for Europe: De Gaulle, the United States, and the Atlantic Alliance*. Trans. Susan Emanuel. Lanham, MD: Rowman & Littlefield, 2001.

Bozo, Frédéric, and Pierre Mélandri. "La France devant l'opinion américaine, Le retour de De Gaulle, debut 1958-printemps 1959." *Relations internationales*, no. 58 (Summer 1989): 195–215.

Bradley, Mark P. *Imagining Vietnam and America: The Making of Postcolonial Vietnam*. Chapel Hill: University of North Carolina Press, 2000.

Branca, Eric. *L'ami américain: Washington contre de Gaulle, 1940–1969*. Paris: Perrin, 2017.

Brinkley, Douglas. *Dean Acheson: The Cold War Years, 1953–1971*. New Haven, CT: Yale University Press, 1994.

Brogi, Allesandro. *A Question of Self-Esteem: The United States and the Cold War Choices in France and Italy, 1944–1958*. Westport, CT: Praeger, 2002.

Brownell, Will, and Richard N. Billings. *So Close to Greatness: A Biography of William C. Bullitt.* New York: Macmillan, 1987.

Buhite, Russell D. *Decisions at Yalta: An Appraisal of Summit Diplomacy.* Wilmington, DE: Scholarly Resources, 1986.

Bundy, McGeorge. *Danger and Survival: Choices About the Bomb in the First Fifty Years.* New York: Random House, 1988.

Burns, James Macgregor. *Roosevelt: The Soldier of Freedom, 1940–1945.* New York: History Book Club, 2006.

Buteux, Paul. *The Politics of Nuclear Consultation in NATO, 1965–1980.* Cambridge: Cambridge University Press, 1983.

Carrère d' Encausse, Hélène. *Le Géneral de Gaulle et la Russie.* Paris: Fayard, 2017.

Cattui, Georges. *L'Homme et son Destin.* Paris: Fayard, 1960.

Cerny, Philip. *Politics of Grandeur: Ideological Aspects of de Gaulle's Foreign Policy.* Cambridge: Cambridge University Press, 1980.

Chafer, Tony. *The End of Empire in French West Africa: France's Successful Decolonization?* Oxford: Berg, 2002.

Chalaby, Jean K. *The de Gaulle Presidency and the Media: Statism and Public Communications.* New York: Palgrave-Macmillan, 2002.

Christofferson, Thomas R., with Michael S. Christofferson. *France During World War II: From Defeat to Liberation.* New York: Fordham University Press, 2006.

Clark, Thurston. *JFK's Last Hundred Days.* New York: The Penguin Press, 2013.

Clemens, Diane Shaver. *Yalta.* New York: Oxford University Press, 1970.

Cleveland, Harlan. *NATO: The Transatlantic Bargain.* New York: Harper & Row, 1970.

Clinton, Adam. *Jean Moulin, 1899–1943: The French Resistance and the Republic.* London: Macmillan, 2002.

Cogan, Charles. *Oldest Allies, Guarded Friends: The United States and France since 1940.* New York: Praeger, 1994.

Cointet, Jean-Paul. *Pierre Laval.* Paris: Fayard, 1993.

Cointet, Michèle. *De Gaulle et l'Algérie française, 1958–1962.* Paris, Librairie Académique Perrin, 2012,

Coles, Harry L., and Albert K. Weinberg. *Civil Affairs: Soldiers Become Governors.* Washington, DC: Center of Military History, 1964.

Collot, Claude, and Jean-Robert Henry. *Le Mouvement Nationale Algérien: Textes 1912–1954.* Algiers: Office des Publications Universitaire, 1981.

Cook, Don. *Charles de Gaulle: A Biography.* New York: G.P. Putnam's Sons, 1983.

Costigliola, Frank. *France and the United States: The Cold Alliance since World War II.* New York: Twayne, 1992.

Coutau-Bégarie, Hervé, and Claude Huan. *Darlan.* Paris: Fayard, 1989.

Crémieux-Brilhac, J.-L. *De Gaulle, la République, et la France Libre, 1940–1945.* Paris: Perrin, 2014.

Creswell, Michael. *A Question of Balance: How France and the United States Created Cold War Europe.* Cambridge, MA: Harvard University Press, 2006.

Creswell, Michael, and Marc Trachtenberg. "France and the German Question, 1945–1955." ProjectMuse. www.sscnet.ucla.edu/polisci/faculty/trachtenberg/cv/jcws5.3creswell01.pdf.

Crozier, Brian. De Gaulle: The First Complete Biography. New York: Scribner's, 1973.

Dallek, Robert. Flawed Giant: Lyndon Johnson and His Times. New York: Oxford University Press, 1998.

———. Franklin D. Roosevelt and American Foreign Policy. New York: Oxford University Press, 1979.

———. Nixon and Kissinger: Partners in Power. New York: HarperCollins, 2007.

———. "Roosevelt and De Gaulle." In De Gaulle and the United States: A Centennial Reappraisal, ed. Robert O. Paxton and Nicholas Wahl, 49–60. Oxford: Berg, 1994.

David, François. "John Foster Dulles, Sécretaire d'Etat, et la France." Doctoral Dissertation, Université de la Sorbonne, Paris IV (2006). 4 volumes.

Davidson, Carolyn. "Dealing with de Gaulle: The United States and France." In Globalizing de Gaulle: International Perspectives on French Foreign Policies, 1958–1969, ed. Christian Nuenlist, Anna Locher, and Garret Martin, 111–134. Plymouth, UK: Lexington Books, 2010.

Démaret, Pierre, and Christian Plume. Target de Gaulle: The True Story of the 31 Attempts on the Life of the French President. Trans. Richard Barry. New York: The Dial Press, 1975.

DePorte, A. W. De Gaulle's Foreign Policy, 1944–1946. Cambridge, MA: Harvard University Press, 1968.

Devillers, Philippe. Histoire du Viet-Nam de 1940 à 1952. Paris: Le Seuil, 1952.

DiLeo, David L. "Catch the Night Train for Paris: George Ball and Jean Monnet." In Monnet and the Americans: The Father of a United Europe and his U.S. Supporters, ed. Clifford P. Hackett. Washington, DC: Jean Monnet Council, 2001.

DiNardo, R. L. "German Armour Doctrine: Correcting the Myths." War in History 3, no. 4 (1996): 384–397.

Dockrill, Saki. Eisenhower's New-Look National Security Policy, 1953–1961. London: Macmillan, 1996.

Doenecke, Justus D., and Mark A. Stoler. Debating Franklin D. Roosevelt's Foreign Policies, 1933–1945. Lanham, MD: Rowman & Littlefield, 2005.

Donnison, F. S. V. History of the Second World War, UK Military Series, Civil Affairs and Military Government: Central Organization and Planning. London: Her Majesty's Stationery Office, 1966.

Donovan, Robert J. Conflict and Compromise: The Presidency of Harry S. Truman, 1945–1948. New York: Norton, 1977.

Dougherty, James J. The Politics of Wartime Aid: American Assistance to France and Northwest Africa, 1940–1946. Westport, CT: Greenwood Press, 1978.

Doughty, Robert A. "De Gaulle's Concept of a Mobile Professional Army." Parameters, no. 4 (1974): 23–34.

Drachman, Edward R. United States Policy Toward Vietnam, 1940–1945. Cranbury, NJ: Fairleigh Dickinson University Press, 1970.

Duchêne, François. *Jean Monnet: The First Statesman of Interdependence*. New York: Norton, 1994.

Duchin, Brian. "The 'Agonizing Reappraisal': Eisenhower, Dulles, and the European Defense Community." *Diplomatic History* 16, no. 2 (April 1, 1992): 201–221.

Dufour, Frédérique. "Charles de Gaulle dans les actualités cinématographiques amércaines durant le Second Guerre mondiale." *Espoir* (Revue de la Fondation et de l'Institut Charles de Gaulle), no. 136 (September 2003).

Ehrlich, Blake. *Resistance: France, 1940–1945*. Boston: Little, Brown, 1965.

Eichengreen, Barry. *The European Economy Since 1945*. Princeton, NJ: Princeton University Press, 2007.

Eisenberg, Noah. *The Life, Legend, and Afterlife of Hollywood's Most Beloved Movie*. New York: WW. Norton, 2017.

Epstein, Klaus. "Adenauer and Rhenish Separatism." *The Review of Politics* 4 (October 1967): 536–545.

Evans, Martin. "Algeria and the Liberation: Hope and Betrayal." in *The Liberation of France: Image and Event*, ed. H. R. Kedward and Nancy Wood, 255–267. Oxford: Berg, 1995).

———. "Reprisal Violence and the Harkis in French Algeria, 1962." *International History Review* 39, no. 1 (2017): 89–106.

Farago, Ladislas. *Patton: Ordeal and Triumph*. New York: Ivan Obolensky, 1963.

Fenby, Jonathan. *The General: Charles De Gaulle and the France He Saved*. New York: Skyhorse, 2012.

Ferro, Maurice. *De Gaulle et L'Amérique: Une Amitié Tumulteuse*. Paris: Plon, 1973.

Fontaine, André. *Un seul lit pour deux rêves: Histoire de la "détente" 1962–1981*. Paris: Fayard, 1982.

Foulon, Charles. *Le Pouvoir en province à la liberation*. Paris: Colin, 1975.

Francisco, Charles. *You Must Remember This: The Filming of "Casablanca."* Englewood Cliffs, J: Prentice Hall, 1980.

Funk, Arthur L. *Charles de Gaulle: The Crucial Years, 1943–1944*. Norman: University of Oklahoma Press, 1959.

———. "Negotiating the Deal with Darlan." *Journal of Contemporary History* 8, no. 2 (April 1973)

Gallup Poll. *Public Opinion, Vol. III, 1959–1971*. New York: Random House, 1972.

Gamrasni, Michel. "France/Etats-Unis: le grand malentendu." In *De Gaulle et l'Algérie, 1943–1969*, ed. Maurice Vaisse. Paris: Armand Colin, 2012.

Gavin, Francis J. *Gold, Dollars, and Power: The Politics of International Monetary Relations, 1958–1971*. Chapel Hill: University of North Carolina Press, 2004.

Gellman, Irwin F. *Secret Affairs: Franklin Roosevelt, Cordell Hull, and Sumner Welles*. Baltimore: Johns Hopkins University Press, 1995.

Giauque, Jeffrey Glen. *Grand Designs and Visions of Unity: The Atlantic Powers and the Reorganization of Western Europe, 1955–1963*. Chapel Hill: University of North Carolina Press, 2002.

Giles, Frank. *The Locust Years, 1946–1958*. London: Secker and Warburg, 1991.

Gillois, André. *Histoire Secrète des Français à Londres, de 1940 à 1944*. Paris: Hachette, 1973.

Goldman, Eric F. *The Tragedy of Lyndon Johnson*. New York: Knopf, 1968.

Gordon, Philip H. *A Certain Idea of France: French Security Policy and the Gaullist Legacy*. Princeton, NJ: Princeton University Press, 1993.

Goscha, Christopher, and Maurice Vaisse, *La Guerre du Vietnam et l'Europe*. Brussels: Bruylant, 2003.

Gottschalk, Louis R. "Our Vichy Fumble." *The Journal of Modern History* 20, no. 1 (March 1948): 47–56.

Gravel, Senator Mike, ed. *The Pentagon Papers: The Defense Department History of United States Decision-making on Vietnam*. Boston: Beacon Press, 1971.

Grosser, Alfred. *French Foreign Policy under De Gaulle*. Trans. Lois Ames Pattison. Boston: Little, Brown and Company, 1967.

Guderian, Heinz. *Panzer Leader*. Trans. Constantine Fitzgibben. London: Michael Joseph, 1952.

Guéna, Yves. *Historique de la Communauté*. Paris: Fayard, 1962.

Gun, Nerin. *Les Secrets des archives américaines: Pétain, Laval, Pétain*. Paris: Albin Michel, 1979.

Gunston, Bill. *Bombers of the West*. New York: Scribner's, 1973.

Hackett, Clifford. "Jean Monnet and the Roosevelt Administration." In *Monnet and the Americans: The Father of a United Europe and his U.S. Supporters*, ed. Clifford P. Hackett, Washington, DC: Jean Monnet Council, 2001.

Haftendorn, Helga. "The NATO Crisis of 1966–1967: Confronting Germany with a Conflict of Priorities." In *The Strategic Triangle: France, Germany, and the United States in the Shaping of the New Europe*, ed. Helga Haftendorn et al. Baltimore: Johns Hopkins University Press, 2006.

Haight, John McVickar. *American Aid to France, 1938–1940*. New York: Atheneum, 1970.

Harmetz, Aljean. *Round Up the Usual Suspects: The Making of "Casablanca": Bogart, Bergman, and World War II*. New York: Hyperion, 2017.

Harrison, Michael M. *The Reluctant Ally: France and Atlantic Security*. Baltimore: Johns Hopkins University Press, 1981.

Hautreux, François-Xavier. "De Gaulle face au problème des harkis." In *De Gaulle et l'Algérie, 1943–1969*, ed. Maurice Vaisse, 264–277. Paris: Armand Colin/Ministère de la Défense, 2012.

Haynes, John Earl, and Harvey Klehr. VENONA. Decoding the Soviet Espionage in America. New Haven, CT: Yale University Press, 1999.

Hazareesingh, Sudhir. *In the Shadow of the General: Modern France and the Myth of De Gaulle*. New York: Oxford University Press, 2012.

Hershberg, James G. "'Marigold': Franco-American Relations, and Secret Vietnam Peace Diplomacy, 1966-1967." *Diplomacy and Statecraft* 28, no. 3 (2017): 403–430.

———. *Marigold: The Last Chance for Peace in Vietnam*. Stanford, CA: Stanford University Press, 2012.

Hildebrand, Robert C. *Dumbarton Oaks: The Origins of the United Nations and the Search for Postwar Security*. Chapel Hill: University of North Carolina Press, 1990.

Hill, John S. "De Gaulle's Strategy for Economic Reconstruction." In *De Gaulle and the United States: A Centennial Reappraisal*, ed. Robert O. Paxton and Nicholas Wahl, 103–115. Oxford: Berg, 1994.

Hitchcock, William. *France Restored: Cold War Diplomacy and the Quest for Leadership in Europe*. Chapel Hill: University of North Carolina Press, 1998.

Hoffmann, Stanley. *Decline or Renewal? France Since the 1930s*. New York: The Viking Press, 1974.

Hurstfield, Julian G. *America and the French Nation, 1939–1945*. Chapel Hill: University of North Carolina Press, 1986.

Jackson, Julian. *De Gaulle*. Cambridge, MA: Harvard University Press, 2018.

———. *France, The Dark Years (1940–1944)*. New York: Oxford University Press, 2001.

Jauvert, Vincent. *L'Amérique Contre De Gaulle: Histoire Secrèt, 1961–1969*. Paris: Seuil, 2000.

Jenkins, Roy. *Churchill: A Biography*. New York: Farrar, Straus & Giroux, 2002.

Jennings, Eric T. *Vichy in the Tropics: Pétain's National Revolution in Madagascar, Guadeloupe, and Indochina, 1940–1944*. Stanford, CA: Stanford University Press, 2001.

Jordan, Robert S. *Norstad: Cold War NATO Supreme Commander*. New York: St. Martin's Press, 2000.

Journoud, Pierre. *De Gaulle et le Vietnam, 1945–1969*. Paris: Tallendier, 2011.

Kaiser, Charles. *The Cost of Courage*. New York: Other Press, 2015.

Kammerer, Albert. *Du débarguement africain au meutre de Darlan*. Paris: Flammarion, 1949.

Kaspi, André. *La Mission de Jean Monnet à Alger, Mars–Octobre 1943*. Paris: Publications de la Sorbonne, 1971.

Kedward, H. R., and Nancy Wood, eds. *The Liberation of France: Image and Event*. Oxford: Berg Publishers, 1995.

Kennedy, Senator John F. "The Algerian Crisis: A New Phase?" *America* 101 (October 5, 1957).

Kersaudy, François. *De Gaulle et Churchill: Le mésentente cordial*. Paris: Perrin, 2010.

———. *De Gaulle et Roosevelt: Le Duel au Sommet*. Paris: Perrin, 2006.

Kettle, Michael. *De Gaulle and Algeria, 1940–1960: From Mers El-Kébir to the Algiers Barricades*. London: Quartet Books, 1993.

Keylor, William R. "France and the Illusion of American Support, 1919–1939." In *The French Defeat of 1940: Reassessments*, ed. Joel Blatt, 204–244. Providence, RI: Berghahn, 1998.

———. *Jacques Bainville and the Renaissance of Royalist History in Twentieth-Century France*. Baton Rouge: Louisiana State University Press, 1979.

———. "Leading from Behind When No One is in Front: Eight Years of Frustration with the International Community's Failure to Share the Burden of Preserving World Order," in *Les Etats-Unis à la Fin de la Grande Stratégie: Un Bilan de la Poli-*

tique Étrangère d'Obama, ed. Maud Quessard and Maya Kandel. Poitiers: *Étude de l'Institut de recherché stratégigue de l'École militaire*, 2017.

———. "Versailles and International Diplomacy." In *The Treaty of Versailles: A Reassessment After 75 Years*, ed. Manfred Boemeke, Gerald Feldman, and Elizabeth Glaser, 469–505. Cambridge: Cambridge University Press, 1998.

Kimball, Jeffery. *Nixon's Vietnam War*. Lawrence: University of Kansas Press, 1998.

Kinzer, Stephen. *The Brothers: John Foster Dulles, Allen Dulles, and Their Secret World War*. New York: Henry Holt, 2013.

Klehr, Harvey, John Earl Haynes, and Fridrikh Igorevich Firsov. *The Secret World of American Communism*. New Haven, CT: Yale University Press, 1995.

Kohl, Wilfred L. *French Nuclear Diplomacy*. Princeton, NJ: Princeton University Press, 1971.

Kolodziej, Edward A. *French International Policy under De Gaulle and Pompidou*. Ithaca, NY: Cornell University Press, 1974.

Kraslow, David, and Stuart H. Loory. *The Secret Search for Peace in Vietnam*. New York: Random House, 1968.

Lacouture, Jean. *De Gaulle, The Rebel 1890–1944*. Trans. Alan Sheridan. New York: Norton, 1993.

———. *De Gaulle, The Ruler, 1945–1970*. Trans. Alan Sheridan. New York: Norton, 1993.

———. *Ho Chi Minh*. Trans. Peter Wiles. Harmondsworth, UK: Penguin Books, 1968.

LaFeber, Walter. "Roosevelt, Churchill, and Indochina, 1942–1945." *American Historical Review* 80 (December 1975): 1277–1295.

Langer, William L. *Our Vichy Gamble*. New York: Norton, 1966.

Larcan, Alain. "L'Europe de l'Atlantique à l'Oural." In *De Gaulle et la Russie*, ed. Maurice Vaisse, 285–313. Paris: CNRS Editions, 2006.

Lasterle, Phillipe. "Could Admiral Gensoul Have Averted the Tragedy of Mers el-Kebir?" Journal of Military History 67, no. 3 (2003): 835–844.

Lawrence, Mark Atwood. *Assuming the Burden: Europe and the American Commitment to War in Vietnam*. Berkeley: University of California Press, 2005.

———. "Forging the 'Great Combination': Britain and the Indochina Problem, 1945–1950." In *The First Vietnam War: Colonial Conflict and Cold War Crisis*, ed. Mark Atwood Lawrence and Frederik Logevall, 105–129. Cambridge, MA: Harvard University Press, 2007.

Lázár, Peter. "The Mansfield Amendment and the U.S. Commitment in Europe, 1966–1975." MA Thesis, Naval Postgraduate School, Monterey, Calif. (2003).

Ledwidge, Bernard. *De Gaulle*. New York: St. Martin's Press, 1982.

Lelyveld, Joseph. *His Final Battle: The Last Months of Franklin Roosevelt*. New York: Vintage, 2017.

Lerner, Daniel. *France Defeats EDC*. New York: Praeger, 1957.

Lévêque, François. "Les relations entre l'Union soviétique et la France Libre." In *De Gaulle et la Russie*, ed. Maurice Vaisse, 19–44. Paris: CNRS Editions, 2012.

Lichtheim, George. *Europe and America: The Future of the Atlantic Community*. London: Thames and Hudson, 1963.

Logevall, Fredrik. *Choosing War: The Last Chance for Peace and the Escalation of War in Vietnam*. Berkeley: University of California Press, 1999.

———. *Embers of War: The Fall of an Empire and the Making of America's Vietnam*. New York: Random House, 2013.

Ludlow, Piers. *The European Community and the Crises of the 1960s: Negotiating the Gaullist Challenge*. New York: Routledge, 2006.

Lynch, Francis M. B. "Resolving the Paradox of the Monnet Plan: National and International Planning in French Reconstruction." *Economic History Review* 37, no. 2 (May 1984).

Maier, Charles, and Dan S. White. *The Thirteenth of May: The Advent of de Gaulle's Republic*. New York: Oxford University Press, 1968.

Maillard, Pierre. *De Gaulle et l'Allemagne: Le rêve inachevé*. Paris: Plon, 1990.

Malraux, André. *Felled Oaks: Conversations with de Gaulle*. Trans. Irene Clephane. New York: Holt, Rinehart and Winston, 1971.

Mansfield, Senator Mike. Guest column for Andrew Tully, "The Case for the Europeanization of NATO," August 7, 1970. Cited in William R. Keylor, "Leading from Behind When No One is in Front: Eight Years of Frustration with the International Community's Failure to Share the Burden of Preserving World Order." In *Les Etats-Unis à la Fin de la Grande Stratégie: Un Bilan de la Politique Étrangère d'Obama*, ed. Maud Quessard and Maya Kandel. Poitiers: Étude de l'Institut de recherché stratégigue de l'École militaire, 2017.

Marr, David G. *Vietnam, 1945: The Quest for Power*. Berkeley: University of California Press, 1995.

Martin, Garrett Joseph. *General de Gaulle's Cold War: Challenging American Hegemony, 1963–1968*. Providence, RI: Berghahn Books, 2013.

Mayers, David. *FDR's Ambassadors and the Diplomacy of Crisis*. Cambridge: Cambridge University Press, 2013.

Mayne, Richard. "Jean Monnet: A Biographical Essay." In *Monnet and the Americans: The Father of a United Europe and his U.S. Supporters*, ed. Clifford P. Hackett. Washington, DC: Jean Monnet Council, 2001.

McCullough, David. *Truman*. New York: Simon & Schuster, 1992.

Melnick, Constantin. *De Gaulle, les services secrets, et l'Algérie*. Paris: Nouveau Monde Editions, 2012.

Mendl, Wolf. *Deterrence and Persuasion: French Nuclear Armament in the Context of National Policy, 1945-1969*. London: Faber & Faber, 1970.

Michelet, Édmond. *Le Gaullisme, passionnante aventure*. Paris: Fayard, 1962.

Mioche, Philippe. *Le Plan Monnet: Genesis et elaboration, 1941–1947*. Paris: Publications de la Sorbonne, 1987.

Moise, Edwin E. *Tonkin Gulf and the Escalation of the Vietnam War*. Chapel Hill: University of North Carolina Press, 1966.

Morse, Edward L. *Foreign Policy and Interdependence in Gaullist France*. Princeton, NJ: Princeton University Press, 1973.

Munholland, J. Kim. *Rock of Contention: Free French and Americans and Americans at War in New Caledonia, 1940–1945*. New York: Berghahn, 2005.

———. "The Trials of the Free French in New Caledonia, 1940–1942." *French Historical Studies* 14, no. 4 (Fall 1986): 547–579.

———. "The United States and the Free French." In *De Gaulle and the United States: A Centennial Reassessment*, ed. Robert O. Paxton and Nicholas Wahl, 61–94. Oxford: Berg, 1994.

Narinsky, Mikhail. "Le retrait de la France de l'organisation militaire de l'OTAN vu de Moscou," in *De Gaulle et la Russie*, ed. Maurice Vaisse, 258–269. Paris: CNRS Editions, 2012.

Neiberg, Michael. *The Blood of Free Men: The Liberation of Paris, 1944*. New York: Basic Books, 2012.

Nettlebeck, Colin. *Forever France: Exile in the United States, 1939–1945*. London: Bloomsbury Academic, 1991.

Newhouse, John. *De Gaulle and the Anglo-Saxons*. New York: The Viking Press, 1970.

Nouailhat, Yves-Henri. "Nixon-De Gaulle: Un episode original des relations franco-américains." *Revue Française d'Etudes Américaines*, no. 32 (April 1987): 310–318.

———. "Richard Nixon et Charles de Gaulle." In *Le Général De Gaulle et Les Presidents des Etats-Unis*, 107–116. Paris: Fondation Charles de Gaulle, Cahiers no. 6, 2006.

Nouzelle, Vincent. *Des Secrets Si Bien Gardé*. Paris: Fayard, 2009.

Novick, Peter. *The Resistance Versus Vichy: The Purge of Collaborators in Liberated France*. London: Chatto & Windus, 1968.

Offner, Arnold A. *Hubert Humphrey: The Conscience of the Country*. New Haven, CT: Yale University Press, 2018.

Paxton, Robert O. *Vichy France: Old Guard and New Order, 1940–1944*. New York: Knopf, 1972.

Paxton, Robert O., and Nicholas Wahl. *De Gaulle and the United States: A Centennial Reappraisal*. Oxford: Berg, 1994.

Pfaltzgraff, Robert L. Jr. *The Atlantic Community: A Complex Imbalance*. New York: Van Nostrand Reinhold Co., 1969.

Pogue, Forest C. *George Marshall, Organizer of Victory*. New York: Viking, 1973.

Poidevin, Raymond. "Frankreich und die Ruhrfrage 1945–1951." *Historische Zeitschrift* 228, no. 2 (April 1979): 317–334.

Polayret, Jean-Marie, Helen Wallace, and Pascaline Winand, eds. *Victims, Votes, and Vetoes: The Empty Chair Crisis and the Luxemburg Compromise Forty Years On*. Berne: Peter Lang, 2006.

Porter, Gareth, ed. *Vietnam: The Definitive Documentation of Human Decisions, Vol. I, The First Indochina War and the Geneva Agreements, 1941–1954*. Stanfordville, NY: Coleman Enterprises, 1979.

Pouget, Jean. *Un certain capitaine de Gaulle*. Paris: Aubéron, 2000.

Reyn, Sebastian. *Atlantis Lost: The American Experience with De Gaulle, 1958–1969*. Amsterdam: Amsterdam University Press, 2009.

Rimbaud, Christiane. *L'Affaire du Massiglia*. Paris: Seuil, 1984.

Ripaux, Alain. *Charles de Gaulle: Une certain idée du Québec*. Appilly: Ripaux, 2017.

Robertson, Charles L. *When Roosevelt Planned to Govern France*. Amherst: University of Massachusetts Press, 2011.

Romerstein, Herbert, and Eric Breidel. *The Venona Secrets: Expanding Soviet Espionage and America's Traitors*. Washington, DC: Regnery History, 2001.

Rossi, Mario. *Roosevelt and the French*. Westport, CT: Praeger, 1993.

Roussel, Eric. *Jean Monnet, 1888–1979*. Paris: Fayard, 1996.

Ruehl, Lothar. *La politique militaire de la Ve République*. Paris: Presses de la Fondation Nationale des Sciences Politiques, 1976.

Sainderichin, Pierre. *De Gaulle et le Monde*. Paris: Le Monde, 1990.

Salat-Baroux, Fréréric. *De Gaulle-Pétain: Le destin, la blessure, la leçon*. Paris: Robert Laffont, 2010.

Sapp, Steven. "Jefferson Caffery, Cold War Diplomat: American-French Relations 1944–1949." *Louisiana History*, no. 23 (1982).

Schlesinger, Arthur M. Jr. *The Bitter Heritage: Vietnam and American Democracy, 1941–1966*. London: André Deutsch, 1967.

Schlesinger, Stephen. *Act of Creation: The Founding of the United Nations*. Boulder, CO: Oxford, 2003.

Schoenbaum, Thomas J. *Waging Peace and War: Dean Rusk in the Truman, Kennedy, and Johnson Years*. New York: Simon and Schuster, 1988.

Schwartz, Hans Peter. *Konrad Adenauer: A German Politician and Statesman in a Period of War, Vol. II, The Statesman (1952–1967)*. Providence, RI: Berghahn Books, 1997.

Schwartz, Thomas A. "The De Gaulle Challenge: The Johnson Administration and the NATO Crisis of 1966–1967." In *The Strategic Triangle: France, Germany, and the United States in the Shaping of the New Europe*, ed. Helga Harftendorn et al. Baltimore: Johns Hopkins University Press, 2006.

———. *Lyndon Johnson and Europe: In the Shadow of Vietnam*. Cambridge, MA: Harvard University Press, 2003.

Shannon, Marie and Tony Shannon. "Jacques Maritain." Catholic Truth Society. maritain.nd.edu/jmc/etext/lives.htm.

Shennan, Andrew. *Rethinking France: Plans for Renewal, 1940–1946*. New York: Oxford University Press, 1989.

Sherman, David. *Camus*. New York: John Wiley, 2009.

Sherwood, Robert E. *Roosevelt and Hopkins: An Intimate History*. New York: Bantam Books, 1948.

Shipway, Martin. *The Road to War: France and Vietnam, 1944–1947*. Providence, RI: Berghahn, 1966.

Silj, Alessandro. *Europe's Political Puzzle: A Study of the Fouchet Negotiations*. Cambridge, MA: Harvard University Press, 1967.

Singer, Barnett. *The Americanization of France: Searching for Happiness After the Algerian War*. Lanham, MD: Rowman & Littlefield, 2013.

Soutou, Georges-Henri. *L'Alliance Incertain: Les rapports politico-stratégiques franco-allemands, 1954–1996*. Paris: Fayard, 1996.

———. *La Guerre de Cinquante Ans: Les Relations Est-Ouest, 1943–1990*. Paris: Fayard, 2001.

Spears, Major General Sir Edward. *Two Men Who Saved France: Pétain and De Gaulle*. New York: Stein & Day, 1966.

Spector, Ronald H. *Advice and Support: The Early Years of the U.S. Army in Vietnam, 1941–1960*. New York: The Free Press, 1985.

Steel, Ronald. *Pax Americana*. New York: The Viking Press, 1968.

———. *Walter Lippmann and the American Century*. Boston: Little, Brown-Atlantic Press, 1980.

Stora, Benjamin. *De Gaulle et l'Algérie*. Paris: Fayard, 2010.

Stromseth, Jane E. *The Origins of Flexible Response: NATO's Debate over Strategy in the 1960s*. New York: Palgrave-Macmillan, 1988.

Sulzberger, C. L. *The Last of the Giants*. New York: Macmillan, 1970.

———. *The Test: De Gaulle and Algeria*. New York: Harcourt, 1962.

Tauric, Michel. *Vivre avex De Gaulle: Les derniers témoins raconte l'homme*. Paris: Plon, 2008.

Thompson, Christopher. "Prologue to Conflict: De Gaulle and the United States, From First Impressions Through 1940." In *De Gaulle and the United States*, ed. Robert O. Paxton and Nicholas Wahl, 13–32. Oxford: Berg, 1994.

Thompson, Dale C. *Vive le Québec Libre*. Toronto: Deneau Publishers, 1988.

Tonnesson, Stein. "Franklin Roosevelt, Trusteeship, and Indochina: A Reassessment." In *The First Vietnam War: Colonial Conflict and Cold War Crisis*, ed. Mark Attwood Lawrence and Frederik Logevall, 56–73. Cambridge, MA: Harvard University Press, 2007.

———. *Vietnam 1946: How the War Began*. Berkeley: University of California Press, 2010.

———. *The Vietnamese Revolution of 1945: Roosevelt, Ho Chi Minh, and de Gaulle in a World at War*. London: Sage Publications, 1991.

Torikata, Yuko, "Reexamining de Gaulle's Peace Initiative on the Vietnam War." *Diplomatic History* 31, no. 5 (November 2007): 909–939.

———. "The U.S. Escalation in Vietnam and de Gaulle's Secret Search for Peace." In *Globalizing de Gaulle: International Perspectives on French Foreign Policies, 1958–1969*, ed. Christian Nuenlist, Anna Locher, and Garret Martin. Plymouth, UK: Lexington Books, 2010.

Tournoux, Jean-Raymond. *Jamais dit*. Paris: Plon, 1971.

———. *Pétain et de Gaulle: Un Demi-Siècle d'Histoire Non Officielle*. Paris: Plon, 1964.

Trachtenberg, Marc. *A Constructed Peace: The Making of the European Settlement, 1945–1963*. Princeton, NJ: Princeton University Press, 1999.

United States–Vietnam Relations, 1945–1967. Study Prepared by the Department of Defense [The Pentagon Papers], 12 vols. Washington, DC: U.S. Government Printing Office, 1971.

Vaisse, Maurice. *Alger: Le Putsch.* Brussels: Editions Complex, 1983.

———. "Aux origins du memorandum de September 1958." *Relations internationals* 38 (Summer 1989): 253–262.

———. ed. *De Gaulle et l'Algérie, 1943–1969.* Paris: Armand Colin/Ministère de la Défense, 2012.

———. ed. *De Gaulle et la Russie.* Paris: CNRS Editions, 2012.

———. "De Gaulle et Willy Brandt: Deux non-conformistes au pouvoir." In *Willy Brandt und Frankreich*, ed. Horst Muller and Maurice Vaisse. Munich: Oldenberg, 2005.

———. *La Grandeur: Politique etrangere du general de Gaulle.* Paris: CNRS Editions, 2013.

———. *La Puissance ou L'Influence?: La France dans le monde depuis 1958.* Paris: Fayard, 2009.

———, ed. *L'Europe et la crise de Cuba.* Paris: Colin, 1993.

———. *Vers la paix en Algérie: Les négociations d'Evian dans les archives diplomatiques françaises 15 janvier–26 juin 1962.* Brussels: Bruylant, 2003.

Vaisse, Maurice, and Jean Doise. *Politique étrangère de la France: Diplomatie et outil militaire, 1871–1991.* Paris: Seuil, 1987.

Vaisse, Maurice, Pierre Mélandri, and Frédéric Bozo, eds. *La France et l'OTAN, 1949–1966.* Paris: Complex, 1996.

Vaughn, Hal. *Sleeping with the Enemy: Coco Chanel's Secret War.* New York: Knopf, 2011.

Verrier, Anthony. *Assassination in Algiers: Roosevelt, Churchill, de Gaulle, and the Murder of Admiral Darlan.* New York: Norton, 1990.

Vinen, Richard. *The Unfree French: Life under the Occupation.* New Haven, CT: Yale University Press, 2006.

Viorst, Milton. *Hostile Allies: FDR and De Gaulle.* New York: Macmillan, 1965.

Virgili, Fabrice. *Shorn Women: Gender and Punishment in Liberated France.* Oxford: Berg, 2002.

Wall, Irwin. "Les Accords Blum-Byrnes, la Modernisation de la France at la guerre froide." *Vingtieme Siecle*, no. 13 (January–March 1987): 45–63.

———. *France, the United States, and the Algerian War.* Berkeley: University of California Press, 2001.

———. "Harry Truman and Charles de Gaulle," in Paxton and Wahl, eds., *De Gaulle and the United States, op. cit.*, 117–129.

———. *The United States and the Making of Postwar France, 1945–1954.* Cambridge: Cambridge University Press, 1991.

Wallace, Brenton G. *Patton and His Third Army.* Harrisburg, PA: Military Service Publishing Company, 1946.

Weber, Eugen. *The Nationalist Revival in France, 1905–1914*. Berkeley: University of California Press, 1968.

White, Dorothy Shipley. *Seeds of Discord: De Gaulle, Free France, and the Allies*. Syracuse, NY: Syracuse University Press, 1964.

Williams, Andrew. "France and the Origins of the United Nations, 1944–1945: Si la France ne compte plus, qu'on nous le dise." *Diplomacy and Statecraft* 28, no. 3 (June 2017): 216–217.

Williams, Charles. *The Last Great Frenchman: A Life of Charles de Gaulle*. New York: Wiley, 1993.

Winand, Pascaline. *Eisenhower, Kennedy, and the United States of Europe*. New York: St. Martin's Press, 1996.

Woolner, David. "Canada, Mackenzie King and the St. Pierre and Miquelon Crisis of 1941." *London Journal of Canadian Studies* 24 (2008–2009): 42–84.

Young, John W. *Britain, France, and the Unity of Europe*. London: Salem House Publishers, 1984.

———. *France, the Cold War, and the Western Alliance, 1944–1949*. Leicester, UK: Leicester University Press, 1990.

Zahniser, Marvin R. *Uncertain Friendship: American-French Relations through the Cold War*. New York: John Wiley & Sons, 1975.

Index

OAS. *See* Secret Army Organization
offensive, military doctrine of, 7, 14
Office of Strategic Services (OSS), 63,
  102, 123, 126
Ophuls, Marcel, 273n62, 276n121

Palewski, Gaston, 106, 138
Paris: Commune, 284n273; Kennedy
  and, 181–82; liberation of, 89–93;
  Nixon and, 251–52; Roosevelt and,
  112; and Vietnam peace talks, 243
parliament, 150; de Gaulle and, 12;
  Fourth Republic and, 136
Partial Test Ban Treaty, 215
Passy (André Dewavrin), 28, 102–3, 133
Patch, Alexander, 55–56, 116
Patti, Archimedes, 126
Patton, George, 34, 68, 89, 99, 116
Paul-Boncour, Joseph, 119
Pearl Harbor, 50–55
Pearson, Lester, 239
Péguy, Charles, 6
People's Republic of China. *See* China
Perse, Saint-John. *See* Leger, Alexis
Pershing, John J., 47–48, 86
Pétain, Henri-Philippe: and Chambrun,
  46; early relationship with de Gaulle,
  7, 9–11, 15, 19; and empire, 49–50,
  62, 64; later life, 104; and Roosevelt,
  34, 76; and surrender, 18, 20; and
  U.S., 37–38; and Vichy government,
  23–25, 35, 50, 57
Peyrefitte, Alain, 178, 184
Peyrouton, Marcel, 21, 73
Pflimlin, Pierre, 144–46
Pham van Dong, 236
Philip, André, 61–62, 65–66, 73, 102
Piaf, Edith, 276n121
pieds noirs, 143–45; Kennedy and, 176;
  term, 142, 296n23
Pinay, Antoine, 140
Pleven, René, 19, 102, 118–19, 133,
  257; and Africa, 29; and cabinet,

73; and EDC, 141, 267n43; and
  Free France finances, 25; and U.S.,
  41–45
Pleven Plan, 140, 267n43, 295n14
Poland, 8–9, 13–15, 107
Polaris submarines, 173, 196
political cooperation, 188–92
Pompidou, Georges, 216, 227, 245, 255
Pondicherry, 29
postwar international order: France and,
  95–114; Roosevelt and, 85–86
Potsdam Conference, 121–22, 132
Powers, Francis Gary, 166
Prague Spring, 245–47
proportional deterrence doctrine, 199,
  312n110, 312n112
Provisional Government of the French
  Republic, 79–80
provisional recognition, term, 97
public opinion, French: on Algeria, 149,
  152; on de Gaulle, 54, 72, 83, 255;
  on NATO, 227; on U.S. leadership,
  221; on Vietnam, 210
public opinion, German, on political
  cooperation, 190
public opinion, U.S.: on aid to France,
  45; on de Gaulle, 154; on France,
  221; on Vietnam, 211, 242

Québec, de Gaulle and, 239
Quebec Conference, 97
Quemoy, 158

Radical party, of France, 147
radio broadcasts by de Gaulle: on
  exclusion from Yalta, 110; "flame of
  resistance," 20–21; on franchise, 59;
  on Mers-el-Kébir, 28; and Operation
  Torch, 62, 64–65
Rains, Claude, 63
Ramadier, Paul, 137
Rassamblement du Peuple Français
  (RPF), 137–38, 140–41

~

About the Author

William R. Keylor received his BA from Stanford University and his MA and PhD from Columbia University. He is the author of four previous books and editor of three books on the history of international relations and the history of modern France. Keylor has been a Guggenheim, Fulbright, Woodrow Wilson, Earhart, and Whiting Fellow. He has been named Chevalier de l'Ordre National du Mérite by the French government and has served as the president of the Society for French Historical Studies. He is professor emeritus at the Frederick Pardee School of Global Studies at Boston University.